A B C

of

Immigration

Disclaimer
The views expressed in this publication are those of the author and do not reflect the views of the publisher.

A B C

of

Immigration

A compilation by

Simon Sherbrooke

British Library Cataloguing in
Publication Data.
A catalogue record for this book
is available from the
British Library

ISBN: 978-1-84104-597-9

This book is dedicated to the betrayed and to the girls of Derby, Blackpool, Rochdale, Rotherham, Oxford et cetera.

Acknowledgements

I gratefully acknowledge the permission of the *Salisbury Review* and *The Times Literary Supplement* as to Raymond Honeyford's two articles one of which is in full in the chapter H is for Ray Honeyford and the other in appendix VI.

Apart from the books and reports listed in the bibliography, what I quote are from newspapers – *The Daily Telegraph*, much more usually the daily as opposed to the Sunday, *The Times*, again daily rather than Sunday, the *Independent*, the *Financial Times*, the *Daily Mail*, *The Sun*, the *Evening Standard* and the *Guardian*: for the most part what I quote from are articles in such newspapers but occasionally I quote a news item itself. And periodicals – inter alia the *Spectator*, *The Economist*, the *Investors Chronicle* and the *Week*, and letters to such.

Occasionally I wanted more on the point and so, as is recorded in the notes, I retrieved the story from such as *AsianImage*, *Bahama Rugby*, *Luton on Sunday*, *Somaliland Sun* and *Watford Observer*.

I appreciate that by far the greater part of the contents of this book is what others have written (or occasionally said) and copyright thereof is in the relevant author but I hope that (because this is a book and not a newspaper or periodical, because this book is about a matter of great current concern) my use of the copyright material is "fair dealing" as I comply with the precondition that the author is acknowledged. And in the case of books, as sometimes requested, when I asked for permission, I name the publisher. But I thank all those I quote.

The following (in alphabetical order) are the authors of such articles (and the occasional newspaper piece when the writer is named) and other writings/sayings which are quoted (from) in this book. (The title MP or MEP is (where relevant) stated even though the individual was also a minister or is no longer an MP/MEP.)

Diane Abbott MP, George Allagiah, John L. Allen, Professor C. Allen, Graeme Archer, David Ashton, Annushka Asthana, Bagehot of The Economist, Ed Balls MP Richard Barratt, Tom Benyon MP, Katharine Birbalsingh, Julie Blacker, David Blunkett MP, Roger Bootle, Tom Bower, James Brokenshire MP, Liam Brown MP, Christopher Caldwell, Charlemagne of The Economist, Simon Collins, Philip Congdon, Yvette Cooper MP, Nick Cohen, Peter Cosgrave, Simon Cross, Lord Crisp, Michael Curtis, Theodore Dalrymple, Roger Daltrey, Jon Gower Davies, James Delingpole, Mary Dejevsky, John Denham MP, Chris Dillow,

G.W. Dipper, Stanley Eckersley, Johnathan Evans, Ambrose Evans-Pritchard Nigel Farage, Frank Field MP, Judith Flanders, Hannah Fletcher, James Forsyth, A.A. Gill, David Goodhart, Andrew Gilligan, John Glanville, DS (retd.) Mick Gradwell, Peter Graystone, Andrew Grimson, Liam Halligan, Daniel Hannan MEP, Mark Harper MP, Allister Heath, Peter Hitchens, Boris Johnson MP, Philip Johnston, Judith Keeling, Jane Kelly, Stephen D. King, Charlie Klendijan, Victoria Lambert, Roland Lee, Sam Leith, Rod Liddle, Andrew Lilico, Penelope Lively, Danny Lockwood, Nick Lowles, Matthew Lynn, Kenan Malik, Theresa May MP, Andrew Mason, Thomas Mayer, Melanie McDonagh, Martin Meredith, Nicky Morgan MP, Charles Moore, Tim Montgomerie, Helena Morrissey, Katie Morley, Douglas Murray, Ferdinand Mount, Harry Mount, Richard Munday, V.S. Naipul, Dianna Nammi, Ogden Nash, Fraser Nelson, Andrew Norfolk, Peter Oborne, Stephen Oppenheimer, Andrew Oxlade, Alasdair Palmer, Andrew Parker, Lara Pawson, Allison Pearson, Jeffrey Pearson, William Pender, Eric Pickles MP, David Pilling, Trevor Phillips, Libby Purves, Gideon Rachman, Jeff Randall, John Redwood MP, Rachel Reeves MP, Xan Rice, Mary Riddell, Matt Ridley, Jasper Ridley, James A. Robinson, Stephen Robinson, Chief Rabbi Johnathan Sacks, Philip Carl Salzman, Roger Scruton, Tony Sewell, Jacqui Smith MP, Merryn Somerset Webb, Nicholas Soames, Janet Street-Porter, Anna Soubry MP, David Starkey, Jack Straw MP, Steerpike, Lord Tebbitt, Taki Theodoracopulos, Damian Thompson, Nicholas Wade, Mary Wakefield, Anne Marie Watson, Jeremy Warner, Lady Warsi, Peter Watt, Ed West, Mike West, Merryn Westfield, Anna White, David Willetts MP, Michael Willis, David Williams MP, Toby Young.

Additionally I quote from letters that were written to (and published by) newspapers or periodicals namely those from -

Richard Ashpole FRCS, David Ashton, George Baggaley (The Next Generation Party), W.H. Bailey, Professor S.F. Bush, Simon Collins, Alan Craig, Ruth Dowding, Stuart Eckersley, Gary Fedtschyschak, Mick Ferrie, S.M. Freedman, John Glanville, Dr Robert Hanson, Yugo Kovach, L. Langrick, Professor Richard Layard, Rob Mason, Richard Munday, Jeffrey Pearson, Simon Ross (Population Matters), Professor Robert Rowthorn, Gregory Shenkman, Baroness Thomas of Winchester, John Waine and Mike West.

There are others who I quote but I don't think they need acknowledging – save in the notes. (Many are politicians and their raison d'être is to get their message out.)

I express my thanks to those who worked on my (so called) manuscript. (Remaining) errors are entirely mine and at least partly due to my continuing additions. The last (in time) of those is down to *Race and Faith: The Deafening Silence* by Trevor Phillips (from Guyana and founding chair of the Equality and Human Rights Commission) published by Civitas in 2016. The publication also includes two commentaries (and a response by Mr Phillips). The first *A Guide through the Maze* is by David Goodhart the author of *The British Dream* and the second *Immigrants Come From Somewhere (Else)* is by Jon Gower Davies. Apart from adding the latter's figures to an existing statement of the number of Muslims in jail (*see* the chapter C is for crime) and similarly as to what is the number of Muslims under surveillance by the security services (*see* the chapter C is for cost) plus additional law (*see* the chapter L is for increase of law) I repeat, here, just a few sentences of what was in his commentary:

> In essence, while we Brits once had an empire of which we are now ashamed, Muslims once had an empire which they are ashamed to have lost and to the restoration of which they aspire.
>
> Their distance from or antipathy to us is not because of what or who we are but *because of what we are not* – we are 'not Muslim'.
>
> The major Muslim organisations are exercises in apologetics and camouflage.

No wonder that the working title of the draft of Mr Phillips' book (as sent to Goodhart and Davies for comment) was *Race: The Silence of the Damned.*

Simon Sherbrooke
31 May 2016

I had to draw a line somewhere with the continuous flow of material for this book. The line was drawn without thought as to the EU referendum. I have not used the following period to effect any apparently relevant changes: after all, at the end of 2016 we still didn't know whether Brexit will be hard or soft.

Introduction

This book was started at least as long ago as 2010. I then envisaged something in the nature of "notes". I apologise if the "feel" of the book ever reflects that history; likewise that the tense (or grammar) reflects that long gestation.

I perceive that the explanation for this book having taken so long and that it has grown so much include the following factors. First of all and despite the conclusion of the House of Lords' Select Committee on Economic Affairs in 2008 (*see* E is for the economics of immigration) and David Cameron's representation in 2010 (*see* D is for disingenuous) the amount of immigration has continued or even increased. Secondly investigation into an item produces leads so that, for example, that committee's report led back to the evidence it received. Thirdly the sources listed below and in the bibliography were mainly unknown to me in 2010: in other words, when one investigates one finds "there is so much more out there". Fourthly as time went on, there were (or came to my notice) further examples of the original point plus the publication of reports such as by Peter Clarke (as the result of the publication of the so called *Trojan Horse* letter) and by Professor Jay (as the extent of child sexual exploitation in Rotherham began to come out, which report was followed by Louise Casey's) and the Serious Case Review into CSE in Oxfordshire from the experiences of Children A, B, C, D, E and F plus judicial decisions such as BAPIO v Royal College of General Practitioners and the General Medical Council in 2014 and as to the Tower Hamlets mayoralty election of that year.

Time and again, I found an item could go under more than one chapter and chopped and changed what the chapter should be. Where I had most difficulty was with disingenuous. Upon looking for something else, I considered 'dissemble' and 'platitude' plus "economical with the truth" (Sir Robert Armstrong as to *Spycatcher*) and "the actualitie" (Alan Clark as to Matrix Churchill). That search brought up 'weasel words' and the newspeak of George Orwell's *1984*. I settled upon disingenuous I am not sure I reached the right decision. I leave it to others to come to a view.

I don't think the book's contents have been cherry-picked and that is shown by the following. In January 2015 there was a small item in a newspaper, that twenty years before receipt of the Trojan Horse letter, the Department for Education had received warnings of Islamist infiltration of schools in Birmingham. An internet search showed that the Department's Permanent Secretary, Chris Wormald, had conducted an investigation the result of which was his *Review into possible warnings to DfE relating to extremism in Birmingham schools*

He found six instances where concerns were raised with the Department. The first had been in 1994 when the headteachers of three schools in Birmingham had written to the Department expressing concerns about Hizb ut-Tahir [the *Party of Liberation* which seeks a caliphate and by one description first converts, secondly establishes a network of secret cells and thirdly tries to achieve its aims by infiltration]. Additionally that year there had been a letter from Revd. John Ray who after 25 years as principal of a school in Srinagar, Kashmir had, for 10 years (to 1991) been chair of the governors of Golden Hillock School: the result had been a meeting, in Westminster, with the Minister of State for Education.

Those alerts had got nowhere because the Department 'lacked inquisitiveness' and the policy at the time was for delegation from central to local government.

(But as to the latter reason) Peter Clarke (of the Clarke Report) concluded 'senior officers of (Birmingham City Council) were aware of practices subsequently referred to in the Trojan Horse letter as early as 2012, and discussions on this issue took place between officers and elected members in May 2013' and yet eight weeks after receipt (in late 2013) of the Trojan Horse letter the 'focus of the Council was very much on the potential community cohesion impact...'.

That search (for the Department's investigation) brought up four reports by *Birmingham Mail* showing, as I see it, a result of immigration (for Birmingham):-

First, Shaid Salim's Pizza Pan in Aldridge Road, Perry Bar had been shut down following environmental health officers, apparently on a routine visit, finding cockroaches.

Second, Ishmaeel Akbar, Yusaf Akbar, Ralph McLeod, Anthony McLeod, Lewis Poyser, Kofi Poyser, Kadeem Poyser, Jermaine Campbell, Lemar Grant and Ricardo Grant had all been imprisoned for or in connection with kidnapping, cutting off the victim's finger and providing that to the victim's family to support a ransom demand.

(Four of them were also sentenced for an earlier assault: all four pleaded guilty but sentencing had been deferred so as not to affect the kidnap trial.) On line, there was a rogues' gallery from which it appeared that (at least)

Campbell, the two McLeods and the two Grants are not indigenous but are of a so called ethnic minority.

Third, there had been instituted a private prosecution of Dr Palaniappan Rajmohan of Calthorpe Clinic in Edgbaston for gender selective abortion.

Fourth, Heartlands Hospital had dealt with 1,500 cases of FGM (female genital mutilation) in the last five years and was now seeing six every week.

All those items are referred to or reflected in some way by the contents of this book.

A is for African, Asian and alien

Being at the northwest corner of Europe, we are about as far as one can get from both Africa and Asia so that necessarily Africans and Asians are alien. But not just geographically. Common African beliefs such as wanting to eat albinos; fearing spirit children, being polygamous,[1] considering twins 'unlucky' and having faith in witch doctors, apparently stay with them despite moving here:

- 'Adam's' torso was found beside the Thames. His stomach revealed traces of matter used in west African magic ritual. He may have come here from Germany, having been in the care of a Nigerian woman following the deportation of his parents. A policeman from Africa who came to assist the investigation explained that *muti* murders are not always reported because an 'Investigative officer tasked to deal with this might be a bit hesitant because of his own traditional beliefs'.[2]

- Kristy Bamu, aged fifteen, died after being beaten and tortured by his sister Magalie and her partner Eric Bikubi because they thought he was bewitching other children – *kindoki*, which pervades the Congo, from whence came both Magalie and Eric. Two years earlier, the two of them had mistreated Naomi Ilonga so as to 'release [her from] witchcraft'.

- Alex Kanneh, as a psychiatric nurse, used the threat of voodoo to stop a (vulnerable) patient revealing their affair.

- Lorraine Mbulwa was born in Zimbabwe in 1991. Her father suddenly collapsed and died in 2000. Two years later, her mother and Lorraine came here. In 2009, then aged eighteen, having been here for seven years and at school studying for A levels, Lorraine stabbed her mother because she believed spirits were making her do it.

- Rubina Maroof lured Alfusaine Jabbi, a Gambian faith healer, to her home in Luton where Jabbi was beaten, stabbed and had salt rubbed in his wounds before his body was dumped in a nearby car park, all because Maroof had paid large sums to Jabbi against his (unfulfilled) promises to solve her problems by sacrificing camels in Gambia. In connection with Jabbi's murder, Tariq Malik and Imran Khan were jailed for life; Maroof, having first tried to disappear by going to Pakistan, was jailed for ten years for manslaughter and conspiracy to commit unlawful imprisonment.

1

Many Africans and Asians have belief in the efficacy of human body parts and of animal parts (viz. African *muti*). Chow Hok Kuen, who has a British passport but is of Taiwanese origin, was arrested in Thailand with a suitcase of human foetuses as part of *Kuman thong*.

Many Africans and Asians, anyway if Muslim, are polygamous. Apart from that not being part of this country's culture:

> Our goal was to understand why monogamous marriage has become standard in most developed nations in recent centuries, when most recorded cultures have practised polygamy. Our findings suggest that institutionalised monogamous marriage provides greater net benefits for society at large by reducing social problems that are inherent in polygamous societies.[3]

We treat male and female babies of equal value: many Asians do not. We do not abort a foetus just because it is female: many Asians do. When Dr Prabha Sivaraman of the Pall Mall Medical clinic in Manchester was asked to effect an abortion as the child was female, she replied, 'I don't ask questions, if you want a termination ... That's my job, I don't ask questions' and added that the mother's address could be 'fictitious ... I don't mind.' Dr Rajmmohan of the Calthorpe Clinic in Birmingham, to avoid the problem of the baby being female, falsified the reason for termination. The two doctors were suspended. The Crown Prosecution Service decided not to prosecute, leaving it to the General Medical Council to deal with.[4]

> While the overall United Kingdom birth ratio is within normal limits, analysis of birth data for the calendar years from 2007 to 2011 has found the gender ratios at birth vary by mothers' country of birth. For the majority of groups, this variation is the result of small numbers of births and does not persist between years. However, for a very small number of countries of birth there are indications that birth ratios may differ from the UK as a whole and potentially fall outside of the range considered possible without intervention.[5]

Africa and much of the Middle East remain largely tribal societies.

> The tribal system is egalitarian and secures redress of wrongs with a minimum of bureaucracy. Despite these outstanding merits, it has grave flaws. Children are taught from the earliest age that their group is always right and must be supported no matter what[6] ... In terms of national politics, the spirit of tribalism leads to 'monopoly of power, ruthless oppression of opponents and accumulation of benefits,' writes Philip Salzman[7] ... 'In short, it is a recipe for despotism, for tyranny.'

There was nothing equivalent to the steady ratchet mechanism that in England enabled the less violent and more literate to prosper and leave more children like themselves. Because it has always been more rational for its inhabitants to trust the tribe more than the state, tribalism in the Middle East has never disappeared.

In Africa too, tribalism has persisted and interacted poorly with the modern world. Throughout much of Africa, the standard mode of government is kleptocracy; whoever gains power uses it to enrich his family and tribe, which is the way that power has always been used in tribal systems. Extractive institutions, as defined by Acemoglu and Robinson,[8] are prevalent in Africa, particularly in countries rich in natural resources.

Despite substantial amounts of Western aid, many African countries are little better off than they were under colonial rule. Corruption is rampant. Many services for the poor are siphoned off by elites who leave only a trickle for the intended recipients. Some African countries have lower per-capita incomes now than they had in 1980 or, in some cases, in 1960. 'Half of Africa's 800 million people live on less than $1 a day,' writes the journalist and historian Martin Meredith.[9] 'It is the only region where school enrolment is falling and where illiteracy is commonplace ... It is also the only region where life expectancy is falling.'

The root of the problem, Meredith believes, is that African leaders have failed to provide effective government. 'Africa has suffered grievously at the hands of its Big Men and its ruling elites,' he writes. 'Their preoccupation, above all, has been to hold power for the purpose of self-enrichment ... Much of the wealth they have acquired has been squandered on luxury living or stashed away in foreign bank accounts or foreign investments. The World Bank has estimated that 40% of Africa's private wealth is held offshore. Their scramble for wealth has spawned a culture of corruption permeating every level of society.'[10]

Many Africans and Asians do not appear to accept that 'one man, one vote' means just that – one vote per person without improper persuasion (*see* V is for vote rigging). While our politicians are not angels, many African and Asian politicians appear to think that the purpose of politics is personal enrichment. To name but fifteen in alphabetical order of country, rather than in amount received in bribes, creamed off, kickbacks or just plain stolen – members of Afghan President Karzai's family, China's railways minister Liu Zhijun[11], Egypt's Muburak and his sons[12], Equatorial Guinea's Teodorin Obiang or anyway his son Teodoro, Haiti's Duvalier[13], India's telecoms minister Andimuthu Raja, Kenya's Daniel Arap Moi, Libya's Qaddafi or anyway his children, Malawi's Bingu wa Matharika, Nigeria's Abacha (and of the same country James Ibori, as to who (*see* O is for obscenity) quite apart from '419' e*mails*), Pakistan's 'Mr Ten Per Cent'[14], Sudan's Omar al-Bashir, Swaziland's King Mzwati, Tunisia's Ali (or anyway his wife, Leila, aka the Queen of Carthage), Zimbabwe's Mugabe (or anyway his wife Grace).

'Our' venal non-indigenous politicians include Lords Bhatia, Paul and Taylor and Baroness Uddin (as to the last – *see* U is for Uddin). And at the level of school governors, although they are not named by the Kershaw Report, those who encouraged and promoted Islamic principles showed 'an utter disregard for the Nolan principles and have rejected responsibility for displaying integrity, objectivity and honesty in all matters related to the governance of a school as required by regulations'.[15]

Such corruption extends to sport – FIFA officials Jack Warner (of African heritage), Amos Adamu (Nigerian) and Reynard Temarii (Tahitian); and bribe-taking Pakistani cricketers Mohammad Amir, Mohammad Asif and Salman Butt; drug takers such as Ben Johnson.[16] Mahmood Al Zarooni gave steroids to the horses he was training at Godolphin stables. And 'Westfield brings shame to England'.[17]

> By half time in the play-off matches, it was clear something was up. The two teams vying for one promotion spot to Nigerian football's fifth tier had gone into the final round-robin games equal on points and goal difference. Now, with 45 minutes left to play, Plateau United Feeders were winning 7–0, with rivals Police Machine 6–0 up.

> Then both teams really started attacking. Police Machine found the net 61 times in the second half to beat Bubayaro 67–0. Sadly, it was not enough. Plateau United Feeders' 79–0 victory over Akurba pushed them top of the four-team play-off group.[18]

For practical purposes, there were no Muslims here fifty years ago and so they are alien, but not just historically. For the most part they think differently and want to remain separate, within their own community, not to integrate/assimilate albeit wanting to live here. Rather than, with their being newcomers, going out of their way to seek to assimilate, to integrate, to become British, and indeed rather than merely wishing to maintain their own separate identity, even seeking to impose their own beliefs and culture on us (anyway in areas where they are in significant numbers). Where they can, through being so numerous, Muslims appear to want to prevent what they do not approve of – alcohol, ballet, beer festivals, mixing of the sexes, music, pantomime and pork – but certainly will not participate, will not be part of the common behaviour of the indigenous population of this country.

To them:

Football is a cancer that has infected our youth.[19]

And

Nearly every university has a department which is called the music department and in others where the satanic influence is more, they call it the Royal College of Music.[19]

and so attend neither Glastonbury nor Glyndebourne nor have anything to do with *Strictly Come Dancing*.[20]

Muslims will have nothing to do with rum baba, sherry trifle or tipsy cake, and never have it that 'nunc est bibendum'.[21]

Four hundred years ago, we tried and rejected theocracy and being ruled by religious. We are sceptical of prelates and even religious do not push it.[22] Muslims believe the state should be subject to religion – 'there is no secularism in Islam'.[23]

Rather than accept the law of this country, (many[24]) Muslims want sharia law:

- Tarik Mahri, president of the Westminster Student Union,[25] had links to Hizb ut-Tahrir, which advocates the establishment of an Islamic state, as did his vice president, Jamal Achchi.

- Ahmed Faraz, a graduate of Birmingham University, if not the owner anyway worked in Maktabah, a bookshop and publisher in Sparkhill, Birmingham, the customers of which have included Mohammed Sidique Khan (*see* T is for terrorism) and the liquid bombers (*see* L is for Luton). Faraz said the bookshop aimed to show 'Islam as a whole'). His conviction for possessing and disseminating terrorist publications with titles such as *21st Century Crusaders, Religion and Doctrine of Jihad* and *The Army of Madinah in Kashmir* was overturned by the Court of Appeal because no causal link between the books and the terrorism had been shown.

We treat men and women as equal: Muslims do not:

And those women you fear may be rebellious
Admonish; banish them to their couches,
And beat them.[26]

We walk together, the gentleman on the outside: Muslims do not.[27]

- Islam Channel, a Muslim TV channel, broadcast on Sky and Freestat –

'It shouldn't be such a big problem where the man feels he has to force himself upon the woman.' And another presenter discussed 'acceptable' levels of violence against a wife.

In our legal proceedings the evidence of a man and of a woman is equal: that is not so under sharia law.

We believe in the rule of law and that all are equal before it. Queen Victoria proclaimed:

> Firmly relying Ourselves on the truth of Christianity, and acknowledging with gratitude the solace of Religion, We disclaim the Right and Desire to impose our convictions on any of our subjects. We declare it to be Our Royal Will and Pleasure that none be in any wise favoured, none molested or disquieted by reason of their Religious Faith and Observances; but that all shall alike enjoy the equal and impartial protection of the Law.

But in Islamic societies non-Muslims, the dhimmis, are subject to discrete/extra taxation[28] – *jizya* – and to restrictions.

Muslims consider themselves honour-bound to kill the result of an adulterous union and the mother of such child; we consider that murder.

Muslims do not like dogs: we have at least six million of them.[29]

If not confused as to the difference between martyrdom, murder and suicide, the Muslim understanding of each is not ours.[30]

Perhaps uniquely, in England, there was complete freedom of testamentary disposition: that shaped our way of life and outlook, but the Koran has detailed prescription as to inheritance, with the female share being at most half that of the male.[31]

And the Muslim thinking as to truth is not ours. For us, truth is fundamental – the ninth commandment: *via, veritas, vita*; my word is my bond (even if the result is uncomfortable).[32] But for Muslims, lying is justified if they thereby perceive the cause of Islam to be thereby promoted – *taqiyya*.[33]

Muslims do not accept others and so Simon Alam, Akmol Hussein, Azad Hussein and Sheik Rashid attacked Gary Smith with a knife, a metal rod and a brick because he was head of religious education at Central Foundation Girls' School in Bow and, in their words, 'He's mocking Islam and he's putting doubts in people's minds. How can somebody take a job to teach Islam when they're not even a Muslim?' And in the words of the trial judge,

6

'Your belief is that you carried out a duty to your god and you did so with no mercy. If you think that people around you in society present an insult or threat to God then you will not hesitate in attacking again in the way that you have acted.' (Those four were assisted by Badruzzuha Uddin.)[34]

And converts to Islam seem to be at least as prone as cradle Muslims to want to blow us up:

- Richard Dart (with Jahangir Alom and Imran Mahmood) planned to attack Royal Wotton Bassett

- Andrew 'Isa' Ibrahim of Bristol was convicted of explosives offences

- Matthew Newton who was an associate of Munir Farooqi[35]

- Richard Reid, the shoe bomber

- Nick Reilly attempted to bomb a restaurant and a café in Exeter

- Nicholas Roddis of Rotherham was jailed in 2008 for a total of seven years for a bomb hoax and preparing for terrorism: in 2013 he was tried and acquitted of preparing explosives.[36]

And this antipathy seems to be particularly so for those of African heritage:

- Michael Adebowale and Michael Adebolajo, or one of them, mowed down Fusilier Lee Rigby and then almost decapitated him.[37]

- Trevor Brooks is the son of Jamaicans who came to this country in the 1960s. He was born in Hackney. Upon converting to Islam, he changed his name first to Omar Brooks and then, upon styling himself a preacher, to Abu Izzadeen. In 2006, he shouted at the then Home Secretary, 'How dare you come to a Muslim area when over 1,000 Muslims have been arrested ...' In 2008, he was convicted of terrorist fundraising and inciting terrorism overseas. He may be a spokesman for Al Ghurabaa, which was banned for advocating terrorism.

- Germiane Lindsay was born in Jamaica but aged nineteen was one of the four 7 July 2005 suicide bombers. He was married to another convert to Islam – Samantha Lewthwaite. She went on to marry another convert to Islam again from Jamaica, Jermaine Grant. He is in prison in Kenya, for fraudulently seeking citizenship; a charge of conspiracy to improvise an explosive device is progressing. (Kenya got Interpol to issue an arrest warrant for Lewthwaite in respect of the Westgate shopping mall atrocity.)

Rather than

> And still they joke, they laugh, are funny and kind
> Long live England and its open mind[38]

and

> Give me the liberty to know, to utter and to argue freely according to conscience, above all liberties[39]

and

> Freedom of thought. Nothing is more important[40]

Muslims 'reject the idea of freedom of speech and even the idea of freedom'.[41]

The Muslim mind is apparently closed, presumably pursuant to their prophet's – 'Every new matter is an innovation, every innovation is misguidance and every misguidance is in the fire [of hell]'[42] Or alternatively, just 'If Mahommed didn't do it, we don't do it.'[43] And is exemplified by

> For a millennium, Islamic scholars have insisted ....that there's nothing to debate. And what happened? As the United Nations Human Development Programme's famous 2002 report blandly noted, more books are translated in Spain in a single year than have been translated into Arabic in the last thousand years.[44]

When, in 2006, a Christian leader,[45] at the university where years before he had taught, included the following in his lecture entitled *Breadth of the Logos*:

> The emperor certainly knew that in surah 2, 256 it says: 'There is no compulsion in religion.'[46] Experts tell us that this is one of the early surahs from the time when Muhammad was himself powerless and under threat. But the emperor was naturally also acquainted with the instructions on holy war recorded in the Qur'an, which came into being later. Without going into details such as the different treatment of those who have 'The Book' and 'infidels' he addresses his dialogue partner in a tone which sounds surprisingly harsh to our ears and says 'Show me just what Muhammad brought that was new and you will only find evil and inhuman things such as his command to spread the faith with the sword'. After having lashed out in this way, the emperor goes onto substantiate in detail why spreading the faith by force is unreasonable.

effigies of the speaker were burnt and rioting occurred, even in countries outside of the Muslim world, despite the first seven words of the last sentence.

There is another reason why many immigrants are alien, a reason whereby they are likely to remain alien and which is insidious:[47]

> If you go further afield the differences are far greater, and show up even more starkly the links between the social, the political, and the economic. Why is it so hard to establish liberal democracies and effective governments in large parts of the Middle East? It is not ultimately a matter of religion but of cultural traditions associated with some versions of Islam. Their family structure may help explain why Western-style democratic government is so hard to establish in parts of the Muslim world. In Pakistan 50 per cent of marriages are to first cousins. In Saudi Arabia this figure is 36 per cent. The political structure of a society of extended families is completely different from that of a society with small families. It means that voting is by clans: it is hard to have neutral contracts enforced by an independent judiciary when family obligations are so wide-ranging and so strong.

> It is no accident that there is a Muslim brotherhood – brotherhood really does mean something in parts of the Muslim world. It weakens national governments and makes it hard for the neutral contractual arrangements of a modern economy to be created. By contrast, as Dr Johnson observed on brotherhood in England: 'Sir, in a country as commercial as ours, when every man can do for himself, there is not much occasion for that attachment. No man is thought the worse of here whose brother was hanged.' The French Revolutionaries ignored the uncomfortable truth that liberty and equality before the law are hard to reconcile with fraternity. That is why it is such a challenge to integrate communities based on fraternity into a host society where the dominant principles are liberty and equality.[48]

And there maybe something else that is even less apparent but at least as insidious:

> Why are some countries rich and others persistently poor? Capital and information flow fairly freely, so what is it that prevents poor countries from taking out a loan, copying every Scandinavian institution, and becoming as rich and peaceful as Denmark? Africa has absorbed billions of dollars in aid over the last half century and yet, until a recent spurt of growth, its standard of living has stagnated for decades. South Korea and Taiwan, on the other hand, almost as poor at the start of the period, have enjoyed an economic resurgence. Why have these countries been able to modernise so rapidly while others have found it so much harder?

The answers to such questions may lie in a hitherto unexamined possibility, that human social nature has been shaped by evolution and that human groups therefore differ slightly in their social behaviour and in social institutions that depend of that behaviour. This would explain why it is so difficult to export American institutions into tribal societies like those of Iraq and Afghanistan, just as it would be impossible to import tribal systems into the United States or Europe. Persistently poor countries, particularly those that are still tribally organised, have not been through the Malthusian wringer experienced by agrarian populations and may therefore find the transition to a modern state that much harder.

People, unlike institutions, can easily migrate from one society to another. Recall evolution's formula for social success: keep the organisms the same, just transform the social behaviour. Human nature is pretty much universal apart from slight differences in social behaviour, variations in which can lead to very different kinds of societies. Significant human differences lie at this level, not that of individuals.[49]

Notes: A is for African, Asian and alien

1. President Zuma of South Africa has a residence in KwaZulu-Natal that cost a fortune because, apart from incorporating a police station, a clinic and a nuclear bombproof bunker, his four wives have to be catered for. (The president justified the works, costing as much as £15 million of public money, as 'security upgrades' but they include a cattle kraal and a chicken coop; the explanation for the swimming pool was that it was needed as a store of water in case of fire. Following public pressure, Zuma is due to 'pay a reasonable percentage of the cost of the measures as determined with the assistance of the National Treasury.')

King Goodwill Zwelethini of the Zulus has six wives. A finance officer, Lucas Buthelezi, gave up his job because of the difficulty of finding the wherewithal to satisfy the requirement that all the wives be treated the same: there are six palaces.

2. Following the trial of Surjit Atwhal's husband and mother-in-law for Surjit's murder (see H is for honour killing) – the Metropolitan Police Sikh Association issued a press statement: 'The MPSA, taking a clear steer from the Sikh religion, condemns crimes against women, including honour killings. However, we accept that Sikhs, reverting to their Punjabi culture, which is ingrained deeply in their psyche and belief system, are responsible for many girls like Surjit disappearing without trace.'

3. Joseph Henrich, professor of psychology and economics, University of British Columbia, published by Philosophical Transactions of the Royal Society.

4. The two 'doctors' were not prosecuted, despite sufficient evidence, as such would not, it was argued, be in the public interest because either the case 'would be better dealt with by the General Medical Council', or because the Crown Prosecution Service saw the issue as 'sensitive'. Subsequently a private prosecution was stopped by the CPS.

5. Earl Howe, health minister, in answer to a parliamentary question.

6. Which must be at least a contributory reason why communities from tribal societies will not be open about criminal activity by members of that community.

7. *Culture and Conflict in the Middle East* by Philip Carl Salzman, an anthropologist at McGill University.

8. The authors of *Why Nations Fail*, published in 2012 by Profile Books.

9. Martin Meredith is the author of *The Fate of Africa: A History of Fifty years of Independence*.

10. *A Troublesome Inheritance* by Nicholas Wade, published in 2014 by Penguin Press (and *see* note 49 below).

11. This came to light after two high-speed trains collided in 2011. Initially, he was removed for so-called disciplinary violations. Those turned out to be taking bribes. He was sentenced to death with indefinite suspension. (According to James Kynge in the *Financial Times*, a Bloomberg study has shown that the seventy richest members of the National People's Congress have a combined wealth of $90 billion – compared with the $7.5 billion of the 535 members of the US Congress, the president, his cabinet and the Supreme Court.)

12. According to the preface to *Why Nations Fail* by Daron Acemoglu and James A. Robinson, they apparently acquired/were worth $70 thousand million.

13. From the obituary entitled *Hereditary despot whose destructive legacy endures* by Andrew Jack, October 2014. –

> Transparency International dubbed Duvalier one of the world's 10 most corrupt leaders in recent times. He siphoned $300m–$800m out of the country via dozens of state institutions, from the tobacco agency to the retirement fund. Prosecutors discovered that he drew a final cheque for

$169,000 on the eve of his departure as social protests intensified and the US applied pressure on him to leave.

14. Asif Ali Zardari, president 2008–13. His wife was Benazir Bhutto. Apart from houses in France and London, he had Rockwood House in Surrey. (Of her it was said, 'She's as ruthless and conniving as they come – a kleptocrat in a Hermes headscarf.')

You would not think it possible that an Asian sovereign wealth fund could run into trouble but Malaysia's $14bn 1MDM state fund came close to default earlier this year after borrowing too heavily to buy energy projects and speculate on land. Its bonds are currently trading at junk level.

It became a piggy bank for the political elites and now faces a corruption probe, a recurring pattern in the BRICs and mini-BRICs as the liquidity tide recedes and exposes who was swimming naked.

The world must prepare for its dollar-binge punishment by Ambrose Evans-Pritchard, *Financial Times*, March 2015.

15. Paragraph 30 (and also 157) of the Kershaw Report.

The Nolan principles are selflessness, integrity, objectivity, accountability, openness, honesty and leadership.

The Labour Party manifesto for the 1997 general election promised that 'the Nolan recommendations will be fully implemented and extended to all public bodies'.

16. Born in Jamaica in 1961; moved to Canada in 1976. After Johnson had been stripped of world records and Olympic titles for use of banned substances, the Canadian amateur sports minister suggested Johnson return to Jamaica, which Johnson said was by far the most disgusting comment he had ever heard.

17. Meryvn Westfield, of African ethnicity, was a fast bowler for Essex. He was jailed in 2012 for accepting money for conceding runs and bowling, in his words, 'deliberately badly'. He said he was inveigled into this criminality by 'Danish': that is Danish Kaneria, who also played for Essex. The English and Welsh Cricket Board found charges against Kaneria to be proved: an appeal board upheld the life ban. Kaneria went to the High Court, claiming the life ban and order to pay £200,000 costs were wrong. The claim was dismissed; Kaneria was not there to hear this decision; the judge was told he was in Pakistan.

'Danish' does not appear to have anything to do with Denmark – Danish Irfan 'repeatedly and ferociously' smashed his wife's head with a hammer at their home in Alford Terrace, Bradford.

18. Xan Rice in the *Financial Times*, 13 July 2013.

Not about sport but also about Nigeria, from *SMA Mission News* (The journal of The Society of African Missions) by Fr Donal Fennessy of Spring 2014:

> The week after the crisis I passed through Assikio, one of the towns afflicted by the conflict. I was sad to see most of the houses burned down. Most of the trees were cut down, some blocking the main road. The reason for cutting down the trees, I'm told, was because one of the tribes believed that the other tribe had charms that could help them hide inside the trees. So by cutting the trees down they believed they would kill anybody inside them. What a destructive sight, to see all these fine mature trees now all gone ...
>
> As usual we had a great number of candidates wanting to go to the diocesan seminary this year. In all, 67 applicants presented themselves with their academic qualifications on paper. Unfortunately, many got these qualifications by attending 'miracle schools' where a lot of exam malpractice goes on. After giving them some written tests, the number who passed was 27. These were then interviewed and 10 were deemed suitable to undertake seminary studies, one of them from our parish here at Shinge.

19. Yusef Riyadh ul Haq, born in Gujarat in 1971 and moved here three years later, and so resident here for as good as all his formative years plus several following decades. He became an imam in Birmingham and more recently in Leicester.

In 2015 Ofsted inspected various schools in Tower Hamlets. In the case of East London Islamic School it reported 'A pupil in Year 1 explained to inspectors that he would "go to hell" if he participated in music or dance'.

20. *Towards Greater Understanding: Meeting the Needs of Muslim Pupils in State Schools* by the Muslim Council of Britain:

> Dance is one of the activity areas of the national curriculum for physical education. Muslims consider that most dance activities, as practised in the curriculum, are not consistent with the Islamic requirements for modesty as they may involve sexual connotations and messages when performed within mixed-gender groups or if performed in front of mixed audiences. Most primary and secondary schools hold dance in mixed-gender classes and may include popular dance styles in which movements of the body are seen as sexually expressive and seductive in nature ... However, most Muslim parents will find little or no

13

educational merit or value in dance or dancing after early childhood and may even find it objectionable on moral and religious grounds once children have become sexually mature (puberty). Some parents consider it to be acceptable within a single sex context provided the dance movements have no sexual connotations. As dancing is not a normal activity for most Muslim families, Muslim pupils are likely to exhibit reluctance to taking part in it, particularly in mixed-gender sessions.

The Ofsted report for Nansen Primary School, one of the Trojan Horse schools (*see* F is for fifth column) of April 2014 found:

> Pupils do not get a broad education. The governing body has removed some subjects, such as music, from the timetable.

21. Horace (65–8 BC) 'Now is (the time) for drinking.'

Nearer in time and place, Daniel Defoe (1660–1731):

> Good husbandry is no English virtue. English labouring people eat and drink, especially the latter, three times as much in value as any sort of foreigners of the same dimensions in the world.

22. Part of the abbey at Bury St Edmunds was burnt down by the town's populace in 1327 because of disquiet with the monks. Today, evangelists are 'God squad'.

23. A Jordanian academic.

Peculiarly there is a striking similarity between puritanism and Mohammedanism – the emphasis on the Bible in the former and the Koran in the latter, and in both cases the subsidiarity of the state to such higher authority.

As to the former, 'To the puritan, everything – not only religion and theology, but also secular and ecclesiastical government as well as the rules of personal conduct and private life – was laid down in the Bible' (*England under the Tudors* by G.R. Elton) but in 1660 we rejected puritanism.

24. This came from:

> Over here, some of our 'banlieues' have turned into mirror images of African homelands, with more than 20 million Muslims inside the EU. Forty per cent of these Muslims in the UK alone would welcome sharia law (i.e. stoning adulterers to death, chopping off limbs for stealing, and covering up women). And what are we doing about it? Easy. We are worried over the 'relentless hostility towards Islam'.
> (Taki Theodoracopulos, *The Spectator* July 2015).

That 'forty per cent' presumably came from an ICM poll conducted in February 2006. In response to the question 'Would you support or oppose there being areas of Britain which are predominantly Muslim and in which sharia law is introduced?' 40% (of the sample of 500) agreed, the same percentage opposed, 1% refused to answer the question and 18% didn't know.

25. Students of Wesminster University include Mohammed Emwazi who probably became 'Jihadi John', the decapitator of hostages for ISIS and Umar Farouk Abdulmutallab, the 'Underpants bomber'.

26. Chapter 4:38 of the Koran.

27. (*See* the website *Anorak*) – *The Truth about Charlene Downes and Blackpool's Paedophile Gangs*: 'He had no respect for us, the way we dressed, the way we drank, how forward we were. It was as though white girls were asking for it. He'd say that all English girls were slags, unlike Muslim women who wore the hijab and walked five steps behind their husband.'

28. After ISIS took over Mosul in Iraq in July 2014, the Christians were told 'We offer them three choices: Islam, the dhimma contract – involving payment of jizya: if they refuse this they will have nothing but the sword.' This is pursuant to chapter 9:29 of the Koran:

Fight all those who believe not in God and the Last Day
And do not forbid what God and His Messenger
have forbidden – such men as practice not the
religion of truth, being of those who have been given
the Book – until they pay the tribute [jizya] out of hand
and have been humbled.

While I have no Arabic, I perceive the following is clearer and, more importantly, still accurate:

Fight all those who do not believe in God and the Last Day
And (also) those who do not forbid what God and Mohammed have
forbidden – such as being Jews or Christians, are not Mohmmedians
– until they feel subdued and pay tribute.

29. Scottish terriers were used to lead each team at the Commonwealth Games in Glasgow in 2014. A Malaysian politician said, 'This is just so disrespectful to Malaysia and Muslims – especially as it happened during Ramadan. Muslims are not allowed to touch dogs, so the organiser should have been more aware and sensitive on this issue.' ('Jock', the Scottie who

15

was to lead the Malaysian team, was canny: he refused to move as soon as he had his (Malaysian) coat put on and had to be carried.)

30. The following is from *The New Persecution* by John L. Allen Jr:

If a female catechist is killed in the Democratic Republic of the Congo, for instance, because she's persuading young people to stay out of militias and criminal gangs, one might say that's a tragedy but not martyrdom, because her assailants weren't driven by hatred of the Christian faith. Yet the crucial point isn't just what was in the mind of her killers, but what was in the heart of the catechist, who knowingly put her life on the line to serve the gospel. To make her attackers' motives the only test, rather than her own, is to distort reality.

31. (*See* chapter 1 of), *Who We Are* of David Willetts' *The Pinch: How the baby boomers took their children's future – and why they should give it back.*

32. Also, by Leo Tolstoy (1828–1910):

Be bad, but at least don't be a liar, a deceiver.
Anything is better than lies and deceit.

33. According to one view, *taqiyya* is the Islamic art of softening the hearts of those who do not hold that Mohammed to be God's (last) prophet. In his *The Losing Battle with Islam* (published by Prometheus Books in 2005) David Selbourne lists twelve 'devices' (albeit they 'overlap, are related and may be employed serially') of *taqiyya*, of Islamic deception.

The following paragraphs of the Clarke Report are examples of such deception:

4.20 At Park View, three Muslim men were selected to teach SRE to boys: the Pupil Leadership Coordinator, the Head of Modern Foreign Languages and the acting headteacher. Ignoring the scheme of work prepared by the co-ordinator, they prepared their own materials. The lessons for the boys centred on the rights of men and women within marriage. On the lesson worksheets it was written that if a woman said 'No' to sex with her husband, the Angel Gabriel would strike her down and condemn her to an eternity of hell. Following these lessons, there was commotion in the corridors, with boys telling girls that they couldn't refuse them saying, 'We have been told this'. An assembly following the lessons was supposed to put right the SRE teaching but again the boys were in effect told that 'this is what it says in Islam but it is different in the eyes of British society'. Staff reported that one of the teachers who gave the lessons said: 'Luckily we were able to hide all the controversial worksheets very, very quickly and managed to get rid of all of them between the two Ofsted inspections.'

16

4.28 At Golden Hillock, we were informed that boys and girls sat separately for assemblies. After the assembly, boys shook hands with a male teacher and girls with a female when exiting. Staff state that senior leaders checked their classrooms and removed Islamic display materials before the Department for Education visited.

4.33 Friday prayers have been introduced at a number of schools. Their part in the central life of the school is growing, as is the pressure on students and staff to attend. We have been told by staff at Park View that a tannoy to broadcast the 'adhan', the Muslim call to prayer, was installed. It could not only be heard across the whole school site, but also by residents in the local community, and used every day to call students and staff to prayer. However, it was switched off immediately before Ofsted visited the school and also on the days when the Department for Education and Education Funding Council officials visited. I was informed that a member of staff at Park View used a microphone from a high window to shout at students who were in the playground, not attending prayers. Some girls were embarrassed when attention was drawn to them because girls who are menstruating are not allowed to attend prayer. But still, the teacher called to them.

4.34 A member of Park View staff, who had been seconded to Golden Hillock, held Friday prayers outside in the main playground, making a point of using a central space. Photographs of the event were posted on the school's website but were removed the day before the Department for Education officials visited. Students who did not wish to attend prayers had pressure put on them by staff and other students.

The National College for Teaching and Leadership conducted an investigation into the professional conduct of Akeel Ahmed, who taught at Park View Academy. A paragraph of its decision, in February 2016, is as follows:

The panel has dealt with the call to prayer under 1b. Mr Ahmed accepts that as Collective Worship Coordinator until May 2013 he was responsible for arranging the call to prayer. Witness A told the panel they and some of the staff felt uncomfortable about the call to prayer being broadcast daily in a British state school; it did not seem appropriate. The panel notes that the call to prayer was suspended during the 2014 Ofsted inspection as confirmed in evidence before the panel by Witness A who stated that when they asked a member of the SLT why the call was not being broadcast they were told to the effect that 'we have to play the game'. The panel is satisfied that the broadcasting of a call to prayer was to encourage the pupils to pray during the school day.

Islam and 'godless' communism also have in common long-term subversion through education. The following by Charles Moore is from *The Trojan Horse Affair is about subversion and only Gove understood this* and was published by *The Spectator* after Michael Gove (Minister for Education) was 'moved' from education and immediately after publication of the Clarke Report:

> The Clarke Report also highlights the error of the 'securocrats' in discarding the concept of subversion. MI5 proudly boasts on its website that, since the end of the Cold War, it has not investigated subversion. By concentrating only on actual terrorism, it has failed to understand how Islamist extremism works, particularly its power in intimidating fellow Muslims and preaching a pseudo-religious political narrative in which the West is always in the wrong. The Trojan Horse affair is exactly about subversion. As with the original beast, our own guards failed to spot what was within the gates. When Margaret Thatcher was education secretary in the early 1970s, the Chief Rabbi, Immanuel Jakobovits, told her that her job made her 'the real minister of defence in this country'. Islamists understand that concept, and work ceaselessly to weaken that defence. Mr Cameron has moved the only minister who really understands this. As Prime Minister, he directs the security agencies. If he is proud of the Gove legacy, as he says he is, he should charge them to investigate subversion once more.

Although it is only a novel, Michel Houellebecq's *Submission*, about Muslims becoming the largest political grouping in France and thereby obtaining power, has it that they would agree any division of ministries with their coalition partners so long as they had education (because) 'If you control the children, you control the future.'

And yet Abu Usamah, an imam at Green Lane Mosque, Small Heath, Birmingham (*see* note 18 to I is for integration and S is for swarm and swamp) said, 'Part of being a non-Muslim is … that they are liars … usually.'

For the 2014 election for mayor of Tower Hamlets, Mohammed Lutfur Rahman (*see* V is for vote rigging) equated voting for himself with being a good Muslim and 101 local imams said the same (*see* Appendix V). Such election was adjudged to be void by reason of corrupt and illegal practices (*Erlam and others v. Mohammed Lutfur Rahman and another*). Such practices apart, lying was par for the course by Mr Rahman and other Muslims: the following are from paragraphs of the judgment:

> 214 – It must be said that Mr [Councillor Jalal] Ahmed was not a satisfactory witness.

250 – Mr [Alibor] Choudhury [Rahman's election agent] was a very unsatisfactory witness. He was arrogant, indeed cocky, and did not hesitate to tell bare-faced lies in the smug assurance that mere lawyers listening to him would not have the wit to see through them.

543 with an insert from 540 – Obviously a court will be wary of disbelieving evidence given on oath by a cleric, especially a senior cleric, of any faith. The external evidence, however, strongly indicated that Mr Hoque [the chairman of the Council of Mosques] ... one of the witnesses who insisted on an interpreter while making it quite clear that he understood English perfectly well .... had not told the truth about these events. The evidence he gave about the next element was also very unsatisfactory. Sadly, the court was not able to treat Mr Hoque as a reliable witness.

297 – In short, Mr Rahman was evasive and discursive to a very high degree.

298 – Sadly, it must also be said that he was not truthful. In one or two crucial matters he was caught out in what were quite blatant lies.

And *see* O is for obscenity – both Huseen Abase and Lady Uddin.

Thus for adherents thereof, lying is justified if Islam is thereby promoted. And there is a counterintuitive parallel with Marxist Leninism – if the revolution is thereby promoted. For both, truth has to be subjected to the ultimate aim. For both, there is the permanent endeavour for world domination – jihad and the proletarian revolution; how long it takes is not crucial, hence attacking the status quo by subverting the education of children (*see* F is for fifth column and earlier in this note).

A similar point was made by Oriana Fallaci in *The Force of Reason* (*see* note 2 to I is for integration):

The Left is a Church. And not a Church similar to the Church which came out of Christianity, thus open to free will. A Church similar to Islam. Like Islam it considers itself sanctified by a God who is the custodian of the Truth. Like Islam it never acknowledges its faults and its errors, it considers itself infallible and never apologizes.

Like Islam it demands a world at its own image, a society built on the verses of its Prophet. Like Islam it enslaves its own followers. It intimidates them, and makes them feel stupid even when they are intelligent. Like Islam it does not accept different opinions and if you think differently it despises you. It denigrates you, it punishes you. Like Islam, in short, it is illiberal. Autocratic, totalitarian, even when it plays the game of democracy.

34. But many Muslims do seem prepared to accept their children attend Roman Catholic schools: for instance, 90% of the children at Rosary Primary School in Saltley, Birmingham, are, or were before Polish immigration, Muslim. But they then seek to have their cultural norms accepted by such schools (*see* note 6 to I is for invasion).

35. Munir Farooqi was born in Pakistan but came to this country in 1962 when he was five. He was convicted on five counts – one of engaging in conduct in preparation for acts of terrorism, three counts of soliciting murder and one count of dissemination of terrorist publications; (and *see* note 16 to C is for community).

36. Another example is Simon Keeler. Having been jailed for assaulting a police officer at a Muslim demonstration, he was jailed for four years for recruiting Muslims to jihad.

37. Perhaps the explanation is:

> For more than a thousand years the influence of Mohammedanism, which appears to possess a strange fascination for negroid races, has been permeating the Soudan, and although ignorance and natural obstacles impede the progress of new ideas, the whole of the black race is gradually adopting the new religion and developing Arab characteristics.

From *The River War: an account of the reconquest of the Sudan (in 1899)* by Winston Churchill.

The fascination continues – Germaine Lindsay from Jamaica was one of the 7 July 2005 suicide bombers; Basiru Gassama from Gambia was part of the Parviz Khan plot to kidnap and behead a British soldier; Brusthom Ziamani, whose father was from the Congo, planned to emulate his 'legend' Adebolajo; and Grace Dare (born here but of Nigerian parents –*see* B is for the benefit and burden of (im)migration).

38. Stella Mann, born in Austria in 1912, married a British soldier in 1946, founder of The College of Performing Arts.

A draft of this book included, here, the words of Ray Honeyford (*see* H is for Ray Honeyford) – 'the British traditions of understatement, civilised discourse and respect for reason' – on the basis that Muslims did not ascribe thereto. However on checking I found that those words were preceded by 'an influential group of black intellectuals of aggressive disposition, who know little of...'

I still think the point is appropriate. Quite apart from the contents of note 33, following the murder of Fusilier Lee Rigby in Woolwich on 22 May 2013, by one or more converts to Islam of African ethnicity, Tell Mama (measuring anti-Muslim attacks) complained there had been a 'wave of attacks' against Muslims, with its founder Fiyaz Mughal saying, 'I do not see an end to this cycle of violence.' In fact, fifty-seven of the incidents were online, only seventeen of the 212 incidents – 8% – were physical and, rather than 'unprecedented', the attacks were slightly fewer than after the bombings of 7 July 2005. Mughal complained to the Press Complaints Commission. The PCC ruled that Tell Mama had exaggerated the occurrence of anti-Muslim attacks.

And apart from that complaint to the PCC, Mughal/Tell Mama claimed that *The Daily Telegraph* had libelled him/it (*see* the last two paragraphs to H is for hegemony and note 35 thereto) and was defamatory. The judgment was followed by the author, Charles Moore, commenting and asking:

> Not long after the murder of Drummer Lee Rigby in Woolwich [in May 2013] I wrote a piece in *The Daily Telegraph* criticising the concentration on the alleged backlash against Muslims. I attacked an organisation called Tell Mama, run by Fiyaz Mughal, for appearing to suggest that the unpleasant EDL was as monstrous as al-Qu'eda. Later in the piece, I wrote that, when you publish on such matters, you are all too often 'subject to 'lawfare' – a blizzard of solicitors' letters claiming damages for usually imagined libels. So it proved. Along came a solicitor's letter from the firm of Farooq Bajwa, saying that I had described Mr Mughal as an extremist. Last week, I attended a court hearing. Was the complainant right about the 'natural and ordinary meaning' of my words? This week the judge, Mr Justice Tugenhat, determined that he was wrong, so we won. Mr Mughal, who is, indeed, not an extremist but seems to be a fool, has now lost two legal cases (including mine) and a PCC case on related matters. What is depressing is the habit among some Muslim groups of seeing ordinary unfavourable comment as something to suppress through the law. Why can't they debate not litigate?

39. John Milton (1608–1674).

While conscience (to judge oneself on the basis of one's own conscience) is part of our make up, it is an alien concept to Muslims. The Arabic word for (and presumably concept of) conscience seems only to have appeared a century or so ago, the reason for this being that to Muslims, God's command had been given once and for all, namely the Koran, and it is not for man to (try to) understand it, much less to apply one's own reasoning.

21

40. What Princess Topazia Alliata 1913–2015 replied when asked by a granddaughter what life had taught her: from an obituary.

41. Ustadh Hamza Tzortis, who was a speaker at one of the Park View Educational Trust schools in Birmingham: *see* F is for fifth column.

42. Alternatively, 'Every new matter is an innovation, every innovation is misguidance and every misguidance is in the fire.' Or 'Follow and do not innovate for indeed you have sufficient and every innovation is misguidance.'

43. Mufti Mohammed Pandor, faith advisor to the universities of Bradford and Huddersfield. (*See Why do Muslims have a thing about Guy Fawkes?* by Jane Kelly *Salisbury Review* April 2016).

44. *The slow death of free speech* by Mark Steyn *The Spectator* April 2014. And from Nicholas Wade's *A troublesome Inheritance* (*see* note 49).

> The intellectual tradition of Islam, that the Qur'an and the sayings of Muhammad contained all science and law, created a hostile environment for all independent lines of thought.... Istanbul did not acquire a printing press until 1726 and the owners were allowed to publish only a few titles before being closed down.

Originally, in note 39, I quoted Diderot's *Islam is the enemy of reason.* I eventually found the "source" namely in the chapter *Sarrasins* of Diderot's *Encylopedié.* I cannot find a (decent) translation (into English) but two (consecutive) sentences are

> *Ce fut le raisonnement d'après lequel un des généraux sarrazins fit chauffer pendant six mois les bains publics avec les précieux manuscrits de la bibliothèque d'Alexandrie. On peut regarder Mahomet comme le plus grand ennemi que la raison humaine ait eu.*

One explanation (of at least three) for the loss of the (ancient) library of Alexandria is that after the followers of Mohammed took Alexandria in 642 the general asked the caliph what to do with the library's contents. He replied that if the books were in accordance with the Koran, they were superfluous and if the books were not in accordance with the Koran there could be no need to preserve them; so destroy the library's contents. Hence, I suppose, Diderot's statement that the (precious) manuscripts heated the public baths in Alexandria for six months.

Today Pervey Hoodbhoy head of physics department Quid-i-Azam University, Islamabad:

> No major intervention or discovery has emerged from the Muslim world for well over seven centuries now.

45. Pope Benedict XVI: part of his lecture in 2006 to the University of Regensburg, entitled *Breadth of the Logos.*

46. (But) in the hadiths, said to be sayings of Mohammed, compiled about two centuries after he died, it is stated that he said, 'Whoever changes his religion, kill him.'

47. [Definition =] '1 stealthy, subtle, cunning or treacherous; 2 working in a subtle or apparently innocuous way, but nevertheless deadly.'

48. *The Pinch: How the baby boomers took their children's future – and why they should give it back* by David Willetts, published in 2010 by Atlantic Books.

As to the levels of first-cousin marriage, Mr Willetts refers to Emmanuel Todd, *After the Empire. The Breakdown of American Order,* Columbia University Press. For the consequences of first-cousin marriage *see* D is for disease as to *Born in Bradford.*

49. Nicholas Wade's preview, May 2014, of his *A Troublesome Inheritance: Genes, Race and Human History,* then to be published by Penguin; and notes 10 and 44 above.

Mr Wade's thesis is that evolution is not just biological but also cultural/sociological and those indigenous to the western edge of the Eurasian landmass have, by evolution, acquired habits that at least currently appear to be conducive to successful societies.

Quite evidently, evolution did not stop with the emergence of Homo sapiens, say 200,000 years ago. We may have all looked alike when, say, about two thirds of the time since then, a few of us wandered out of Africa but today their descendants do not look like the descendants of those who then remained in Africa. That evolution has continued is demonstrated by the indigenous inhabitants of the Tibetan plateau having acquired an adaption to the thin atmosphere: 'It is a great example of human evolution. This adaption stopped Tibetans suffering from hypoxia,' – *Nature Genetics.*

For creationists, suffice it that the various races do not look alike but are all Homo sapiens, and all appear to be descended from one single base.

On the basis of Mr Wade's thesis, the final paragraph of the conclusion of *Immigration Economics* by George J. Borjas, published by Harvard University Press in 2014, namely

The long, long run: Even if all new immigrants were turned away starting tomorrow, the large-scale migration flows that entered the developed countries in the past three decades have already set in motion a series of economic and labor market adjustments that are bound to affect these countries throughout the next century. As a result, it is crucial to find out what will happen to the children and grandchildren of the immigrants and the extent to which ethnic external effects may or may not delay the economic progress of the descendants. The evidence suggests that ethnicity matters, and that it matters a lot, even in such a socially mobile country as the United States. Nevertheless, we need a far better understanding of the role that these ethnic external effects will play in different economic and social settings. The long-term impact of immigration will hinge crucially on the factors that strengthen or weaken ethnic externality.

is particularly worrying.

And A is for the Australian attitude

A former prime minister apparently expressed the Australian attitude to immigrant society:

Immigrants not Australians must adapt. Take it or leave it. I am tired of this nation worrying about whether we are offending some individual or their culture. Since the terrorist attacks on Bali we have experienced a surge in patriotism by the majority of Australians.

This culture has been developed over two centuries of struggles, trials and victories of men and women who have sought freedom.

We speak mainly English, not Spanish, Lebanese, Arabic, Chinese, Japanese, Russian or any other language. Therefore, if you wish to become part of our society learn the language.

Most Australians believe in God. This is not some Christian, right wing, political push but a fact because Christian men and women, on Christian principles, founded this nation and this is clearly documented. It is certainly appropriate to display it on the walls of our schools. If God offends you, then I suggest you consider another part of the world as your new home, because God is part of our culture. We will accept your beliefs and not question why. All we ask is that you accept ours and live in harmony and peaceful enjoyment with us.

This is our country, our land, and our lifestyle and we will allow you every opportunity to enjoy all of this. But once you are done complaining, whining and griping about our flag, our pledge, our Christian beliefs, our way of life, I highly encourage you to take advantage of one other great Australian opportunity, the right to leave.

If you are not happy here, then leave. We didn't force you to be here. So accept the country you accepted.[1]

In late 2013, because the government had 'become increasingly concerned about non-citizens who engage in conduct that is not in line with the expectations of The Australian community', it introduced the requirement that would-be asylum seekers sign up to a code of conduct, namely:

This Code of Behaviour contains a list of expectations about how you will behave at all times while in Australia. It does not contain all your rights and duties under Australian law. If you are found to have breached the Code of Behaviour, you could have your income support reduced, or your visa cancelled. If your visa is cancelled you will be returned to immigration detention and may be transferred to an offshore processing centre.

- You must not disobey any Australian laws including Australian road laws; you must cooperate with all lawful instructions given to you by police and other government officials;

- You must not make sexual contact with another person without that person's consent, regardless of their age; you must never make sexual contact with someone under the age of consent;

- You must not take part in, or get involved in any criminal behaviour in Australia, including violence against any person, including your family or government officials; deliberately damage property; give false identity documents or lie to a government official;

- You must not harass, intimidate or bully any other person or group of people or engage in any antisocial or disruptive activities that are inconsiderate, disrespectful or threaten the peaceful enjoyment of other members of the community;

- You must not refuse to comply with any health undertaking provided by the Department of Immigration and Border Protection or direction issued by the Chief Medical Officer (Immigration) to undertake treatment for a health condition for public health purposes;

- You must co-operate with all reasonable requests from the department or its agents in regard to the resolution of your status, including requests to attend interviews or to provide or obtain identity and/or travel documents.

I [name to be written] agree to abide by this Code of Behaviour while I am living in Australia on a Bridging E visa. I understand that if I do not abide by the Code of Behaviour my income support may be reduced or ceased, or my visa may be cancelled and I will be returned to immigration detention.

Notes: A is for the Australian attitude

1. Allegedly said by Julia Gillard, the prime minister of Australia, 2010–13, but perhaps it was only revamped comments of earlier prime ministers, John Howard and Kevin Rudd.

This attitude is not unique. In December 2006 Tony Blair in his speech *The Duty to integrate Shared British Values* said 'Our tolerance is part of what makes Britain, Britain. So conform to it, or don't come here.' And in August 2015 (with the tide of migrants into Europe via Greece) Milos Zeman, the president of the Czech Republic, said (to the migrants), 'If you do not like it, just go away.'

B is for being assaulted in one's own country because one is of it

- Airmen from RAF Wittering, by Peterborough, are told not to wear their uniform in the town because of verbal abuse from immigrants.

- Andrew Goodram suffered a punctured lung and two broken ribs when four Asian men attacked him in Queens Park, Bolton, shouting, 'white bastard'.

- Rhea Page was assaulted by Somalis – Ambaro, Ayan and Hibo Maxamed and their cousin Ifrah Nur, who allegedly shouted, 'Kill the white slag' and 'white bitch'. According to Miss Page, 'They were taking turns to kick me in the head and back over and over. I honestly think they attacked me just because I was white. I can't think of any other reason.' (The assailants escaped prison after the judge decided the attack was not racially motivated and heard in mitigation that the assailants were not used to alcohol because their religion, Islam, does not allow it.)

And B is for the benefit and burden of (im)migration

For benefit, ask the family of Police Constable Keith Blakelock.[1] Ask the family of Philip Lawrence.[2] Ask the family of Stephen Lawrence.[3] Ask the family of Fusilier Lee Rigby.[4]

Ask the users of the midwifery services and of A & E. Ask the parents trying to find a school place for their child.

Ask the (white) working class (see B is for betrayal). Ask the (white) girls of, inter alia, Blackburn, Derby, Oxford, Rochdale, Rotherham and Telford (see D is for Derby).

Listen to Anjem Choudary.[5]

Consider that 'Jihadi John'[6] was educated in this country, and hear the following story: Grace (Dare) was born here in 1991 to immigrants from Nigeria. While at Sydenham Girls School she became a Muslim and changed her name to Khadijah. She attended Lewisham Islamic Centre[7] and Lewisham College (as to media and film studies, psychology and sociology). She married a Turk and had a son, Isa. In 2013, she married Abu

Bakr (who several months later was killed fighting in Syria) and after the killing of James Foley[8] she posted a picture of Isa with a Kalashnikov and tweeted:

> Any links 4 da execution of journalist plz. Allahu Akbar. UK must b shaking up ha ha. I wna b da 1st UK woman 2 kill a UK or US terrorist!

For benefit, ask the (indigenous) people of this country, when they find the following additions to poetry in the English language:

> I draw for a shank
> You boys will get poked
> We do not pet to do murders
> Come round here, you'll get bored
> That don't work out, draw your sword.[9]

> Let us make jihad
> Move to the front line
> To chop chop head of the kuffar swine
> It's not as messy or as hard as some may think
> It's all about the flow of the wrist.[10]

Or when they read the following newspaper heading/item:

> Return of 250 British jihadis is serious threat, says minister.

> [Followed by] Britain is facing a 'significant and growing' threat from up to 250 British-based jihadis who went to train and fight in Syria and have returned home, a minister has warned.

> James Brokenshire, a Home Office minister, said the security services were facing a 'big problem' for the 'foreseeable future' from 'jihad tourists'. His comments came amid claims that security services were monitoring 250 individuals, more than five times the number previously reported ...[11]

Or when they read these tweets by 'British' girls gone to Syria:[12]

> Happy#9/11 Happiest day of my life. Hopefully more to come In Sha Allah #Is [12.1]

> May Allah protect all the mujahideen in Franceeee!!!Shooting was maaaad!![12.2]

> Vans, Nike, Chelsea FC, beheading kafirs[12.3]

For burden:

> Kieran McKay seldom smiles. He lives with his three brothers in a council flat in southeast London, his mother works punishing hours at a hospital,

his father long ago returned to Jamaica and, for a nine-year-old, he is disarmingly melancholy.

But for this young black boy from Peckham, an area known for crime-ridden estates, sink schools and violence, as well as strong support for Millwall Football Club, one thing makes him happy. For two years Kieran has played rugby for the Southwark Tigers.

Many of the players come from single parent families and some attend special schools. On Sunday morning, these hoody-clad youths drift through holes in fences and clamber over upturned trolleys into Burgess Park – near where Damiola Taylor was murdered in 2000 – and train in the shadow of the surrounding tower blocks.

It is a far cry from the well-kept pitches of the public schools, where so many international players learnt their sport. Very few members of the latest England team went to comprehensive schools and only two were black.[13]

I am surprised that, in calling for a free-for-all immigration policy, the Bishop of Dudley and others have failed to realise that they are urging the Government to strip developing countries of their most energetic and able people.[14]

Nick Clegg, the [former] Deputy Prime Minister, says that our health service would 'fall over' if it were not for foreign nationals working within it. This may be true, but it seems to lack any appreciation of the questionable morality of this position.

Is it fair for a wealthy country such as ours to poach health professionals from poorer countries, whose own health services may then be in danger of 'falling over'?

We read that midwives are being recruited from Bulgaria at a salary of £35,000 a year. This may be great for the midwives concerned but one wonders how this will affect the service available to mothers in Bulgaria.

This seems even more unfair if one considers the Bulgarian taxpayers have paid for the training of these folk. Surely we should be striving to train our own health workers rather than relying on foreign workers who are trained at someone else's expense. [15]

This problem is particularly acute in the health sector. A particularly striking example was given to us by Patrick Taran of the International Labour Organisation (ILO), who had been told when in southern Africa recently that half the wards in the national public health hospital in the capital of Botswana had been closed down because of shortages of nursing staff, who had been recruited to work in the United Kingdom and other western countries. A similar situation can arise in Europe.

29

Madame Quinn noted that Romania was losing many doctors, who were well trained but badly paid, to the old Member states.[16]

Notes: *B is for the benefit and burden of (im)migration*

1. Hacked to death in a riot in Broadwater Farm, Tottenham, in 1985, the first constable to be killed in a riot since 1833. Winston Silcott (of African ethnicity) was initially convicted of his murder but subsequently acquitted but remained in prison for another murder.

2. Headmaster of St George's, Maida Vale. In 1995, he went outside the school gates to the aid of a pupil who was being attacked by a gang that included Learco Chindamo, then aged fifteen. Chindamo's father is Italian, his mother a Filipino; she moved here with her son when he was six. Chindamo successfully resisted deportation, to Italy, on the basis of having lived here for so long (albeit ten of those years were in prison).

3. Stabbed to death by indigenous youths in 1993 in south-east London. The murder, or rather the performance of the police, was the reason for the Macpherson Report.

4. Run down and then almost decapitated outside Woolwich Barracks because he was British soldier.

5. Apart from anything else, Choudary argues that because the Koran has the words 'obey not the unbelievers' (chapter 33), he should not have to obey the laws of this country (despite having been a solicitor).

I was not able to get to the source but read that the founding chapter of the Muslim Parliament of Great Britain had – has? – this:

For a Muslim, the observance of his host country's laws is optional. A Muslim must obey the Sharia and the Sharia alone.

Anjem Choudary appears in Stacey Dooley's report of her home town of Luton. Watch/listen to www.youtube.com/watch?v=SgKM1wVOpn, (and *see* L is for Luton).

There is an historical parallel – the Puritans. A.L. Rowse wrote in *The England of Elizabeth*, 'she was disgusted by their hateful Biblical intolerance'. And G.M. Trevelyan: 'certainly there was more chance that [the Queen's Church of England] would be acceptable to the English than the scripture pedantry of the Puritan who must find a text to justify every act of daily life ...'

In the century after Elizabeth's death, the Puritans first took over but were then rejected by the people who wanted their old ways of Christmas, drink and maypoles.

6. Thought to be Mohammed Emwazi: (*see* note 25 to A is for African, Asian and alien and note 33 to I is for integration).

7. The killers of Fusilier Lee Rigby also attended such mosque.

8. It is alleged that he was murdered by Jihadi John: (*see* note 6).

9. From a (song) recorded by Donnel Carty. "Shank" is knife; "poked is stabbed"; "pet" is fear; "bored" is knifed; "sword" is knife: apparently Jamaican patois.

Carty with Delano Brown, neither indigenous, at about 11pm on 12 January 2006 near Kensal Green tube station robbed Kurshid Ali and half an hour later sought to rob Thomas ap Rhys Pryce: in the following fight, Thomas the great-grandson of a general, was stabbed at least three times, once in the heart.

10. Samina Malix, 'the lyrical terrorist': (*see* I is for integration).

Another example is *Inglan is a Bitch* by Linton Kwesi Johnson, who was born in Jamaica in 1952 and came here in 1963.

11. *The Daily Telegraph*, 17 February 2014. The number has subsequently multiplied – in October 2015 the *Evening Standard* stated it to be more than 750.

Some will not return. First, suicide bombers such as Abdul Waheed Majeed of, appropriately, Martyrs Avenue, Crawley, and Talha Asmal (aka Abu Yusuf al Britany of Dewsbury). Secondly, those killed in fighting such as Hasan Blidi (from Algeria via Southwark) and Walid Hussain and Mohammed and Akram Sebah.

12. *Isis takes its British schoolgirl jihadis seriously. Why don't we?* by Mary Wakefield, *The Spectator*, October 2015.

12.1. Zahra Halane from Manchester.

12.2. Her twin sister Salma upon learning of the Charlie Hebdo massacre in Paris in early 2015.

12.3. Um Ayoub … listing a few of her favourite things.

13. Hannah Fletcher in *The Times* of 1 December 2007 … and reproduced, later that day, in *Bahamas Rugby*.

14. Jeffrey Pearson, letter to a newspaper. The same point has been made about the Gurkhas and Nepal.

15. John Glanville, letter to a newspaper, December 2013.

16. From paragraph 33 of *Economic Migration* to the EU House of Lords' European Economic Committee, 14th report of Session 2005–06 (HL Paper 58).

And **B** is for betrayal

In his speech to the Labour Party Conference in October 1996, Tony Blair said, 'Ask me my three main priorities for government and I tell you, Education, Education, Education.' In the forward to his party's manifesto for the 1997 general election, Mr Blair set out ten commitments, the first of which was 'Education will be our number one priority, and we will increase the share of national income spent on education as we decrease it on the bills of economic and social failure.'

And yet, and despite a (published) letter to the *Financial Times* in 2002 including

> There is a huge amount of evidence that any increase in the number of unskilled workers lowers unskilled wages and increases the unskilled unemployment rate. If we are concerned about fairness, we ought not to ignore these facts. Employers gain from unskilled immigration. But the unskilled do not.[1]

and that part of the letter being read out to the House of Lords' European Union Committee on 8 June 2005[2]

and part of the evidence in 2007 to the House of Lords' Select Committee on Economic Affairs, being that immigration 'undermines the labour market position of the most vulnerable and least skilled sections of the local workforce ...'[3]

- In 2010, at the end of thirteen years of the Labour Party being in government, there were about a million NEETs (young not in education, employment or training), an increase over those thirteen years of 70%:

- In August 2014, 'Even after the fall in UK youth unemployment this month [August 2014] about 17pc of 16–24-year-olds here are neither employed nor in education compared with just 7.8pc in Germany'[4]:

- In 2015, 'one in five children still leaves school unable to read well enough to succeed at secondary school – a figure that rises to one in three of our poorest children'[5]

from 2004 there was uncontrolled immigration from at least the A8 countries because, allegedly, the skills were needed.

But in 2009 the number of foreign workers rose by 175,000 and the number of British workers fell by 46,000; of the (2.5 million) extra persons in employment since 1997, three quarters are foreigners.

Mr Duncan Smith's department this week released figures showing that under the previous Labour government, the number of Britons in jobs dropped by 413,000 between 2005 and 2010 while the number of working foreigners rose by 736,000.

Since the formation of the Coalition, the number of Britons in jobs has risen by 538,000 while the number of working foreigners increased by 247,000.[6]

Our politicians are so obsessed by race that they have forgotten the importance of class. They agonise about racial segregation while generally ignoring the exclusion of the white working class from our politics. Lord Bruce-Lockhart, the head of the Local Government Association, last week recommended ethnic quotas for state schools, to end the division of neighbouring schools along ethnic lines.

But while ethnic divisions are certainly deep in some areas, they are nothing like as widespread – and in many respects nothing like as pernicious – as the scornful treatment by our overwhelmingly bourgeois political establishment of the white working class. While a brilliant campaign has been waged against racial prejudice, prejudice against the white working class has flourished as never before.

...In our politics, the unions, which used to give the working class a stake in the system, have been crushed. Labour has spent the past decade taking the working class for granted. It has gone after the trendy middle-class vote, with great success. The Government has encouraged mass immigration, a change of which I am in favour, for I believe these newcomers are an asset to our country and will rapidly become British.[7] But no heed has been paid to those members of the indigenous working class who have found their wages undercut by cheap foreign competition and have difficulty getting council housing.

It was reported last week that 100,000 people are being paid incapacity benefit because they are alcoholics or drug addicts. These lost souls can be found during the day sitting listlessly in our pubs. The state gives them enough money for drink and drugs, and has encouraged them to become incapable of work. The rest of us choose to believe that the state is caring for them. They are certainly nothing to do with us. Any sense of common nationhood which transcends class has disappeared, except during football tournaments.

If Lord Bruce-Lockhart is worried by the failure of ethnic minorities to integrate themselves into society, he should consider what kind of society we are asking them to join. Are we one nation, or has that nation dissolved?[8]

Those of us who feel culturally enriched by the benefits of migration and who are insulated from the competition for jobs, housing and public services that is potentially posed by immigrants, often find these views [the perception that migrants jump the queue] difficult to appreciate.

The affluent often are able to see opportunities within change and uncertainty; whereas those who are less insulated from potential drawbacks may see the same change as a risk or threat.

Crudely expressed, the higher you are in the pecking order, the more likely you may be to benefit from immigration.

If immigration makes it easier for you to find a plumber or cheaper for you to hire a cleaner[9] then you clearly and directly benefit. But for many others you may see them as a direct threat to your own interests.[10]

Of course, during the boom years there were some serious economic benefits that flowed. Business had a ready supply of labour, skilled and unskilled, and that helped to hold down wages and prices. But by the same token, the policy hit the very people that had traditionally been identified by Labour as its core vote – people who found, or certainly believed, that they were losing jobs, homes and benefits to the incomers; and their fears were by no means always groundless.

There is some evidence, for example, that British building companies cancelled training projects for British workers because they found they could just hire Poles and other East Europeans who needed no training.[11]

That is not to say there are no winners from the injection of a very large number of workers into the economy. It acts, in effect, like a King John tax, transferring resources from the poor to the rich. For the employer class, in particular London's metropolitan elite, immigration provides a ready supply of nannies,[12] ironing ladies and odd-job men willing to work for the minimum wage.

By contrast, for locals at the bottom of the employment ladder, the impact is deleterious. According to Cambridge University's Professor Robert Rowthorn,[13] it's bizarre that the Labour Party, champion of the vulnerable (or so it claims), intentionally created what Marx called 'a reserve army of labour': a pool of workers whose presence ensures that rates of pay for unskilled staff can be kept low.[14]

Take immigration. The left was instinctively in favour of it because it made its Conservative opponents uncomfortable. It also introduced two million Labour voters onto the electoral rolls but these intensely political motives have stored up more trouble than almost anything else in modern times.

What will happen (as is starting to happen now) when liberal intellectuals realise this level of immigration is a de facto incomes policy? When it is accepted that working class wages are kept down by an oversupply of unskilled workers? That the 'cost of living crisis' promoted by the Labour leadership was created by Labour's own policy of 'rubbing the noses of the Right in diversity'?[15]

I just can't believe that where local authorities can whistle up plentiful supplies of eager and energetic baristas[16] and beanpickers from central Europe, this has no effect on local wage rates. I do think that if Marx and Engels were with us today they would be telling us immigrants are the new reserve army of labour in Britain.[17]

... the only experience the average BBC manager has of immigration is a cheap au pair, cleaner and a fascinating little restaurant down the road.[18]

Even if immigrants are not competing directly for the same jobs in many cases, they may still have a strong indirect effect on depressing wages for resident workers. Professor Blanchflower found that wage growth slowed in both the UK and Ireland following A8 accession although both economies were booming. He attributed this to a rise in the fear of unemployment caused by high immigration, which in turn leads to lower wage settlements [paragraph 73 of the House of Lords Report].[19]

The available evidence suggests that immigration has had a small negative impact on the lowest-paid workers in the UK, and a small positive impact on the earnings of higher-paid workers. Resident workers whose wages have been adversely affected by immigration are likely to include a significant proportion of previous immigrants and workers from ethnic minority groups [paragraphs 78 and 217 of the House of Lords Report].[19]

In fact, the imposition of a minimum wage is the ultimate stealth tax. It is beloved by bankrupt governments and their civil servants because it transfers wealth from the middle class to the poor, cuts welfare spending, and is a net vote-winner as the losers are unaware their pockets are being picked. Like all taxes on production inputs, it increases prices to the consumer and cuts demand for the goods produced, but with a sinister and unique facet. Ceteris paribus, it also decreases the demand for labour but raises the supply of labour, and in particular makes illegal immigration a much more attractive venture. Whether or not illegal immigrants command the minimum wage or operate at a discount, their effective rate will certainly rise in response to an increase in the minimum wage.

Analysts who seek to demonstrate that a minimum wage does not cause job losses are looking in the wrong place – ironically, low wage employment can actually rise in a recession as consumers trade down. It is rampant immigration, immense youth unemployment and cheap imports that tell the true consequences.[20]

For example, British companies have little incentive to train domestic employees if they are able to import foreign staff with higher skills and a stronger work ethic.[14]

How much easier it was in the Labour years to forget [those on incapacity benefit] and airbrush them out of the unemployment figures. How much easier to import workers from abroad, and grow the economy with immigrants instead. But [the present employment minister] is trying to make progress while Mr Brown was trying to fake progress.[21]

... So it was refreshing to dip into A Classless Society, the third volume of Alwyn Turner's history of Britain since the 1970s. This time, his subject is the 1990s and his thesis is that the massive increase in income inequality that characterised that decade went hand-in-hand with a concurrent increase in social equality.

Take mass immigration. Between 1991 and 1999, net immigration averaged 104,000 a year and in lots of ways that contributed to rising inequality. Plentiful supplies of cheap labour helped fuel the economic boom that began in the autumn of 1992 and ended with the credit crunch of 2007 – a boom that resulted in the gap between the highest and lowest earners growing ever wider. The increasing number of new arrivals as a percentage of the population also undermined the social cohesion that anchored the welfare state and, by extension, the redistributive taxation associated with Old Labour, a point made by David Goodhart in The British Dream.

Yet, at the same time, the multiethnic character of modern Britain resulted in a steep decline in racial inequality. Britain's indigenous African-Caribbean population, particularly the men, may not have shared much in Britain's prosperity during the 1990s but other ethnic groups did. More importantly, it was the decade in which any manifestation of racial prejudice became taboo. In London, which has the highest density of foreign-born residents in the UK, Ken Livingstone launched a successful mayoral bid by appealing to a patchwork quilt of different groups.[22]

I will never forgive the Labour Party for allowing this mass immigration with no demands put on what people should be paid should they come into this country. I will never forgive them for destroying the jobs of my mates, because they allowed their jobs to be undercut with stupid thinking on Europe, letting them all in, so they can live five, ten to a room, working for Polish wages.[23]

It wasn't as if the Labour Party, and everybody else,[24] had not been warned. By 2004, the detrimental effect on earnings and employment, for the indigenous population, by immigration was well known:

What should more seriously alarm the political Left is the finding that, in EU countries, for every hundred migrants eighty-three indigenous workers eventually lose their jobs. This is the most recent research (June 2003) and mirrors disturbing results of US studies (November 2002) showing labour at the bottom of the market experiencing pay cuts of 20 per cent through migrant competition.

A 2003 report by Professor George Borjas[25] of Harvard, the world's leading economist regarding immigration, puts it at about 10 per cent, still a substantial effect. Although our economy differs from both the continental European model and that of the USA – falling somewhere in between the two – it is highly unlikely that there is something peculiar to the UK situation that protects us from this adverse impact on both pay and jobs.[26]

For too long, the benefits of immigration went to employers who wanted an easy supply of cheap labour, or to the wealthy metropolitan elite who wanted cheap tradesmen and services – but not to the ordinary, hardworking people of this country.[27]

And yet supporters of immigration, myself included, have to accept that it has downsides as well as upsides. EU membership has been good for those who hire immigrants – as office workers, nannies,[12] architects or plumbers. Not so good for people who compete with them – for jobs, school places or social housing. For years, Labour treated concerns with contempt, an attitude encapsulated by Gordon Brown referring to a voter who asked about immigration as a 'bigoted woman'. The Lib Dems are taking the same approach, deriding every criticism as an attempt 'to turn our back on the world'.[28]

The well educated can afford to embrace immigration, diversity and change: they are confident and capable, and see globalisation as an opportunity rather than a threat. For them Europe's open borders provide 'cleaners, not competition'.[29]

Ed Miliband recognised the detriment to anyway part of the indigenous population:

> Worrying about immigration, talking about immigration, thinking about immigration, does not make them [his constituents of Doncaster North] bigots. Quite simply, we became too disconnected from the concerns of working people.
>
> We too easily assumed those who worried about immigration were stuck in the past.
>
> Unrealistic about how things could be different.
>
> Even prejudiced.
>
> And people's concerns were genuine.
>
> At least by the end of our time in office, we were too dazzled by globalisation and too sanguine about its price.
>
> By focusing too much on globalisation and migration's impact on growth, we lost sight of who was benefiting from that growth – and people were being squeezed. And to those who lost out, Labour was too quick to say 'like it or lump it'.
>
> First of all, as a result of immigration combined with weak labour standards in some sectors, there was a direct effect on wages, especially in lower skilled jobs.
>
> If you wanted some building work done in your home, you were probably better off.
>
> If you were working in construction, you often weren't.
>
> The ready supply of temporary low-wage, low-skill migrant labour has further pushed some businesses to take a short-term low-skill approach.
>
> And it has discouraged too many firms from training and developing their own workers.
>
> Far too many British firms in construction today find it is in their interests to hire foreign-trained workers, rather than to train up workers from Britain themselves.[30]

And also Ed Balls:

> There have been real economic gains from the arrival of young, committed and hardworking migrants from Eastern Europe over the past six years. But there has also been a direct impact on the wages, terms and conditions of too many people across our country – in communities ill-prepared to deal with the reality of globalisation – including the one I represent.[31]

But,

If Ed Miliband is serious about wiping the slate, he should tell us what the real motivation was for his party to force social, cultural and economic upheaval on many British communities without ever consulting them.[14]

Tony remarked, reasonably enough, that no one had ever asked a single East Ender if they were happy with the levels of immigration that had altered his birthplace so much. His reward for this was to be called a racist by the interviewer, as though a Londoner owning a holiday home in Spain is equivalent to what governments have done to Whitechapel in the past 30 years. Despicable.[32]

Only 17% of the inhabitants of Newham, the East End borough ... are classified as 'white British'. It is the epicentre of the mass immigration that has transformed many British cities in recent decades, which is appropriate. The East End – broadly speaking, the poor, sprawling area north of Docklands and Victorian housing east of the City and north of the Thames – has seen many waves of immigration since the late seventeenth century, when over 29,000 Protestant Huguenots fled there from France. Irish and Chinese, then Russian and Polish Jews followed, making the gateway to London the melting pot of the world. By the end of the nineteenth century there were more than 42,000 Russians and Poles in the borough of Stepney alone. Yet the recent waves, from Bangladesh, west Africa and Eastern Europe, are bigger. Newham has 16,000 newcomers – representing 5% of its population – every year. Coinciding with a period of socioeconomic tumult, this immigrant horde has not melted into Cockney society, as previous ones did, but displaced it. Between 2001 and 2011, Newham lost 37% of it white British residents.[33]

There is one additional issue I have not so far raised, which I would like to talk about today. That is the decision of the past government to invite up to 5 million new people to the UK over little more than a decade. The UK has a workforce of around 30 million, so the increase in the potential workforce from large-scale immigration must have had some impact on the UK labour market. More than 2m jobs have been taken by people born overseas. Business likes the ability to recruit people from around the world, and likes a plentiful supply of good value labour. Employees of UK companies already settled here need income levels that sustain a reasonable lifestyle in one of the dearer locations in the world. The issue is one of balance. Allow too little migration, and business might find it difficult to set up or continue here without access to the affordable skills they need. Let in too many new people, and you must depress wages and make it more difficult for unemployed people legally settled here to find a job. Part of the issue of wages is tied up in the potential supply of labour. Over the last decade the UK has had an unprecedented expansion of its labour supply, which is part of the background to stagnant wages.[34]

The free movement of people is a different story [to the EU's free movement of capital]. Clearly this has a huge effect on some EU members. The UK, for one, has experienced substantial net immigration from Eastern Europe. Has this been a good thing? This is a tricky area and there are evidently some significant losers from the process, not least the indigenous workers who now find themselves in keener competition with immigrant labour and often, given the rigidities in the labour market, finding themselves unemployed as a result.[35]

Immigration is an interesting case study. For affluent political correspondents, it made domestic help cheaper, enabling them to pay for the nannies,[12] au pairs, cleaning ladies, gardeners and tradesmen who make middle-class life comfortable.

These journalists were often provided with private health schemes and were therefore immune from the pressure on NHS hospitals from immigration. They tended to send their children to private schools. This meant they rarely faced the problems of poorer parents whose children find themselves in schools where scores of different languages were spoken in the playground. Meanwhile corporate bosses who funded all the main political parties (and owned the big media groups) tended to love immigration because it meant cheaper labour and higher profits.

Great tracts of urban Britain have been utterly changed by immigration in the course of barely a generation. The people who originally lived in these areas were never consulted and felt that the communities they lived in had been wilfully destroyed. Nobody would speak up for them: not the Conservatives, not Labour, not the Lib Dems. They were literally left without a voice.[36]

However tough it is for that elastic cohort, the squeezed middle, to pay energy and food bills, the Waitrose woes of the moderately affluent are not to be compared with the plight of the destitute. A report published [in the last week of May 2014] by Save the Children reveals that a record five million children could be living in poverty by 2020. With food prices soaring and the costs of nursery places for infants up 77 per cent in the past decade, children's lives are being stunted in ways that shame a rich nation.[37]

One reason for the lack of wage growth is that there is still a massive excess supply of labour. Although figures this [second] week [of September 2014] showed that the official measure of unemployment has fallen to 2.02m – the lowest since late 2008 – they also showed that there are 2.3m people outside the labour force who would like a job, and another 1.3m who are working part-time who would prefer a full-time job.[38]

It's time we took a long, hard look at lifting Britain's working-class back to a position of pride.

I recognise this all too clearly in my constituency of Rochdale. Blue-collar workers continually tell me that an influx of Eastern European workers have sucked them into a race to the bottom in wages. Whether it's the electrician who says he's being undercut to the point where it makes no economic sense to continue, or the builder who says he's been priced out by silly quotes, there is a sense that a deeply unfair playing field is making it impossible for some Britons to compete.

We must dump the myopic view that you can only be for or against immigration. That's not the case. Immigration is valuable, but it can't be a free-for-all. It needs to be controlled and managed. And where Europe's concerned, we need to be pushing for reform on the principle of free movement in order to create fair movement.[39]

Inflation-targeting under an Independent central bank, in combination with the Thatcher labour market reforms, seemed finally to do the trick [of dealing with inflation] but you have to wonder how much of the subsequent, well-behaved inflation of the Great Moderation was really down to the genius of policymakers, and whether it wasn't mainly the disinflationary pressures of globalisation – cheap imports, and cheap labour from immigration.[40]

Those at the top of the British social scale have generally done pretty well out of the globalisation they occasionally decry: their salaries are higher, their houses are worth more, their horizons and those of their children are broadened by living in one of the most internationally connected countries in the world.

The impact of the globalisation on the poorer parts of the country is much more ambiguous. It is the working class whose wages are most likely to be held down by competition with immigrants, and whose areas are most likely to be transformed by mass immigration.[41]

... Workers' bargaining power is not as strong as you might infer from the fact that the unemployment rate, at 5.3 per cent, is at its lowest since early 2008. This is because the official unemployment rate greatly understates the excess supply of labour. As well as the 1.75m unemployed, there are almost 2.3m people who would like a job but are classified by the ONS as 'economically inactive': these include some of the retired, home-makers and students. And 'inactivity' is a misnomer. In the third quarter, 541,000 'inactive' people moved into work. That's 23.3

per cent of all the 'inactive' who wanted a job. This means that the 'inactive' are almost as likely to move into work as the unemployed, 27.6 per cent of whom did so in the third quarter.

With the supply of labour so high – and I'm not even mentioning migration – the result is lowish wage growth.[42]

The economic impact of immigration is essentially a distributional one. Immigration shifts wealth away from those who compete with the skills and abilities that immigrants bring into the country, and toward those who employ or use those immigrant resources. As with many redistribution schemes, the people who lose from immigration tend to be quite diffused – there are many of them, they are dispersed geographically, and they are not well organised. In contrast, the winners are much more concentrated and better organised – many immigrants tend to be employed in a few industries, and employers in those industries probably gain substantially.[43]

Notes: *B is for betrayal*

1. The letter (to the editor of the *Financial Times*) was published on 20 May 2002. It was from Professor Richard Layard. It should not have been ignored by the government of the day because:

- in 1990, Layard founded the Centre for Economic Performance;

- in 2000, Layard was appointed a Labour life peer (*see* immediately following note);

- the four sentences were quoted in Steve Moxon's book *The Great Immigration Scandal*, (first) published in 2004.

2. Read out by Sir Andrew Green (now Lord Green of Deddington) in his oral evidence to the House of Commons' European Union Committee on 8 June 2005. He preceded those words with:

I would like to quote Lord Layard, one of your colleagues, who, as I am sure you know, helped to design the government's Welfare to Work programme. He is very close to the present government and is a considerable expert.

3. This is part of the evidence of Professor Rowthorn to the committee (*see* the part of E is for economics to which note 8 applies).

4. *Starting money lessons early is just the first step* by Helena Morrissey, *The Daily Telegraph*, August 2014.

5. *Let's get each child reading widely and well* by Nicky Morgan and David Williams, *The Daily Telegraph*, August 2015.

6. *The Daily Telegraph*, 23 January 2014. Mr Duncan Smith was then and remained the secretary of state for work and pensions until March 2016 when he resigned.

7. But *see* notes 4 and 5 and 15–18 of I is for integration.

8. *Why is the white working class so roundly despised?* by Andrew Grimson, *The Daily Telegraph*, October 2006.

9. For example Lady Amos of Scotland and (one-time) immigration minister Mark Harper.

10. John Denham, Communities Secretary to Policy Network, December 2009.

11. *Britain needs immigrants, but it also needs tough border controls* by Boris Johnson, *The Daily Telegraph*, September 2010.

12. For example the (wife of the) prime minister. Nigel Farage, leader of UKIP, commented: 'This is a perfect illustration of an uncomprehending wealthy metropolitan elite who now so dominate politics in the UK. Ordinary decent British people are paying the price through loss of jobs and wage depreciation.'

Vince Cable, while Business Secretary, had a Polish cleaner.

13. Professor Rowthorn gave evidence to the House of Lords' Select Committee on Economic Affairs for its report: (*see* note 8 to E is for economics). He has since written *The Costs and Benefits of Large-Scale Immigration*.

14. *Now for Labour's lies about immigration* by Jeff Randall, *The Daily Telegraph*, September 2013.

(And) Karl Marx wrote:

> The main purpose of the bourgeois in relation to the worker is, of course, to have the commodity labour as cheaply as possible, which is only possible when the supply of this commodity is as large as possible in relation to the demand for it.

15. *Res Publica* by Simon Carr, *The Oldie*, February 2015.

16. Baristas seem to have become a benchmark: the following is from *Always trust wise voters, not the dumb elites* by Tim Montgomerie, *The Times*, October 2014:

Immigration is the issue that most exposes the gap between the elites and the great unwashed. Debates about the benefits and cost of allowing four million more people into this country over the last decade will go on. Both sides have good arguments.

What cannot be questioned is that voters never gave their consent. Tony Blair didn't even ask for it. The Conservatives promised to control immigration but Boris Johnson now admits that EU membership means control is 'impossible'. Voters aren't wrong to be furious. They're not wrong to link immigration with house-price inflation and the greatest squeeze on the incomes of the low-paid since Victorian times.

Immigration may only be one ingredient of the globalisation that is providing cheap baristas and nannies for those at the top and stiff job competition for those at the bottom – but it is most certainly one factor.

In the past 20 years political and journalistic elites have advocated the euro, allowed uncontrolled immigration, poured money into an unreformed welfare state and tried to invade two countries on the cheap. On each occasion the masses have been sceptical – and on each occasion the masses have been right.

17. Ferdinand Mount – (possibly November) 2013.

18. Nigel Farage, former leader of UKIP, commenting on Helen Boaden, director of radio at the BBC, stating that the corporation had a 'deep liberal bias'.

19. The report of the House of Lords: (*see* note 7 of the economics of immigration).

20. W.H. Bailey of Eire – letter to the *Financial Times*, February 2013.

And Bridging the poverty gap calls for bold ideas by Jeremy Warner, *The Daily Telegraph*, January 2014:

As a sticking-plaster solution, there's surprisingly little that's actually wrong with higher minimum wages. Obviously, there are drawbacks. Traditional neo-classical theory puts wage regulation in the same category as price controls: if you artificially attempt to lower wages, it will both increase demand and reduce supply. Pretty soon you get product shortages. By the same token, raising the cost of labour theoretically reduces the demand for it. The poorest and the young tend to get hit the hardest – as happens in France, where the very high minimum wage seems to have permanently excluded large elements of its youth from the jobs market.

21. *Sticking with Gordon Brown's flawed policy keeps people in poverty* by Fraser Nelson, *The Daily Telegraph*, March 2012.

And see his *Brown has exploited immigration to hide from deep problems*, September 2008, in *The Spectator*, which included:

> Take for example, the Prime Minister's mantra-like boast that he has 'created three million new jobs'. The Statistics Commission discloses that 68 per cent of the increase can be attributed to immigrants......Narrow the field to working-age people, and immigrants account for 82 per cent of the job increases......But the grim fact remains that there still 700,000 Londoners on benefits.

22. Toby Young, *The Spectator*, August 2013.

23. Roger Daltrey, November 2013.

24. For instance, the House of Lords. (And *see* the next note.)

25. The author of *Heaven's Door: Immigration Policy and the American Economy, 1999*, and *The Labor Demand Curve is Downward Sloping: Re-examining the Impact of Immigration on the Labor Market, 2002*.

And *see* what has note 43 to it.

26. *The Great Immigration Scandal* by Steve Moxon, published in 2004 by Imprint Academic.

27. James Brokenshire, immigration minister, March 2014.

28. *Only one person is laughing at the Farage–Clegg EU pantomime* by Fraser Nelson, *The Daily Telegraph*, March 2014.

29. The Week – *Clegg vs Farage. Who came off best?* April 2014.

30. Ed Miliband, MP for Doncaster North since 2005, leader of the opposition 2010/15; to the Institute for Public Policy Research, June 2012.

Miliband's 'we lost sight of who was benefiting from that growth' is probably another example of the failure to realise that it is per-capita income rather than GNP, which is what is fundamental: (*see* E is for economics, and particularly note 1 thereto).

31. Ed Balls, MP 2005/15 latterly for Morley and Outwood, West Yorkshire; into the Treasury in 2006; ultimately shadow Chancellor of the Exchequer.

32. Tony, a cabbie, 'reported' by Graeme Archer – June 2012 [In the thirty years to 2011, the population of Tower Hamlets increased from 168,000 to 254,000 and the indigenous population became a minority.]

33. *Cockney funerals*, *The Economist*, December 2013.

The words 'which is appropriate' at the end of the second sentence is a puzzle. There is no obvious reason for their inclusion, or why it is appropriate that Newham should be the epicentre of mass immigration; the words are at odds with the tone of the later 'horde'. Perhaps the words are just a reflection of where the author comes from, of the 'right way to think': (*see* note 29 of H is for hegemony).

It is to be noted that 'this immigrant horde has not melted into Cockney society', in other words has not integrated. And rather over a third of the members of that 'Cockney society' have moved away.

Another example of displacement (of the native population) by immigrants is by Stephen Williams (MP for Bristol West, January 2015):

> In my own constituency, lots of pubs have closed but it is usually because of demographic change. Particularly in some parts of my constituency, which used to have a white working-class community 20 or 30 years ago are now populated primarily by recently-arrived Somalis and other people. Obviously the pubs in that area have closed.

34. *Mass immigration must have depressed wages* by John Redwood (MP since 1987 for Wokingham) January 2014. [I thought I saw this in the *Financial Times* but all I can find on line was *The Commentator*.]

35. *The Trouble with €urope* by Roger Bootle, February 2014, published by Nicholas Brealey Publishing.

36. *Ukip's triumph* by Peter Oborne, *The Spectator*, May 2014.

37. *Has Ed Miliband trapped himself on the wrong side of history?* by Mary Riddell, *The Daily Telegraph*, May 2014.

38. *Rate rise a "long way off"'* by Chris Dillow, *Investors Chronicle*, September 2014.

39. *Cheap immigrant labour has cost blue-collar Britain dear* by Simon Danczuk, MP for Rochdale since 2010, *The Daily Telegraph*, November 2014.

40. *Sadly for all our futures, cheap money is here to stay. Just get used to it* by Jeremy Warner, *The Daily Telegraph*, January 2015.

41. *Globalisation has moved the goalposts for Britain* by Gideon Rachman, *Financial Times*, January 2015.

42. *Wage Woes* by Chris Dillow, *Investors Chronicle*, November 2015.

43. From the conclusion of *Heaven's Door* by George J. Borjas, published in 1999 by Princetown Press, apparently in succession to *Knockin' on Heaven's Door* published in 1973. Borjas is the son, as he puts it, of 'a Cuban refugee' who moved to the USA just before the Cuban missile crisis in 1962, which shut the door to any more such movement. (And *see* the paragraph that has note 25 to it.)

And **B** is for bussing

Bussing was introduced in the USA following the Supreme Court judgment[1] that 'separate educational facilities are inherently unequal' and so where school catchment areas were too predominately of one ethnicity, children had to be bused to another school.

In 1963, Edward Boyle, the then education secretary, suggested that no school should have a 'minority roll' of more than 30%.

The Asians in the schools where the roll is over 90% 'Asian', for example, Bradford and Burnley, and Leicester, Luton and Swindon (and *see* S is for swarm and swamp) should be bussed, if there is to be any chance of those pupils integrating and becoming British, but even then real assimilation and integration are not necessarily the result (*see* I is for integration).

- Henry Webster suffered multiple blows to his skull when attacked by a group of young Asians. This was on the tennis courts at Ridgeway School, Wroughton, Swindon, which was criticised for not preparing for the consequences of a new policy to bring Asian children from inner-city Swindon to the school. The school's Serious Case Review includes, '[The school] knew well in advance that a significant number of British Asian pupils were joining the school after the London bombings in July 2005. The likely influence of all pupils' communities and families on pupil behaviour was not understood.'[2]

Notes: **B** *is for bussing*

1. *Brown v. Board of Education* [1954].

2. The headline of *exposingislam.blogspot* (posted by English kaffir) was '7 Muslims of Pakistani descent convicted in Henry Webster case', which was followed by 'Four teenagers – Wasif Khan eighteen, Amjad Qazi nineteen and two boys aged fifteen and sixteen were found … Nazrul Amin nineteen, and two teenagers had previously admitted inflicting grievous bodily harm.'

C is for Lord Carlile

In late 2010, Lord Carlile the reviewer of terrorism legislation wrote:

> We know that there may be up to 2,000 terrorists living in the United Kingdom. They aim to cause death and damage here, and to British soldiers and other assets abroad. Many are British citizens, male, young, well educated, and radicalized to a violent heresy. Most are orchestrated from abroad. Some are prepared to kill using their bodies as bombs. Policing them is a huge challenge, demanding large resources and eternal vigilance. ... To watch and listen to all suspects at all time would demand unavailable financial and expert resources.

And C is for common sense

> I can't feel sympathy for either party. Neither had the courage or the common sense to oppose mass immigration. As a result Britain will soon – for the first time – suffer the fate of countless foreign countries and have to build its policies around religious and ethnic enclaves.[1]

Notes: C is for common sense

1. Damian Thompson, April 2012 – the month after Ken Livingstone promised to make London 'a beacon of Islam'.

And C is for community

The term can be used to refer a discrete group, usually of immigrants, or to everyone in the locality or indeed the country; sometimes to both – if not in the same sentence, at least in the same paragraph:

- 'Somali community divided over criminalisation of khat.'

- [Chewing khat] 'helps our community come together. If our young people didn't have a place to talk through their problems, they could fall in with the wrong people – gangs, or radicals in the mosque.'[1]

- 'We need to deal with [immigration scams] because otherwise it becomes a real source of tension and misunderstanding within our community here in this country.'[2]

- '[Electoral fraud] is predominately within the Asian community.'[3]

- 'foster hatred which may lead to intra-community violence in the UK.'[4]

- 'Councils are committed to continually improving services. We recognise that we need to address the diverse needs of different people in our community. We also want to address any inequality and ensure fair access to our services. In order to do this we need to ask for and keep certain information about you (and your family). Please leave any questions that you do not want to answer.'[5]

- 'These are serious matters and custody appears to be appropriate in this case. Also what troubles me, although this is not something which bears on sentence, [is that] he has been here for nigh on 20 years and he requires an interpreter. I suspect he lives within his own community and has never bothered to learn English.'[6]

- 'I hope this action shows the communities of Rochdale that we take the issue of sexual exploitation of children extremely seriously.'[7]

- 'These are closed communities essentially and I worry that in these communities there are people who knew what was going on and didn't say anything, either because they're frightened or because they're so separated from the rest of the communities, they think "Oh, that's just how white people let their children carry on, we don't need to do anything".'[8]

- 'It is only when communities know the government is serious about tackling FGM and that offenders cannot get away with it, that we will see girls in this country protected against this heinous crime.'[9]

- 'Slough Council said that some of the Pakistani community in the borough felt that their jobs were being lost to the new incoming Polish community, which is higher skilled and prepared to work for lower wages.'[10]

- 'There is no such thing as surveillance of the Muslim community. What the security services are trying to do is to get information about plots to commit terrorist attacks. The security services neither have the resources nor the energy nor the inclination to look at a whole community. It is trying to find those few people within a community who are a threat.'[11]

- When the trial in Burnley County Court of a Muslim for raping his wife collapsed because she had been placed [by her community] under

49

'enormous emotional pressure' and so retracted her statement, the judge ordered the matter to remain on file and commented: 'This will not be tolerated. It is not for individuals or sections of the community to attempt to resolve matters outside the court.'

- 'I am absolutely clear that this problem [of endemic corruption] is not attributable to any one community, as I know very well from my many years promoting community cohesion.'[12]

- 'an inclination to demonstrate prejudice against certain sections of our community'.[13]

- 'There is a real dilemma when you get communities coming into part of our country and then they behave in a way that people find quite difficult to accept. They behave in a way that people sometimes find intimidating, sometimes offensive. We have every right to say that if you are in Britain and are coming to live here and you are bringing up a family here, you have got to be sensitive to the way life is lived in this country. If you do things that people find intimidating, such as large groups hanging around on street corners, you have got to listen to what other people in the community say.'[14]

- 'Responsible people in our communities need to reflect on what they said before in light of what this case has shown.'[15]

- 'We know this is an emotive issue within our community and we have met regularly with representatives from local mosques, elected members and others to hear their views.'[16]

- 'Nobody should underestimate the fears that Britons have over immigration. Young migrant families make it harder to find school places in communities. There are legitimate cultural concerns that need to be addressed by ensuring that migrants speak English and are properly integrated into local communities.'[17]

- In 2012 'insurgents', disguised in American uniform, got into Camp Bastian, Afghanistan, killing two soldiers and effecting a great deal of damage. Nearly two years later there 'came out' pictures of two members of the British forces, each with his thumb up, beside the body of a killed insurgent. The British senior officer at the time, Colonel Richard Kemp, in the course of being interviewed on the radio expressed concern about the pictures 'inflaming outrage among our community at home'.[18]

- 'I think the community will be able to recognise this person and I am sure that many in the community will be keen to do so, the intelligence community certainly but also the community from which this man comes.'[19]

- 'Like many writers and broadcasters covering the Rotherham sex abuse scandal, Colin Brewer refers to the alleged offenders as 'Asian' (*Does social work work?*) If I was a member of South Yorkshire's Chinese or Indian community I would find this offensive.'[20]

- 'In carrying out the assessment a distinction must be made between a sophisticated, highly educated and politically literate community and a community which is traditional, respectful of authority and, possibly, not fully integrated with other communities living in the same area.'[21]

Notes: *C is for community*

1. Headline to an item in the *Financial Times*, September 2013, followed by part of the conversation with a supplier of the leaf. Khat was subsequently criminalised. One can only hope young 'Somalis' did not then 'fall in with the wrong people'.

2. Tony Blair in the spring of 2004, following the resignation of the immigration minister, Beverley Hughes: *see* note 1 to I is for identity.

3. Lady Warsi: *see* V is for vote rigging.

4. The Home Office's *Exclusion or deportation from the UK on non-conducive grounds: Consultation Document*: *see* C is for non-conducive.

5. Bournemouth/Dorset/Poole questionnaire as to Skills & Learning courses. It asks for ethnic origin, listing seventeen alternatives plus 'Any other ethnic group'.

6. Judge King when sentencing Zamal Uddin, an unlicensed taxi driver, with a council flat, for sexual assault.

7. Chief Superintendent John O'Hare following the arrest in Rochdale of a group of non-indigenous people accused of the sexual grooming and exploitation of girls: *see* D is for Derby.

8. Trevor Phillips, Chairman of the Equality and Human Rights Commission, May 2014, in respect of the grooming of white girls in Rochdale by Asian men.

9. Efua Dorkenoo, advocacy director of *Equality Now*.

10. Paragraph 74 of the House of Lords Report.

11. Dame Eliza Manningham Buller, December 2013, Director General of MI5 for five years from 2002.

12. Dominic Grieve, QC, MP for Beaconsfield since 1997, Attorney General 2010–14, after speaking about many immigrants coming from a favour culture, and perhaps Pakistan being the worst example.

13. Mohammed Ajeeb, the mayor of Bradford, in 1984 calling for the dismissal of Ray Honeyford. The word 'community' was being used to denote the whole but as about 95% of the pupils at Drummond Middle School, Bradford, of which Mr Honeyford was headmaster, were 'Asian', perhaps the mayor was correct: *see* H is for Ray Honeyford.

14. Nick Clegg (MP for Sheffield Hallam from 2005, leader of the Liberal Democrats from 2007, Deputy Prime Minister from 2010–2015) about the Roma community in the Page Hall area of Sheffield (which is in the constituency of David Blunkett, as to who *see* note 19 of R is for racism).

15. The assistant chief constable of West Midlands Police after Parviz Khan admitted plotting to behead a British soldier and others admitted related offences. The plot was stopped by a large raid early on 31 January 2007 on eight homes and four businesses; eight men were arrested, with another later in the day. Three of those were released without charge, one complaining that Britain had become a police state for Muslims.

16. Assistant Chief Constable Dawn Copley of Greater Manchester in answer to Munir Farooqi's daughter complaining, 'Leaving three generations of a family homeless, including an eight-month old baby, is disgusting. It's not British law, it's just wrong and inhumane.'

Munir Farooqi, a Pakistani-born British citizen, was jailed in 2001. Following release, he returned home and turned the house into a 'production centre' with a collection of 50,000 books, DVDs and CDs for which, and trying to persuade other Muslims to fight in Afghanistan, he received four life sentences. His house was subject to forfeiture because of the use to which Farooqi had put it.

According to the police, the Farooqi family had two other properties.

17. *Financial Times*, (second) leader, 8 March 2014.

18. Radio 4's *Today*, 10 May 2014.

19. (According to a newspaper) Richard Barratt a former director of counter-terrorism at the Secret Intelligence Service after the murder of James Foley by ISIS, August 2014, as to identifying a masked man pictured holding a knife, with a British accent who may have effected Foley's beheading. (Perhaps this should go under M is for mangled!).

Another example of the varied meaning of the word 'community' is in the (first two paragraphs of the) open letter of August 2011 from United Platform against Racism and Fascism (by Shaheed Bhavan of the Bangladesh Welfare Association):

> We, the undersigned, call on the authorities to ban the proposed march by the English Defence League (EDL) in Tower Hamlets on Saturday 3 September. The EDL is a violent racist organisation that seeks to vilify communities and damage community relations. Its planned march is designed to whip up fear and incite violence.
>
> We reject entirely the EDL and its racism and we don't see why the people of Tower Hamlets should pay for its march of hate. There can be no excuse for this march of hate. It is not right for one or two thousand racists to bring fear and trouble into somebody else's community. We have to stop the EDL from marching.

20. Simon Collins, September 2014, letter to *The Spectator* wherein there had been the article *Does social work work?*

21. Part of paragraph 159 of the judgment in *Erlam v. Rahman* (which found that Rahman's election as mayor of the London Borough of Tower Hamlets in 2014 was voided by corrupt and illegal practices. And *see* V is for vote rigging).

And **C** is for non-conducive

In 2005, the Home Office asked for views as to its *Exclusion or Deportation from the UK on Non-Conducive Grounds*, the proposal being that the power to exclude or deport (foreign nationals) should be extended to enable exclusion and deportation because of behaviour which the Government considers to be unacceptable namely to:

- Foment terrorism or seek to provoke others to terrorist acts
- Justify or glorify terrorism
- Foment other serious criminal activity or seek to provoke others to serious criminal acts

- Foster hatred which may lead to intra-community violence in the UK
- Advocate violence in furtherance of particular beliefs
- And those who express what the Government considers to be extreme views that are in conflict with the UK's culture of tolerance

One response was from the Muslim Council of Britain (MCoB),[1] which argued that the list of unacceptable behaviours was too wide and lacked clarity, and exclusion and deportation for behaviours that the government appeared to consider unacceptable (as listed above) 'have the serious potential of stifling legitimate expression of views with such draconian consequences as to cause deep alienation and anguish'. The inference is that the MCoB considers:

- those who foment terrorism or seek to provoke others to terrorist acts
- those who justify or glorify terrorism
- those who foment other serious criminal activity
- those who foster hatred that might lead to intra-community violence here
- those who advocate violence in furtherance of particular beliefs, and
- those who express views that the government considers to be extreme or to conflict with this country's culture (of tolerance).

should not be excluded/deported but should be free to continue with such behaviour in this country.

Another submission was from Article 19, which 'is an international human rights organisation which defends and promotes freedom of expression of information all over the world'. Part of its submission was:

In those cases where deportation or exclusion is seen as the only answer, we urge that Home Secretary's powers are not used in a way that would violate the right to freedom of expression contained in Article 10 of the European Convention on Human Rights and Article 19 of the International Covenant on Civil and Political Rights. In the light of this, we have serious concerns with regard to the following items on the list:

- justifying or glorifying terrorism;
- fostering hatred which may lead to intra-community violence in the UK;
- advocating violence in furtherance of particular beliefs;

- the expression of views that the Government consider to be extreme and that conflict with the UK's culture of tolerance.

The first of the behaviours listed by the government as unacceptable, namely fomenting terrorism or seeking to provoke others to terrorist acts, is omitted from that list so that the inference is that Article 19 accepts that those who foment terrorism or seek to provoke others to terrorist acts may be deported, but holds that:

- those who justify or glorify terrorism,

- those who foment other serious criminal activity or seek to provoke others to serious criminal acts,

- those who foster hatred that might lead to intra-community violence in the UK,

- those who advocate violence in furtherance of particular beliefs, and

- those who express what the government considers to be extreme views (which conflict with the UK's culture of tolerance)

should not necessarily be deported but perhaps allowed to continue to do so (here).

The first to be so deported, for non-terrorist behaviour, was Frezel Poku from Ghana. His record included convictions in 2008 for robbery and attempted robbery, and arrests for numerous gang-related 'group' robbery offences on public transport; and there was a YouTube video of him threatening to stab members of other gangs.

Another to be so deported was Lincoln Farquharson (*see* H is for human rights). Others to be so deported were the following eight under Operation Bite:

- Andrew Drummond from Jamaica, sentenced in 2000 to four years for rape and in 2005 to five years for two armed commercial robberies, plus arrests for firearms and vehicle offences. He had been shot in 2005 and again two years later, the latter time with a MAC-10 machine gun, which was used in 2009 to murder an associate. (His brother was shot fatally in 2000.)

- Everald Howell from Jamaica; gang member, convicted of affray and theft plus possession of a firearm and heroin.

- Jerman Jarrett from Jamaica; deemed such a risk that he was detained before Operation Bite when only 17; convictions for possession with intent to supply crack cocaine, possession of an offensive weapon and heroin, arrested for attempted murder/GBH by stabbing.

- Xhafer Nezaj from Albania; upon being arrested for affray he was found to be in possession of false identity documents.

- Roosevelt Odigie from Nigeria; convicted of possession of a butterfly knife, robbery, theft, assault, breach of supervision and community punishment order.

- Omar Wildman from Jamaica; gang member, convicted of robbery, possession of heroin and cocaine, arrested for possession of a firearm with intent.

- Andrew Williams, and his twin Anjay, from Jamaica; convictions for robbery with a firearm.

Notes: *C is for non-conducive*

1. The MCoB's submission, notwithstanding the secular nature of the proposal, was prefaced, 'In the name of Allah the Most Beneficent and the Most Merciful'.

And C is for contradiction

Assimilation and diversity are contradictory. You can have one or the other but not both. It is the same with integration and multiculturalism.

And C is for the cost of immigration

First of all, generally,

> Despite their partial subjectivity and regional concentration, the wider welfare consequences of rising population density need to be considered in a serious manner, as many of them will involve economic consequences. For example, Lord Turner, in his LSE lecture, explained how a home owner, faced with a new noisy motorway or rail line nearby, would often be compensated for the loss in value of their home. Such compensation costs will rise as population density increases, creating a clear economic impact. Failure to compensate fully for the loss of individuals' welfare in such cases will, according to Lord Turner, lead to

more 'Nimbys' (Not In My Back Yard), who attempt to block public infrastructure and transport developments. Lord Turner argued that Nimbys are more prevalent in Britain than France or the US due to the much higher population density in the UK. It is thus the UK's higher population density, rather than its planning system, which often makes it much slower and more costly to build large infrastructure projects compared to other countries. (Paragraph 183 of the House of Lords Report).[1]

Second, expenditure on housing and general infrastructure such as hospitals, law enforcement, schools, security etc. consequential on rapid/sudden population increase.

One cost of immigration has been publicly acknowledged for about fifty years. By the end of the 1960s, it was stated that the cost of housing immigrants in Birmingham was adding 4d in the pound to the city's rates.[2]

With increased population density, there is more building, there is more hard surface and so more immediate run-off of rainwater and so greater propensity to flood; the greater population density exacerbates pressure to build on floodplains and so further increases the danger of flooding, all of which increases insurance premiums.

Third, specifically:

- The 'large resources and eternal vigilance' necessitated by the 'up to 2000 terrorists'[3] identified by Lord Carlile – the cost of which is likely to continue because 'It remains the case that there are several thousand Islamist extremists here who see the British public as legitimate target'.[3.1]

- The cost (and inconvenience) of bag searching in public spaces such as the Royal Opera House, Covent Garden and Chelsea Flower Show, plus courts.

- The compensation paid to terror suspects because, for reasons of national security, it is inadvisable to disclose the evidence held against such suspects: (it may be that such payments already total £15 million but confidentiality agreements with the suspects are prayed in aid of not disclosing the amounts).

- The cost of checking on all those whose movements are restricted under the Terrorism Acts.

- The cost of tuberculosis immunisation for babies born in areas of high relevant immigration.

- The cost of keeping in prison all those convicted under the Terrorism Act 2000, the Anti-Terrorism, Crime and Security Act 2001, the Prevention of Terrorism Act 2005, the Terrorism Act 2006 and the Counter-Terrorism Act 2008.

- The cost of keeping in prison all those non-indigenous convicted of 'mere' criminality.

- The cost of the legal fight to deport non-indigenous criminals at the conclusion of their sentence (or at any other time).

- In 2007, the chief constable of Cambridgeshire reported that her force's bill for interpreters had risen from £224,000 to £805,000 in four years.

- In 2007/8, thirty-seven out of the forty-three police forces in England and Wales spent £24.1 million on translation, an increase of 64% over 2004.

- Southwark Council provides a free interpretation service into more than seventy languages.

- In 2010/11, the UK Border Agency paid out £14.2 million in pay-outs and legal fees, in some cases even where the application for asylum failed.

- Fadi and Hayat El-Dinnaoui came here in 1997 from Lebanon and were granted asylum. They objected to being housed on the 16th floor because of her fear of heights (albeit they presumably flew here). The civil war in Lebanon finished years ago so they could return 'home' but no doubt there they would not have been provided with social housing.

- Kent County Council was reported as spending £2 million a year supporting unsuccessful applicants for asylum whom the Border Agency had failed to deport.

- The extra cost of educating children whose first language is not English. By mid-2013, according to the Department for Education, 1,061,010 schoolchildren did not have English as their first language. In mid-2013, in Westminster, 72% of schoolchildren did not have English as their first language but there are many schools where the percentage of the children whose first language is not English is well over 90%: (*see* S is for swarm and swamp). (It is alleged that there is no detriment to the education of children whose language at home is English by classmates whose first language is not English, but if nothing else there is the (extra) cost of engaging specialist foreign-language speakers for the children who have insufficient English.)

- The assistance to applicants for asylum whose applications were rejected.

- Between 2005 and 2010, over £109 million was spent on flights effecting deportation.

- In the seventeen months to the autumn of 2011, the charge for cancelled flights to carry home failed asylum seekers and illegal immigrants was £3.2 million.

- The standard 'accompaniment' of security on a flight to repatriate illegal immigrants is two to one: it has been 100 guards to thirty-five returnees on a flight to Jamaica.[4]

- The cost of policing 'honour violence': *see* H is for honour killings.

- The Metropolitan Police's Trident Gang Crime Command Unit at one stage was costing £60 million a year.

- The cost of the Prevent strategy.[5]

- The cost of the Jay Report into the Rotherham child sexual exploitation scandal plus the ensuing report by Louise Casey: *see* D is for Derby.

- The cost of the investigations into the so-called Trojan Horse letter – the Clarke Report, the Kershaw Report, West Midlands Police's report, the Department for Education's *Review into Possible Warnings to DfE Relating to Extremism in Birmingham Schools*, Ofsted's reports together with the time and expense of Birmingham City Council's own investigations, plus the compromise payments to headmasters etc. such as Balwant Bains of Saltley School and Specialist Science College.

- 'In the light of the Trojan Horse experience…. increasing the size of the Department for Education's Due Diligence and Counter Extremism Division DDCED to 25 staff…. further strengthening the DDCED, increasing its size to 36 and establishing it as a Group (DDCEG) under a newly-recruited Director with sole responsibility for this area of work'.[6]

- '[Translating services by local authorities] are also very expensive and a poor use of taxpayers' money. Independent research has suggested that local authorities alone spend nearly £20 million a year translating a variety of documents. Across the wider public sector, it has been estimated that translation and interpretation costs reached over £100 million in 2006.'[7]

- The cost of treatment, in the period 2010 to mid-2013 in London hospitals, of 2,115 FGM patients with at least 298 reversal operations.

- In mid-2010, Abdi Nur from Somalia was unemployed. He, his wife and their seven children were having their £2,000-a-week rent paid for them.

- The legal costs of getting Abu Qatada out of the country. (He entered this country on a forged passport, and so was an illegal immigrant; he left behind a wife and children continuing to live in tax-payer-funded housing.)

- The Lagos shuttle.[8]

- The Migrant Impacts Fund.[9] (Rushmoor Borough Council, wherein is Aldershot, was being so overwhelmed by former Gurkhas and their families that central government provided £1.5m to meet 'immediate resource needs'.)

- Quangos such as the North West Strategic Migration Partnership.

- The chairman of the Metropolitan Police Federation said that migration had had a 'huge' impact on police resources, adding,

    It is a problem when you get someone in who can't speak English and we wait hours for an expensive interpreter to hear their side of the story. Even in trivial case where you might be giving just a caution officers could be off the street for five or six hours – which is a massive expense.

Fourth, probably incapable of valuation in monetary terms but rather in terms of loss of social capital,[10] reduction in social cohesion,[11] destruction of social fabric by sudden expansion of villages into towns and towns into cities and likewise by tenant farmers being thrown off their land for development (particularly by the local authority, which wants the money and is the local planning authority), reduction in national identity and of national solidarity and reduction of common understanding and enjoyment of innuendo and double entendre.[12] And the contra of the cost of promoting 'community cohesion'.[13]

Fifth, the cost of the 'race industry'.[14]

Sixth the cost of the 'race card'.[15]

Seventh, again probably incapable of valuation in monetary terms, but immigration brings into the country aliens with other social norms, people with whom one has less in common and so is less likely to trust; but trust lowers transaction costs[16] and

You must trust and believe in people or life becomes impossible.[17]

We all began as sectarians: it's in our selfish genes. We've been squabbling since our Rift Valley days, wasting time and lives locked in clan-on-clan vendettas. As Paul Collier says in his terrific book *Exodus: Immigration and Multiculturalism in the 21st Century*: 'Trust and cooperation do not arise naturally. They are not primordial attributes of the "Noble savage" that get undermined by civilisation: Jean-Jacques Rousseau was spectacularly wrong. The evidence suggests precisely the opposite: trust and cooperation beyond the family are acquired as part of the functional attitudes that accumulate in a modern prosperous society. One reason that poor societies are poor is that they lack these attitudes.' So trust grows and develops over time, from small to big. You trust yourself first, your family, then your clan and, only slowly and hesitatingly in the right conditions, something bigger; your country. Once you've grown this fragile sense of nation, you trash it at your peril. [18]

Eighth,

New names sought for jailed couple's children.

Two young children currently being placed for adoption should be given new identities to prevent their abusive parents tracking them down through an internet campaign, the High Court has been told.

Social workers also want to sever all contact between the children, aged two and three, and their five older brother and sisters to make it more difficult for their Nigerian parents, who are currently in prison, to re-establish contact.

But Mr Justice Holman urged caution over the 'highly unusual' plan set out by social workers from Haringey, north London, and urged them to 'pause for thought'. He said that while it was common for children to be given new surnames on adoption, it was highly unusual to give children new first names. He warned such a change could have a profound effect on them, particularly on the older of the two, a girl who is now almost four.

Adjourning the case for further expert views to be taken, he said he was 'frankly astonished' that there had been such an expectation he would reach a decision in a single day's hearing, as previously planned. Details of the Family Division case emerged in a judgment published yesterday. A further hearing will take place next week.[19]

Ninth, reduction in what would have been the economy's growth rate by the size of the state increasing.[20]

Tenth, the added welfare bill and cost of (child) poverty by immigration driving down the wages of the lowest earnings deciles. Plus the cost of the increase in inequality resulting from such earnings reduction.

And from abroad we have this view:

> Another potential source of labour is immigration. The Keidanren, the main business lobby, has periodically come up with eye-catching estimates suggesting Japan needs to import millions of workers if it is to make up a labour shortfall of 6 million people by 2025. Given that Japan is home to only around 2 million 'non-Japanese', many of them long-term Korean residents, it is impossible to imagine it opening the floodgates to that extent. Some years ago, I asked a senior Japanese official, urbane in the extreme, about the latest Keidanren report urging mass immigration. He visibly shuddered. 'For the rewards you get in terms of economic rejuvenation the costs are simply too high,' he said without explanation, though he was clearly alluding to the perceived social problems in multicultural western societies. 'We've seen what has happened in the US and Europe.'[21]

Notes: C is for the cost of immigration

1. The Report of the House of Lords' Select Committee on Economic Affairs, entitled *The Economic Impact of Immigration*, published 1 April 2008.

2. Sir Neville Bosworth: 1918/2012 Birmingham councillor for forty-six years and its lord mayor, 1969/70.

3. *See* C is for Lord Carlile.

3.1 Andrew Parker: (new) head of UK Security Service, April 2013.

In March 2014 Boris Johnson, the then mayor of London wrote 'Every day in London and other big cities, there are thousands of counter-terrorism officers doing a fantastic job of keeping us safe … There are a few thousand people in London – the 'low thousands', they say who are of interest to the security services …'

In 2016 Jon Gower Davies in *Immigrants Come From Somewhere (Else)* put it thus 'In the UK alone, there are currently 3,000 Muslims under surveillance by the security services.'

John Gieve, Permanent Secretary to the Home Office 2001–05 (*see* what has note 27 to it of I is for integration) put the number of al-Qaeda activists at 15,000. Perhaps the explanation is a different level of surveillance.

4. In response to the furore over the *In the UK illegally? Go Home or face arrest* van adverts, the then immigration minister, Mark Harper, said the average cost of an enforced removal (from the country) was £15,000.

5. In 2009 The TaxPayers' Alliance listed the following grants:

- Preventing Violent Extremism grants distributed by local authorities ranging from £17 to Yorkshire Purchasing Office for 'Work with BME women to tackle extremism and Islamophobia and celebrate diversity, including focus groups and awareness sessions' and £300 (twice) to Barking Mosque for 'Lunch for workshops for young Muslims', to £38,000 to Islah for 'Islah Youth Project', totalling £4,489,466 in 2007–08 and £7,511,856 in 2008–09.

- 'Prevent' funding given to the official affiliates of the Muslim Council of Britain, ranging from £1,000 to Islamic Society of Britain – Redbridge, to the Muslim Cultural Heritage Centre totalling, over three years, £857,761.

- DCLG grant payments made to organisations to deliver specific projects, 2006–07, ranging from £811 to GSN Displays for 'Support forum to discuss solutions to violent extremism and Islamaphobia' to £160,000 to Sufi Muslim Council for 'Support for events to tackle extremist ideology, and for work to build the capacity of the Sufi Muslim Councils, including developing SMC website to promote key work areas', totalling £1,007,618.

6. *Review into possible warnings to DfE relating to extremism in Birmingham Schools* by Chris Wormald the Permanent Secretary, January 2015.

7. Eric Pickles (MP for Brentwood and Ongar from 1992, Secretary of State for Communities and Local Government 2010/15), *Guidance on translation into foreign languages*, March 2013.

Only Muslim women can reform Islam by Allison Pearson, *The Daily Telegraph*, January 2016:

> The UK is spending £100 million a year on interpreters. One hospital trust in the North West uses interpreters 74 times a day. In the NHS, the sum spent on foreign language services has risen 41 per cent over the last four years to at least £33 million.

8. Taiwo Aromokum had an emergency caesarean, shortly after arrival in this country, for twins. According to her, they arrived three months early but

she had a lavish baby shower before leaving and there is nothing in the Nigerian press – she is a leading actress there – about the delivery being premature. Mrs Aromokum came here on a six-month general visa so might not have been due to pay for her medical care. But Bimbo Ayelabola was apparently open about coming here for the birth, of quintuplets, and so should have paid for medical care.

9. This was 'launched in 2009 to assist with public service providers to deal with transitional pressures of immigration'. It was to be funded by an increase in migrant fees but when in 2010 it came to abolish the fund, the minister said, 'In the light of the overall fiscal position and the need for urgent action to tackle the deficit the Government concluded it was not a priority funding stream.'

10. *See Bowling Alone* by Robert D. Putnam.

In *E Pluribus Unum: Diversity and Community in the 21st Century*, Putnam wrote, 'in the short run … immigration and ethnic diversity tend to reduce social solidarity and social capital'. And that in diverse communities, people are liable to 'distrust their neighbours, regardless of the colour of their skin, to withdraw even from close friends, to expect the worst from their community and its leaders, to volunteer less, give less to charity and work on community projects less often, to register to vote less, to agitate for social reform more but have less faith that they can actually make a difference, and to huddle unhappily in front of the television.'

11. Matt Ridley's blog of 2 December 2013, a paragraph of which is quoted under C is for culture, is headed *Immigration versus social cohesion* followed by *The elite benefit, so it's becoming a leftish issue.*

12. Apart from in *Carry On* films, the *Just a Minute* radio programme and books such as *Rumpole of the Bailey.*

13. Dominic Grieve MP: (*see* note 12 to C is for community).

14. *Understanding East London's Somali Communities*, a study conducted for the East London Alliance, August 2010, by Options UK (Joanne Hemmings, PhD) is 107 pages long.

15. Four officials of Unison were accused by the Union of racism when they criticised the leadership for failing to listen to the membership, by a cartoon of the three wise monkeys (these representative figures of 'hear no evil', 'speak no evil' and 'see no evil' date from at least as long ago as seventeenth century Japan but probably are far older and 'from' China).

Apart from £49,000 of damages, the legal costs must have been several/many times as much. The four officials included Onay Kasab, who doesn't sound very indigenous.

16. *See*, for example: *The role of trustworthiness in reducing transaction costs and improving performance: Empirical evidence from the United States, Japan and Korea* by Jeffrey H. Dyer and Wujin Chu, Organization Science, 14(1), 2003:

> Our findings indicate that perceived trustworthiness reduces transaction costs and is correlated with greater information sharing in supplier–buyer relationships. Moreover, the findings suggest that the value created for transactors, in terms of lower transaction costs, may be substantial. In particular, we found that the least trusted automaker spent significantly more of its face-to-face interaction time with suppliers on contracting and haggling when compared to the most trusted automaker. This translated into procurement (transaction) costs that were five times higher for the least trusted automaker ... Our findings provide empirical evidence that trustworthiness lowers transactions costs and may be an important source of competitive advantage.

17. Anton Chekov (1860–1904).

18. *Why it's uncivilised to sneer at patriotism* by Mary Wakefield, *The Spectator*, November 2014.

The extract from Professor Collier's *Exodus*, which she quotes, was there followed by:

> Two brilliant new studies of Africa illustrate how a lack of trust has been perpetuated. One draws on the painstaking reconstruction of Africa's deep past that historians have achieved over recent decades. Cumulatively, historians have now recorded over eighty violent intergroup conflicts that occurred prior to 1600. Timothy Beesley and Marta Reynal-Querol thought to code all these conflicts by their spatial coordinates and investigate whether they were correlated with modern conflicts. The correlation turned out to be remarkably strong: the violence of over four hundred years ago proved to be disturbingly persistent today. So by what mechanism has this persistence occurred? The researchers suggest that the transmission mechanism is the lack of trust created by violence that echoes down the decades....

> Among the societies with which I am familiar, the one with the lowest level of trust is Nigeria. I find Nigeria exhilarating and vibrant: people are engaged and witty. But Nigerians radically, deeply, do not trust each other. Opportunism is the result of decades, probably centuries, in which trust would have been quixotic, and it is now ingrained in ordinary behaviour.

If it were not principally about institutions the following extract from *When the Money Runs Out* by Stephen D. King would be in the body of this book. Chapter 6, poignantly entitled *Loss of Trust, Loss of Growth*, concludes with:

> If people trust each other, and the institutions they represent, they are more likely to trade. That means more in the way of profitable exchanges and, hence, greater opportunities to specialize. And with heightened levels of trust, there is less need for bureaucracy: rules, regulations and legal enforcement can be reduced without wider costs. Meanwhile, higher levels of trust are also associated with more effective financial markets: savers are prepared to put their money into projects with uncertain returns believing, rightly or otherwise, that they will be fairly treated. And higher levels of trust in financial markets will surely facilitate the cross-border movement of funds between creditors and debtors, allowing savers to hunt for the best global returns and, thus, allowing capital to be allocated in the most efficient way to maximize income.
>
> Without trust, economic growth will be in short supply. And with neither trust nor growth, society is in danger of disintegrating.

19. Newspaper item, *The Daily Telegraph*, 4 April 2014. The following eight questions arise,

(i) Why were the Nigerians allowed into this country in the first place?

(ii) What was the crime(s) for which both parents were both imprisoned?

(iii) What was the cost of the police investigation and judicial process whereby both parents were both imprisoned?

(iv) What was the cost of keeping each of the parents in prison?

(v) What was the cost of taking the children into care upon their parents being arrested/imprisoned?

(vi) What was the weekly cost of caring for each of the seven children (while their parents were in prison)?

(vii) What was the cost of the judicial process as to the proposed adoption of the two youngest of the seven children?

(viii) Why weren't the parents deported immediately and accompanied by all seven of their children?

20. *See Government Size and Implication for Economic Growth* by Andreas Bergh and Magnus Henrekson, published (in the USA by The AEI Press) in 2010'...there is a negative correlation between government size and

economic growth, where government size increases by ten percentage points, annual growth rates decrease by between 0.5% and 1%.

Or possibly even more – '…a percentage point increase in the share of total revenue …. would decrease output by 0.12 and 0.13 percentage points': *Government size, composition, volatility and economic growth* Working Paper No. 849 January 2008 of the European Central Bank by Antonio Afonso and Davide Furceri.

According to Andrew Lilico in *What Jonathan Portes gets wrong and why* (*conservativehome*, January 2013), 'In standard studies, conducted since the mid-1970s and now having achieved a high degree of academic consensus, each additional percentage point of GDP of government consumption spending reduces GDP growth by 0.1–0.15 percentage points'.

21. *Bending Adversity: Japan and the Art of Survival* by David Pilling, published by Allen Lane in 2014: the conversation of 'some years ago' was in 2003.

And C is for crime committed by immigrants

On 30 June 2005, one quarter of those in prison were 'non-white ethnic'.

In 2010 more than 91,000 non-indigenous were arrested upon suspicion of crime, compared with fewer than 52,000 in 2008.

By the end of 2011, one in seven of the women in jail were foreigners, the number thereof having risen by nearly half in the preceding decade.

On 15 November 2012 it was reported that Maria Di Natale had been sentenced to five years for stealing from a design business while there as a temporary financial controller. An internet search did not reveal her ethnicity but that she lived in Kilburn. The *Brent & Kilburn Times* reported the story and on the same day had an item entitled *Brent Police reveal 10 most wanted burglary suspects*. Those suspects were Ayman Ben Ali, Darius Alexsander, Ahsan Baloch, Joel Cirstean, David Dragon, Marchin Gadacek, Pawel Harasim, Yousef Hammoumi, Florin-Avram Lucescu and Felix Morrehouse. Perhaps none of the ten were convicted. Another item was entitled *12 Most wanted suspects*, namely Peter Gavin Abeygunarayne – robbery; Hamdi Abdelaziz – recall to prison and immigration offences; Jose Correla – harassment; Denny Desilva – recall to prison; Charles Joseph Dhillon – notification offences and fraud; Rafal Filonowicz – failing to appear accused of possession with intent to supply drugs; Adrian Losiewcs

– burglary; John Oatway – burglary, GBH and flytipping; Manjindir Singe – failing to appear for taking a vehicle; Marco Vario – failing to appear for cultivation of drugs (together with two of Brent Police's ten most wanted burglary suspects). Again, all twelve were merely suspects. But in both cases, on the basis of their names, nearly all would appear to be non-indigenous.

(Most of Kilburn is in the London Borough of Brent. The Council's profile at the beginning of 2010 stated that 59% of the population were black, Asian and minority ethnic groups; 71% of the population were from a group other than white British; 48% of the population were born outside of the UK and 130 different languages were spoken in the borough's schools).

This [of Diarrassouba] may be the first actual killing on Oxford Street since 2008 but two male teenagers were stabbed outside an H&M shop in August. A year last March a 15-year-old was lynched by a mob of more than 100 teenagers who pursued their quarry through Victoria Station at rush-hour (*see* Victoria Osteku in Appendix I). In recent months I have witnessed several incidents of minor violence on and around London buses during daylight and other threatening behaviour often between different races. And, of course, there were the August riots which brought members of a whole urban sub-culture to the streets, of whom a disproportionate number were black, most of whom were already on the wrong side of the law.

You do not need to immerse yourself in the intricacies of so-called gang culture to draw two conclusions. The first is that visible policing, whether of city estates or of public spaces, such as Oxford Street is absurdly inadequate. The liabilities of relying on CCTV to detect crime after-the-fact should be obvious: vastly better street lighting would also help.

The second is that established, middle-class, family Britain is in retreat from the capital in a way which that risks an American style hollowing out with the very rich, the very poor and the newly arrived concentrated in an urban circle and everyone else clustered around the edge. Look at the last election results for London and the South-east. Look at the extent of de-facto racial segregation in London's schools.

Bear in mind that more than half of all children born in London are to foreign mothers, compared with 25 per cent nationally. Then ask whether the killing of Seydou Diarrassouba outside Foot Looker on Boxing Day [2011] was a tragic accident, or – if these social trends continue – a sign of things to come.[1]

Diarrassouba, a Muslim whose parents moved to Britain from Ivory Coast in west Africa, was the 15th young person to be murdered on the streets of London [in 2011].

Intelligence shows that 27% of all those arrested for a criminal offence are foreign nationals.[2]

The convention that neither side should carry guns is obviously over. Paul Collier,[3] a professor of economics at Oxford who discusses the contrast between the reaction to Roberts and to Duggan in his fascinating book *Exodus*, thinks the arrival in Britain of criminal gangs from other countries may have started the process which has led to the convention's demise. The murder rate in Jamaica is more than 50 times the rate in the UK. There, criminals have always carried guns, as have the police.[4]

There are about 500,000 Sikhs in the UK, and about 700,000 Hindus. Criminal Sikhs in the prisons of England and Wales number 777 and criminal Hindus number 456. Thus together, they provide 1,232 prisoners in the prisons of England and Wales: and if you add Buddhists and Jews to this, these minorities provide 3,241 prisoners.... Muslims on their own provide 11,248 being 13 per cent of the prison population – well above their due statistical 'share' – and growing.[5]

See Appendix I

While not here as immigrants:

- They flew in from the Baltic for each job – Janno Heinola, Algo Toomits, Joonas Jarsvoo, Sarik Sander, Rauno Kuklase, Ivo Parn, Regio Janes and Raivo Loige robbed numerous jewellers, including one in Leeds four times in three years.

- Libyan soldiers at Bassingbourn Barracks to be trained – army cadets Moktar Ali Saad Mahmoud and Ibrahim Abugtila were both sentenced to twelve years for raping and aiding and abetting rape of a man. Until this conviction, it could not be reported that on the same night, again in Cambridge, three other Libyan cadets carried out sex attacks – Khaled El Azibi admitted sexual assault and theft, Naji El Maarfi admitted three counts of sexual assault, exposure and theft and Mohammed Abdalsalam admitted two counts of sexual assault, using threatening abusive or insulting words, and theft.

Notes: *C is for crime commited by immigrants*

1. *The hollowed-out city invites lawlessness* by Mary Dejevsky, Civil Liberty, December 2011.

In the month before his death, Diarrassouba had appeared in court, accused of theft of a phone from Nile Downes, and assault of Downes and his brother Yafeu.

Thulani Khumalo and Jermaine Joseph were tried for Diarrassouba's murder and acquitted.

2. Assistant Commissioner Mark Rowley, November 2012, announcing Operation Nexus – collaboration between the Metropolitan Police and UK Border Agency.

3. *See* notes 15 to P is for progression.

4. *All guns blazing or How did Britain ever have unarmed criminals?* by Alasdair Palmer, *The Spectator,* November 2014.

5. *Immigrants Come From Somewhere (Else)* by Jon Gower Davies in his comment on Trevor Phillips' *Race and Faith: The Deafening Silence* published by Civitas June 2016.

And C is for culture

[... immigrants] come from societies where they have been brought up to believe you can only get certain things through a favour culture.

... we have minority communities in this country which come from backgrounds where corruption is endemic.

Yes it's mainly the Pakistani community, not the Indian community. I wouldn't draw it down to one. I'd be wary of saying it's just a Pakistani problem.[1]

The unprecedented wave of immigration that Britain received between 1997 and 2010 (about 3.2 million net immigrants) did not just put pressure on housing and welfare; it also put pressure on culture. The more that immigrants fail to integrate, either by sheer numbers or by the encouragement of multiculturalism, the more resented they will be. What America did so well for so long was to suck in millions of people from Ireland, Germany, Italy and Africa but turn them into flag-waving democrats who loved free enterprise.[2]

Notes: *C is for culture*

1. Dominic Grieve QC, Attorney General, 2010/14; MP for Beaconsfield, November 2013. (The constituency adjoins Slough, as to which *see* V is for vote rigging. Mr Grieve had to apologise for this statement *see* H is for hegemony.)

2. Matt Ridley's blog *Immigration versus social cohesion?* followed by *The elite benefit, so it's becoming a leftish issue* of 2 December 2013.

D is for Derby

Derby is where men from Mirpur (in Kashmir and *see* M is for Mirpur) groomed, abused and raped teenage girls.

At the culmination of Operation Retriever, through 2010, there were three split trials. The men described as the ringleaders – Abid Mohammed Saddique and Mohammed Romaan Liaquat – pleaded guilty to at least one of charges of rape, false imprisonment, sexual assault, sexual activity with a child, perverting the course of justice and aiding and abetting rape, and were both given indefinite prison sentences. Others convicted of at least one of such crimes included Farooq Ahmed, Akshay Kumar, Faisal Mehmood (subsequently deported to Pakistan), Mohammed Imran Rehman and Liaquat's brother, Nawed Liaquat.[1]

Derby turned out not to be a one-off or the first. If no one else had known of this Asian threat, decades before, the police did. Mick Gradwell, a former detective superintendent, observed:

> When I joined in 1979 one of my first tasks was to police around a Blackburn nightclub where one of the issues was Asian men cruising around in BMWs and Mercs trying to pick up young drunken girls.

But this Asian behaviour was not confronted, immigration continued and

- in 2003, Charlene Downes disappeared, and Paige Rivers in 2007. In 2012, a kebab shop in Blackpool was refused a hot food licence;[2]

- in August 2008, the police attended the Balti House in Heywood, Rochdale, and arrested a fifteen-year-old, who came to be referred to as Girl A, on suspicion of causing criminal damage: she was attempting to smash up the place. The reason for this, she told police, was that she had been repeatedly plied with vodka and then raped. As a result, Kabeer Hassan and Defendant X were arrested but, despite the latter's DNA being found on Girl A's underwear, no prosecution followed.[3] A new Chief Crown Prosecutor for North West England, Nazir Afzal, re-examined the file and, in December 2010, Defendant X and Kabeer Hassan were re-arrested, with nine others to follow;

- on Saturday, 28 November 2009, Amar Hussain and Shamrez Rashid took two girls, then aged sixteen and fifteen, from Telford to a hostel in Birmingham, where they were joined by Amer Islam Choudhrey, Jahbar

Rafiq and Adel Saleem. To the five men, 'It was Eid. We treated [the girls] as our guests. OK so they gave us [sex] but we were buying them food and drink.' Between them, the five men were convicted of rape, attempted rape, attempted sexual assault and child abduction;

- in 2010, Mohammed Ditta and Mirza Baig, both of Manchester, in their thirties and married, were jailed indefinitely for plying three fifteen-year-olds with vodka, ecstasy and cocaine and then sexually assaulting them;

- in 2010, Adil Hussain, Moshin Khan, Zafran Ramzan, Umar Razaq and (his cousin) Razwan Razaq, (all) of Rotherham, were jailed for grooming, in 2008, girls who at the time were aged twelve and thirteen, and in one case of raping a sixteen-year-old;

- in 2012 there was posted[4] the following:

The Rotherham grooming case[5] shows the dangers of confusing criminality with culture.

If you are a parent then there are some things that scare you more than others. Someone else hurting your children is pretty high up that list.

The details emerging from Rotherham over the last few months about the systematic abuse of young girls are truly the stuff of parental nightmare. But it's all made worse because it now seems that for over ten years those charged with protecting children and young girls failed. In fact, worst of all, they decided to look the other way!

They made a choice; protect children in the face of overwhelming evidence of sexual abuse and cruelty or worry more about some misconceived notion of 'cultural sensitivities'; as if there is any culture where rape is acceptable.

They chose the latter.

It is important to say that The Times has led the way in exposing both the abuse and the cover-up. And some of the details that they have uncovered from confidential reports are some of the most shocking that you can imagine. The documents revealed by The Times give details of events over the years for which no one was prosecuted such as:

- fifty-four Rotherham children were linked to sexual exploitation by three brothers from one British Pakistani family, 18 identifying one brother as their "boyfriend" and several allegedly made pregnant by him;

- a 14-year-old girl from a loving, supportive family was allegedly held in a flat and forced to perform sex acts on five men, four of them Pakistani, plus a 32-year-old Iraqi Kurd. She gave a filmed police interview and identified her abusers;

- one girl, 15, spent days in hospital after a broken bottle was allegedly forced inside her by two young British Pakistani men in a park, causing her to bleed extensively;

- a 13-year-old girl was found at 3am with disrupted clothing in a house with a large group of Asian men who had fed her vodka. A neighbour reported the girl's screams. Police arrested the child for being drunk and disorderly but did not question the men.

But the police and local authorities knew – and did nothing!

As *The Times* says:

"A 2010 confidential report by the police intelligence bureau warning that thousands of such crimes were committed in the county each year.

It contains explosive details about the men responsible for the most serious, co-ordinated abuse. 'Possibly the most shocking threat is the existence of substantial and organised offender networks that groom and exploit victims on a worrying scale,' the report says.

'Practitioners throughout the force state that there is a problem with networks of Asian offenders both locally and nationally. This was particularly stressed in Sheffield, and even more so in Rotherham where there appears to be a significant problem with networks of Asian males exploiting young white females. 'Such groups are said to have trafficked South Yorkshire child victims' to many other cities including Bristol, Manchester, Birmingham, Bradford and Dover".

But nothing was done; why? Well, in 2010 the Rotherham Safeguarding Children Board produced another report. The board is made up of senior representatives from local schools, social services, voluntary sector and the police. Now remember that no one has been prosecuted but enough was clearly known and there were enough concerns for a report to be commissioned into what had been going on, in fact is still going on. They helpfully noted that the crimes (presumably they meant alleged) had:

"cultural characteristics ... which are locally sensitive in terms of diversity."

And for the avoidance of doubt as to where priorities lay:

"There are sensitivities of ethnicity with potential to endanger the harmony of community relationships. Great care will be taken in drafting ... this report to ensure that its findings embrace Rotherham's qualities of diversity. It is imperative that suggestions of a wider cultural phenomenon are avoided."[6]

- in May 2012, under newspaper headlines such as *Men who helped themselves to easy meat* and *Why did no one listen to teenage victims of sex gang?*[7], it was reported that Shabir Ahmed,[8.1] Mohammed Amin,[8.2] Abdul Aziz,[8.3] Adil Khan,[8.4] Kabeer Hassan,[8.5] Abdul Qayyum,[8.6] Abdul Rauf,[8.7] Mohammed Sajid,[8.8] and Hamid Safi,[8.9] had been convicted of one or more of rape, arranging and/or inciting child prostitution, allowing premises to be used therefor, sexual activity with a child and trafficking;

- in 2012, from Telford or thereabouts, Ahdel Ali and his brother Mubarek, Tanveer Ahmed, Mohammed Ali Sultan, Mohammed Islam Choudrey and Mohammed Younis were convicted of one or more of sexual activity with a child, controlling child prostitution, inciting child prostitution, inciting a child to engage in sexual activity, meeting a child after sexual grooming, and trafficking a child within the UK for sexual exploitation;

- in 2012, from Keighley and Halifax, Bilal Hussain and Shazad Rehman were convicted of raping two girls and assaulting others. Their modus operandi was to drug and then rape young girls after cruising the streets looking for 'fresh meat': one victim, a fourteen-year-old, said, 'The choice was either have sex with both or get beaten up';

- in May 2012, Azad Miah from Bangladesh, of The Spice of India in Carlisle, was jailed for fifteen years having been found guilty on ten of eighteen charges – paying for the sexual services of a child, child prostitution and keeping a brothel (mainly 'staffed' by teenagers. A twelve-year-old had complained to the police three times about Miah before giving up, as nothing was done). Three years later Azad's brother, Ata, of The Indigo in Carlisle, was jailed for a year for harassment: according to one of Azad's victims, Ata had pulled up in his car beside the victim, saying he was 'keeping an eye on her' as she had 'put the boss away';

- in February 2013, Hamza Ali, Surin Uddin and Mohamed Sheikh were convicted of taking a thirteen-year-old from a bus stop in London to a house in Ipswich where she was treated 'like a piece of meat' for four days;

- in May 2013, Bassan and Mohammed Karrar, Akthar and Anjum Dogar, Kamar Jamil, Zeesham Ahmed and Assad Hussain collected, between the seven of them, nineteen convictions for rape; ten convictions for conspiracy to rape; five convictions for rape of a child under thirteen; four convictions for conspiracy to rape a child under thirteen; eight convictions for arranging or facilitating prostitution; five convictions for trafficking for sexual exploitation; four convictions for sexual activity with a child; and one conviction for each of conspiracy to commit a sexual assault of a child, sexual assault of a child under thirteen by penetration, using an instrument to procure a miscarriage and supplying a class-A drug. This was the result of Operation Bullfinch.

Nearly two years later, Oxfordshire Safeguarding Children Board (OSCB) issued its 114-page (plus appendices) *Serious Case Review in to Child Sexual Exploitation in Oxfordshire: from the experiences of Children A, B, C, D, E, and F.* Part of its paragraph 2.6 is:

Adding cases where there was some certainty to those where there was a formal conviction of offences against them, there are grounds for believing that over the last 15 years around 370 girls may have been exploited in the ways covered by this SCR.

And three entire paragraphs of that Review are:

1.29 Terminology around ethnicity: The perpetrators in this case were predominately of Pakistani heritage. (Five were of Pakistani and one of North African heritage and the other said he was born in Saudi Arabia.) In this report the word 'Asian'[9] is used more than 'Pakistani'. This is not to hide any specific ethnic origin, but because this was the description mainly used by the victims[10] and in agency case records. It is believed that when the term 'Asian' was used it did often refer to those of Pakistani heritage, but 'Asian' seems to be the word used in common professional parlance.

1.30 The victims were white British girls.

4.25 Community relations: With the known perpetrators of group CSE [child sexual exploitation] being significantly of Pakistani heritage, there is considerable work to build relationships with these communities (and others), increase their understanding of CSE and help build a preventative approach. Some examples:

o The Children's Society runs 12-week induction programmes for young unaccompanied asylum seekers, on which CSC [child sexual contact] and the Police provide input on CSE and age of consent issues.

76

o The City Council is appointing a Pakistani Father Support project worker, and has developed a new mentoring programme to prevent CSE amongst at risk BME/South Asian males.

o The Superintendent in charge of the Oxford Police (who also chairs the OSCB CSE subgroup) meets Mosque leaders every two months, with for example discussions on CSE warning signs. In 2015 it is planned to extend this to include the City and County Councils.

o The Superintendent also has a bi-monthly Independent Advisory Group which includes all faiths. CSE is always on the agenda, and the Group is briefed for example on disruption operations.

o Police officers attend the Mosque Friday Prayers weekly.

o The OSCB's revised CSE strategy will have a major new section on community engagement.

o The Local Authority Designated Officer (LADO) has led work with the Oxfordshire Mosques and their linked Madrassas on safeguarding children and has worked to ensure safeguarding arrangements are in place including DBS checks, basic training and a safeguarding policy.

o Seven faith leaders attended a top-level briefing on CSE progress in September 2014.

o In October 2014 Muslim representatives attended a CSC/TVP meeting, discussing trafficking and CSE with other religious leaders.

o A meeting was held in February 2015 between Police, City and County representatives and the OSCB Chair with Muslim community leaders.

• in August 2013, Aabidali Mubarak Ali, Rakib Iacub, Hamza Imitiazali, Chandresh Mistry, Bharat Modhwadia and Wajud Usman, all of Leicester – five Muslim and one Hindu – pleaded guilty to offences against a sixteen-year-old girl;

• in September 2013, Naeem Ahmed, Nabeel Ahmed and Hassan Raza were sentenced in Snaresbrook Crown Court to fourteen, eight and two years respectively for rape and/or sexual assault of an eighteen-year-old. During a seven-week trial, six girls gave evidence about the three men. The initial arrest was pursuant to investigations into the suspected abuse of two girls in the care of Essex County Council;

• in November 2013, Rochdale came up again: Manchester Crown Court jailed Rufiq Abubaken a Kurd; Abdul Huk and Roheez Khan, both of Pakistani heritage; and Chola Chansa and Freddie Kendakumana, both from the Congo, for sexual activity with an underage girl (the jury failed to reach a verdict as to Mohammed Ali and Asrar Haider);

- in March 2014, the furore over the trial of Abid Miskeen, aged thirty-two, of Bradford, was not over what he had done (he had had intercourse with a girl who was then aged fourteen) but that his victim was kept in custody overnight to ensure she gave evidence. The trial was delayed for a few hours; the girl went outside for a smoke and disappeared. The judge issued a warrant for her and three other witnesses. She was kept in a police station overnight and for four hours the next day. The jury took less than two hours to return a unanimous guilty verdict. Miskeen was sentenced to the maximum possible, namely seven years. Miskeen, father of two, made the girl pregnant. He had a string of previous convictions including robbery, assault and dangerous driving. In 2012, he was given a community order for punching his partner and was in breach of that order when he had intercourse with the girl;

- in April 2014, Nazakat Mahmood, Ghulfaraz Nawaz, Haroon Rauf and Omar Sharif – three of Chesham and one of Amersham – were convicted of sexual activity with a girl who at the time was fourteen;

- in July 2014, Mohammed Sadiq of Leeds was convicted of sexual assault on a child a third of his age. His counsel, Zia Chaudry, in mitigation, told the court that he continued to deny the offences. He was sentenced to five years (with three years extended licence);

- in July 2014, Matab Ali, Umber Farooq and Anees Hanif of Burton-upon-Trent were sentenced to five and a half years for sexually abusing a girl when she was between thirteen and fifteen, with Junaid Ali also being jailed for attempted rape, and Ameer Arshad for blackmail;

- in August 2014, there was published Professor Jay's *Independent Inquiry into Child Sexual Exploitation in Rotherham 1997–2013*:

  > No one knows the true scale of child sexual exploitation (CSE) in Rotherham over the years. Our conservative estimate is that approximately 1,400 children were sexually exploited over the full inquiry period, from 1997 to 2013.[11.1]

  > By far the majority of perpetrators were described as 'Asian' by victims [11.2]

- in November 2014, Birmingham City Council obtained an order that ten men should not approach in public places 'any female under 18' with whom they were not personally associated, the names of six to be identified namely Omar Ahmed, Shah Alam, Mohammed Amjan, Sajid Hussain, Mohammed Javed and Naseem Khan;

- in February 2015 there was published *Report of Inspection of Rotherham Metropolitan Borough Council* by Louise Casey: this was at the instigation of the government pursuant to the findings of the Jay Report

- in March 2015, ten men of Blackley, Burnley, Ilkeston, Prestwich, Rochdale and various prisons were charged with one or more of rape, conspiracy to rape, sexual activity with a child, aiding and abetting rape, assault occasioning actual bodily harm, between 2005 and 2013, at a time when the eight victims were aged between thirteen and twenty-three. Assistant Chief Constable Ian Wiggett said,

This investigation is one of a number of cases which comes under the umbrella of Operation Doublet, which is the continued investigation into Child Sexual Exploitation that arose following the 2011 investigation into CSE in Rochdale … So far 65 people have been arrested as part of Operation Doublet.

- in July 2015, Asif Hussain, Mohammed Imran, Arshad Jani, Akbari Khan, Taimoor Khan and Vikram Singh (four of Aylesbury and one of each of Milton Keynes and Bradford) were convicted of sexual activity with two girls of twelve or thirteen. Between the six of them, they were jailed for a total of eight-two years. The prosecutor told the jury:

The scale of it is, you may agree, horrifying. [One of the girls] estimated that she had sex with about 60 men – six zero – almost all Asian.

(The trial was also of five other men: four were found not guilty and the jury could not decide on the eleventh.)

- in August 2015, Bilal Ahmed, Dilon Rasul (who came here from Iran in 2009) and Hassan Ali were convicted of offences relating to two teenage girls and a teenage boy living in care homes in Rochdale; Jubair Rahman had already pleaded guilty to child abduction;

- in February 2016, Arshid Hussain and his brothers Basharat and Bannaras, all of Rotherham, were convicted (and in the third case at the eleventh hour admitted) between them of multiple counts of rape, indecent assault, buggery, child abduction and false imprisonment against eleven children, and their uncle Qurban Ali of conspiracy to rape. The evidence of one girl, thirteen at the time, included:

> There was a graveyard. When it was dark I'd be taken there by Pakistani men. They were all a lot older than me. It got to the point where it was a different man nearly every day. A Pakistani man would go with you a couple of times and then pass you on to his friends. It was as though once they'd used you and had sex with you they didn't want to know.

Moving from criminals from Asia to those from Africa, in November 2014, there could be reported the trial in Bristol that ended in June with the conviction of Liban Abdi, Abdulahi Aden, Mustafa Deria, Mustafa Farah, Arafar Osman, Idleh Osman and Said Zakaria (aged between twenty and twenty-two). That publication was on the conviction of Zakaria on further charges plus Jusuf Abdizirak, Abdirashid Abdulahi, Mohamed Dahir, Mohamed Jumale, Omar Jumale and Sakariah Sheik (aged between twenty and twenty-four). (Apart from drug dealing) the thirteen men abused, raped and trafficked teenage girls. Apparently seven of the thirteen are British citizens but all are of Somali ethnicity: Muna Abdi of the Bristol Somali Forum said, 'I am hoping people will look at this as a crime and not just a crime for the Somali community. The community is deeply shocked and shaken.'

Notes: *D is for Derby*

1. Ziafat Yasin was cleared of sex charges but pleaded guilty to being concerned with the supply of cocaine, and Graham Blackman was convicted of breaching a sexual offences prevention order.

2. (The website) *for our daughters Charlene Downes and Paige Rivers* has

> Charlene Downes (14) disappeared in 2003 and is presumed dead. Paige Rivers (15) went missing in 2007 and is also presumed dead.
>
> The two girls were linked to alleged sexual grooming and exploitation focussed upon fast food outlets in Blackpool. Following Charlene Downes' disappearance in 2003, police found more than 60 girls were being groomed for sex around 11 Blackpool takeaways. They were mainly aged between 13 and 15, but some were as young as 11. It is alleged the children involved were offered food, alcohol and cigarettes in return for sexual activity.
>
> Two restaurant owners were acquitted of Charlene Downes' murder in 2007 and the crime remains unsolved. A jury failed to reach a verdict on charges that Iyad Albattikhi, a Jordanian, had murdered Charlene Downes while his landlord Mohammed Reveshi, an Iranian, had disposed of her body. A retrial collapsed in 2008 amid failings in the police investigation and the men were paid almost £250,000 each in

compensation. The defence had successfully questioned the integrity of the recorded evidence and the accuracy of the transcription.

Claims were made in court that takeaway staff had joked that Charlene's remains had 'gone into the kebabs'. Recordings, later discredited, were alleged to reveal the accused talking about the disposal of the body. In 2012, the kebab shop, now renamed, was refused a hot food licence amid reports of continued 'sexual activity' linked to the premises, but the applicants reportedly blamed a police vendetta and appealed. FOD could find no reports as to whether that appeal was successful.

There have been allegations that a police report produced after Charlene Downes vanished in 2003 was suppressed, because of the racial mix of alleged abusers, most of whom were Asian or middle eastern in origin, and victims, most of whom were white. Lancashire Police denied a cover-up, sayng the report had been available online since 2007 but had never been intended for publication. Assistant Chief Constable Andy Rhodes said his officers were making significant progress in tackling child sex exploitation across Lancashire, regardless of the background of the culprits. However, former Detective Superintendent Mick Gradwell warned that research into the problem was being hampered by 'concerns about upsetting community cohesion'.

Paragraphs 21 and 22 of Appendix 4 to the Jay Report are:

In November 2003, a Blackpool teenager, Charlene Downes, disappeared. She was believed to have been the subject to sexual exploitation. Charlene has never been seen since this time and is believed to have been killed by her abuser/s. A subsequent investigation revealed 'endemic' sexual abuse in the town and the 'Project Awaken' Team was set up as a response. The team brought together professionals from licensing, social services, education and police. It aimed to root out and arrest the abusers before they did serious harm, and to protect children from exploiters. Officers targeted what they called 'honey pots', likely to attract both children and offenders, such as takeaways, amusement arcades and the pier, which Charlene visited the night she vanished. The *Guardian* journalist Julie Bindel wrote in May 2008, 'Early on in the investigation, police became aware that Charlene and a number of other girls had been swapping sex for food, cigarettes and affection. Police are certain that Charlene was sexually abused by one or more men, over a period of time before she went missing, and that her death was linked to the abuse.'

In 2012, the trial of two men accused over Charlene's murder was halted when the jury failed to reach a verdict. The subsequent retrial collapsed owing to concerns over a key prosecution witness. Both men were cleared of the charges. The case is still open.

3. Girl A's father appeared on *File on 4*'s 'Rochdale: Failed Victims' on 26
March 2013. A relevant part of the programme was:

Father:

> At first, the evidence really was gathered around two men and basically
> it was treated as a one-off rape. I know evidence was gathered from one
> of the takeaways, mattresses and things like that, from my daughter's
> knickers. You know, if you've got DNA evidence, how can this not
> proceed?

Interviewer:

> The police passed a file to the Crown Prosecution Service, where it was
> looked at by two lawyers.

Father:

> Six months later I think it was, five or six months later, I received just a
> letter from the Crown Prosecution Service informing us there wasn't a
> reliable prospect of prosecution or conviction and therefore the case was
> dropped. My overall impression was the police were trying their best, but
> it seemed like their hands were tied. As soon as I read the letter I screwed
> it up in a ball and threw it is the dustbin. So much anger, and I just
> thought, well, fantastic, justice – Rochdale. Fantastic. And it's transpired
> the CPS made the decision that my daughter wouldn't have been a
> credible witness.

Interviewer:

> Within a week his daughter was back in the grip of her abusers, being
> raped by up to five men a night. She only escaped when she got pregnant
> and stopped being of use. She would eventually become Girl A – the
> main witness at the trial. Tessa was also arrested. At fifteen, she was put
> in a police cell and questioned, along the lines of being some sort of pimp
> – recruiting her friends to be raped. She denies that and the police didn't
> charge her. But Tessa's mother says nor did they investigate the men.

Tessa's mother:

> Tessa gave them a list of names, phone numbers, taxis they drove.
> There must have been about two pages of it; is it A4 and nothing was
> done with none of it. I used to go to case conferences and I'd ask why
> these people were still riding round in Rotherham taxis, taking young girls
> to school when you know that they had been doing things to my daughter.
> I can't tell you how bad the feelings are. It's horrendous.

4. This posting, *The Rotherham grooming case shows the dangers of
confusing criminality with culture* (*Labour Uncut*, labour-uncut.co.uk,

September 2012) was by Peter Watt, one-time general secretary of the Labour Party.

Although the posting does not state the author of the article in *The Times*, it was probably Andrew Norfolk. He pointed out Rotherham Council's apparent failure to understand that someone who is under the age of sixteen cannot, in law, consent to sexual activity (and so intercourse with such is necessarily rape). He provided evidence both to the House of Commons' Home Affairs Committee for its report *Child Sexual Exploitation and the Response to Localised Grooming* and to the *Independent Inquiry into Child Sexual Exploitation in Rotherham 1997–2013* by Alexis Jay.

The posting continued:

So scores of girls aged 12–16 from a small geographical area are groomed, gang raped and then intimidated into silence by a small group of men of Pakistani origin and:

"It is imperative that suggestions of a wider cultural phenomenon are avoided."

What bloody planet are these people on? No one is suggesting that all Pakistani men are rapists for god's sake. There is nothing genetic or cultural about criminality.

But a sick and distorted sense of political sensitivity allowed criminals to go unprosecuted and worse the horror to continue for years for young girls in Rotherham.

The irony is that this "culturally sensitive" approach will be seen as manna from heaven to the racists who will surely exploit this to the max.

Sadly the voices of most local families of Pakistani origin won't be heard. Their horror, their sense of shame about an incredibly small and nasty group of misogynist men from their community, will be missed by many.

And in reality they were let down by the decisions taken by the local police and local authorities. Local MP Dennis McShane has been a refreshingly strong voice this week saying:

"There's a culture here of denial and cover-up and a refusal to accept the reality that we have men living in the Rotherham community who treat young girls as objects for their sexual pleasure. It's time to tell the truth. We must root out this evil."

He is right. Andrew Mitchell may well be a pompous prat who is rude to [a] policeman. Nick Clegg may have been making another 'make or break speech'. But please can we get a sense of priority! The really big story this week has been the uncovering of what surely must be one of the most shocking and largest scale child abuse scandals ever. And quite frankly it is that we should be getting hot under the collar about and demanding a full public enquiry into.

Or is industrial scale rape not newsworthy enough?

Originally I did not include that (latter) part of the posting: it seemed to be just politically correct comment and a reflection of the hegemony of 'immigration is good' rather than unbiased reporting.

But the final part of the posting is here in the notes and so readers can, hopefully after reading at least the rest of this chapter (D is for Derby) make up their own minds – whether there is anything 'cultural' (in the behaviour of Pakistani men) that produces CSE. A local MP suggested there was; *see* M is for Mirpur.

As to (Mr Watts') 'as if there is any culture where rape is acceptable' *see* 20 and 21 of Q is for questions.

5. Presumably this was the immediately preceding case of 'Five Rotherham men jailed for child sex offences'. It was also reported that 'The men, all British-born Pakistanis … were found guilty of a string of sexually related offences against the girls, one aged twelve, two aged thirteen and one aged sixteen.'

6. Andrew Norfolk in *The Times*, had this last paragraph as follows:

Although the alleged perpetrators are of Asian origin and the victims are white, this is the factuality of these cases alone; nothing more can be drawn from that. It is imperative that suggestions/allusions of a wider cultural phenomenon are avoided. These assertions are without foundation.

4-6. *See Broken and Betrayed* by Jayne Senior, published by Pan Books, 2016.

7. But *see* note 3 as to what was said by Girl A's father. (That was Rochdale: in Rotherham, two fathers who tracked down their daughters and tried to remove them from where they were being abused were arrested – para 5.9 of the Jay Report.)

8. Sources include *Daily Mail, Evening Standard, Manchester Evening News, The Times* – Andrew Norfolk, *The Daily Telegraph* – Allison Pearson. The respective ages of the nine, in 2012, were reported as being between fifty-nine and twenty-five.

8.1 Shabir Ahmed is probably Defendant X of August 2008 and probably, anyway, initially the ringleader of the other eight.

Ahmed could not, initially, be named as he was facing trial on another matter – repeated rape of a young Asian girl over more than ten years, for which he was sentenced to twenty-two years.

Ahmed was sentenced to nineteen years for conspiracy, rape, aiding and abetting a rape, sexual assault and trafficking for sexual exploitation. Ahmed called the judge a 'racist bastard'. His defending counsel told the court he did not wish to attend the sentencing because

- [Ahmed] has objected from the start for being tried by an all white jury.
- He believes his convictions have nothing to do with justice but result from his faith and the race of the defendants.
- He further believes that society failed the girls in this case before the girls even met them and now that failure is being blamed on a weak minority group.

In 2016 there was heard the first stage of the Home Office's wish to strip Ahmed of British citizenship – he was born in Pakistan and came here in 1967 when he was fourteen – and thereby to be able to deport him; likewise, three others of the nine.

8.2. Mohammed Amin, known as 'Car Zero', worked as a driver for Eagle Taxis with Abdul Aziz. Jailed for five years for conspiracy and one year for sexual assault.

8.3. Abdul Aziz, came here in 2000; known as either 'The Master' or 'Car 40'. Jailed for nine years for conspiracy and nine years for trafficking for sexual exploitation.

8.4. Adil Khan, known as 'Billy', denied making one of the girls pregnant until presented with DNA evidence that he was the father. Jailed for eight years for conspiracy and eight years for trafficking for sexual exploitation.

8.5. Kabeer Hassan (*see* August 2008) jailed for nine years for rape and three years for conspiracy.

8.6. Abdul Qayyum, a driver for Streamline Taxis in Middleton, Manchester, and known as 'Tiger'. Jailed for five years for conspiracy.

8.7. Abdul Rauf came here in 1993 and worked as a teacher in a mosque. Jailed for six years for conspiracy and six years for trafficking for sexual exploitation.

8.8. Mohammed Sajid, known as 'Saj', came here in 2003 knowing Aziz (note 8.3) because they both came from the same village in Pakistan. Jailed for twelve years for rape, six years for conspiracy, one year for trafficking and six years for sexual activity with a child.

8.9. Hamid Safi – the only one of the nine who is not from Pakistan, but from Afghanistan. Apparently he got here in 2008, having stowed away in a lorry: he applied for but was refused asylum. Jailed for four years for conspiracy and one year for trafficking.

9. 'Asian' is the common term but the perpetrators are most likely to be Pakistani. Others – *fahrenheit 211, Vanguard News Network Forum, kafircrusaders* (tags Media Blackout and Grooming Gang), *Brenner Brief* and especially *'Easy Meat': Multiculturalism, Islam and Child Sex Slavery* by Peter McLoughlin published in 2014 by the Law and Freedom Foundation – are more specific and refer to verse 49 (and on) of chapter 33 of the Koran and to *malak ul-yameen*.

The Serious Case Review, following the conviction in May 2013 of the CSE ring in Oxford, lists ten examples of 'building relationships' with 'communities' of which five are in respect of Muslims.

10. Paragraph 3.8 of the Oxford SCR records girls saying:

- It was exciting – Asian boys with flash cars.

- They left you in a house with Asian men and didn't even ask my age. Asian men felt they ran Oxford. That was exciting. People were afraid of them. I felt protected. People respected them.

- It was always Asian men.

11.1. The first paragraph of the Jay Report's Executive Summary.

11.2. The full paragraph is in the part of H is for hegemony to which note 7 applies.

1-11. The list from Derby via Rochdale and Rotherham to Bristol is not (and is not intended to be) a complete list of immigrant led CSE. For that go to *Easy Meat Multiculturalism, Islam and Child Sex Slavery* aka *Easy Meat – Inside Britain's Grooming Gang Scandal* by Peter McLoughlin published by the Law and Freedom Foundation and/or the video *https://www.youtube.com/watch?v=Y9e3LXzyBo8*.

And **D** is for disease

Disease in this country following immigration includes increase in Aids/HIV, HBV[1] multiple myeloma, scabies, sickle cell disease, tuberculosis, rickets[2] and birth defects due to consanguinity.

3.4% of the babies born in Britain are of Pakistani origin but they account for 30% of children born with genetic illnesses. Nearly one third of children whose parents are of Pakistani origin suffer from either mild or severe genetic disability.

Bradford Royal Infirmary estimates that nearly half of the children born of parents of Pakistani origin have special needs at school.[3]

Pakistani men have the highest rate of heart disease in the UK and the risk of dying early from heart disease is twice as high among South Asian groups compared with the general population.

People from South Asian communities are five times more likely to have type 2 diabetes than the general population.

Tower Hamlets and Newham have the lowest life expectancy of all London boroughs.[4]

Men of Afro-Caribbean heritage have a one in four chance of getting prostate cancer – we're not sure why yet. And black men have been shown to be diagnosed five years earlier than white men on average ...[5]

- Jaymin Abdulrahman 'put' her newborn baby down a rubbish chute of a block of flats thereby causing the girl a skull fracture and brain injuries: she was eventually committed to be detained in a mental hospital.

- Polly Chowdhury, at the instigation of Kiki Muddar, tortured her eight-year-old daughter Ayesha to death upon the basis that the girl needed to be punished to 'stop the gates of hell from opening'.

- Deyan Deyanov, from Bulgaria, stabbed Jennifer Mills-Westley repeatedly in the neck and cut off her head.

- Phillip Simelane, from Swaziland, randomly stabbed to death a schoolgirl on a bus to school.

*Notes: **D** is for disease*

1. In 2002 the Chief Medical Officer estimated hepatitis B cases in the UK to be 180,000. In 2007 the Hepatitis B Foundation, estimated such cases to

be 326,000: (*see* its report *Rising Curve: Chronic Hepatitis B Infection in the UK*).

I have not been able to see such report but it looks as if its cover included *UK: Majority of chronic HBV infection results from the migration of HBV carriers*.

David Mutimer, Professor of Clinical Hepatology at Birmingham University commented:

> It's pretty obvious that the number of patients is increasing exponentially year on year and it is quite clear the effect that migration is having on the numbers.

And according to *Nursing in practice* Eddie Chan, director of the Chinese National Living Centre, commented:

> With a surge in migration from countries with a high HBV prevalence rate we are not surprised by these figures. Britain needs migrant workers and in return Britain must set in place the infrastructure to deal with the changing health demographics. Today we are joining with the Hepatitis B Foundation to call for the government to develop a strategy and set in place an action plan to halt the rapid increase in the numbers of people infected with chronic HBV.

2. *From Out of Africa's Eden: The Peopling of the World* by Stephen Oppenheimer:

> In North Asia ... and Europe there is less sun and a lower risk of skin cancer, but there is the ever present risk of rickets, a bone disease caused by lack of sunlight that was still killing London children even at the beginning of the twentieth century ... Rickets, or osteomalacia, came back in a small way in the second half of the twentieth century, but affected the families of children from the Indian subcontinent. Part of the reason for this was their darker skin colour, which filtered out some of the already meagre sunlight.

And from an obituary of Dr Malcom Arthurton 1918–2016, a consultant paediatrician in Yorkshire, first in 1953 at Dewsbury, and then from 1957 at the Bradford Group Hospitals:

> ... and drew attention to paediatric issues facing Asian populations. He found the combination of lack of sunlight (causing vitamin D deficiency) and the high phytate content of chapatti flour (reducing calcium absorption) resulted in severe rickets in some children.

3. *Born in Bradford* by Bradford Royal Infirmary.

The rate of infant abnormality in Bradford is 300 per 100,000 births, which is about twice that of the whole of the UK: 37% of parents who live in Bradford of Pakistani origin are married to their first cousin.

4. *World's largest community genetics study launches in East London*, March 2015. The study was to be conducted by Queen Mary University of London – of Mile End Road, London E1.

5. *Should you take the prostate test?* by Victoria Lambert, *Spectator Health*, February 2015.

And **D** is for disingenuous

In January 2010, when leader of the opposition, David Cameron said:

In the last decade, net immigration in some years has been sort of 200,000, so implying a 2 million increase over a decade, which I think is too much. We would like to see net immigration in the tens of thousands, rather than the hundreds of thousands. I don't think that's unrealistic.[1]

In April 2011, after he had become prime minister, Mr Cameron said:

Between 1997 and 2009, 2.2 million more people came to live in this country than left to live abroad ...

Yes, Britain will always be open to the best and brightest from around the world and those fleeing persecution. But with us, our borders will be under our control and immigration will be at levels our country can manage. No ifs. No buts. That's a promise we made to the British people. And it's a promise we are keeping.[2]

In March 2013, Mr Cameron said:

But while I've always believed in the benefits of migration and immigration, I've also believed that immigration has to be properly controlled. Without proper controls, community confidence is sapped, resources are stretched and the benefits that immigration can bring are lost or forgotten. As I've long argued, under the previous government immigration was far too high and the system was badly out of control. Net migration needs to come down radically from hundreds of thousands a year, to just tens of thousands, and as we bring net migration down we must also make sure that Britain continues to benefit from it.[3]

I am told by senior officials in Border Force that there is an explanation for the pattern of failure on the e-borders scheme. It isn't that the computer systems don't work. It is that ministers do not actually want to have the information that e-borders, if successfully implemented, would provide – because if they had it, they would have to reveal it, and that would almost certainly show that there were at least 200,000 additional illegal immigrants coming into Britain every year.

A successful passenger information programme would not merely demonstrate that the Government was miles away from its goal of reducing immigration into Britain to 'tens of thousands' a year. It would also expose the fact that the real figure for net migration into this country is running at more than double the officially recognised rate.[4]

In September 2014, Mr Cameron's 'immigration minister' wrote:

Our reforms mean that people with no legal right to benefits are refused them: that illegal immigrants will be unable to rent homes, open bank accounts or obtain driving licences. We have also cut the number of appeal routes through which too many people tried to abuse the British legal system. The Immigration Act which became law earlier this year is already delivering important results: for example, we have revoked more than 3,500 driving licences in little over a month.

By reforming family and work visa routes, cracking down on abuse in the student sector and cutting access to benefits, we have cut net migration by a quarter since its peak under Labour. But we will do more. We are stopping immigrants using public services to which they are not entitled: taking driving licences from illegal immigrants; fining landlords who rent homes to people who have no right to be here; and reducing the legal routes for migrants to abuse the system.[5]

But,

... with the barriers to victory getting higher, Mr Cameron promised to limit net migration to 'tens of thousands' by 2015. The PM might as well have pledged to a ceiling on the ladybird population. For as long as Britain remains in the EU[6] and retains an open border policy, the tally of those entering and leaving is beyond his control.[7]

And,

By declaring that they would bring the figure for net migration ('no ifs, no buts'), Mr Cameron and Theresa May, the Home Secretary, set themselves up for a battle they could not win. Very few of the elements are in their control. They cannot alter the departing side of the net calculation – emigrants. They cannot, by treaty,[6] affect the largest element of the arrivals – EU citizens. And they dare not do much about the human-rights obligations which guarantee others – family members, for example – the right of entry.

So net migration stands at 300,000, nearly 0.5 per cent of our total population added in one year, and even higher than the Blair/Brown era average of 277,000. The population of England alone has reportedly risen by 565,000 since 2011, two thirds attributable to EU migrants. All the Government can do (and is doing) is throw up bureaucratic barriers against the sort of above-board immigrants whom most of us would probably welcome – skilled professionals from friendly countries such as Australia or the United States.[8]

The Office for National Statistics[9] has it as follows:

24 November 2011 – Final figures for 2010 show that annual net migration to the UK was 252,000, the highest calendar year figure on record.

24 May 2012 – Estimated total long-term immigration to the UK in the year to September 2011 was 589,000. This compares to 600,000 in the year to September 2010 and has remained at a similar level since 2004.

29 November 2012 – Latest provisional data show that there was a net flow of 183,000 migrants in the year ending March 2012, which is significantly lower than the net flow of 242,000 in the year ending March 2011.

23 May 2013 – 500,000 people immigrated to the UK in the year ending September 2012, which is significantly lower than the 581,000 who migrated the previous year.

28 November 2013 – 503,000 people immigrated to the UK in the year ending June 2013, compared to the 517,000 people who immigrated during the previous year.

27 February 2014 – There was an estimated net flow of 212,000 long-term migrants to the UK in the year ending September 2013, a statistically significant increase from 154,000 in the previous year.

22 May 2014 – Net long-term migration to the UK was estimated to be 212,000 in the year ending December 2013, not a statistically significant ... increase from 177,000 the previous year and unchanged from the net migration figure previously reported for the year ending September 2013.

28 August 2014 – Net long-term migration to the UK was estimated to be 243,000 in the year ending March 2014, a statistically significant increase from 175,000 in the previous 12 months.
560,000 people immigrated to the UK in the year ending March 2014, a statistically significant increase from 492,000 in the previous 12 months. Two thirds of the increase is accounted for by immigration of

EU citizens (up 44,000 to 214,000).
28,000 EU2 (Romanian and Bulgarian) citizens immigrated to the UK in the year ending March 2014, a statistically significant increase from 12,000 in the previous 12 months.
265,000 non-EU citizens immigrated to the UK in the year ending March 2014. This ends a steady decline since the recent peak of 334,000 in 2011.

27 November 2014 – Net long-term migration to the UK was estimated to be 260,000 in the year ending June 2014, a statistically significant increase from 182,000 in the previous 12 months.
583,000 people immigrated to the UK in the year ending June 2014, a statistically significant increase from 502,000 in the previous 12 months. There were significant increases in immigration of EU (up 45,000) and non-EU (up 30,000) citizens.
National Insurance Number registrations to adult overseas nationals increased by 12% to 668,000 in the year ending September 2014 from the previous year. Romanian citizens had the highest number of registrations (104,000), followed by Polish citizens (98,000).

26 February 2015 – Net long-term migration to the UK was estimated to be 298,000 in the year ending September 2014, a statistically significant increase from 210,000 in the previous 12 months, but below the peak of 320,000 in the year ending June 2005.
624,000 people immigrated to the UK in the year ending September 2014, a statistically significant increase from 530,000 in the previous 12 months. There were statistically significant increases for immigration of non-EU citizens (up 49,000 to 292,000) and EU (non-British) citizens (up 43,000 to 251,000).
37,000 Romanian and Bulgarian (EU2) citizens immigrated to the UK in the year ending September 2014, a statistically significant increase from 24,000 in the previous 12 months. Of these, 27,000 were coming for work, a rise of 10,000 on year ending September 2013, but this change was not statistically significant.

21 May 2015 – Net long-term migration to the UK (immigration less emigration) was estimated to be 318,000 in the calendar year 2014. This was just below the previous peak (320,000 in the year ending (YE) June 2005) and a statistically significant increase from 209,000 in 2013.
641,000 people immigrated to the UK in 2014, a statistically significant increase from 526,000 in 2013. There were statistically significant increases for immigration of EU (non-British) citizens (up 67,000 to 268,000) and non-EU citizens (up 42,000 to 290,000). Immigration of British citizens increased by 7,000 to 83,000, but this was not statistically significant.

27 August 2015 – Net long-term international migration = +330,000 (up 94,000 from YE March 2014), in the s March 2015.
Immigration = 636,000 (up 84,000), in the year ending (YE) March 2015.
Emigration = 307,000 (down 9,000), in the year ending (YE) March 2015.
The net migration figure was a statistically significant increase from 236,000 in YE March 2014 and is the highest net migration on record.
Net migration of EU citizens showed a statistically significant increase to 183,000 (up 53,000 from YE March 2014). The increase in non-EU net migration to 196,000 (up 39,000) was also statistically significant and is a result of an increase in immigration (not statistically significant) and a decrease in emigration (statistically significant).
The increase in long-term international immigration included a statistically significant increase for EU citizens to 269,000 (up 56,000), the highest recorded level for this group; and an increase for non-EU nationals to 284,000 (up 23,000) (not statistically significant).
53,000 Romanian and Bulgarian (EU2) citizens immigrated to the UK in YE March 2015, a statistically significant increase and almost double the 28,000 in the previous 12 months.
290,000 people immigrated for work in YE March 2015, a statistically significant increase of 65,000 from 225,000 in YE March 2014 continuing the upward trend.

26 November 2015 – Net long-term international migration = + 336,000 (up 82,000 from YE June 2014) in the year ending (YE) June 2015.
Immigration = 636,000 (up 62,000 from YE June 2014).
Emigration = 300,000 (down 20,000 from YE June 2014).
The net migration figure was a statistically significant increase from 254,000 in YE June 2014 and remains the highest net migration on record. This is a result of a statistically significant increase in immigration (from 574,000 in YE June 2014) and a decrease in emigration (from 320,000 in YE June 2014 (not statistically significant)).
Net migration of EU citizens showed a statistically significant increase to 180,000 (up 42,000 from YE June 2014). Non-EU net migration also had a statistically significant increase, to 201,000 (up 36,000).
The increase in long-term international immigration included a statistically significant increase for EU citizens to 265,000 (up 42,000) and an increase for non-EU citizens to 286,000 (up 17,000) (not statistically significant).

25 February 2016 – Net Long-term international migration = + 323,000 (up 31,000 from YE September 2014).
Immigration = 617,000 (up 2,000 from YE September 2014).

Emigration = 294,000 (down 29,000 from YE September 2014).
Net migration in YE September 2015 was 13,000 lower (not statistically significant) then the peak level of 336,000 published for YE June 2015. Net migration of EU citizens was estimated to be 172,000 (compared with 158,000 in YE September 2014; change not statistically significant). Non-EU net migration (191,000) was similar to the previous year (188,000).

26 May 2016 – In the year ending December 2015
Net Long-Term International Migration =+ 330,000 (up 20,000 from YE 2014)
Immigration = 630,000
Emigration = 297,000
There were 630,000 National Insurance Number registrations by EU nationals in YE March 2016, an increase of 1,000 on the previous year. For non –EU nationals, there were 195,00 NNo registrations in YE March 2016, an increase of 2,000 on the previous year.

Notes: *D is for disingenuous*

1. This was while being interviewed by Andrew Marr. Mr Cameron also said, 'I'm in favour of immigration, we've benefited from immigration but I think the pressures – particularly on our public services – have been very great.'

2. Mr Cameron to Conservative Party members, April 2011.

3. Mr Cameron to Ipswich University, March 2013.

4. *This border control fiasco could be hiding a more sinister truth* by Alasdair Palmer, *The Daily Telegraph*, August 2014, just after an arbitral tribunal awarded Raytheon £220 million because the Home Office cancelled a contract. (Shortly afterwards, a letter to a newspaper pointed out that there would be no confusion as to a passenger's identity because of misspelling (especially Mohammed) as the e-reader was otherwise configured.)

5. *New border laws are both fair and tough* September 2014, *The Daily Telegraph* by James Brokenshire, MP since 2005 for Old Bexley, and Sidcup since 2010, Minister for Security and Immigration (in succession to Mark Harper, who resigned following the disclosure that his cleaner was an illegal immigrant).

6. Article 48 of the Treaty of Rome and 45 of the Treaty of Maastricht (*see* note 1 to E is for European Union) provides for the free movement of workers throughout the European Union.

A Conservative Party election communication for the EU elections in May 2014 (which sought to show that which had been promised and that which had been achieved) had against 'controlling immigration' what the government had done, namely 'So we've taken all the action we can under the current EU agreements to fix our immigration system and limited migrants' access to benefits'.

7. *David Cameron will pay a heavy price in 2015 for alienating immigrant voters* by Mary Riddell, *The Daily Telegraph*, April 2014. She continued:

> But while Miliband can rely on the support of ethnic minority citizens, regardless of their class his natural blue-collar voters are less accommodating. With immigration in voters' top three issues, Labour MPs are assailed by lifelong supporters complaining that immigrants are filching the houses, jobs and benefits that should rightfully be theirs.

Her reference to Miliband relying on the support of ethnic-minority citizens is ambiguous because many immigrants who are not citizens can vote – citizens of a Commonwealth country, albeit not a citizen of this country, can vote here, as soon as they have an address here *see* V is for voting and V is for vote rigging.

8. *Don't take the voters for granted on immigration and defence* by Charles Moore, *The Daily Telegraph*, March 2015.

9. The following paragraphs are extracts from ONS' *Migration Statistics Quarterly Reports*. With the release of that for February 2016, *The Sun* (26 February 2016) under the front page headline: *The Great Migrant CON: MPs accused of a "cover-up" as we reveal that 630,000 registered to work here in 2015. Official stats say just 257,000 came from the EU sparking controversy among MPs*, reported:

> Total immigration into Britain, not taking into account people who left was 617,000.
>
> Romanians and Bulgarians now make up a fifth of the Europeans pouring into Britain …

And *The Sun*'s leader included:

> The greatest trick the Government ever pulled was convincing the world it cared about immigration.
>
> Bear that in mind and you'll understand both why our population continues to soar – and the extraordinary cynicism behind the minuscule tweaks David Cameron 'won' from Brussels.

The total number of immigrants from the EU is 257,000. Some 55,000 are Romanians and Bulgarians.

The true number may be far more, since 630,000 Europeans registered to work in 2015 ...

And **D** is for diversity

The word is either a statement of the subject being non-indigenous or the encouragement of immigrants to continue to be forcign(ers) despite their seeking to live here permanently and become British citizens.

The creed of multiculturalism and endeavour for equality requires identifying and labelling, and so

- a housing association (serving a non-metropolitan area) in a survey of its tenants, asks:

    Please tell us about your ethnicity and that of other members of your household [offering the following eighteen alternatives]:
    White British; White Irish; White Other; Gypsy/Romany; Traveller of Irish Heritage; Mixed: White & Black Caribbean; Mixed: White & Black African;

    Mixed: White & Asian; Mixed Other; Asian or Asian British: Indian;

    Asian or Asian British: Pakistani; Asian or Asian British: Bangladeshi;

    Asian or Asian British: Other; Black or Black British: Caribbean; Black or Black British: African; Black or Black British: Other; Chinese; Other.[1]

- Manchester University's *Dynamics of Diversity Evidence from the 2011 Census* lists the ethnic-minority groups as:

    Indian, Pakistani, African, Caribbean, Bangladeshi, Chinese

    Mixed: White-Caribbean, White-African, White-Asian, Mixed Other

    Other Asian, Other Black, Arab, Other

- Wiltshire Council's *Wiltshire's Diverse Communities Results* from the Census 2011 Profile of Ethnicity in Wiltshire and lists the following ethnic groups:

    English/Welsh/Scottish/Northern Irish/British; Irish; Gypsy or Irish Traveller; Other white; White and Black Caribbean; White and Black Caribbean; White and Black African; White and Asian; Other Mixed;

96

Indian; Pakistani; Bangladeshi; Chinese; Other Asian; African; Caribbean; Other Black; Arab; Any other Ethnic Group.

Do any of you still like the dread word diversity, one that's proudly flung around by those who squirm when the name of the great Enoch Powell comes up? If anything, Powell was a prophet, and after the latest London outrage, his so-called Rivers of Blood speech sure comes to mind. He got it right while midgets such as Heath and Howe sold and keep on selling the country out to diversity. Can you imagine a time when a British soldier was unsafe wearing a military uniform in his own country? Well, yes, when the IRA was blowing up horses and soldiers near the Hyde Park barracks, but Tony Blair made nice with them and those same nice guys collect English pounds and don't even bother to attend Parliament.[2]

Notes: *D is for diversity*

1. Synergy Housing (now part of Aster).

2. Taki Theodoracopulos, *The Spectator,* 1 June 2013, namely just after Fusilier Lee Rigby was run down and then hacked to death in the street outside his barracks in Woolwich.

E is for the economics of immigration

If when the population was 55 million, the country's economic output was 55x and a decade later the population had increased to 60 million and economic output to 60x, we would have been no richer: while the country's GDP had increased, output per head was the same.

The reality was and is worse. In October 2006, the National Institute of Economic and Social Research's Economic Review showed that in the period 1998/2005 immigration boosted economic growth by 3% but the population had increased by 3.8%, so, over that period, GDP per head reduced. Similarly, an April 2011 paper of the National Institute found that since the arrival of 700,000 people from Eastern Europe since 2004, output had increased by 0.4% (but that with the population increase being more) there had been a fall in GDP per head for the resident population.

> I have deliberately focused on per-capita gains: overall increases in GDP can be distorted through demographic change, in the short term and obviously through waves of emigration and immigration. Too often, people fail to make the distinction between per-capita and total gains.[1]

But that axiom appears to have been unknown to or ignored by

- the prime minister,[2] who in 2004 'is determined not to allow abuses of the system to poison the whole idea of managed migration which brings enormous benefits to the whole country'.

- Liam Byrne,[3] who in November 2007 said, '… there are obviously enormous economic benefits of immigration … There is a big positive impact on the economy which is worth about £6 billion.'

- Jacqui Smith,[4] who in December 2007, spoke of the 'purity of the macroeconomic case for migration'.

It would seem this ignorance or avoidance of reality continues – in April 2013, the then prime minister[5] said, 'Uncontrolled immigration was a source of economic growth. But it's not a sustainable way to grow your economy so we need to grow our economy the proper way.'

Even those critical of the 1997/2010 government, and at least sceptical of its successor, appear not to accept the axiom, so we have:

... Yesterday, for example, David Cameron was boasting about record employment figures. But he did not quite get round to admitting that three quarters of the rise has been due to the immigration he claims to be stamping down on.

Over the past 15 years, the number of foreign-born workers here has doubled ... this week there were signs that the Treasury has succumbed to [being addicted to immigration]. Its economic forecasting unit, now called the Office for Budget Responsibility (OBR) is fretting about what the country would look like if [immigration stopped] ... One 'low' forecast envisages 140,000 arrivals annually ... With this inflow, the OBR says, the debt pile will be just about manageable. But without immigrants ... ending up as the new Greece.

This sums up the lazy thinking that has reigned at HM Treasury since the days of Gordon Brown. Immigration is seen as a wonder drug with the bright new workers bringing in far more than they take out. Certainly, under Labour, mass immigration made it possible to enlarge the economy without going through the political pain of sorting out the welfare problem. With newcomers accounting for almost half of all the increase in employment, at least four million people were left on out-of-work benefits. And while David Cameron talks about curbing immigration, the number of EU workers in Britain has risen by a quarter since he has become Prime Minister.[6]

In 2005, *Migration Watch* asserted that the government was exaggerating the benefit of immigration, arguing that the government was 'at best being disingenuous' in claiming immigrants contributed 0.5% of GDP: after costs such as housing, *Migration Watch's* view was that the real figure was 0.1%.

On 1 April 2008, there was published the report by the House of Lords' Select Committee on Economic Affairs entitled *The Economic Impact of Immigration*.[7] One of those who provided evidence to the Committee was Professor Rowthorn of Cambridge University. The abstract of his memorandum to the committee began with:

Since 1997 a new UK immigration policy has displaced previous aims, which were focused on minimizing settlement. Large-scale immigration is now seen as essential for the UK's economic well-being, and measures have been introduced to increase inflows. The benefits claimed include fiscal advantages, increased prosperity, a ready supply of labour and improvements to the age-structure. Fears that large-scale immigration might damage the interests of unskilled workers are discounted.

This submission examines these claims. It concludes that the economic consequences of large-scale immigration are mostly minor, negative or

99

transient; that the interests of the most vulnerable sections of the domestic population may well be damaged and that the economic benefits are unlikely to bear comparison with its substantial impact on population growth. Such findings are in line with those from other developed countries.

Although it does not benefit the UK population as a whole, large-scale immigration does benefit migrants, their families and sometimes their countries of origin. It can be argued that UK migration policy should take the interests of these other parties. This issue is not addressed in the present submission.

Immigration has been increasing for many years, but the pace has accelerated noticeably since Labour came to power in 1997. The net inflow of non-British citizens into the UK trebled in the eight years from 1997 onwards, and there was also an increase in the net outflow of British citizens. In 2005, 474,000 non-British citizens entered the country as long-term immigrants and 181,000 left, making a net gain of 292,000 (after rounding). In the same year, 198,000 British citizens left the country as long-term emigrants and 91,000 returned from long-term emigration making a net loss of 107,000. Many people fear that cumulated over decades, these flows will have a serious impact on the sense of national identity and historical continuity, especially viewed against the background of increasing separatist tendencies in Wales and Scotland. Opinion polls regularly show widespread public concern about these developments. However, in this document I restrict myself to narrower economic issues.

I argue that, taken as a whole, the large-scale immigration is of minor economic benefit to the existing population of the UK, as a whole, although it is certainly of benefit to the immigrants, their families and sometimes their countries of origin. Large-scale immigration will lead to a rapid and sustained growth in population with negative economic and environmental consequences in the form of overcrowding, congestion, pressure on housing and public services, and loss of environmental amenities. It also undermines the labour market position of the most vulnerable and least skilled sections of the local workforce, including many in the ethnic minority population, who must compete against the immigrants. There are, of course, domestic beneficiaries of large-scale migration. These include employers who can obtain good workers at close to the minimum wage, or even less, and the consumers of goods and services that rely heavily on migrant labour.[8]

Another submission of evidence was from the Home Office,[9] part of which was:

4.2 The labour market impact of immigration: theory.

4.2.1 In theory, immigration could have a number of impacts on the labour market and in particular the labour market outcomes of natives. Depending on the characteristics of migrants and the labour market adjustment process, impacts could be seen on both employment and wages.

4.2.2 There is no theoretical reason why immigration need either depress native wages or increase native unemployment. Given that there is a strong long-run correlation between the size of the labour force and employment, there is no 'lump of labour'; it is not true to say that there are only a fixed number of jobs to go round. It is increasingly recognised that, given sound macroeconomic management, unemployment is primarily a structural phenomenon. If that is the case, then migrants will have no effect on the job prospects of natives (in the medium or long term); and the appropriate policies for Government to pursue to address unemployment among natives (and to the extent relevant, among past and present migrants) are active labour market policies designed to connect people with the labour market, including by increasing their skills and employability. This is what the Government is doing with its current programme of welfare reform. A key element of this is a new jobs pledge that aims for major employers to offer a quarter of a million job opportunities to local people at a disadvantage in the labour market. This pledge will be delivered through Local Employment Partnerships.[10]

The committee's conclusion was:

Overall GDP, which the Government has persistently emphasised, is an irrelevant and misleading criterion for assessing the economic impacts of immigration on the UK. The total size of an economy is not an index of prosperity. The focus of analysis should rather be on the effects of immigration on income per head of the resident population. Both theory and the available empirical evidence indicate that these effects are small, especially in the long run when the economy fully adjusts to the increased supply of labour. In the long run, the main economic effect of immigration is to enlarge the economy, with relatively small costs and benefits for the incomes of the resident population. (The second paragraph of the abstract)

GDP – which measures the total output created by immigrants and pre-existing residents in the UK – is an irrelevant and misleading measure for the economic impacts of immigration on the resident population. The total size of an economy is not an indicator of prosperity or of residents' living standards. (Paragraphs 49 and 212)

Rather than referring to total GDP when discussing the economic impacts of immigration, the Government should focus on the per-capita income (as a measure of the standard of living) of the resident population. (Paragraph 51)

In respect of labour shortages, the committee reported:

Although clearly benefiting employers, immigration that is in the best interest of individual employers is not always in the best interest of the economy as a whole. If, as Liam Byrne MP[4] says, the Government is 'not actually running British immigration policy in the exclusive interests of the British business community', it is important to examine the economic basis of the arguments that immigrants are needed to fill and reduce vacancies, and that immigrants have a superior work ethic, and thus are needed to do the jobs that British workers cannot or will not do. (Paragraph 102)

As Prime Minister, Tony Blair argued that immigration was needed to lower the number of vacancies. But as Figure 4 shows, the recent increase in immigration to the UK has not resulted in a decline in the number of overall vacancies in the UK, which has remained around or above 600,000 since 2001. The recent ITEM Club report cites data from a survey carried out by the British Chamber of Commerce, showing that the proportion of firms reporting recruitment problems across all skill levels has not substantially declined since 2000. (Paragraph 103)

Rising immigration has not resulted in a decline in vacancies because the number of jobs in an economy is not fixed. Immigration increases both the supply of labour and, over time, the demand for labour, thus creating new vacancies. As William Simpson of the CBI explained, 'immigrants do not just plug holes in the labour market ... they create new demands for products and services which are already available, but also those that cater to the immigrant population. So this will, in a dynamic economy, lead to creating new vacancies' as companies seek to recruit more employees to increase production to meet the extra demand. In other words, because immigration expands the overall economy, it cannot be expected to be an effective policy tool for significantly reducing vacancies. Vacancies are, to a certain extent, a sign of a healthy labour market and economy. They cannot be a good reason for encouraging large-scale labour immigration. (Paragraph 104)

It is clear that various low-wage sectors of the UK economy (in both private and public sectors) are currently heavily dependent on immigrant labour. Increasing wages to attract more British workers to produce or provide a certain product or service can be expected to lead to an increase in the price and thus affect consumers of that product or service. In the public sector, higher labour costs could result in higher taxes and/or require a restructuring of the way in which some services such as social care are provided. Nevertheless, the fundamental point remains that labour demand, supply and thus the existence and size of labour shortages critically depend on wages – the price of labour. Arguments about the 'need' for migrant labour that ignore price adjustments are meaningless and misleading. (Paragraph 116)

Nevertheless, the argument that sustained net immigration is needed to fill vacancies, and that immigrants do the jobs that locals cannot or will not do, is fundamentally flawed. (Part of paragraph 228)

The overall conclusion from existing evidence is that immigration has very small impacts on GDP per-capita whether these impacts are positive or negative. This conclusion is in line with findings of studies of the economic impacts of immigration in other countries including the US. The Government should initiate research in this area, in view of the paucity of evidence for the UK. (Paragraph 215)

Although possible in theory, we found no systematic empirical evidence to suggest that net immigration creates significant dynamic benefits for the resident population in the UK. This does not necessarily mean that such effects do not exist but that there is currently no systematic evidence for them and it is possible that there are also negative dynamic and wider welfare effects. (Paragraphs 69 and 216)

The committee also refuted another argument for immigration:

Arguments in favour of high immigration to defuse the 'pensions time bomb' do not stand up to scrutiny as they are based on the unreasonable assumption of a static retirement age as people live longer, and ignore the fact that, in time, immigrants too grow old and draw pensions. Increasing the official retirement age will significantly reduce the increase in the dependency ratio and is the only viable way to do so. (Paragraph 234)

It was not just the committee who saw the wood for the trees:

We already know the general tenor of their report, and it would be a surprise, given the evidence, if they conclude anything other than that the economic benefits of immigration to the country as whole have been marginal, even non-existent. This is not to say that nobody benefits. Clearly an immigrant who earns far more than at home gains, and his remittances will help his family and his country's economy.

So, too, do householders who pay a plasterer/nanny/plumber half the amount they would do to a domestic worker. So, also, does the employer by using cheaper labour. I have never understood the enthusiasm of the trade unions for large-scale immigration since it depresses wages, but they may judge that low-paid workers mean more numbers ... Last autumn, in evidence to the committee, a joint study by the Home Office and the Office for National Statistics said immigration boosted GDP by £6 billion in 2006, which sounds impressive but is irrelevant since it also added to the population. On a per-capita basis, the increase in economic output could be measured in pence.[11]

Messrs Blair and Byrne and Ms Smith were apparently also unaware of, or chose to ignore, the law of supply and demand.[12] This is not new.[13]

Ex-convicts and in fact many new free settlers also wanted transportation of ex-convicts from Britain to stop, because it created competition in the labor market and drove down wages. The Squatters liked low wages, but they lost. In 1840 transportation to New South Wales was stopped, and in 1842 a legislative council was created with two-thirds of its members being elected (the rest appointed).[14]

And the law of supply and demand was acknowledged in the Report:

The recent ITEM Club report points to the potential negative impact of immigration on youth unemployment. The report notes that youth unemployment increased by about 100,000 since early 2004 and the participation rate has dropped from 69.4% to 67.4%. Given that age and skill profile of many of the new immigrants, it is possible that 'native youngsters may have been losing out in the battle for entry-level jobs'. The Royal Society of Edinburgh also noted that a high proportion of A8 migrants were under 24 years old and said that further research was needed on the impact on the youth labour market. (Paragraph 84)

The available evidence is insufficient to draw clear conclusions about the impact of immigration on unemployment in the UK. It is possible, although not proven, that immigration adversely affects the employment opportunities of young people who are competing with young immigrants from the A8 countries. More research is needed to examine the impact of recent immigration on unemployment among different groups of resident workers in the UK. (Paragraph 85)

That the law of supply and demand is relevant to immigration is not just the opinion of the House of Lords:

Why might immigration affect natives' wages or employment rates?

Basic laws of supply and demand imply that increasing the supply of labour should reduce wages for native workers in the short run, since more people are willing to supply their labour at a given wage. If wages cannot adjust (for example, because of a minimum wage or union activity) we might see increased unemployment instead of wage reductions.

At the same time, however, businesses are expected to respond to immigration by hiring more people: they increase production of the goods that immigrants produce, raising the demand for labour and pushing up wages again. In a small open economy like the UK, wages are eventually expected to return to the 'pre-immigration' level.

This simplified model treats immigrants and natives as homogeneous 'units of labour'. In practice, of course, the two have different skills and abilities. On the whole, the more different they are, the less 'competition' there will be between them in the labour market. For this and other reasons, immigration is most likely to lead to reductions in wages or employment in the case of low-skilled or low-wages jobs: these jobs, by their nature, require less training or education than more highly paid work, making it more feasible to substitute immigrants for native workers.[15]

A more recent report by the Institute for Public Policy Research largely replicates these results, finding that a one per cent increase in the share of immigrants in the working-age population would reduce wages by about 0.3 per cent.[15.1]

... Using the area comparison methodology usually associated with a low estimated impact of immigration, Christopher Smith finds that a 10 per cent increase in the immigrant share of the labour market (equivalent to slightly more than the average increase experienced in US cities between 1990 and 2000) reduced teenage employment rates by 4.8 percent – over three times the effect found for adults.[15.2]

And there's another factor that creates a labour surplus: immigration. Where once Britain was a net exporter of people we're now net importers. At the end of 2009 there were 3.72 million non-UK-born people in employment in the UK, and that is a trend that has been continuing for years. That is to be expected: in the last decade about a half a million people came to Britain – mostly to work – every year. And from an economic perspective this has an obvious effect: just like unemployment, it adds to the labour surplus and drives down earnings. Young people in Britain bear the brunt of it too – between 2004 and 2006, 82 per cent of the 600,000 new migrants from the EU accession states were aged 18–35 and so are in direct competition with them for millions of jobs.[16]

And the economists who favour large-scale immigration often seem to forget how markets work. If people had not been so easily importable in the past fifteen years, price signals would have changed – in other words the pay for certain jobs would have gone up – and existing citizens would have responded. In a few cases companies would have had to improve their training programmes, instead of just buying already trained foreigners off the shelf.[17]

The only bad numbers obvious at the moment are those on income growth. An example: the starting wage for the average new employee in

2007 was £8.50 an hour. Six years of inflation later it is £8 ... Low paid jobs are clearly better than no jobs and you could argue that the high percentage of low paid jobs in the UK relative to much of Europe merely reflects the fact that we have a relatively young population (and lots of immigration). But you can also argue ...[18]

In the year to the middle of 2014, GDP grew by approaching 3%, the number of registered unemployed fell by 437,000 but base pay by 0.6%, while inflation was between 1.9 or 2.6% (CPI and RPI respectively) so wages fell – 'cheaper workers are boosting demand for labour'.[19]

In May 2015 the Governor of the Bank of England said:

In recent years labour supply has expanded significantly owing to higher participation rates among older workers, a greater willingness to work longer hours and strong population growth partly driven by higher net migration. These positive labour supply shocks have contained wage growth in the face of robust employment growth. Wages have grown by about 2 per cent in the past year – less than half the average rate before the global financial crisis – and a key risk is that these subdued growth rates continue.

Which produced the following:

This should come as no surprise to anyone who has ever thought for more than a couple of minutes about the effect of migration. If you provide more of something, the price tends to go down. Specifically if foreign workers arriving in the UK at a rate of about 250,000 per year (for this is the current rate of increase) employers are less likely to compete for staff by raising wages.

And to be clear, the general point that an influx of workers from abroad represents a weight on the pay of the indigenous population is a statement of the overwhelmingly obvious: it is simply a version of the law of supply and demand that the price of anything falls when supply rises relative to demand.[20]

When people complain about free movement of labour, it's not the big picture economics of migration they tend to focus on; it's about feeling like a foreigner in their own country, pressure on services, and so on. Nor do you need a doctorate in economics to realise that an inexhaustible supply of cheap migrant labour is bound to depress wages and productivity in industries it invades, at least in the short term.[21]

If we had control over our borders, then the jobs issue would be dead in the water.[22]

... Wednesday's numbers are likely to show wage inflation is less than 1 per cent, implying that wages are still falling in real terms. And Friday's GDP data could show that the strong rise in consumer spending in the third quarter was caused by a drop in the savings ratio – something that is not sustainable for long.

However, this slowdown doesn't mean the general economy is doing badly. Monday's CBI survey is likely to show that output growth and orders in manufacturing at close to 18-year highs. And Wednesday's figures could report another drop in the unemployment rate, to 7.5 per cent – although there are almost as many people out of the labour force who would like a job as there are officially unemployed.

So mass unemployment helps to explain why wage inflation is so low.[23]

In December 2015, there was published the Bank of England's Staff Working Paper[24] No. 574 entitled *The Impact of Immigration on Occupational Wages: Evidence from Britain.* It stated:

... a 10 percentage point rise in the proportion of immigrants working in semi/unskilled services ... leads to a 1.88 per cent reduction in pay.

And the Paper's conclusion included:

... the immigrant–native ratio has a significant small impact on the average occupational wage rates ... Closer examination reveals that the biggest effect is in the semi/unskilled services sector, where a 10 percentage point rise[25] in the proportion of immigrants is associated with a 2 per cent reduction in pay.

with the conclusion's final sentence being:

These findings accord well with intuition and anecdotal evidence, but do not seem to have been recorded previously in the empirical evidence.

which would presumably account for the following letter to a newspaper:[26]

At last there is an admission[27] – from Mark Carney, the governor of the Bank of England – that immigration is driving down the wages of our lower paid workers. How is it that it takes our leaders so long to come to a simple conclusion that anyone with common sense realised years ago?

It is obvious that if supply outweighs demand, then prices (wages) are driven down and job vacancies are reduced. It is also obvious that the more people that come into the country and visit the hospitals, the more stretched they become, which creates longer waiting times; and the more children that go to our schools, the bigger the classes will be. It is also obvious that the main cause of all of this is the EU.[28]

Wider afield:

> Apart from foreigners on holiday in Yugoslavia, foreign currency was also brought into the country by Yugoslavs working abroad. Many Yugoslavs went to work in Germany and Austria. Most of them came from Slovenia and Croatia, which were nearer than the other republics to the Austrian border. This emigration helped to ease the unemployment problem ...[29]

> He cites the example of how Park's government engineered a 30 per cent jump in wages through a massive shrinkage of the labour force. It was achieved, he explains, by making education compulsory up to the age of 12, removing at a stroke millions of children from the labour pool.[30]

> [Emigration] has reduced Ireland's unemployment rate and the burden on the state's overstretched finances.[31]

> [At the start of 2014 when Latvia joined the euro], real GDP remains 8pc below its peak even now. The unemployment rate has been flattered by emigration.[32]

In the not so longer term, immigration limits economic progress. In no particular order, first migrants migrate, at least in part for economic reasons, moving from societies that are unsuccessful, but, following arrival, (naturally) join their fellow countrymen and in so doing are likely to perpetuate the deficiencies of the society from where they came, to continue with the same habits, to continue with the same social structures of that unsuccessful society. For instance, Somalis continue their tribalism; Yeminis so cover their females that (anyway), at this latitude, girls are liable to rickets; Jamaican criminals carry guns; Pakistanis marry their cousins and bear the consequences of consanguinity and continue their 'favour culture'.[33] And so the economic performance of this country is undermined by the deficiencies of the unsuccessful societies, the deficiencies from which the migrants were (perhaps) seeking to escape.

Secondly, economic growth (of this country) will be adversely affected by immigration because economic activity depends on trust but between strangers, between different and separate communities. There is not the trust found in homogenous societies?[34]

Thirdly, the availability of cheap labour obstructs innovation:

> Professor Christian Dustmann pointed out 'there is evidence that technology adjusts to the availability of labour in particular parts of the skill distribution'. He gave the example of 'the wine industry in Australia and California which is highly labour intensive in California and highly mechanised in Australia, the reason being that it is very easy to get

unskilled workers in California but not in Australia'. (Paragraph 120 of the House of Lords Report)

If, in 1780, easy assembly instructions for the spinning jenny had been available, it would have hardly been worth building in France; in India the effort would have been loss-making but in the UK, where energy was cheap but labour expensive, the annual return on the investment would have been nearly 40%.[35]

... mechanisation of the tomato-processing industry after the end of the 'bracero' programme in the 1960s, as evidence that immigration slows down the adoption of labour-saving technology.

On the other hand, an implication of this trend is that immigration slows down gains in productivity.[15.3]

More controversially, the fall in productivity might have something to do with an apparently inexhaustible supply of cheap workers, both from mass immigration and greater employment participation, particularly among the elderly. Employers have chosen cheap and easy-to-get-rid-of labour over the capital cost of investment.[36]

Despite the reasonably robust growth of the past few years, UK productivity has remained subdued, with increases in output met mainly through an increase in total hours worked. It's been a jobs-rich recovery, but also a half-baked and unbalanced one in which relatively high levels of net immigration – driven primarily by the deep slump in Europe – and increased labour market participation have acted to depress productivity and wages. Asset prices have risen strongly, but incomes have failed to keep pace. The monetary accommodation judged necessary to support growth has helped ease the pain of the post-crisis adjustment, but it has also left the economy vulnerable to repeated bouts of financial instability.[37]

Strong GDP and employment growth throughout 2013 has highlighted productivity's continued weakness. At the onset of the recession in Q1 2008, productivity initially fell. However, it has not recovered and remains 4% below the pre-crisis peak on an output per hour basis. Productivity has now fallen back to where it was in Q4 2005. Without improvements, we will have lived through almost a decade of stagnant productivity.

The average growth in productivity between Q1 1971 and Q1 2008 was 2.6%. If it had continued on this trend, then productivity would be 20.5% higher than it is now. That is to say that for every hour worked in our economy, we would be producing 20.5% more output if we had not experienced this stagnation.[38]

Fourthly, with cheap and plentiful labour removing the incentive to innovate, the result is a weak and devaluing currency:

> A weak currency implies weak terms of trade and hence a modest level of economic welfare. In other words, when the exchange rate of a country is weak the residents have to produce and exchange more of their products against imports than in a situation where the exchange rate is strong. A weak exchange rate is therefore not a good thing for consumers who want to buy imports from abroad.

> Why is it then that so many governments want the exchange rate of their country to be weak? The answer is that a weak exchange rate benefits existing companies that want to sell their products abroad. In the short term this is good for exports and therefore for domestic production and employment. Most governments care mainly for the short term and hence tend to prefer weak exchange rates to strong ones. In the long term, however, a weak exchange rate discriminates against new companies wanting to come up with new products, better technologies or more efficient production methods. A weak exchange rate keeps incumbent companies in business, even if they produce outdated products in inefficient ways, as they can sell these products abroad at a discount and still make money in domestic currency terms. It protects the owners and employees of these companies at the cost of consumer welfare and new, innovative entrepreneurs who have to compete with the existing companies for capital, labour and raw materials. In contrast, a strong exchange rate forces companies to constantly upgrade products, technologies and production methods or exit their business, freeing resources for new companies adding more value. As a result, countries with strong exchange rates tend to have more innovative industries using more up-to-date technologies to produce products that consumers like and therefore can be sold at a premium price.[39]

And in conclusion:

> It was little more than a couple of weeks ago that Tony Blair stated that he did not regret the Labour Party's immigration policy. Indeed, we were constantly told during the Labour years that high immigration was good for the economy. Yet here we are: the welfare system is buckling, the roads are congested, the police are struggling to cope, the NHS is falling apart, the schools are overcrowded and, of course, the economy is on its knees. Mr Blair and his collaborators have changed this country forever, no doubt to serve their own purposes.[40]

> ... The immigration about which Powell got himself worked up numbered less than 50,000 across several years: we have perhaps ten times that amount in a single year. There is plenty of evidence to suggest that, at the very best, the economy receives a brief spurt as a consequence of

this inward migration, and certainly in the short term some businesses benefit. But that's about it: in the long term it is financially and socially ruinous, even if the rivers are not perpetually foaming with blood, but do so only occasionally.[41]

Notes: *E is for the economics of immigration*

1. Note 2 to the Introduction to *When the Money Runs Out: The End of Western Affluence* by Stephen D. King, published by Yale University Press in 2013.

The same point had been made earlier by Wolfgang Lutz – 'It's this human capital, not crude numbers, that correlates best with economic growth' (about the tiger economies of east Asia). And also by Jeff Randall in *Now for Labour's lies about immigration*, *The Daily Telegraph*, September 2013 – 'Yes output went up but GDP per head did not because the cake had to be shared amongst more people.' Similarly, Jeremy Warner in *Harsh Truths about the decline of Britain*, *The Daily Telegraph*, October 2013, stated:

Analysis released by the Office for National Statistics [the last week of October 2013] shows that disposable income has risen somewhat since the start of the crisis – but this is entirely accounted for by population growth, lower interest rates and higher employment. Real income per household is going backwards, and is now no higher than it was 10 years ago.

In the summer of 2014, it was reported that in the second quarter GDP had exceeded that of the preceding high in the first quarter of 2008 so there were these headlines: *Recovery passes the pre-crisis peak at last* (*The Daily Telegraph*) and *Longest slump in a century ends* (*Financial Times*) but only in one was the proviso of 'But the population has grown in the meantime.'

In November 2014 Liam Halligan in *The Sunday Telegraph* in *UK Recovery? The feel-good factor remains elusive* did make the point

... why is the feel-good factor so elusive?

The reason is obvious if you look at the date. It's true that UK GDP has just about recovered to its pre-crisis level and is now 0.6pc higher than in early 2008 (or just over 2pc higher if you consider recently implemented accounting changes including various forms of informal economic activity). Yet, factor in a 4pc population rise since early 2008 and GDP per head (even under the new data rules) remains around 1pc lower than before the Lehman collapse.

2. Tony Blair, prime minister from 1997 to 2007. This statement by his spokesman came after Beverley Hughes resigned as immigration minister (*see* note 1 to I is for identity).

3. Liam Byrne became MP for Birmingham Hodge Hill in a by-election in 2004. Between May 2006 and October 2008 he was Minister of State for Borders and Immigration during which time he commented that immigration 'affects the ability of public servants to deliver education and health services'.

On 17 July 2007 the House of Commons, at the instigation of Nicholas Soames MP for Mid Sussex, had a debate on immigration. Mr Soames said:

> Talk of Britain as a nation of immigrants is absurd.

And set out the background namely:

> Net immigration is a new phenomenon and initially was quite small. Between the mid 1980s and the mid 1990s, it hardly exceeded 50,000 a year. Since 1997, however, it has quadrupled to some 200,000 a year.

He explained that the massive increase in immigration was in part due to the government's failure during its first five years in office to get a grip with asylum claims; in part to allowing a massive increase in work permits and in part to abolishing the primary purpose rule, so that

> Looking ahead the government's projections we anticipate that we will add 1 million to our population every five years. Of that increase 83 per cent will be added due to new immigrants and their descendants. Even that forecast is based on the cautious assumption that immigration will fall by about 30 per cent, from its present level and remain flat.

> If proof were needed, consider the Prime Minister's speech to the House last week. After 10 years in government, he has discovered that there is a housing crisis, particularly in respect of affordable homes. Why? Because for years, demand has outstripped supply. The Government have permitted – indeed encouraged – the arrival of 2 million immigrants since 1997, but have completely failed to build the necessary homes or the wider social infrastructure that is so vital. They have not even built enough social housing to match the number of grants that they have made of asylum and other forms of protection. All these people qualify for social housing and many, but not all, will take it up.

> The infrastructure of schools, hospitals and roads must also be considered because immigration levels mean we are committing ourselves to building a city the size of Birmingham every five years.

The pressure on our education system has also increased, not only because of the numbers of immigrants, but because many pupils arrive with no English.

...there is also major concern about, and question mark, over social cohesion.

and explained that even using the Government's

own calculations, the arithmetic shows that [benefit per head] amounts to around 73p per head per week, at the most. Similar results have been found in major studies in the US, Canada and Holland. I challenge the Government to produce any evidence that immigration makes a significant difference to GDP per head, and therefore to the indigenous population.

The reality is that most of the economic benefit goes to the immigrants themselves, which is, of course, why they come.

Frank Field, the MP for Birkenhead, said he thought Mr Soames' figures were "modest", and said:

The debate is of course about numbers, but it is also about what it means to create and maintain a community. If the government do not change track very smartly on this issue, the sense of national identity might be lost, and then we are in totally new territory.

And made four points/proposals

It is not sustainable to have those open borders within Europe when some countries will not begin to approach our current living standards....the future of the European Union is an unsure one if we continue to turn our eyes away from what is now a mass movement of people within Europe as well as.....people coming from beyond the European borders

to be able to trace people from this country into Europe and from Europe to the terror training camps

we should insist that anyone coming here should speak English

we are undermining one of the cornerstones of our society by allowing Tom, Dick and Harry to qualify [for welfare]

Nick Clegg, the MP for Sheffield Hallam, said

I return to the legacy of the large numbers of people living invisibly and illegally in this country. What are we to do about them? The Conservative proposal that we should somehow deport those 600,000 people is entirely fanciful.

The reply from Mr Byrne as the minister included

> There is a degree of consensus on the level of EU migration.......the position that both sides of the House have settled on is that we should accept free movement of people inside Europe.

but ignored Mr Soames' challenge and the points made by Mr Soames and Mr Field.

4. Jacqui Smith was the MP for Redditch between 1997 and 2010 and Home Secretary between 2007 and 2009. More comprehensible, during her time as Home Secretary she said, as to excluding certain visitors to this country – 'If you can't live by the rules that we live by, the standards and values that we live by, we should exclude you from this country and what's more we will make public those people we have excluded.'

5. David Cameron, Prime Minister from 2010.

6. Fraser Nelson, 18 July 2013, *The Daily Telegraph*. The next day John McDermott in the *Financial Times* in *Public finances are heading for another big squeeze* put the OBR's view of immigration as follows:

> Under the last government, Britain received the largest peacetime migration in recent history. Politicians are acutely aware that, for some, too many came too fast. Immigration is near the top of issues people tell pollsters they care about. The government has pledged to limit net inward migration to the tens of thousands. (It was 153,000 in the year to September 2012.) The OBR says this will be expensive because it assumes migrants are young and pay more in to the state than they take out. If net inward migration were nearer zero, public debt would balloon, the watchdog says. People will disagree about the assumptions but the OBR's conclusion is inescapable: curbing immigration would come at a large fiscal cost ...

> Time is the justice that examines all offenders. The OBR report forms the deep context for many of the most sensitive areas of government. Parties have begun the arduous road towards their manifestos for the 2015 general election. These will be sold as strategies for the country. But strategies require choices. The OBR implies Britain cannot limit migration without paying a cost, or protect the state pension without putting pressure on school budgets. For in the long run we may be all dead, but first many of us grow old. (*Financial Times*)

7. The House of Lords' Select Committee on Economic Affairs' Report entitled *The Economic Impact of Immigration* published 1 April 2008. A paragraph thereof is particularised by '(Paragraph ...)'.

8. Memorandum [of evidence] by Professor Robert Rowthorn of Cambridge University to the House of Lords' Select Committee on Economic Affairs (for its report).

At the end of 2015, there was published by Civitas, Professor Rowthorn's *The Costs and Benefits of Large-scale Immigration*. It included (in the 'Overview'):

> Unskilled workers have suffered some reduction in their wages due to competition from immigrants. [And] Even on optimistic assumptions, the economic and fiscal gains for existing inhabitants and their descendants from large-scale immigration are small in comparison to its impact on population growth.

9. *The Economic and Fiscal Impact of Immigration*, by the Home Office in partnership with the Department for Work and Pensions, October 2007.

10. Local Employment Partnerships – 'LEPs'.

There are various ways to assess unemployment but, according to the IMF in 2007, the UK's unemployment rate was 5.4% and in 2010 it was 7.858%. In 2010 the DWP wrote:

> LEPs were not a programme or a scheme but an approach and a way in which we, in Jobcentre Plus, work in partnership with employers to create opportunities for people who are some distance away from the labour market. Because this way of working is now very much how we do business with employers, a decision was made in June 2010 to remove the label to this approach, i.e. the LEP branding. We know that LEPs have been successful and the CIPD Recruitment and Retention Survey 2009 showed that over half of employers surveyed have changed their recruitment practices as a direct result of LEPs. All the Jobcentre Plus services for employers that were delivered under the LEP banner are still very much available, for example Work Trials and sifting and matching of applications.

11. *Official: immigration doesn't benefit Britain* by Philip Johnston, *The Daily Telegraph*, March 2008. Another part of the article is under M is for misfeasance, there referred to by note 3.

12. In a competitive market, the unit price for a particular item will vary until it settles at a point where the quantity demanded by consumers will equal the quantity supplied by producers, resulting in an economic equilibrium of price and quantity. Or put more shortly and specifically to labour, the law of supply and demand is that with a surplus of labour, wage rates will lower.

13. Labourers' wages doubled in the century after the Black Death, which had killed up to half the population and thereby decreased the supply of labour.

14. *Why Nations Fail* by Daron Acemoglu and James A. Robinson, published in 2012 by Crown Publishers in the USA and by Profile Books in the UK: from chapter 10, *The Diffusion of Prosperity*.

15. *Immigration and the Labour Market: Theory, Evidence and Policy*, published March 2009 by Will Somerville and Madeleine Sumption of the Migration Policy Institute; page 9. Their note to the secondly quoted paragraph is:

> In economic language, two things are happening. First the labour supply curve is shifting right, which means that wages fall but employment rises (although not by as much as the increased supply of workers.) Second (and with a time lag), the labour demand curve shifts right, further increasing employment, but also raising wages again. The magnitude of this shift in the demand curve is uncertain (for reasons discussed at length in this paper) and hence must be resolved empirically.

15.1. The same authors, page 14 of the same paper.

15.2. The same authors, page 17 of the same paper.

15.3. The same authors, page 25 of the same paper.

16. *Jilted Generation: How Britain has Bankrupted its Youth* by Ed Howker and Shiv Malik, published by Icon Books in 2010.

17. *The British Dream: Successes and Failures of Post-War Immigration* by David Goodhart published by Atlantic Books in 2013.

18. Merryn Somerset Webb, *Financial Times,* September 2013.

19. *Britain's great paradox: the economy is booming and yet wages are falling* by Allister Heath, *The Daily Telegraph,* August 2014.

20. Nicholas Simpson – blog.

21. *Here's why migrants want to come to Britain* by Jeremy Warner, *The Daily Telegraph,* March 2014.

22. This is taken out of the following paragraph of the *Financial Times* at the end of November 2013, namely:

> John Allen, a member of the Northampton branch of Ukip, is a case in point. Allen, a third-generation military veteran, has been out of work for five years. The 63-year-old puts this down to a mix of age discrimination

and immigration. 'If we had control over our borders, then the jobs issue would be dead in the water,' he says. 'I'm looking at Ukip on the same basis as the wartime campaign my father fought.'

23. *The shrinking state* by Chris Dillow in the *Investors Chronicle* for the third week of December 2013.

The rate of unemployment can be measured in various ways but Izabella Kaminska in *The mystery of UK slack, FTAlphaville* of August 2013:

Due to friction in the labour market there is always some unemployment in the economy

..... job-finding rates and job creation suggests that the natural rate was just over 5%...

Nevertheless, the current unemployment rate is likely to be well over its long-run equilibrium....The unemployment rate has now remained elevated for five years, and the proportion of unemployed people who are long-term unemployed has increased from just over 20% in the pre-crisis period from 2000 to 2007 to around 35% in 2013

stated that the proportion of unemployed who are long-term unemployed was horrendous and would appear to acknowledge that there were more unemployed than there should have been.

24. (And so) there was a disclaimer – the views expressed therein were solely of the authors and not to be taken to represent those of the Bank.

25. The Working Paper also included:

... the net inflow of immigrants to the United Kingdom has risen from around 50,000 individuals in 1995 to just under 300,000 in 2014.

and

Having been stable at around 8 percent between 1984 and 1995, ['the immigrant–native ratio'] has grown to nearly 20 percent by 2014.

26. From Gary Fedtschyschak, January 2016.

27. Strictly this is not correct (*see* note 24 above). The authors were Stephen Nickell and Jumana Saleheen, the former an honorary fellow at Nuffield College, Oxford, and the latter apparently only of the Bank.

28. In fact less than half of immigrants come from the EU: *see* number 39 of W is for what is to be done?

29. *Tito: A Biography* by Jasper Ridley.

30. Ha-Joon Chang (author of, inter alia, *23 Things They Don't Tell You About Capitalism*) from 'Lunch with the FT', David Pilling, *Financial Times*. ('Park' was the autocratic leader of South Korea between 1961 and 1979.) (This 'David Pilling' is probably the same as the author of the book quoted from in note 21 to C is for the cost of immigration.)

31. *Celtic Metamorphosis: Is Ireland a model of adjustment through austerity* by Charlemagne – in *The Economist* of 12 January 2013.

32. *Latvia joins euro against the will of its people* by Ambrose Evans-Pritchard, *The Daily Telegraph*, December 2013 (when the population had 'shrunk by 7 per cent since 2007').

33. *See* C is for culture.

34. *See Bowling Alone* by Robert D. Putnam.

35. *See The Industrial Revolution in Miniature: The Spinning Jenny in Britain France and India* by Robert C. Allen, Professor of Economic History, Oxford University, Department of Economics, Working Paper 375.

And from The Knowledge: How to Rebuild our World from Scratch by Lewis Dartnell:

> And eighteenth century Britain presented a peculiar confluence of factors that provided the impetus and opportunity necessary for industrialisation. At that time Britain possessed not only abundant energy (coal) but an economy with expensive labour (high wages) coupled with cheap capital (the ability to borrow money to undertake large projects). Such circumstances encouraged the substitution of capital and energy for labour: workers were replaced by machines such as automated spinners and looms.

36. *Our productivity is still a national disgrace* by Jeremy Warner, *The Daily Telegraph*, March 2015. Earlier in the article he had written:

> On some measures, Britain is now around a fifth less productive per worker than the G7 average, and a jaw-dropping 40 per cent below the US.

37. *Britain's shameful productivity deficit must be tackled head-on* by Jeremy Warner, *The Daily Telegraph*, May 2015.

38. *Productivity's Lost decade – and How to Avoid Another* by Adam Memon, Brian Sturgess and Tim Knox, published by the Centre for Policy Studies, May 2015.

39. *Europe's Unfinished Currency: The Political Economics of the Euro* by Thomas Mayer, published by Anthem Press in 2012.

40. W.H. Bailey, letter to a newspaper, February 2013.

41. *Once more, the spectre of Enoch Powell is raised to stop debate about immigration* by Rod Liddle, *The Spectator,* January 2014.

And **E** is for education

In primary schools, 16.8% of pupils do not speak English as a first language; in Tower Hamlets, the figure is 78%; in secondary schools, the figure is 12.3%.[1]

> English is not the first language of more than half a million pupils in Britain's primary schools. The language spoken at home by 567,888 children aged between four and 11 could be any one of the hundreds of foreign languages now used by migrants from across the globe who have settled in this country. No one should be surprised by the statistic, because it is a straightforward consequence of the enormous amount of migration into Britain over the past decade: the more foreigners who come here to live, the more of their children will be educated in British schools – and the more our schools will have to deal with pupils whose first language is not English or who do not speak it at all.[2]

> In the last two decades, children have come to the UK from an increasing range of different countries. The LGA and Dr Janet Dobson both pointed to increasing costs that schools have consequently incurred on translation, English language training and books such as bilingual dictionaries. The National Union of Teachers referred to Government figures showing that almost 790,000 school children in England – 12% of all pupils in 2007 – did not speak English as their first language, up from 9.7% in 2003.[3]

> One wonders how many teachers in China and South Korea are confronted by students who do not speak the national language – a situation that pertains in a good many schools here. This may have contributed to the decline of education in this country.[4]

> Just 13% of the poorest white children in Britain get a degree, compared with 53% of the poorest British Indians and 30% of the poorest black Caribbeans.[5]

(And *see* H is for Ray Honeyford for his *Education and Race – an Alternative View* and Appendix VI for his *Multiracial Myths*.)

Notes: *E is for education*

1. It is to be noted that the percentage is greater in primary than in secondary schools. (*See* P is for progression and S is for swarm and swamp).

2. *All you need to know about immigration in Britain today* by Alasdair Palmer, *The Daily Telegraph*, March 2009.

3. Paragraph 139 of the House of Lords Report.

4. Letter to a newspaper, Judith Keeling, December 2013 (just after the OECD PISA results for 2010 showing Britain's very average attainment despite spending per pupil in Shanghai, Singapore and South Korea (which scored so well) being less than in the UK (and classes there are bigger than here).

5. The Institute for Fiscal Studies, reported by *The Week*, November 2015.

And **E** is for examples perhaps encapsulating where we are

- When KA arrived here in the back of a lorry, he claimed to be fifteen years old. He was assessed to be over eighteen. In March 2010, an immigration tribunal decided he had 'fabricated' what he said as to coming to this country. In November 2011, a higher tribunal also dismissed his account. On further appeal it was held he should be given the benefit of the doubt. On yet further appeal it was decided his age was a simple question of fact and the earlier tribunals had properly considered the matter.

- Sani Adil Ali arrived here in 2003 from Sudan and two years later was given refugee status. Within months he admitted rape. Upon release from three years of imprisonment, he appealed against a deportation order: that was rejected but he appealed again, successfully.

- Diamond and Tiny Babamuboni, aged seventeen and fifteen, with Jude Odigie, aged sixteen, all from Nigeria, plus another seventeen-year-old, in 2005, robbed a christening party and, with a 9mm handgun, killed the woman holding the baby; all four were convicted of murder. The Babamuboni brothers came here with their mother, who was refused refugee status: Odigie was an overstayer who had been refused leave to remain here. All three had a string of convictions. The woman who was murdered was a refugee from Sierra Leone. The Home Office offered its sympathy to her family but did not comment on the murderers, save 'We want to make it clear that we will not accommodate those that abuse our hospitality and sanctuary by becoming involved in crime.'

- Bashir Barrow, from Somalia, was refused asylum following his arrival in 1995 but later granted exceptional leave to remain. Within a year he was jailed for indecent assault, theft and breach of a community order. He went on to commit other offences and returned to jail. At the end of that second term he appealed against deportation, at one hearing being so drunk as to cause the hearing to be delayed. On appeal, he has been granted the right to claim damages for being kept in custody: otherwise he is in council accommodation.

- Moazzam Begg was born in, Sparkhill, Birmingham, (in 1968) and/but has dual nationality – British and Pakistani. In 2001, he and his family moved to Afghanistan. The next year he was arrested in Pakistan and transferred to Bagram air base in Afghanistan. He was moved to Guantanamo and released in 2005. In 2010, he and other persons who had been detained in Guantanamo settled their claim against the government for having been complicit in his mistreatment by the Americans. In 2011, he and his wife paid £395,000 for a house in Hall Green, Birmingham. In 2013, he was stopped at Heathrow and his passport taken away. In 2014, Begg and three others were arrested on suspicion of facilitating terrorism overseas.

- Amada Bizimana, an illegal immigrant, was jailed in 2008 for possessing false identity documents; when due for release he was kept in a deportation centre as his country of origin could not be identified and so his detention was unlawful and he was entitled to compensation. (While here, by another African, he fathered a child and, it having been born here, such child is 'automatically' a British citizen.)

- Mohamed Bouzalim claimed asylum in 2001, purporting to be an Afghani whose father had been killed by the Taliban. His application was rejected but he was given leave to remain. He subsequently claimed benefits on the basis of being paralysed but was filmed dancing at his wedding. He was arrested together with his parents and siblings. His sister and brothers also admitted fraud. Three Bridges Hospital described him as a 'malingerer'.

- Rolands Brize may be known because his sentencing for attempted rape was adjourned eleven times (because of, inter alia, the need for psychiatric reports and a translator) but he is included here as Brize is Latvian. He was in a mental health institute there after burning down his family home. After release, he came here but initially returned home, and, after again being in such an institute, he came back here again and went on to attempt to rape.

- Joland Giwa ('Dexter')[1] arrived in 1999 on a flight from Lagos, aged ten, with his twin brother and without any identity documents. He claimed asylum, which was refused, but was allowed to stay for four years. In 2005, he was given indefinite leave to remain despite having a conviction for handling stolen goods. Over the following years he was convicted of a string of robberies and thefts that, in 2009, resulted in a twenty-seven-month sentence. Release was to immigration detention because, with the length of his sentence, he was liable to automatic deportation; however, he got moved on to Belmarsh because it was thought he was smuggling drugs into the detention centre. Both Nigeria and Sierra Leone refused to accept him. He was due to be released because detention pending deportation cannot be indefinite. (His brother has been jailed for trying to smuggle heroin and SIM cards into Belmarsh.)

- Mustafa Hussain, with five others, hijacked a Sudan Airways airbus in 1996 to land it at Stanstead. All six were convicted. The Court of Appeal quashed those convictions, concluding the jury should have been given the chance to consider the defence of duress. Two others of the hijackers, including the ringleader, were granted indefinite leave to remain. In July 2012, the Home Secretary was ordered to consider the same outcome for Hussain.

- Aso Mohammed Ibrahim was still in the country despite his original application for asylum having been refused, had a criminal record including criminal damage, driving while disqualified and without insurance, burglary, theft, harassment and possession of cannabis when he ran over twelve-year-old Amy Houston and fled the scene, and then claimed he had a right to a family life in this country.

- Mustaf Jama came to this country from Somalia in 1993. He, with Muzzaker Shah, Raza ul-Aslam, Faisal and Hassan Razzaq and Pitta Ditta Khan, were the gang, one of whom killed PC Sharon Beshenivsky. He had (already) accumulated twenty-one convictions and, when released from his fourth stretch of imprisonment, the Home Office deemed it unfair to send him back to Somalia. However, following the policewoman's murder, he fled there, using a false passport.

- Choudry Kanwal entered the country in 2007 on a six-month visitors' visa. He tried to stay here permanently by way of a 'marriage'. That was to Marcela Tancosva from Slovakia, where she has a husband (she was pregnant by a third man). The 'marriage' and others was arranged by

Sajid Mehmood, who when arrested had a list of requirements, for marriage, written in Urdu. Mehmood, who had already served a term of imprisonment for fixing sham marriages, was given a community order of 200 hours of unpaid work. Kanwal jumped bail and, when Tancosva and Mehmood were sentenced, was still on the run.

- Mohammed Kendeh attempted to rape in 2003; two years later he was sentenced to jail for four years plus two on licence; he was released in 2007; in 2009 he was convicted of robbery but by pleading Article 8 of the European Convention on Human Rights was able to delay his deportation to Sierra Leone until early 2012.

- Aziz Lamari from Algeria was jailed for robbery and claimed compensation for being kept in custody for too long while attempts were made to deport him.

- Johnathan Limani, from Albania, was convicted in Switzerland in 1999 of trafficking heroin; he skipped bail and claimed asylum in Sweden, where he was twice sectioned. Here, having killed his manager over a row about smoking breaks, Limani sawed off the manager's head with a cheese knife.

- Rhomaine Mohan came here in 2000, aged twenty, from Jamaica on a one-month visa. He served terms of imprisonment for driving offences and possessing class-A drugs with intent to supply. He has three children by two women. A rehearing of Mohan's case to stay in this country was ordered as there was no 'overwhelming' public interest in his deportation.

- Karmal Mustafa, by giving different addresses, bank account details and national insurance numbers, managed over seven years to claim income support, council and housing benefit amounting to nearly £39,000. In mitigation, the court heard how despite Mustafa having a wife in Somalia, another woman, who came to this country in 2007 and by whom he has two children and who does not speak English, is 'utterly dependent' on him.

- Suleman Maknojioa 'touched up' an eleven-year-old girl while teaching her and her two brothers the Koran. His defending counsel told the court, 'This is a man who doesn't pose any risk to his children. He has problems with his kidneys and is due to go back into hospital for a further follow-up operation. He is married with six children; that family unit depends on him. His wife doesn't work and speaks very little

English, they are dependent on him to lead their lives and with the running of the household.' The judge told Maknojioa, 'There could be no greater recognition of trust than between a minister of religion and pupils whose care is entrusted to him by parents. You breached that trust deliberately and repeatedly. I bear in mind that social services conducted their own assessment and found that you do not pose a risk. You are now unemployed, living on state benefits', and sentenced him to forty weeks suspended for two years plus supervision for two years and subject to a sexual offences prevention order for ten years.

- Rebecca Muwonge came here from Uganda in 1996; she is now about fifty but purported to be Proscovia Kasozi, her eighteen-year-old niece (which does not say much, or does say volumes, for the vigilance of the Border Agency). Later that year she married Samuel Bisaso, who was subsequently ordained into the Church of Uganda but went on to be chaplain to the Mission of Seafarers near Grimsby. They separated and she purported to marry again. In 2011, Muwonge and Bisaso were both convicted of immigration offences and sentenced to eighteen months. As soon as she got into this country, Muwonge, under a false name, obtained accommodation from the London Borough of Newham and housing benefit; under her real name she also obtained benefits from the London Borough of Enfield. She wrote to Newham, purportedly from her brother-in-law, that she was homeless and was rehoused by it and then applied for a second house in Enfield. She was able to buy her house in Newham at a discount and later made £60,000 when the council bought it back. Following a joint investigation, she has now been prosecuted for false accounting, failing to notify a change of circumstances so as to obtain welfare benefits and obtaining property by deception, all the while still seeking citizenship.

- Justice Ngema, an illegal immigrant from South Africa, left a nurse bound, gagged and blindfolded in the boot of her car while he used her credit card. (Ngema claimed asylum in 2001; his application was rejected and he was removed from the UK in 2002. Three months later he re-entered using his brother's passport.)

- Felista Peters from Kenya used a fake British passport to be admitted to the University of the West of England; the NHS paid £26,000 for her to train as a radiologist.

- Idreez Popoola came here from Nigeria in 2005 on a twelve-month visa; upon expiry, there was a temporary extension. He married and had a child. At the end of 2011, he was arrested upon allegation of assault and found to be an overstayer. He was told he would be deported but appealed successfully on the basis of his family here – Article 8 of the Human Rights Act. Subsequently, he persuaded a woman to take her back to her home but no sooner was he in the door than he raped her. When sentencing Popoola to seven years, the judge told him that he would be automatically deported on release from prison.

- Chrisodoulos Sotiriou was jailed for life in 1991 after stabbing to death a man after the two of them bumped into each other in a swimming pool. Sotiriou was released in 2001 after serving a ten year minimum term and told the Probation Service he was moving to Cyprus. He was released from all licence restrictions but did not leave the country, rather continuing to occupy the same flat as where he had lived before the murder. While in prison, Sotiriou practised his metalwork skills and, after release, used the flat to produce an arsenal of weapons and ammunition: a cache of thirty-six guns was found buried in Epping Forest.

- SSA from Pakistan overstayed his visa, had his marriage application refused, disappeared and then married a different woman and appealed following his detention for removal from the country, for it to be held that such would be a breach of his right to a family life.

- Gbenga Sunday was sent back to Nigeria in 2005 and again in the following year. In early 2012, he was arrested again and was due to be made to leave on 18 May but the day before made an application on the basis of being in a relationship with a European resident so that removing him would breach his right to a family life.

- John Thuo was a member of a criminal mob in Nairobi, *Mungiki*, which apparently enforces its rule by beheading. He admitted to an immigration tribunal that he had killed 'about 100 to 400 people' but successfully claimed that returning him home would be contrary to his human rights because 'If I go back they'll [namely *Mungiki*] kill me. They'll behead me.'

- TM, a Pakistani who has made fifteen attempts to stay in this country since his arrival in 1998, will (be forced to) leave, the Court of Appeal commenting, 'Here we have one of those whirligig cases where an asylum seeker goes up and down on the merry-go-round, leaving one wondering when the music will ever stop', and holding that the secretary of state was entitled to take steps to remove TM.

- Ai Vee Ong was jailed for using illegal immigrant workers, selling counterfeit goods and money laundering. The immigration appeal tribunal accepted her argument that the shame she would encounter at home in Malaysia (where her imprisonment was not known of) would result in a breach of her human rights if she were deported (home).

Such examples can be contrasted with that of Imran Mahmood, who was deported from Pakistan (for) having overstayed his visa. Upon his arrival at Heathrow, it was seen that Mahmood's rucksack was tainted with traces of explosives. In 2013, Mahmood, together with Jahangir Alom, who had been in the TA and a PCSO, plus (convert) Richard Dart pleaded guilty to preparing acts of terrorism. Alom's wife, Ruskana Begum, pleaded guilty to possession of information likely to be useful to a terrorist, namely, on a SIM card, an edition of *Inspire* with information as to making bombs; two of her brothers were convicted of the plot to bomb, inter alia, the Stock Exchange.

The case of Derrick Kinsasi is a more recent example and perhaps particularly exemplifies where we are. He was born on 15 November 1991. 'There was no record of his lawful entry into the UK. He claimed that he and his brother entered with an agent on 9 April 2002. The next day they attended the Asylum Screening Unit and claimed asylum as unaccompanied minors. On 12 July 2002 asylum was refused' but they were granted exceptional leave to remain until 10 October 2006. On 31 January 2005, Kinsasi and his brother were included on their mother's application for indefinite leave to remain under the family exercise. That was granted.

On 24 October 2011, Kinsasi was convicted of burglary and theft. The sentencing judge related how Kinsasi with a number of others 'were engaged in the violent entry to the back of a store containing high-value portable items. There was one group breaking into the front of [the] Comet Store while you and others were at the back. All of this you have admitted. That behaviour was on the second day of the 2011 riots; he was sentenced to eighteen months' imprisonment.

By letter of 18 November 2011, Kinsasi was informed that in the light of his conviction he was liable to deportation. He asserted that to deport him would be a breach of his right under Article 8 of the European Convention on Human Rights (the right to respect for private and family life).

The secretary of state considered Kinsasi's relationship with his 'mother and siblings and wider family' did not constitute family life for the purposes of Article 8 (without more which had not been produced), he did not have a partner or issue in the UK and so had not established family life here. It was noted Kinsasi had not lived continuously in the UK for at least twenty years/half of his life, he spoke the language of his country of origin and was aware of its cultures and traditions due to spending his formative years there.

The first-tier Tribunal did not find Kinsasi or his mother to be credible witnesses. She did not speak very much English. He had lived with her until he was imprisoned. Due to his time inside, he now spoke English fluently; the Tribunal did not accept his evidence that he only spoke 25% of his native tongue; he was minimising his abilities in that language and so would have little difficulty communicating (there). Further, Kinsasi's claim to have no real recollection of the DRC was lacking in credibility and it was considered that his evidence 'was a further attempt to minimise his knowledge of the DRC and his links to that country'.

The Tribunal pointed out that while it had taken into account what it had been told of Kinsasi's younger brother's offending, it was dealing with Derrick's appeal on its own – there was an important distinction to be made as he was some two years older.

> In so far as Kinsasi's younger brother was concerned he was now over 18. Submissions addressed to the panel on the importance of this relationship to Kinsasi were borne in mind. Account was taken of the fact that the brothers were both adults who had been separated by their offending and consequent custodial sentences.

The Tribunal found that the decision to deport Kinsasi was lawful and in pursuit of a legitimate aim, namely the protection of the public from those who had committed serious criminal offences.

The Tribunal dismissed Kinsasi's appeal. He appealed to the Upper Tribunal, which allowed the appeal, and so, despite

- being trafficked into this country

- committing a serious criminal offence

- neither he nor his mother being credible witnesses

he is being allowed to stay here.(The report of Kinsasi's last appeal does not relate how his mother got to or arrived in this country.)

The ease with which our border controls are evaded, and the comparative robustness of dealing with illegal immigrants, is encapsulated by the report in July 2014 of twenty-eight Bangladeshi, Pakistani, Afghani and Sri Lankans, including two children, being found at Calais, in a Polish lorry driven by a Romanian, having left the UK from Dover. They were shipped back by the French authorities the same day and here the UK authorities said, 'If those questioned are found to have no right to remain in the UK we will take action to remove them.'

Notes: *E is for examples perhaps encapsulating where we are*

1. Giwa was apparently a member of the Croydon gang known as 'Don't say nothing' or DSN. Sergeant Darin Birmingham of the Metropolitan Police gangs unit called him 'a serious threat to the public and other young people'. On a YouTube video, Giwa spoke of shanking, namely stabbing a man in the head. A fellow gang member was on *gangstathug4eva* saying 'My nigga Dexter gonna bang order when he back on road, free of all mandem, now.'

From prison, Giwa was relocated to Newport, whose MP wrote to the Home Secretary, 'If unpalatable decisions are unavoidable, London should be responsible for its own problems and not seek to dump them on Wales and Newport.' Giwa told the South Wales *Argus*, 'I never think I'm perfect but I think the way I've been targeted is worse than a terrorist. I've never killed anyone. I'm not a violent person. Nobody is scared of me. I'm not a harm to the public.' Later in Newport, when questioned by a policeman who saw him sitting in a children's play park, Giwa ran off, leaving a bag that was found to contain cannabis.

And **E** is for European Union

Article 48 of the Treaty of Rome and Article 45 of the Treaty of Maastricht provide for free movement throughout the Union.[1]

In 2004, eight states – the A8 – joined. Most of the existing states had transitional requirements: the then government of this country did not avail itself of this, stating it expected the influx from the A8 to be 15,000.[2] It has been and is many times more:

> As a result of the enlargement of the EU there has also been a particularly high inflow of European migrants over recent years. For example, between the accession of Poland to the EU in 2004 and 2011, the Polish national population of the UK increased from 69,000 to 687,000, and Poles now constitute the highest proportion of all foreign nationals in the UK (ONS). At the same time, migration from more traditional source countries has also continued to grow.[3]

Initially, the Workers Registration Scheme meant that people from such countries who were to work here were to register, but that expired at the end of 2013.

Such immigration has been reinforced by this country's welfare benefits:

Imagine you're a Romanian or Bulgarian looking to escape your 'dismal, corrupt and impoverished homeland'. From the end of [2013], you'll have the right to live anywhere in the EU. Which country would you choose? The answer's obvious, says Minette Marrin. You'd be 'daft' not to pick the UK: it's not just that EU citizens who move here are entitled to free schools, GPs and hospitals; Britain also offers notable generous welfare benefits. In other EU countries, migrants can claim unemployment benefit only after they've contributed to the system; here they can claim it 'more or less on arrival'. According to new research by Migration Watch UK, only three other EU countries – Ireland, Denmark and Luxembourg – offer more generous benefits to low-paid workers, and why would any would-be migrant choose a place that's 'freezing or boring' over a vibrant, multicultural, English-speaking country? You can't blame migrants for seeking a better life, but their choice will eventually force one on the UK. Either we accept that 'a generous welfare state is incompatible with the free movement of people'. Or we 'go broke'.[4]

But large-scale immigration from the EU is not limited to the A8/A2 countries:

By 2030 Britain, Denmark and Sweden could be the only EU states outside [the euro]. Of these three countries, Britain has much the largest economy. So if the eurozone economies converge – and they must if their union is to survive – then Britain, with its different business cycle will end up as the eurozone's safety valve whenever unemployment spikes.

In 2006 before everything went wrong, fewer than 10,000 Spaniards were issued with UK National Insurance numbers. Last year it was more than 50,000. You can see the same trend in terms of immigration from Portugal – from under 10,000 NI numbers issued to more than 30,000 – and Italy has gone from just over 11,000 to 44,000 on the same measure. That's more than 120,000 immigrants to Britain last year from just three long-established EU member states. Such figures make a mockery of Cameron's aim to reduce net migration from the hundreds of thousands to the tens of thousands. They also put in question any policy proposal based on the idea that the problem is just immigration from new member states. Longer 'transitional controls'– tougher immigration conditions for those who have recently joined the EU – would not address the eurozone factor.[5]

At the end of 2013, one third of the vendors of *Big Issue* were from A8/A2 countries and 112,000 European citizens were seeking Jobseekers Allowance, of which 37% had never worked in this country.

By the end of June 2014, the total number of EU workers in the UK was 1,836,000 – up by 187,000 in three months.[6] And in the year to the end of September 2014, EU immigration increased by 43,000 to 251,000.[6/1]

> The problem with mass migration is not so much the misuse of benefits by a minority – though that is wrong – but is the impact of mass, low-waged and unskilled labour upon the wages, employment opportunities and services of this country. I have been campaigning for years, not on the point of benefits, but the impact of the sheer numbers.

> Even Mark Carney, the Governor of the Bank of England, couldn't help but allude to the subject last week as he talked about a 'staggering' 25 per cent slump in demand from Europe for British exports, combined with what he described as the effects of 'more labour supply than we had previously thought'. He went on to comment that we have 'severe' structural problems due to a 'chronic' shortfall in housing. Yes, these things are related.

> Just look at the way that growth is disproportionately helping the rich, who benefit from cheap labour supply, while the low-waged see pay cuts and freezes. The Local Government Association tells us that there will be a shortfall of 230,000 primary school places in the next three years, caused almost entirely by migration and a soaring birth rate among first-generation migrants.[7]

> The best official guess at the number of Brazilians in Britain is upward of 200,000, though Brazilian expats suggest the true figure is much, much higher. Many come as students then stay on, blending into life in the capital, earning their money, paying their taxes, marrying Brits, generally adding to the gaiety of the nation, but somehow failing to register as foreign nationals.

> Brazilians can blag a Portuguese passport on the flimsiest of ancestral grounds, so many thousands of them who drift into London are technically classed as EU citizens, and are therefore barely acknowledged statistically.[8]

> Uncontrolled immigration is both an economic and moral issue. By all means let the market decide pay differentials but it is morally wrong to import labour with the aim of driving down unskilled wages.

> There is unwillingness across the political spectrum to acknowledge that a necessary condition for getting both the poorly paid and chronically unemployed off benefits is a rise in the minimum wage.

Simply curtail immigration and unskilled pay will rise. There will be a transfer of purchasing power from the 'haves' to the 'have-nots' as menial jobs that cannot be outsourced become more costly. Any renegotiation of Britain's EU membership that does not include an opt-out from the EU accord on the free movement of peoples would be sham.[9]

- Linda Kozlovska arrived in this country in 2008, then aged thirty-one, with three children. Four years later, she has had three more children and four others have arrived from Latvia. According to her, 'I have ten children living here with me. I'm the only adult. I am on the council waiting list but we're still here. They don't have a big enough house. I want a bigger house. I don't like it here. When we moved in it had bed bugs', and 'I came to England to live – because we are from Latvia, which is in the EU, I could just come.' She was reported to receive benefits totalling £34,000 a year. A neighbour (in Boston) commented, 'It is almost like a halfway house for people arriving from Latvia, who then move on.'[10]

Notes: *E is for European Union*

1. Article 48 of the Treaty of Rome 1957 is as follows:

1. Freedom of movement for workers shall be secured within the Community by the end of the transitional period at the latest.

2. Such freedom of movement shall entail the abolition of any discrimination based on nationality between workers of the Member States as regards employment, remuneration and other conditions of work and employment.

3. It shall entail the right, subject to limitations justified on grounds of public policy, public security or public health:

(a) to accept offers of employment actually made;

(b) to move freely within the territory of Member States for this purpose;

(c) to stay in a Member State for the purpose of employment in accordance with the provisions governing the employment of nationals of that State laid down by law, regulation or administrative action;

(d) to remain in the territory of a Member State after having been employed in that State, subject to conditions which shall be embodied in implementing regulations to be drawn up by the Commission.

4. The provisions of this Article shall not apply to employment in the public service.

Article 45 of the Treaty of Maastricht (as amended by, inter alia, the Treaty of Lisbon, aka the Reform Treaty) is to the same effect.

(And so) in their flyer for the European elections in 2014 the Conservatives listed

What you told us	What we did
Control Immigration'	So we've taken all the action we can under current EU agreements to fix our immigration system and limited migrants' access to benefits

(And so) in the year ending September 2014, EU immigration increased by 43,000 to 251,000 and from A2 countries from 24,000 to 37,000 (ONS Migration Statistics Quarterly Report of February 2015).

2. *See* M is for mistake.

3. *Social and Public Service Impacts of International Migration at the Local Level* by Jon Simmons, Head of Migration and Border Analysis, Home Office, with Sarah Poppleton, Kate Hitchcock, Kitty Lymperopoulou and Rebecca Gillespie, July 2013.

(By the end of 2015 the number of Poles in the UK was about 800,000.)

4. From *The Sunday Times*, as reported by *The Week*:

At the end of 2013 the minimum wage was then £6.31 per hour and due to increase by 19p per hour at the end of 2014. According to Business Insider, Eurostat the minimum wage (in sterling equivalent) in Spain was (then) £3.61, in Romania £1.08 and in Bulgaria 84p [but that understates the difference when welfare benefits are taken into account].

5. *It's not just Ukip that's changing Cameron's mind about immigration* by James Forsyth, *The Spectator*, October 2014.

6. Office for National Statistics.

6/1 ONS February 2015.

7. *Cameron's EU benefits diatribe fools no one* by Nigel Farage, former leader of UKIP, *The Daily Telegraph,* July 2014. (This item is, of course, also applicable to B is for Betrayal.)

8. *Rich boys from Brazil* by Stephen Robinson, *The Spectator*, September 2014.

9. Yugo Kovach – letter to a newspaper, March 2013.

10. Newspaper report of September 2012.

F is for fifth column

On 1 November 2010, two youths of Asian or mixed-race appearance shouted at sixty-nine-year-old Anthony O'Brien of Fallowfield, Manchester, who was wearing a poppy and wearing an RAF blazer, 'F—ing shoot all you bastards and blow your soldiers up. Death to all soldiers', and then assaulted him.

Following the deaths of six soldiers in Afghanistan, Azhar Ahmed of Ravensthorpe, West Yorkshire, texted, 'All soldiers should die and go to hell.' He said he did not think that was offensive. He was found guilty of sending a grossly offensive communication, fined £300 and ordered to do 240 hours of community service.

At the end of November 2013, Birmingham City Council received what came to be called the Trojan Horse letter.[1] This led to various reports being commissioned, including at the behest of the then secretary of state for education, by Peter Clarke, one-time anti-terrorism chief. The penultimate paragraph of the Clarke Report is as follows:

> There has been a co-ordinated, deliberate and sustained action, carried out by a number of associated individuals, to introduce an intolerant and aggressive Islamic ethos into a few schools in Birmingham. This has been achieved by gaining influence on the governing bodies, installing sympathetic headteachers or senior members of staff, appointing like-minded people to key positions, and seeking to remove headteachers they do not feel to be sufficiently compliant. Some of these individuals are named in this report; most are not. Whether their motivation reflects a political agenda, a deeply held religious conviction, personal gain or a desire to influence communities, the effect has been to limit the life chances of the young people in their care and to render them more vulnerable to pernicious influences in the future.

Mr Clarke was appointed on 15 April 2014. The investigation was to be effected and the report made in time for the autumn school term of that year; it was published in July. Subsequently Mr Clarke said,

> Of course the Government hasn't got to the bottom of the Trojan Horse affair, nowhere near it.

> What I put in my report was the tip of the iceberg. There is a huge amount of material which I didn't put in. I deliberately focused on what appeared to be the epicentre. There were problems elsewhere which I couldn't evidence sufficiently in the time available.[2]

(As per the introduction) it turns out the 'problems' are not just more widespread as stated by Mr Clarke but are long-standing. In 1994, the Department of Education was alerted to Islamist infiltration:

> While I have not found instances of warnings having been ignored or of individuals having acted inappropriately, I have found the department lacked inquisitiveness about this issue, and that procedures could have been tighter than they were.[3]

Another report resulting from the Trojan Horse letter was by Ofsted, whose head, Sir Michael Wilshaw, in November 2014, told the House of Commons' Public Accounts Committee:

> I don't think we've seen the end of the Trojan Horse issues. That's why I've been clear that Birmingham's got to step up to the plate and monitor what's happening in their schools ... much more effectively.
>
> There needs to be a greater sense of urgency. It is astonishing the local authority has not produced an action plan ... after 13 or 14 drafts. These are very, very serious issues.

And in January 2015 he told the Education Committee there had been 'very limited progress', and

> My strong recommendation to the department is that additional funding should be found so that we can recruit good people to these schools very quickly. Because unless that happens and we see improvement across the board then these people who have gone to ground but who want to exploit the situation will do so.

On the first day of 2015, President Abdel Fattah Al Sisi of Egypt (90% of the population of which is Muslim) said:

> I am referring here to the religious clerics. We have to think hard about what we are facing – and I have, in fact, addressed this topic a couple of times before. It's inconceivable that the thinking that we hold most sacred should cause the entire [Islamic world] to be a source of anxiety, danger, killing and destruction for the rest of the world. Impossible!
>
> That thinking – I am not saying 'religion' but 'thinking' – that corpus of texts and ideas that we have sacralized over the centuries, to the point that departing from them has become almost impossible, is antagonizing the entire world. It's antagonizing the entire world!
>
> Is it possible that 1.6 billion people [Muslims] should want to kill the rest of the world's inhabitants – that is 7 billion so they themselves may live? Impossible!

I am saying these words here at Al Azhar,[4] before this assembly of scholars and ulema[5] – Allah Almighty be witness to your truth on Judgment Day concerning that which I'm talking about now.

All this that I am telling you, you cannot feel if you remained trapped within this mindset. You need to step outside of yourselves to be able to observe it and reflect on it from a more enlightened perspective.[6]

Thus (although he disagreed with such thinking) the president was saying that the thinking of Muslims is to want to kill all who are not of their faith.

Notes: *F is for fifth column*

1. Whether or not the letter was genuine and/or merely 'a Christian plot' (as Mr Clarke was told),[A] the name must come from the third, fifth and sixth paragraphs of the first page of what was received by the Council, namely:

Operation 'Trojan Horse' has been very carefully thought through and is tried and tested within Birmingham, implementing it in Bradford will not be difficult for you, especially if you replicate the same relationship that we have with [redacted] I not sure if [redacted] is of the same mindset as [redacted] but if she is keen on the Academy route she will support your plan [redacted] has been very supportive and has helped our agenda progress, in return we will give her the Academies she wants.

The process behind 'Trojan Horse' is simple. It is about seeing our intentions as respectable and our being accepted by the key stakeholders such as the Director of Education and the City Council. The long-term nature of the plan means that we have to have very close relationships with stakeholders and Tahir [Alam][B] has managed this so much so that he is trusted by [redacted] and others.

He has also fine tuned the 'Trojan Horse' so that it is totally invisible to the naked eye and allows us to operate under the radar. I have detailed the plan we have in Birmingham and how well it has worked and you will see how easy the whole process is to get the Head teacher out and our own person in.

Whoever wrote the letter, the term Trojan Horse is apt – it was how something like 3,000 years ago, after ten unsuccessful years (of war), the Greeks took the city of Troy by leaving (the gift of) a horse filled with troops, who in the dead of night let their company into the city:

Into the darkened city, buried deep
In sleep and wine, they made their way
Cut the few sentries down
Let in their fellow soldiers at the gate

And joined their combat companies as planned.
(The Aeneid, Book II, 'How they took the city')

Similarly, on 24 August 410, the Goths took Rome, not by breaching or climbing over the walls but through being let in, through the Salarian Gate, by a fifth column.

2. My thanks to Andrew Gilligan for reporting this, October 2014. But it was also reported by *Jihad Watch*, and *Breitbart* (which states that what Mr Clarke is reported to have said was said on a BBC West Midlands programme).

I haven't found any full transcript of what Mr Clarke said so I don't know if the sentences/paragraphs are in the right order.

Of course, the Trojan Horse letter was apparently addressed to someone in Bradford. There are indications that the plan was – is? – also, being implemented in Dudley and Manchester.

A. By a chair of (school) governors: page 8 of the Clarke Report.

B. 'Tahir' is named in the paragraph at the top of the page. Tahir Alam, as Chair of Education Committee of the Muslim Council of Britain, was the joint author of that Council's *Towards Greater Understanding: Meeting the Needs of Muslim Pupils in State Schools*. In September 2015 (fourteen months after the publication of the Clarke Report), Mr Alam became the first person to be banned (by the DfE) from any involvement with schools because he had engaged in:

- Conduct which is aimed at undermining fundamental British values of democracy, the rule of law, individual liberty, and mutual respect and tolerance of those with different faiths and beliefs.

- Conduct that is so inappropriate that, in the opinion of the appropriate authority, it makes a person unsuitable to take part in the management of independent schools,

- and that because of that conduct he was unsuitable to take part in the management of an independent school (including an academy or Free School). The barring decision also has the effect of disqualifying the person from being a governor at a maintained school.

3. *Review into Possible Warnings to DfE Relating to Extremism in Birmingham Schools* by Chris Wormald, Permanent Secretary to the Department for Education, January 2015.

4. University and mosque dating back to the tenth century.

5. Islamic scholars.

6. Translation by Michele Antaki. *(See* note 1 to W is for we were warned.)

And **F** is for fissiparous

In its report, the House of Lords *(see* E is for economics) recognised this consequence of immigration:

> Our overall conclusion is that the economic benefits of the resident population of net immigration are small, especially in the long run. Of course, many immigrants make a valuable contribution to the UK. But the real issue is how much net immigration is desirable. Here non-economic considerations such as impacts on cultural diversity and social cohesion will be important, but these are outside the scope of our enquiry.[1]

> We are building not so much a multicultural society or a multiracial society; we are building separate societies which really don't have much to do with each other.[2]

Despite living next door to one another for centuries, following the break up of the 'old' Yugoslavia, one ethnic or religious group sought to cleanse another from its area. It is similar in, for example, Lebanon, Palestine, Rwanda and Ulster. This continues with moving to another country: in Malmo (Sweden) the Muslim immigrants attack Jews who have lived in Sweden rather longer than they have; in Palestine newcoming Jews destroy the olive trees of the indigenous Palestinians.

This division of the country into (discrete) communities, indeed Balkanisation, is shown by:

- the division of doctors into us and the British Association of Physicians of Indian Origin;[3]

- the division of engineers into us and the Association of Black Engineers;

- the division of the Crown Prosecution Service into us and the National Black Crown Prosecution Association;

- the division of the police into us and the National Black Police Association, the Metropolitan Black Police Association, the Association of Muslim Police and the Metropolitan Police Sikh Association;[4]

- the division of solicitors into us and Black Solicitors Network (BSN) and the Society of Black Lawyers (SBL), (which accused the Solicitors Regulation Authority of being institutionally racist).

Additionally, there is 'black and Asian minority ethnic' (BAME and sometimes BME); *Black Activists Rising Against Cuts* (BARAC); the Black Training and Enterprise Group (BTEG); Jamaica Teachers' Association; Muslims Against Crusades. Unison (*see* C is for cost) has a National Black Members Committee.

Apart from division between the native population and immigrants, there is division among the latter – the two sides of the Sri Lankan civil war, Shia and Sunni Muslims,[5] Sikhs and Muslims.

The Equality and Human Rights Commission has a BME support group, which, as to the decision not to reappoint a black and a Muslim commissioner to the board, complained, 'We consider [the former's] rejection as symptomatic of a wider culture racial inequality which prevails within the EHRC, a culture which is leading to the loss of two thirds of BME staff ...' This was despite the Commission still employing a far higher proportion of ethnic-minority staff than the Civil Service average.

A local authority survey asking for ethnic origin lists five types of white, five types of Asian, three types of black, four variations on mixed ethnic (quite apart from 'Any other ethnic group' and 'Prefer not to say').

> In the Nineties, when I arrived, this part of Acton was a traditional working-class area. Now there is no trace of any kind of community – that word so cherished by the Left. Instead it has been transformed into a giant transit camp and is home to no one. The scale of immigration over recent years has created communities throughout London that never need to – or want to – interact with outsiders.
>
> It wasn't always the case: since the 1890s thousands of Jewish, Irish, Afro-Caribbean, Asian and Chinese workers among others have arrived in the capital, often displacing the indigenous population. Yes there was hateful overt racism and discrimination I'm not denying that. But, over time, I believe we settled down into a happy mix of incorporation and shared aspiration, with disparate peoples walking the same pavements but returning to very different homes – something the Americans call 'sundown segregation'.
>
> But now, the wishful thinking of multiculturalists, wilful segregation by immigrants is increasingly echoed by the white population – the rate of white flight from our cities is soaring. According to the Office for National Statistics, 600,000 white Britons have left London in the past 10 years.

The latest census data shows the breakdown in telling detail: some London boroughs have lost a quarter of their population of white, British people. The number in Redbridge, north London, for example, has fallen by 40,844 (to 96,253) in this period, while the total population has risen by more than 40,345 to 278,970. It isn't only London boroughs. The market town of Wokingham in Berkshire has lost nearly 5 per cent of its white British population.[6]

After George Galloway[7] in 2012 deliberately sought the 'Asian' vote in the Bradford West by-election, Ken Livingstone in the London mayoralty election campaign promised to make London 'a beacon of Islam'.

In June 2012, Zohaib Ahmed, Mohammed Hasseen, Mohammed Hussain, Omar Mohammed Khan, Mohammed Saud and Jewel Uddin travelled from Birmingham to Dewsbury[8] armed with guns, knives and homemade bombs with the intention of attacking an EDL rally. They arrived too late for the rally; as they returned home, they were stopped: the car insurance was wrong. The weapons and a letter attacking the queen and detailing the plot were found after the car had been in a police pound for two days. The six were sentenced to terms in excess of eighteen years.

So the PM faces an invidious choice. Should he placate the angry voters, many of them white, whose desertion may seal his fate in 2015? Or should he reach out to the ethnic minorities who are likely to make up a third of Britain by 2050 and whose support will be crucial in future elections if the Tories are ever to win again? You do not have to read the rubbishing of Lady Warsi by some former colleagues to deduce that Mr Cameron favours option one.

By way of evidence, the Chancellor's promise to carve another £12 billion in the two years after the election is a sop to those who wrongly demonise incomers as leeches on the social security budget. The stark reality of what George Osborne is planning will become clearer later this month when the Policy Exchange think tank – which has close links to the Conservative Party – publishes a report spelling out the brutal nature of the measures needed to claw back such savings from people of working age.

As reported earlier this month, the report will say that lowering the £26,000 benefits cap to £23,400 for families outside London and the South East could save £100 million a year. It will examine plans, due for inclusion in the Tory manifesto, to debar parents from claiming child benefit for more than four children. I understand it will focus on freezing the current 1 per cent uprating cap on working-age benefits for up to three more years.

Much as British voters, ethnic minorities among them, may appear to clamour for a tougher stance on welfare, Mr Cameron should beware of prising open this Pandora's box. A recent report on the make-up of modern Britain, also the work of Policy Exchange, implies that crude measures would alienate for good the very communities to whom the Tories should be appealing.

For instance, most minority households have more children than their white counterparts. Any ceiling on the numbers of children eligible for benefit, especially one set too low, would therefore risk alienating a section of the population that is growing larger and richer. Since 40 per cent of black people live in social housing, abolishing housing benefit for the under 25s would have a disproportionate effect on another section of the populace whose potential backing Mr Cameron would forfeit at his peril.

Too bad, hard-liners may decide. In their argument, trying to win back Ukip deserters through harsh curbs on welfare and immigration is a far more useful electoral ploy than blandishments to burgeoning ethnic minorities, of whom only 16 per cent voted Tory in 2010. In a sign that even this woeful endorsement may decline, anecdotal evidence suggests the Government's failure to condemn the Israeli bombardment of Gaza is estranging Muslim voters in key Tory seats.

Should the PM continue to offend such powerful groupings (Muslims alone increased from three to 4.8 per cent of the population in the first decade of this century), he will find himself on a short cut to oblivion.[9]

The debate on how best to ensure that religious extremism does not generate terrorism takes place in the context of another one: how to integrate immigrants into British society – secular democracy, freedom of conscience, tolerance and equality of everyone before the law.

The number of immigrants coming to this country increased enormously when Tony Blair relaxed the rules restricting entry. Many of the new immigrants were from Pakistan and Bangladesh. They went into communities in Britain that had been settled and shaped by people who came from the same area, sometimes the same village, as they did.

It is perfectly reasonable that immigrants, arriving in a strange land whose values and even language they did not fully understand, should prefer to be with people who are similar to them and who share their own language and values. But the effect of that preference is to create 'diaspora' communities that do not integrate or adapt to the values of the new society.

Sir Paul Collier, a professor of development economics at Oxford University, has produced a model that shows that it inevitably becomes a self-reinforcing process: each diaspora community gets ever more entrenched in reproducing the values of the society from which the migrants to it come, which in turn attracts more migrants from that society to it, which then ensures that it is less integrated with the host society – and more attractive to the immigrants from the traditional society in Pakistan, India or wherever.

Professor Collier thinks that unless the state takes very definite steps to stop this process happening, it will continue more or less indefinitely, with the result that migrant communities become ever more alienated and remote from the society to which they are supposed to adapt.

That leads directly to the nightmare scenario: a Britain made up of mutually antagonistic 'monocultures' that do not trust each other, do not work together and do not share the values of secular democracy, freedom of conscience and equality of both sexes before the law.

State policy in Britain over the last two decades has fostered the formation of unintegrated diaspora communities: multiculturalism, which was for many years the dominant approach, encouraged communities to hold on to their own values – with the inevitable result that they have become more entrenched.[10]

For the 2015 general election, the Labour Party had six pledges, the fourth of which was *Controls on Immigration*.[11] This was opposed by three members of the shadow cabinet, all of whom are either of immigrant or mixed-race stock, namely Chuka Umunna (Nigerian, Streatham), Sadiq Khan (Asian, Tooting) and Diane Abbott (African, Hackney North and Stoke Newington), the last of whom tweeted:

This shameful mug is an embarrassment. But the real problem is that immigration controls are one of our five pledges at all.

In the spring of 2015, Ione Wells[12] waived her right to anonymity by writing about being sexually assaulted … by a seventeen-year-old[13] who turned out to be a Somali who had been here for ten years. The story was followed by an article[14] by another young woman[15] who was similarly attacked in 1982. She had (then) written a piece in the *Guardian*, stating her attacker was black and speculated on why young men of that community were so violent; she was reported to the 'Race Today Collective'. She concluded her (present) article with:

But it is sad that [Ione Wells] she has learned, as I did, that life in England is frequently about conflict, that walking home alone in London can be a very dangerous thing to do, and much worse than that, attacks on young women may sometimes be political, not just rampant lust but a by-product of ethnic conflict.

Such ethnic conflict can be extremely long lasting:

> 'Carreira and Onambwe, but also Lucio Lara – they were not genuine Angolans, you know.'
> 'Genuine?'
> 'They were not Angolans of origin,' he says.
> 'But they were born in Angola, right?'
> Julio looks to Tito, who looks agitated. 'Listen!' says Tito. 'There were cultural differences, cultural problems. They came from Portuguese families.'
> 'But I've read that Lara's father was a mestico [mixed blood] so possibly the son of a black Angolan mother or father.'
> 'Those three were all born in Angola, it's true,' says Tito, 'but their parents were not of Angolan origin so they were not Angolans by origin ...'[16]

Notes: *F is for fissiparous*

1. The ninth paragraph of the abstract of the Report of the House of Lords.

2. Lord Tebbit, September 2013.

3. BAPIO. And *see* U is for unintended consequences.

4. *See* note 2 to A is for African, Asian and alien.

5. In April 2016 Tanveer Ahmed travelled from Bradford to Glasgow to kill Asad Shah an Ahmadiyya Muslim and a few days later issued this "explanation" through his solicitor "This has happened for one reason and no other issues and no other intentions. Asad Shah disrespected the messenger of Islam, the Prophet Muhammad, peace be upon him."

6. *I feel like a stranger where I live* by Jane Kelly, *The Daily Telegraph*, January 2013. The article included 'It seems that almost overnight it's changed from Acton Vale into Acton Veil'.

7. Member of Parliament since 1987, latterly for Bradford West.

8. *See* H is for hegemony as to the level of Muslim domination of Savile Town, Dewsbury. Dewsbury is the home town of 'Britain's youngest suicide bomber', Talha Asmal, the 7/7 bomber Mohammed Sidique Khan, and of Lady Sayeeda Warsi.

9. *Upsetting minorities will put the PM on a short cut to oblivion* by Mary Riddell, *The Daily Telegraph*, August 2014.

10. *We can't afford the threat of Islamism* by Alasdair Palmer, *The Daily Telegraph*, June 2014. The article 'produced' letters to a newspaper.

From William Pender:

> Alasdair Palmer's penetrating and far-sighted article highlights the growing threat to Britain's internal security from radicalised British nationals, and the Government's reluctance to do anything about it for fear of being accused of xenophobia. This astonishing situation has come about for three reasons.
>
> First, Britain retreated from the principle that immigration should serve the interests of the host country first.
>
> Successive governments did not anticipate that when groups of distant cultural and political traditions arrive in significant numbers, more than merely expressing an ethnic diversity (through festivals or restaurants, for example), they are likely to establish their communities as separate cultural-political entities.
>
> Secondly, the government tried to turn this liability into an asset by promoting multiculturalism. It stopped ascribing any value to integration and assimilation, and began flirting with the notion that host countries are only political frameworks for various co-existing cultures.
>
> Finally, rendering unto Caesar what is Caesar's, and unto God what is God's, is an alien concept in fundamentalist Islam. It considers everything to belong to God and does not allow a person's citizenship to command a higher loyalty than his faith.
>
> When Britain no longer regards itself as a distinct culture with its own culture but as a clean slate for anyone to write on, there will be those ready with their own texts, including some that are ominous.

From Michael Willis:

> Alasdair Palmer's article on Islamic extremism eloquently sums up many of the factors that determine the future of our country as it is affected by mass immigration. But he misses one important factor in the debate: the demographic implications of some immigrant communities having large families.
>
> While the present Government may be able to limit the 'Islamist threat', future governments may not, given that they could be comprised mainly of immigrants or their descendants. They will be able to impose whatever culture they wish, leaving those with 'British values' as an isolated minority culture. Perhaps this is a 'taboo' subject, but it is crucial nevertheless.

11. The other four were: *A strong economic foundation; Higher living standards for working families; An NHS with the time to care; A Country where the next generation can do better than the last*; and *Homes to buy and action on rents.*

The Green Party came up with its own mug – *Standing up for migrants.*

12. A student of twenty who wrote about her attack in the university paper … from where it went national.

13. Being less than eighteen, his name was not published. He was sentenced to two years, meaning that after a year he will be out.

In 1996, one of the Swedish government's own agencies…..said that male immigrants were 23 times more likely to commit rape than the average….

> Attempts to explain these problems as the outcome of sex ratio imbalances have foundered. Similar concerns have arisen in countries and in years where no such imbalance existed – in the UK, and in Germany, Holland and Finland.

(From *Race and Faith: The Deafening Silence* by Trevor Phillips.)

14. *Victim Status or Shame sex, violence and race in 1980s London – and today* by Jane Kelly, *The Spectator*, May 2015.

15. Jane Kelly and *see* note 5 above and 27 to H is for hegemony.

16. *In the Name of the People* by Lara Pawson, published in 2014 by I.B. Tauris. It is about 'Angola's Forgotten Massacre' – on 27 May 1977 – when 'thousands if not tens of thousands' were killed. The extract illustrates that, anyway in Angola, although the Portuguese had been there for hundreds of years, Portuguese settlement goes back to the sixteenth century, the non-indigenous remain culturally different, despite intermarrying and/or being resident for decades or even generations.

And **F** is for flavour

A flavour of where we are – the amount of immigration, the cost, and the pervasiveness of the race industry – is shown by a parliamentary question[1] and what followed. Lord Crisp[2] asked how many executive directors of nursing in the National Health Service were of black or minority ethnic background. Earl Howe[3] – data from September 2012 – estimated that there were 195 nursing directors. Of those, five, representing 3%, identified themselves as being from a black or minority ethnic background and continued

> The government recognises that there needs to be better progress in promoting talented BME nurses to senior and influential positions. Last month, NHS England launched a coaching and mentoring scheme, and it is currently working on a strategy alongside the chief nursing officer's Black and Minority Ethnic Advisory Group.

Lord Crisp:

> My Lords, I thank the noble Earl for that detailed response, and I am pleased to know NHS England is taking some steps on this. This is a hidden problem with fewer than 3% of nursing directors coming from black and minority ethnic backgrounds. This underrepresentation, which is mirrored elsewhere in the NHS, is particularly important because it affects morale, and staff morale in turn, as noble Lords will know, inevitably affects patient care and outcomes. In other words, this is a health issue and not just an equal opportunities one. Will the Minister say a bit more about his plans to deal with this problem and, crucially, whether he will arrange for progress to be monitored and reported publicly by the Care Quality Commission, the Equality and Human Rights Commission or some other independent body?

Earl Howe:

> My Lords, I fully agree with the noble Lord about the importance of this issue. A strong focus on equality and diversity is essential to create services and workplaces that are equitable and where everyone feels that they count. The position at present is highly unsatisfactory. The Chief Nursing Officer has personally assured me that this is a priority for her, and she is working with BME nurse leaders to address how to support BME nurses to prepare themselves for promotion. Forty-six million pounds have been invested at the NHS Leadership Academy in schemes on leadership development being led by the Chief Nursing Officer. At last year's BME nursing conference, she made a public commitment to renew efforts to develop BME nurses more effectively, and that will include monitoring.

Lord Mawhinney:

> My Lords, what figure, set by the Government or Public Health England, would constitute a success for the strategy that my noble friend has just outlined?

Earl Howe:

> We have to be a little careful about doing anything that appears to look like positive discrimination or setting quotas, because we stray into areas of dubious legality if we do that. Having said that, as I have indicated, the priority of the Chief Nursing Officer is extremely clear and substantial resources have been put behind this. I pay tribute to the work that the noble Lord, Lord Crisp, did when he was NHS Chief Executive. We have picked up a lot of the ideas that he promoted at that time. I would be very disappointed if there were not progress within a few years but one has to set a realistic timetable.

Lord Hunt of Kings Heath:

> My Lords, I refer my noble Lords to my health interests. One answer to the question raised by the noble Lord, Lord Mawhinney, would be to point out that 18% of the NHS workforce in England is from a BME background and 14% of the population of England is from a BME background. As 2.6% of nursing directors comes from a BME background, that shows that there is a very long way to go. Is the Minister confident that NHS England is acting in accordance with the Equality Act? If he is not confident, what is he going to do about it?

Earl Howe:

> My Lords, just to correct the noble Lord, the latest figure I have from 2012 is that the total ethnic minority groups in nursing, midwifery and health visitors comprise 19.7% of the workforce. That underscores the basic point that he made. One cannot aspire to 19.7% of those ethnic nurses becoming nurse leaders because there is only a limited number of leadership posts. However, we are clear that this should be a priority for the NHS. The answer to the noble Lord's second question is that the Equality and Diversity Council has published some refreshed guidelines. One of its goals is to have a representative and supportive workforce throughout the NHS. It is putting that in train by asking NHS organisations to monitor their equality performance jointly with their patients, communities and staff.

Baroness Brinton:

> My Lords, ten years ago, the noble Lord, Lord Crisp, described the NHS as being snow-capped – that is, all white at the top. Since his departure as Chief Executive of the NHS in 2005, there are now fewer leaders from visibly different backgrounds and, as we have heard, pitifully few executive directors of nursing. What are the government doing to ensure that this matter is kept at the top of the agenda and to assure us that we will hear about the success of the programme as it continues?

Earl Howe:

> My Lords, I have already mentioned some of the initiatives mentioned that are in train. However, I can tell my noble friend that, within the NHS Leadership Academy, there are two programmes specifically for nurses and midwives that map to foundation, mid and executive level leadership development. There is the front-line leadership programme which is for staff who have leadership responsibilities – for example, ward sisters and nurses working in primary care. We expect 6,000 nurses and midwives to participate in that programme in the first year. There is also the senior operational leaders programme which provides senior nursing clinicians with an opportunity to enhance their leadership skills.

Baroness Manzoor:

> My Lords, a web audit found that only 80 NHS trusts publish annual staff data broken down by ethnicity. Will the Minister reassure the House that all NHS trusts meet their obligations under the Race Relations Act and that all workforce issues faced by black and minority staff are identified?

Earl Howe:

> My noble friend raises a crucial issue about transparency. I can assure her that this is squarely within the sights of the Chief Nursing Officer and her advisory group.

Notes: *F is for flavour*

1. House of Lords on 10 February 2014. (With hereditaries limited to *c*.90, of the order of five sixths of those who can vote in the House of Lords are nominees – nominees of the present and preceding governments.)

2. Lord Crisp. In 2000 he was appointed chief executive of the NHS and Permanent Secretary at the Department of Health and ennobled in 2006.

3. Earl Howe (and *see* note 5 of A is for African, Asian and alien).

G is for joined-up government – or not

Government that has no foresight and/or is not joined up has led to a situation whereby millions from abroad are allowed in without thought as to the extra load on housing, midwifery, schools and the extra loading of rail and road infrastructure.

... Or take the proposed three million new houses. The principal reason for the shortage of housing is the break up of families. But that accounts for only two thirds of the requirement. The other million are needed for immigrants.

A revealing government response to a question from James Clappison, Conservative MP for Hertsmere, last week showed how hopelessly wrong past assessments of the likely impact of net immigration upon housing demand has been. In doing so the answer demonstrated conclusively that the government simply had no idea what it was doing.

It indicated that not long after Labour came to power, Government actuaries – using household projections from 1996 – estimated that a quarter of the 150,000 additional households that would be formed each year between 2001 and 2021 – i.e. 38,000 – would be attributable to net migration into England. By March of this year, the actuarial projection, based on 2004 figures, was that one third of the extra 223,000 households that would be formed annually by 2026 – i.e. 73,000 – would be attributable to immigration.

In other words, the housing requirement caused by immigration to England is twice what was predicted when Labour took office just 10 years ago.[1]

The numbers related to immigration are astonishing. In excess of 600,000 Eastern Europeans have arrived since their countries acceded to the European Union. In London last year, 53 per cent of births were to mothers who were not born in Britain; across England and Wales it was 22 per cent. It does not take a genius to work out that in 18 years, the capital's adult population will be more diverse than now. Even modest population projections, from the Government's own actuary, put the UK population up seven million at 67 million by 2013. Others say it is an underestimate. Try imagining six Birminghams, or the combined population of Wales and Scotland landing on us in the decades ahead and ask yourself if Britain's housing market, transport network, education system and the NHS are built to cope. It is at this point that some idiots of the liberal-Left start using the "R" word to shut down rational discussion. Race has nothing to do with it: this. is about the impracticality of what the Government proposes to let happen because it has lost any sense of how to stop, slow or manage it.[2]

At the heart of [the fact that one in seven parents in England likely to be denied their first choice for their child's primary school] lies denial about the ongoing surge in immigration. The concerns, so widely felt throughout the country, were never driven by racism or xenophobia. It was more about the supply of GP clinics, houses or school places. Under the last government, a refusal to talk frankly about immigration mutated into a failure to consider its implications. Of the children who enrol in primary school this September [2012], one in four will have a foreign-born mother ... The implications of our multilingual baby boom were known about for years, yet preparations were not made.[3]

By the next election some 240,000 places will be needed, but free schools are expected to deliver just 8,000. The next few years will be bulge years.

Mr Gove had not envisaged this when he took over at Education almost three years ago. Officials had not, then, realised that the effect of mass migration in the Labour years would mean a boom in primary school pupils. A quarter of all children under the age of six have foreign-born mothers ...[4]

The last projections showed the population – now around 64 million – increasing to more than 70 million within 12 years. Yet during the 1970s planning was predicated upon a static population. Even as recently as 15 years ago, projections were anticipating that the 64 million would not be achieved until 2031, whereupon it would fall. In fact the population has grown by eight million since 1980 and another 10 million will be added in the next 25 years. Is it any surprise we have too few houses, schools, hospitals and trains to cope?[5]

But the penny is beginning to drop:

- [T]he volume of immigrants may pose serious infrastructure issues.[6]

- Uncontrolled mass immigration can force wages down and house prices up and put pressure on social cohesion and public services. And let me be clear – it can also cause displacement in the labour market.[7]

- Undoubtedly there are certain parts of the country where there has been a huge influx of people. If you don't put the right sort of infrastructure, you don't put the schools and hospitals people get fed up with it.[8]

- We haven't got the schools, we haven't got the hospitals, we haven't got the housing, we haven't got the roads.[9]

Notes: *G is for joined-up government – or not*

1. *Counting the cost of immigration* by Philip Johnston, *The Daily Telegraph*, July 2007.

2. *Like it or not, we must face up to the truth on immigration* by Iain Martin, *The Daily Telegraph*, August 2007.

3. *David Cameron should beware the march of the angry mothers* by Fraser Nelson, *The Daily Telegraph*, April 2012.

4. *Will Michael Gove's schools revolution be just another false start?* by Fraser Nelson, *The Daily Telegraph*, April 2013.

5. *While migrants cross Europe, our population booms* or *We are watching the death of open frontiers in Europe* by Philip Johnston, *The Daily Telegraph*, October 2015.

6. Dominic Grieve QC (Attorney General, MP for Beaconsfield since 1997), November 2013.

7. James Brokenshire (Immigration Minister), March 2014.

8. Anna Soubry (MP for Broxtowe, a defence minister), June 2014.

9. Chris Grayling (MP for Epsom & Ewell since 2001, leader of the House of Commons since 2015), April 2016.

H is for Hackney

The growth of Turkish and Kurdish organised crime closely linked with heroin importation, during the 1990s brought a renewed opportunity for young people in deprived areas to earn a living through the drugs trade. As time progressed, many of the Hackney gangs became heavily involved in controlling local drug markets and equally this gave rise to numerous estate based gangs. There is also a Vietnamese community in South Hackney, an area where organised Asian criminality has taken place, which harbours criminals involved in mass production of cannabis since the turn of the millennium. Cannabis factory worker Khach Nguyen was left for dead on the Frampton Park estate in 2008 after crossing a gang boss.

Nguyen and his chauffer Phuc Tran were go-betweens in a drug deal set up to take place near a McDonalds in Sutton, Greater London. The drug deal involved the sale of £30,000 worth of cannabis. However, the transaction did not materialise as planned and Nguyen and Tran were robbed of the drugs at gunpoint, and naturally they were held responsible by the other members of what was described as a well –organised drugs gang. Nguyen took more responsibility as it was he who was said to have arranged the botched deal. To make good the robbery it was expected that he would stump up the £30,000. It wasn't to be as simple as that and after reporting to the boss Hoc Kim Khoa, he and other members of the gang decided that Nhuyen and Tran had probably stolen the cannabis, or staged or lied about the robbery. Nguyen and Tran were kidnapped, put into a car and driven to a remote farmhouse in a remote area near Horley by Gatwick Airport.

The farmhouse had been rented out earlier that month by the gang. It was here that Nguyen suffered a severe beating being kicked and stamped on by members of the gang in what was described as prolonged physical violence. Tran was a witness to the violence. Following the severe assault Nguyen and Tran were taken back to a house in Loddiges Road, South Hackney in the early hours of July 30th 2008. Emergency services were called on their return however such were Nguyen's injuries that no medical care could have saved him. Hung Mai, Hoc Kim Khoa, Giang Vu and Dioc Vu, all of no fixed address along with Tuam Pham of Watford and Dunt Dinh of Plumstead all denied charges of murder, false imprisonment and kidnap. They were convicted following a six-week trial at the Old Bailey.

... A Vietnamese street gang existed in Hackney borough that was known as VOB (Viets Over Bitches) ...

Four loud bangs were heard. One bullet smashed into a windscreen. Another whizzed by the head of a 10-year-old boy on a bike. Young Jadie Brissett, 18, was hit twice. A bullet smashed into his upper left thigh, and a shotgun blasted a two-inch hole in his chest. Despite his wounds, he clambered over a fence, and finally collapsed and died next to some dustbins. The cycle of violence had started.

Brissett was popular. His only conviction involved possessing cannabis. That same evening his friends and relatives started tracking down those they believed responsible. The resulting retaliation caused more bloodshed and a criminal investigation that culminated in an estimated £5m in police and court costs.

The boy's murder made headlines only in east London. It was barely worth national attention with 'black-on-black' gun murders in the capital taking place every few weeks. Although black people make up around 10% of London's population, they are involved in a staggering 70% of the city's shooting incidents. The same sort of figures are reported from the country's other main areas plagued by gun crime and gang feuds – Manchester, Nottingham, the West Midlands and Bristol. Generally, only those involving children or young women make headlines. Recent cases include the murder of seven-year-old Toni-Ann Byfield shot with her drug-dealing father in his London bedsit: and the teenage girls Letisha Shakespeare and Charlene Ellis, killed in crossfire at a New Year party in Birmingham. In a bizarre murder in 2002, two men were killed by the same bullet at another New Year party in east London. The bullet passed through the neck of the first man DJ Ashley Kenton, went through a wall and into the head of the second man, Wayne Mowatt.

Guns started to be increasingly used in our cities during the 1980s; many of the shootings and murders were associated with turf wars including the spread of crack cocaine. At the time, and during the next decade, Jamaicans were involved in most of the cases and Scotland Yard's response was slow – cynical even. Who cared if black drug dealers were killing each other?

Two events changed that: the outcry over the murder by white racists of the black teenager Stephen Lawrence; and a series of horrific murders, prompting Scotland Yard to attempt to build bridges with the wider black community. One woman was shot dead in front of her two children. Another was tied to a chair, tortured, and then shot in the head, to be found by her three children the next day. With nobody knowing where the gang was going to strike next, activists who had previously branded police racist demanded action from Scotland Yard. Welcoming the opportunity, the Metropolitan Police piled money and resources into the investigation, and for the first time black community leaders began helping the police. The gang was caught in what turned out to be a landmark case leading to Scotland Yard creating Operation Trident, the branch dealing only with black shootings and murders. Such crime, acknowledges the Metropolitan commissioner, Sir Ian Blair, represents the biggest problem after terrorism.

With 360 detectives and civilian staff, Trident has an annual budget of more than £23m, aided by community groups in 'hot-spot' London boroughs. It's an alien world for many Trident detectives. One experienced sergeant vented his frustration after giving evidence in a murder case. The defendant 'made the sign of a gun with his fingers and mouthed mum'. He was threatening to kill my mother, he says. 'I just can't understand the mentality. I live outside London in a nice area. My friends and neighbours know I'm a cop, but they simply cannot comprehend what we're dealing with. When I leave work, it's like I'm going to a different planet.'

Until 2000, most gun crime was being committed by young men from Jamaica. Now British-born blacks are estimated to be involved in 80% of black-on-black gun crime. All of those involved in Brissett's murder and its violent aftermath were born in London and brought up by their mothers. With their fathers either in prison or with other women, they had no positive male role models. All had underachieved at school, had few if any qualifications and had no job. They saw the only way of getting money, girls and respect was through drug-dealing or robbery-often both.[1]

Notes: *H is for Hackney*

1. This item was originally not much more than the last paragraph which was to be under C is for crime (at black on black) but on checking, the article containing it came up – under *londonstreetgangs*. The author is not apparent save that the first half or so of what is quoted appears to be from a *Sunday Times* investigation of 25 September 2005.

And **H** is for Abu Hamza

Abu Hamza began life in Egypt in 1958 as Mustafa Kamel Mustafa. He entered this country as a student. He later lost both hands and an eye (in either Afghanistan or Pakistan); he has a prosthetic hook, and is so known as 'Hook'. In 2006, he was jailed for inciting murder and hate speeches outside the Finsbury Park Mosque. In 2012, after years of legal battle, he was extradited to the USA on charges as to hostage-taking in Yemen and trying to set up a terrorist training camp in Oregon; in 2014, he was found guilty on eleven charges.

Abu Hamza has eight children who include:

- Mohammed, who was jailed for plotting to blow up British tourists.

- Hamza and Mohamed, who, with their father's stepson, Mohssin Ghailam, were convicted in 2009 for their part in a vehicle scam. (As part of the same enterprise, Mohammed Chiadmi and his brother Abdul plus Khalid Jebari and Hamza Mrimou were also convicted.)

- Yasser, who was convicted in 2010 for violent disorder, namely throwing sticks at police and using a police shield, all the time wearing a scarf, which was presumably to hide his identity as he also, later, changed his clothing before being arrested later that same day; he (already) had two convictions for dishonesty.

- Imran, who when on trial in 2012 declared, 'I am not a thief. I am not an armed robber' and 'I feel that this is a plot against my father, myself and my family' and 'Me and my family have been subjected to a witch hunt' and his father's 'fight for innocent people and their beliefs … would go on'. The trial was as to whether a gang used a gun and a sledgehammer in an attack on a jeweller's in Kings Lynn. He was convicted and sentenced to eleven years. The other gang members were Johnathon Abdul, Ossama Hamed and Ahmed Ahmed.

One of Abu Hamza's daughters-in-law is CS.[1] She is from Morocco. On the basis of being married to a British citizen, she was issued with a visa. CS visited her father-in-law in Belmarsh (high-security prison; he had completed his sentence but continued to be held pending an outcome to the USA request for his extradition). On her visit in late 2010, it was found that she had in her jeans pocket, underneath her Islamic dress, a SIM card. In July 2011, there was registered the birth of CS's child. In 2012, CS was convicted for taking a prohibited article into a prison and sentenced to twelve months' imprisonment. Within three weeks she got to the Court of Appeal, before which she appeared with all of her face, save her eyes, covered. She claimed she had put the SIM card into her pocket some days before seeing her father-in-law and forgotten it; the court pointed out that the jury had not believed her. She prayed in aid against her imprisonment the care of her one-year-old child but the court commented that arrangements had obviously been made.

In August 2012 CS was told that upon completion of her sentence (because it was for not less than a year) she would be deported. However, CS then applied for asylum and upon that being rejected appealed to the Immigration and Asylum Tribunal, which found that deportation would be a breach of Article 8 of the Human Rights Act. The Home Office appealed to the Upper Tribunal, which asked the European Court of Justice whether deporting CS would deprive a European-Union-citizen child of enjoyment of his rights; in 2016 the advocate general issued his opinion that deportation of CS would be such a breach.

Notes: *H is for Abu Hamza*

1. The daughter-in-law is referred to by her initials because a court decision, after that of the Court of Appeal, ordered such anonymity. This seems to be pointless – until early 2016, when the advocate general's opinion was publicised (and parliamentary privilege was used), drafts of this book stated CS's full name, and an internet search of Abu Hamza will name the offending daughter-in-law.

And **H** is for hegemony[1]

The (hegemony of) thinking that immigration is good and to question it is racist (and thus wrong) and those who think or even worse say there is a downside to immigration are evil or at least ill; the hegemony of the right way to think, the way of thinking of the bien pensant, of the commentariat, of the metropolitan elite, is that foreigners are cleverer, are better educated and trained and work harder so we are advantaged to have them here; diversity and multiculturalism are good; the hegemony of the thinking that any requirement for assimilation is contrary to the immigrant's human rights. And if one doesn't like immigration, or diversity or multiculturalism, one has to 'like it or lump it'.[2]

> So uncongenial was Fraser's message to all right-thinking Britons that 60 publishers to whom he sent the book turned it down. In a country that publishes more than 10,000 books monthly, not many of which are imperishable masterpieces, there was no room for what it said, though it would take no great acumen to see its commercial possibilities in a country crowded with crime victims. So great was the pressure of the orthodoxy now weighing on the minds of the British intelligentsia that Fraser might as well have gone to Mecca and said that there is no God and that Mohammed was not His prophet. Of course, no publisher actually told him that what he said was unacceptable or unsayable in

public: his book merely did not 'fit the list' of any publisher. He was the victim of British publishing's equivalent of Mafia omerta.

Fortunately, he did not give up, as he sometimes thought of doing. The 61st publisher to whom he sent the book accepted it. I mean no disrespect to her judgment when I say that it was her personal situation that distinguished her from her fellow publishers: for her husband's son by a previous marriage had not long before been murdered in the street, stabbed by a drug-dealing Jamaican immigrant, aged 20, who had not been deported despite his criminal record but instead allowed to stay in the country as if he were a national treasure to be at all costs cherished and nurtured. Indeed, in court his lawyer presented him as an unemployed painter and decorator, the victim of racial prejudice (a mitigating circumstance, of course), a view that the prosecution did not challenge, even though the killer had somehow managed alchemically to transmute his unemployment benefits into a new convertible costing £34,000.[3]

More insidious yet was the great 'middle ground' confidence trick ... This proceeds by, first, insisting that political choices are necessarily arranged along a one-dimensional spectrum from left to right. Secondly, anything near the ends of the spectrum is called 'extreme' – and by implication weird and mad – and anything in the middle is correspondingly 'moderate' – and by implication reasonable and sane. The third step is to stipulate that support for [immigration] is in the middle ground – and therefore, QED, moderate, sensible, sane – so right.[4]

The reason the BBC can never talk honestly about the immigration problem, in other words, is that it is largely responsible for shaping the cultural and dialectical mindset that made it possible.

That would explain another of the programme's sleights of hand – the way it concluded by offering a false dichotomy, between continued economic growth on the one hand and (relative) cultural homogeneity on the other. Even Nigel Farage was co-opted into conceding this point, saying that he would prefer Britons to have lower average incomes if that was the price to be paid for less immigration. (You wonder how much else of what he said, rather less convenient to the BBC's narrative, was left on the cutting-room floor. Acres, I'm guessing.)

But this just isn't true. As the 2008 House of Lords Economic Affairs Committee report on the Economic Impact of Immigration found, 'immigration has very small impacts on GDP per capita'. Even the NIESR – one of the BBC's favourite left leaning think tanks – agreed in 2011 that the impact of eight Eastern European countries joining the EU between 2004 and 2009 would have a 'negligible' long-term impact on UK GDP per capita.

So all this overcrowding, all this destruction of social cohesion, all this unwelcome pressure on our schools, hospitals and transport infrastructure, all this dilution of what used to be our national identity has been inflicted on us, by our remote political class, against our wishes, to no useful purpose whatsoever. What a fantastically interesting subject for a documentary that would be. Now I wonder who is going to make it.[5]

Whatever else was already changing, that day[6] signalled a cataclysmic shift of relationships in this town. Ultimately both white and Asian communities alike would be failed by politicians and police, but mostly by the liberal zealots of the race industry. Their agenda permeates every level of public life, forbids criticism and stifles debate. The effect has been to create a sense of absolute preference for a migrant culture, and the alienation of the host population. People count the cost of that on a daily basis. This town is on its knees both economically and socially – and it pays too high a price in human lives.[6.1]

By far the majority of perpetrators were described as 'Asian' by victims, yet throughout the entire period, councillors did not engage directly with the Pakistani-heritage community to discuss how best they could jointly address the issue. Some councillors seemed to think it was a one-off problem, which they hoped would go away. Several staff described their nervousness about identifying the ethnic origin of perpetrators for fear of being thought racist; others remembered clear direction from their managers not to do so.[7]

In March 2015, Channel 4 broadcast a programme about the 1964 parliamentary election in Smethwick (the constituency where and the election when the electorate was warned that a vote for Labour would mean an immigrant as one's neighbour). A review of the programme concluded with 'Today Smethwick is multicultural ...', the inference being that such is an improvement.

The programme's most common term was 'white community' even though, rather than there then being a 'white community', the constituency was white. Today the term is correct:

With the exception of Smethwick, Sandwell towns have seen increases in the proportion of residents in all Minority Ethnic groups, and a contrasting decline in the White British group since 2001. The White British population in Smethwick has fallen from 54.6% in 2001 to 37.9% in 2011. There has also been a decrease in the proportions of Indian and Black Caribbean residents in the town, and the Indian population has fallen in actual numbers (albeit a small decrease at – 81). However, there has been a contrasting increase in the Pakistani population in Smethwick town (from 8.3% in 2001 to 12.6% in 2011, an increase of +2,904 in number).[8]

And yet, when in 2007, Nigel Hastilow, the Conservative Party candidate for Halesowen and Rowley Regis, wrote in the *Birmingham Post*,

> When you ask most people in the Black Country what the single biggest problem facing the country is, most say immigration.

> Many insist 'Enoch Powell was right'. Enoch, once MP for Wolverhampton South-West was sacked from the Conservative front bench and marginalised politically for his 1968 'rivers of blood' speech, warning that uncontrolled immigration would change our country irrevocably.

> He was right. It has changed dramatically.

he had to 'resign'.[9]

This hegemony manifests itself in

- an absence of immigrants being described as a loss:

> [Grimsby] was once the liveliest, gutsiest fishing port in Europe. Now it does a bit of processing when the Icelanders pass on stuff they're too busy to handle. It suffers all the dull litany of deprivation: high youth unemployment, lack of investment, worn-out infrastructure, under-achievement, bad education, and is one of the least diverse and pasty white pockets of England.[10]

- in diversity being 'a good thing', so

> Welcome to Redbridge – find more about the borough.
> - o Redbridge is an outer London Borough situated ...
> - o Known as the 'leafy' suburb, Redbridge enjoys one of the best living environments in London
> - o Redbridge has a thriving, vibrant multi-cultural community ...
> - o Redbridge is the fourth most diverse borough[11] in the country and approximately 66 per cent of its population hail from a minority ethnic background ...[12]

- in diversity crowding out all else, and so the strapline of Balham Baptist Church[13] is not prayer or repentance or redemption, or even baptism, but 'Where diversity matters'

- in having to apologise if the truth is spoken[14]

- in failing to enforce the law[15]

- in racial profiling being beyond the pale, despite the experience of

Derby, Rochdale, Rotherham (and more), and so

In her 2006 report [Dr Heal] stated that 'it is believed by a number of workers that one of the difficulties that prevent this issue of Child Sexual Exploitation being dealt with effectively is the ethnicity of the main perpetrators'.

She also reported in 2006 that young people in Rotherham believed at that time that the Police dared not act against Asian youths for fear of allegations of racism. This perception was echoed at the present time by some young people we met during the Inquiry, but was not supported by specific examples.

Several people interviewed expressed the general view that ethnic considerations had influenced the policy response of the Council and the Police, rather than in individual cases. One example was given by the Risky Business Project Manager (1997–2012) who reported that she was told not to refer to the ethnic origins of perpetrators when carrying out training. Other staff in children's social care said that when writing reports on CSE cases, they were advised by their managers to be cautious about referring to the ethnicity of the perpetrators.[16]

- in the following

Because when immigration is too high, when the pace of change is too fast, it's impossible to build a cohesive society. It's difficult for schools and core infrastructure like housing and transport to cope. And we know that for people in low-paid jobs, wages are forced down even further while some people are forced out of work altogether.

… not all of the consequences can be managed, and doing so for many of them comes at a high price. We need to build 210,000 new homes every year to deal with rising demand. We need to find 900,000 new school places by 2024. And there are thousands of people who have been forced out of the labour market, still unable to find a job.[17]

being described as 'lurching Rightwards to deliver an unpleasant anti-migrant diatribe' and 'migrant bashing'[18]

- in 'concerns about upsetting community cohesion' obstructing investigation of criminal depravity[19]

- and when eleven students were to be arrested upon suspicion of terrorism, one of the authorities' principal concerns was 'Community Impact, Engagement and Reassurance' even though ten of the eleven were foreigners here on student visas[20]

159

- in deference to the non-indigenous – despite the BBC's tendency to repeats, it won't show *It Ain't Half Hot Mum* but it produces (for UK viewers) *Rastamouse*

- in a primary school having a sign of 'Welcome' on the outside, with such word in English, Arabic and Bangla[21]

- in 'The main pressure police have is being called institutionally racist if they highlight a trend like this. There is a fantastic reluctance to be absolutely straight because some people might take offence'[22]

- in deference to diversity

    The alleged perpetrators are of Asian origin and the victims are white this is the factuality of these cases alone: nothing more can be drawn from that … Great care will be taken in drafting this report to ensure that its findings embrace Rotherham's qualities of diversity. It is imperative that suggestions of a wider cultural phenomenon are avoided …[23]

    I was aware that as a white person I had to be sensitive to the feelings of people of all races and backgrounds, both clinically and with professionals. Maybe some social workers felt they knew more about black children than I did.[24]

- in having to obscure the truth

    You are certainly required, as a journalist, to point out, when reporting yet another repulsive incident of what has come to be called the 'grooming' and subsequent assault of underage white girls by Muslim men, that the majority of sexual offences against children in this country are carried out by lone white males of various religious denominations. The reason for this absurd caveat is simply crowd control – and also a wish on behalf of the spineless journalist to make clear that while Muslims can from time to time behave naughtily, we whitey Christians are even more naughty, really.

    Which is, in the case of sexual abuse against underage girls, deluding, because according to the 2001 census data only 2.7 per cent of the population of the UK is Muslim.[25]

- and simply in the indigenous being crowded out and/or forgotten, so

    One of the patients I see regularly as a voluntary hospital visitor, who has been in hospital for weeks, seems to be getting better. Still skeletally thin he is now sitting up and complaining. His problem is that he longs for a jacket potato with just butter. He hates beans. But he might as well ask for gravlax and dill. On the hospital menu, baked potatoes only come with baked beans.

> There are in fact a great many dishes on the long laminated menu card. You can have curried goat, ackee[26] and saltfish, Arabic halal, Asian halal and Asian vegan but no plain potato, ice cream, custard, diabetic desserts or anything freshly cooked.[27]

Ed Miliband, in 2011, one year after he became leader of the Labour Party, told its annual conference that his family were immigrants and said, 'My family hasn't sat under the same oak tree for the last 500 years.' Presumably, Mr Miliband thought his audience would be impressed that he was of immigrant stock – that was, he thought, a plus point; he thought those to whom he was speaking would think he was better for being of immigrant stock.[28]

In the spring of 2013, a respected columnist wrote:

> Most residents of Ipswich – a port town with a thousand-year history of trade, where the body of a thirteenth century African was recently exhumed – claim to feel inundated by foreigners. Yet Ipswich's immigrant population is only 12% of the total.[29]

('Only' is (defined as) single or very few in number; 12% is more than one in ten, is almost one in eight. In fact, the percentage of the general population that is 'immigrant' is more (*see* P is for population) so, arguably, if the immigrant population of Ipswich is 12%, the word 'only' is appropriate.)

> If you compare life in James Turner Street (Benefits Street's real name) today with the equivalent pre 1914, you will see some striking differences. One is family ... Another difference is work ... A third is race. In James Turner Street, a big group of Romanians, worried about their gangmaster, flits in and out. Africans, Asians, West Indians, probably outnumber whites. The cultural and religious uniformity that makes loyalty easier to build was overwhelming in 1914 and now it isn't. Diversity is the fact; indeed, it is the creed.[30]

> In 'Live from the Vatican – You're to be a cardinal' (Interview, February 15), Archbishop Vincent Nicholls, in discussing immigration, says: 'It would appear that no political party is prepared to speak in moderate terms about its beneficial effects. Fear is being fed for political gain.'

> He can't have seen the Second Reading of the Immigration Bill in the Lords on February 10, where speakers from all three major political parties spoke forcefully about the beneficial effect of immigration. The only speakers notable by their absence from the debate were the two Ukip peers.[31]

The preamble to the Immigration Bill, now Act, is:

> To make provision about immigration law; to limit, or otherwise make provision about, access to services, facilities and employment by reference to immigration status; to make provision about marriage and civil partnership involving certain foreign nationals; and for connected purposes.

The second reading of the Bill was moved in the House of Lords by Lord Taylor of Holbeach, the parliamentary Under-Secretary of State, Home Office, the first paragraph of whose speech was:

> My Lords, as a country we welcome the benefits migrants bring to our industries, educational institutions and communities. We know that most migrants are here lawfully and benefit our country, but some are not: they enter the country illegally, overstay their permission to be here, work illegally, undercutting the resident labour market, contribute to overcrowded housing, claim benefits and damage social cohesion.[32]

So the millions of migrants who have been given permission to be here – either by way of free movement throughout the EU or otherwise – do not, Lord Taylor of Holbeach believes, undercut resident labour, do not contribute to overcrowded housing, do not claim benefits and do not damage social cohesion; it is (only) the unnumbered illegal migrants who do so.

Andrew Young[33] was aged forty when he died on 7 November 2013. The day before, he remonstrated with Victor Ibitoye for bicycling on the pavement, outside Tesco Express in Charminster, Bournemouth, and was then punched by Ibitoye's friend, Lewis Gill, who (already) had convictions for handling stolen goods and robbery. Gill's mother is Sherron O'Hagan; Ibitoye's father has been described as from Nigeria; Gill's conviction was reported immediately by *Daily Guide: Ghana's Favourite Newspaper*. The 'story' also produced the following:

> Last week in London, a black thug was sentenced to four years – he will serve only two – for killing a sick white man with one punch. The judge said his intent was not to kill him. I beg to differ. Winding up and throwing a punch at someone who was not looking is called murder in my book. Boxers throw short punches because if they wind up and throw it, it will not land. It's called telegraphing. The thug in question wound up and punched a man half his size looking elsewhere. It would have been a miracle if the man had lived. The thug deserved ten years minimum. Just think what a white thug would have received had he cold cocked a small black man suffering from Asperger's syndrome? First and foremost, it would be called a hate crime, and no judge would dare not call it murder. Second degree, that is.[34]

All journalists experience this disparity. If we attack the EDL for being racist, fascist and pro-violence, we can do so with impunity, although we are not strictly accurate. If we make similar remarks about Islamist organisations, we will be accused of being racist ourselves. 'Human rights' will be thrown at us. We shall also – this has happened to me more than once – be subject to 'lawfare'. A blizzard of solicitors' letters claiming damages for imagined libels. Many powerful people in the Civil Service, local government, politics and the police, far from backing up our attacks on extremism, will tut-tut at our 'provocative' comments.

Much more important – from the point of view of the general public – you frequently find that Muslim groups like Tell Mama get taxpayers' money (though, in its case, this is now coming to an end). You discover that leading figures of respectable officialdom share conference platforms with dubious groups. You learn that Muslim charities with blatantly political aims and Islamist links have been let off lightly by the Charity Commission. And you notice that many bigwigs in Muslim groups are decorated with public honours. Fiyaz Mughal, for example, who runs Tell Mama, measuring anti-Muslim attacks, has an OBE. Obviously it would be half laughable, half disgusting, if activists of the EDL were indulged in this way; yet they are, in fact, less extreme than some of those Muslims who are.[35]

Notes: *H is for hegemony*

1. (With apologies to) Antonio Gramsci (1891–1937), who argued that capitalism keeps control (of the proletariat) not through force but by (the momentum of) the established way of thinking.

I am indebted to Nick Cohen for the following explanation of hegemony:

If it is to win next time, if indeed there is a next time, the SNP has to achieve what we old Marxists call 'hegemony': the cultural as well as the political domination of Scottish society.

To achieve hegemony, 'opinion formers' must assure the public that independence is the only way forward. Nationalism must become the common speak of Scottish life. If the opinion formers lack the required enthusiasm, the SNP must persuade them to think twice before speaking out.

(And so) opinion formers assure us that immigration is a good thing; the common speak is to the same effect; those who think otherwise must be persuaded to think twice before speaking out.

Language, indeed thought, is being limited to reflect the orthodoxy:

> Decent people are not only afraid of voicing certain thoughts, they are uncertain even if their right to think those thoughts.

That is from *Education and Race – an Alternative View* by Raymond Honeyford, which is reproduced in the next chapter but one. Therein Honeyford referred to Professor Honey, who (in an echo of Wittgenstein's 'the limits of my language are the limits of my world') wrote, 'language has the power to condition thought': and also to George Orwell. The following is from the appendix entitled *The Principles of Newspeak* to his *Nineteen Eighty-Four*:

> The purpose of Newspeak was not only to provide a medium of expression for the world-view and mental habits proper to the devotees of Ingsoc, but to make all other modes of thought impossible. It was intended that when Newspeak had been adopted once and for all and Oldspeak forgotten, a heretical thought – that is, a thought diverging from the principles of Ingsoc – should be literally unthinkable, at least so far as thought is dependent on words.

2. What Ed Miliband said, after becoming leader of the Labour Party in 2010, had been its answer to those who did not agree with its immigration policy: *see* note 30 to B is for betrayal.

3. 'Fraser' was David Fraser, who had been a probation officer and was the author of *A Land Fit for Criminals*, published in 2006 by The Book Guild.

The quoted paragraphs are from *Not with a Bang but a Whimper: The Politics & Culture of Decline,* by Theodore Dalrymple, published in 2009 by Monday Books.

4. This comes from a completely other context – the word 'immigration' is in italics and in square brackets because it has been substituted for another, but the thinking demonstrates the hegemony of the right way to think. The original, by Peter Jay, was in the foreword to *Guilty Men* by Peter Oborne and Frances Weaver (published by the Centre for Policy Studies in 2011) which showed that the right way to think was to be in favour of the EU and the euro and that to question such way of thinking was to be mad or at least bad.

An edited extract of that foreword was subsequently in *The Times*, under the heading *How Britain was betrayed to the Bonapartists*.

Guilty Men also included:

> [The BBC] allied itself with the left/liberal elite, and framed the debate in a way that the supporters of the Euro were bound to win. The methods used were insidious. BBC broadcasters tended to present the pro-Euro

position itself as centre-ground, thus defining even moderately euro-sceptic voices as extreme, meaning that they were defeated even before they had entered the debate.

The creation of the Euro was the most important financial story of the age, and the FT got it hopelessly wrong. It ceased to be a sober-minded reporter of financial affairs, becoming instead the enthusiastic propaganda arm of what was, at bottom, a political project.

'Ten more lessons' [to prevent being overwhelmed by the right way to think, the first being,] 'Conventional wisdom is very often wrong'.

[For the 'euro' substitute immigration, and for the 'FT' substitute *The Economist* and move to *No flood, after all* in note 29 below.]

This book is not about the euro, but Roger Bootle's *The Trouble with €urope* (*see* note 35 of B is for Betrayal) explains how 'People can drown in an intellectual consensus' –

The essential question is why so many clever and sophisticated people were so readily taken in ... my point is that it is plainly possible for many intelligent and well-meaning people to be thoroughly misled about the great issue of the day. People can drown in an intellectual consensus. Consensus views take on a life of their own and once entrenched, are tricky to shift. People can be led to believe what they want to believe, because it gives a comfortable view of the world and its future. Such intellectual bromides are like a drug and the addiction is very difficult to shake off.

5. *Truths and fallacies* or *'The Truth About Immigration' is anything but* by James Delingpole, *The Spectator*, January 2014, about the BBC programme *The Truth about Immigration*.

As to House of Lords' Report, (*see* E is for economics of immigration), where the complete sentence was 'The overall conclusion from existing evidence is that immigration has very small impacts on GDP per capita, whether these impacts are positive or negative.'

6. 'That day' was Saturday, 24 June 1989, when the Scarborough Hotel on the corner of Savile Road and Orchard Street, at the effective 'entrance' to the already predominately Muslim enclave of Savile Town, Dewsbury, was ransacked.

The word 'already' (as to the situation in 1989) is to be noted. According to the 2011 census, Savile Town was then more than 98% South Asian with 'white British' at less than twenty (that is in number rather than percentage).

6.1. *The Islamic Republic of Dewsbury* by Danny Lockwood, published by The Press News Ltd in 2011.

7. From the Executive Summary of the Jay Report, published August 2014.

8. Research, Sandwell Smethwick ethnic mix.

Another example of Channel 4's view was to describe the multiplicity of ethnicities and languages in a school in Peterborough as 'inspirational': this was Jon Snow in the lead up to the 2015 general election.

9. George Osborne, the then shadow Chancellor of the Exchequer said: 'Candidates of any party – Conservative, Labour, Liberal Democrat – have to exercise great caution in the language they use about immigration.'

David Davis, the then shadow Home Secretary (MP for Haltemprice and Howden since 1997) said, 'You cannot just stumble around throwing out comments which are insensitive or inflammatory.'

Mary Docker, chairwoman of the local Conservative Association said, 'He's basically just raising issues that have been asked with him when he has been canvassing the area. All he is doing is just relaying the views of the public, which is what a politician should do.'

10. *Tanked up Britain* by A.A. Gill, *The Sunday Times* Magazine, December 2013.

11. The more diverse boroughs, in increasing order of diversity, are the three London boroughs of Ealing, Brent and Newham, plus Slough.

12. Redbridge Council's home page.

13. Ramsden Street in the London Borough of Wandsworth.

14. Such as Dominic Grieve: *see* note 13 to C is for the cost of immigration, and note 1 to C is for culture.

Mr Grieve said:

> [corruption was growing in this country] because we have minority communities in this country which come from backgrounds where corruption is endemic. It is something we as politicians have to wake up to. I can see many of them have come because of the opportunities they get. But they also come from societies where they have been brought up to believe you can only get certain things through a favour culture. One of the things you have to make absolutely clear is that that is not the case and it's not acceptable.

Yes, it's mainly the Pakistani community, not the Indian community. I wouldn't draw it down to one. I'd be wary of saying it's just a Pakistani problem.

Sajjad Karim, the Conservative Party's legal affairs spokesman in the European Parliament, complained:

As a member of the British Pakistani community myself, I found these comments to be offensive, divisive: I do think they were ill-advised and I'm afraid the very general way in which Dominic is trying to make the points that he is making will have the net effect of being seen as purely populist in nature.

And so Mr Grieve had to "clarify" matters:

The point I was making is that as a law officer it's my duty to ensure the rule of law is upheld, and one of the issues that I feel requires close attention is any potential for a rise in corruption to undermine civil society. I believe this is an issue which needs to be addressed calmly and rationally. I am absolutely clear that this problem is not attributable to any one community, as I know very well from my many years promoting community cohesion.

If I gave the impression that there is a particular problem in the Pakistani community, I was wrong. It is not my view. I believe the Pakistani community has enriched this country a great deal as I know full well from my extensive contact with the community over a number of years. I am sorry if I have caused offence.

But *see* V is for vote rigging in Slough – adjacent to Mr Grieve's constituency.

After Michael Fallon, MP for Sevenoaks and Secretary of State for Defence in 2014, said when explaining that

[measures to limit immigration are] still being worked on at the moment to see what we can do to prevent whole towns and communities being swamped by huge numbers of migrant workers.

In some areas, particularly on the east coast, yes, towns do feel under siege from large numbers of migrant workers and people claiming benefits. It is quite right that we look at that.

a government source responded, 'He accepts he should have chosen his words better', and Mr Fallon said, 'I was a bit careless with my words, I accept that.'

The Labour Party was split as to Mr Fallon's statement. Keith Vaz, chairman of the House of Commons' Home Affairs Select Committee, said Mr

Fallon's words were 'nasty, inappropriate and wrong'. And Diane Abbott said that the use of the word 'swamped' was 'unfortunate' as 'we are talking about children here, not raw sewage'. (Keith Vaz was born in Aden; Diane Abbott was born in London but to Jamaican parents.)

But David Blunkett wrote:

> Just because immigration is deeply controversial, that cannot mean that we should avoid talking about it.

> It is interesting that in both cases, our critics focused largely on the language used – not on the points we made. If we had deployed the word 'overwhelmed', which according to the Oxford English Dictionary, means almost exactly the same as 'swamped' it is unlikely that there would have been so many protests.

On 6 October 1985, PC Keith Blakelock was on the Broadwater Farm estate in Tottenham, protecting the fire brigade, when he died of forty wounds including from a six-inch knife having been buried in his neck, an event of which Bernie Grant (from Guyana), council leader of the London Borough of Haringey and member of parliament for Tottenham, said, 'The youths around here believe that the police were to blame for what happened on Sunday and what they got was a bloody good hiding.'

In the preceding month there had been disturbances in Brixton and Handsworth.

Oliver Letwin (MP since 1997 for West Dorset) and in 1985 a member with Hartley Booth of the then prime minister's Policy Unit, produced a memo that included '… when things were very bad in the great depression of the 1930s, people in Brixton went out, leaving their grocery money in a bag at the front door … Riots, criminality and social disintegration are caused solely by individual characters and attitudes. So long as bad moral attitudes remain, all efforts to improve the inner cities will founder … will set up in the disco and drug trade.'

That extract from the memo is in Volume Two of Charles Moore's authorised biography of Margaret Thatcher, published in the autumn of 2015. So Mr Moore was 'a bit surprised' when release of the memo (under the thirty year rule) right at the end of 2015 produced a media brouhaha. That media torrent reported that the memo included the word 'Rastafarian', thus clarifying the ethnicity of the rioters.

Darcus Howe, race activist, born in Trinidad in 1943 and came here, first, eighteen years later, said Letwin's words were 'bordering on criminality'.

Today, use of firearms by black criminals is fifty times that of their white counterparts and 59% of Caribbean children are fatherless compared to 44% of African children.

Letwin had to backtrack – 'Following reports tonight, I want to make it clear that some parts of a private memo I wrote nearly 30 years ago were both badly worded and wrong. I apologise unreservedly for any offence these comments have caused and wish to make clear that none was intended.'

(Between the 2001 and 2011, the residents of Haringey increased from 216,507 to 254,926, of whom white British dropped from 96,028 to 88,424 while 'black' increased from 43,377 to 47,830.)

15. Examples include –

- FGM, which has been illegal since 1985, and since 2003 it has been unlawful to take a girl abroad for such. Estimates for the number of women in the country who have been 'cut' range from 60,000 to 137,000 but there was not one prosecution until 2014. (In September 2014, the NHS found 467 cases of FGM; a further 1,279 previously identified were treated. In the second quarter of 2015, there were 1,036 newly recorded cases in England).

- Mobile poster vans with the words *In the UK illegally? Go home or face arrest* are criticised as offensive and in areas of high 'ethnicity' as irresponsible as likely to damage community relations (and later condemned by the Advertising Standards Authority for using incorrect data).

- The police procrastinated about taking action against the defacement of advertisements in Tower Hamlets.

- 'Travellers' (apparently) commit trespass and criminal damage with impunity.

16. Paragraphs 11.5 to 11.7 of the Jay Report into child sexual exploitation in Rotherham.

17. Theresa May, then Home Secretary, to the 2015 Conservative Party Conference.

18. *It falls to a broken Labour Party to keep this country in Europe* by Mary Riddell, *The Daily Telegraph,* October 2015.

19. *See* D is for Derby and, indeed, the final paragraph of H is for hegemony.

It is similar in Sweden, where, after it emerged that Afghani youths harassed girls at the We Are Sthlm music festival, the central Stockholm police chief admitted, 'Sometimes we do not dare to say how things really are ...'

20. *See* P is for Pakistan and Operation Pathway.

21. Nansen Primary School – one of the subjects of the Trojan Horse letter *see* F is for fifth column.

22. Retired Detective Superintendent Mick Gradwell about investigating the problem of sexual exploitation of (white) girls by (brown) men.

23. Rotherham Safeguarding Children Board.

But Trevor Phillips, of Guyanese ethnicity, the head of the Commission for Equality and Human Rights (EHRC), said, 'Anybody who says that the fact that most of the men are Asian and most of the children are white is not relevant – that's just fatuous.'

Rotherham Borough Council's strapline is 'Where Everyone Matters' and the main objective of its Safeguarding Children Board is 'to ensure the effectiveness of all work done to safeguard and promote the welfare of children and young people in Rotherham'.

Despite, or perhaps because of, its failings to the white girls of the borough, Rotherham Borough Council has an Interpretation and Translation Service.

(Moving over the Pennines) Rezgar Nouri and Mohammed Ibrahim were convicted of raping Lucy Walsh in Preston. Araz Latif Najmaden is wanted in respect of the same facts. Lucy said, 'I truly believe that had the third man been white, the police would have made more effort to find him. To me, it feels as if they didn't want to make waves and upset the immigrant community.' Her father said, 'The way it seems to us is that the police are so worried about upsetting the local immigrant community that they have done little to track this man down and allowed him to walk free.' Mohammed Ibrahim was an illegal immigrant. He applied for British citizenship before the attack. It was granted while he was in prison awaiting trial.

24. Dr Mary Rossiter, consultant paediatrician, North Middlesex Hospital, to Lord Laming's enquiry into Victoria Climbié's death.

25. *What are we supposed to say when a grooming ring comes to light?* by Rod Liddle *The Spectator,* September 2013. (According to the 2011 census, the Muslim percentage of the population was then 4.8%). The article continued:

> The latest report of the grooming of a non-Muslim girl comes not from the white working class, who were always treated with suspicion when they took their complaints to the impeccably liberal middle-class authorities and marked down as racists, but from the Sikhs – who had an even harder time of it convincing the Old Bill, and the social services that something seriously remiss was going on. The authorities seem to have decided that the Sikhs were racist too. So a bunch of some 50 Sikh men reportedly trashed a Muslim-run restaurant in the multicultural nirvana of Leicester after having failed to gain redress through the more appropriate and official channels. (The restaurant was adjacent to an apartment at which some of the abuse took place, apparently.) Some of these Sikh men have since been arrested. So, too, at last have some of the Muslim men said to have been involved in the grooming ring.

The restaurant, Moghul Durbar in East Park Road, of the Spinney Hills area of Leicester, was certainly trashed – in January 2013 – for which seven men, from Derby and Oldbury, were jailed … 'mob rule' and 'lawless anarchy' according to the judge. Six men from Derby – five Muslims and one Hindu – were jailed for the abuse of the then sixteen-year-old girl. Aabidali Mubarak Ali was jailed for five years for paying for the sexual services of a child and facilitating child prostitution. In mitigation, his barrister said he was an immigration 'overstayer' and the consequences for his wife and three children would be 'grave' if he were deported. The other five – Rakib Iacub, Wajid Usman, an illegal immigrant from Afghanistan, Hamza Imtiazali, Bharat Modhwadia and Chandresh Mistry – were sentenced to less time.

26. Traditional Jamaican dish.

27. *Hard to swallow. Hospital food isn't a joke. It's a scandal* by Jane Kelly, *The Spectator*, September 2013.

28. Perhaps it is merely coincidental, rather than a further example of hegemony, but the two colleagues Mr Miliband (when leader of the Opposition) conferred with on immigration are not of indigenous heritage – while both Abbott and Khan were both born here, both are of an ethnic-minority ethnicity. As to Ms Abbott, *see* of R is for racist/racism.

29. Bagehot in *The Economist* of 30 March 2013. In the same article that columnist wrote:

> Mr Miliband reiterated his regret that the previous Labour governments, under Tony Blair and Gordon Brown, had taken such a laissez-faire view of the matter – allowing net immigration to rise by 2m in a decade. Still two years from the next general election, a grim pattern has emerged. Immigration, once unmentionable in polite political circles, will be one of

the big issues in a painfully protracted campaign.

In fact, *The Economist* is pro-immigration – the following is from *No flood, after all* of 17 May 2014:

> At the very end of 2013, as other newspapers warned of a terrible deluge, The Economist invited Bulgarians and Romanians to come and work in Britain. So we are sad to report that, since working restrictions imposed when the two countries joined the EU were lifted on January 1st, rather few seem to have taken up our offer. Official figures published on May 14th suggest that the number of Romanians and Bulgarian-born people working in Britain actually fell between December and March, from 144,000 to 140,000.
>
> The figure is an estimate based on a large survey and is not definitive, says Carlos Vargas-Silva of the Migration Observatory at Oxford University. But it does at least suggest there has been no spectacular surge of immigrants. That fits with more anecdotal evidence. On January 1st tabloid journalists – and Keith Vaz, a publicity-hungry Labour MP – gamely conquered their hangovers and flocked to Luton Airport to interview new arrivals. They found barely a handful.
>
> The number of Bulgarians and Romanians moving to Britain was always likely to undershoot expectations. Partly this is because forecasts were so inflated: media outlets and politicians reported the combined population of the two (some 27m) as though every single citizen would up sticks and come to Britain. But mostly it is because, as Ion Jinga, Romania's ambassador to Britain points out, by January most of the Romanians and Bulgarians who wanted to move had already done so.
>
> Between 2007, when Romania and Bulgaria joined the European Union, and March, the number of people from those countries working in Britain increased fivefold. Even before labour-market controls were lifted, skilled migrants were able to get work permits while unskilled ones could be self-employed. Data from the Labour Force Survey analysed in February found that 59% of Romanian and Bulgarians in Britain were self-employed at the end of last year, compared with 14% of the British-born population. Men have had no trouble getting grey-market jobs on building sites, suggests Mr Vargas-Silva.
>
> The lifting of restrictions mostly means that those workers can now get proper jobs, so pay full taxes and national insurance, instead of waiting on street corners for casual and often exploitative work. For both migrants and Britain, that seems like an excellent outcome.

Thus the explanation for there being no flood at the beginning of 2014 was that those who wanted to be here were so already (*see* note 1 as to I is for identity). Was the one-legged roof tiler from Bucharest self-employed? – *see* Steve Moxon's *The Great Immigration Scandal.*

30. *How socialism created a moral no man's land* by Charles Moore, *The Daily Telegraph,* February 2014. And two months later he wrote:

> On the other hand, the angry atheists are surely speaking truth when they say that 'we are a largely non-religious society'. If there is a battle in Britain nowadays between something explicitly Christian and something secular, the latter usually wins. Look at Sunday shopping, mass abortion, the growing desire to kill old people (sorry, let them 'die with dignity'), divorce, surrogate motherhood and so on. For better or worse, religious objections couched as such tend to be disliked and rejected (unless they are made by Muslims, in which case people get scared of causing offence).

And a year later David Ashton wrote to *The Spectator:*

> Wouldn't the expensive upkeep of its virtually empty buildings be mitigated if the Church of England actually tried to convert the population to the Christian religion, or is any such possible futile mission prevented in any case by the new state ideology of 'diversity and equality'?

31. Baroness Thomas of Winchester (Lib Dem), letter to a newspaper, February 2014.

32. The speech concluded with: 'The Bill renews the legal foundations for proper enforcement of our immigration laws. That enforcement is necessary to build public trust in the system. It is also necessary to enable us to reap the benefits of migration as a nation.'

33. This item originally was in B is for the benefit and burden of (im)migration – among (PC) Keith Blakelock, (headmaster) Philip Lawrence, (Fusilier) Lee Rigby. Andrew Young wasn't so well known, so the item was in a footnote. But I then saw the reproduced paragraph, and although no name (of either the victim or the criminal) is stated, or the place, there looks to be a match.

Andrew Young's mother called Mr Gill's sentence 'a joke'. The attorney general sought to have the sentence increased. The Court of Appeal held: 'In this judgment the sentence imposed was not one which can be described as unduly lenient.'

34. Taki Theodoracopulos, *The Spectator* March 2014.

35. *Woolwich outrage: we are too weak to face up to the extremism in our midst* by Charles Moore, *The Daily Telegraph*, July 2013.

The article resulted in a claim for defamation – *Fiyaz Mughal v. Telegraph Media Group Ltd* (2014 EWHC 1371), which was unsuccessful.

And **H** is for Ray Honeyford[1]

Multiracial myths? by Raymond Honeyford was published in November 1982 by the *Times Educational Supplement*. It had the footnote, 'Raymond Honeyford is headmaster of a middle school with 80 per cent[2] ethnic-minority children covering 11 mother tongues.' The school was Drummond Middle School in Bradford.

It was his article *Education and Race – an Alternative View*, published two years later[3] which 'led to his downfall', namely:

> The issues and problems of our multi-racial inner schools are frequently thrown into sharp relief for me. As the headteacher of a school in the middle of a predominantly Asian area, I am often witness to scenes which have the raw feel of reality and the recipient of vehement criticism, whenever I question some of the current educational orthodoxies connected with race.

> It is very difficult to write honestly and openly of my experiences, and the reflections they evoke, since the race relations lobby is extremely powerful in the state education service. The propaganda generated by multi-racial zealots is now aggravated by a growing bureaucracy of race in local authorities. And this makes freedom of speech difficult to maintain.

> By exploiting the enormous tolerance traditional in this country, the race lobby has so managed to induce and maintain feelings of guilt in the well-disposed majority, that decent people are not only afraid of voicing certain thoughts, they are uncertain even of their right to think those thoughts. They are intimidated not only by their fear of giving offence by voicing their own reasonable concerns about the inner cities, but by the necessity of conducting debate in a language which is dishonest.

> The term 'racism', for instance, functions not as a word with which to create insight but as a slogan designed to suppress constructive thought. It conflates prejudice and discrimination, and thereby denies a crucial conceptual distinction. It is the icon word of those committed to the race game. And they apply it with the some sort of mindless zeal as the inquisitors voiced 'heretic' or Senator McCarthy spat out 'Commie'.

> The word 'black' has been perverted. Every non-white is now, officially, 'black', be he Indian, Pakistani or Vietnamese. This gross and offensive dichotomy has an obvious purpose: the creation of an atmosphere of

anti-white solidarity. To suppress and distort the enormous variations within races which I every day observe by using language in this way is an outrage to all decent people whatever their skin colour.

And there are other distortions: race riots are described by the politically motivated as 'uprisings', and by a Lord of Appeal as a 'superb and healthy catalyst for the British people' and the police blamed for the behaviour of violent thugs; rather like the patient blaming the doctor because he has a cold in the head.

'Cultural enrichment' is the approved term for the West Indian's right to create an ear splitting cacophony for most of the night to the detriment of his neighbour's sanity, or for the Notting Hill festival, whose success or failure is judged by the level of street crime which accompanies it. At the schools' level the term refers to such things as the Muslim parent's insistence on banning his daughter from drama, dance and sport, i.e. imposing a purdah mentality in schools committed to the principle of sexuality equality; and the determined efforts of misguided radical teachers to place such as the following alongside the works of Shakespeare and Wordsworth.

Wi mek a lickle date
fi nineteen seventy eight
An wi fite and wi fite
An defeat di state (From 'Inglan is a Bitch', by Linton Kwesi Johnson)

No one, of course, is allowed to describe first-generation black or coloured immigrants as 'immigrants' though no other collective noun exists. In the courts it has been revealed that we now have laws on the statute book which insist that Sikhism is a race, which, as three distinguished lords of appeal were able to demonstrate, contradicts the best available dictionary definitions.

We have, therefore, officially perverted words to such a degree that it would be perfectly reasonable in law to describe a member of the Church of England or the Labour Party as a member of an ethnic group, a manifest absurdity. (It is worth noting that in his judgment of this case, Lord Justice Kerr commented of The Commission for Racial Equality, 'The commission seemed to have created discord where there had been none before', a view, I suspect, which is shared by the vast majority of the public with regard to most of the C.R.E.'s activities.)

We in the schools are also enjoined to believe that creole, pidgin and other non standard variants have the same power, subtlety and capacity for expressing five shades of meaning, and for tolerating uncertainity, ambiguity and irony as standard English. A generation of cultural relativists in the field of linguistics has managed to impose on the schools the mindless slogan, 'All languages are equally good' – a myth recently and convincingly demolished by Professor John Honey in The Language Trap, a monograph published by the National Council for Educational Standards.

Those of us working in Asian areas are encouraged, officially, to 'celebrate linguistic diversity', i.e. to applaud the rapidly mounting linguistic confusion in those growing number of inner-city schools in which British-born Asian children begin their mastery of English by being taught in Urdu.

In Politics and the English language George Orwell said, 'Political language is designed to make lies sound truthful and murder respectable, and to give an impression of solidity to pure wind.' Race speak is the language of a politics committed to that sort of deceit. There is little hope of our coming to terms with the monumental significance for our future of New Commonwealth and Pakistani immigration until we invent a language by means of which doubts, fears and aspirations can be expressed openly and honestly.

What, in the meantime, can one do? In the absence of the coinage of honest discourse, one can perhaps make a start by reporting and commenting on one's everyday experiences. I recall, for instance, the meeting called to explain to Asian parents the importance of regular school attendance for their offspring's future. A very high proportion of Asian immigrants have a habit of sending children to the Indian sub-continent during term time with obvious, deleterious educational consequences. Not only is the practice inadvisable, it is almost certainly illegal though no local education authority has had the courage to bring a test case, and the Department of Education and Science turns a blind eye.

After much badgering from the schools, the local authority had agreed to impose on brown parents the same obligations it demanded from white and black parents with regard to school attendance. Against all normal expectations the meeting was packed. There had obviously been a local 'three-line whip' from the Pakistani leadership. It quickly became evident that what had been proposed as an act of reconciliation, based on the school's concern for the child, was to descend into a noisy and unseemly demonstration of sectarian bitterness.

The hysterical political temperament of the Indian sub-continent became evident an extraordinary sight in an English School Hall. There was much shouting and fist waving. The local authority was accused of 'racism'; the chairman insulted. One anglicised Asian stood near the door and, at regular intervals, shouted 'bullshit' at the chair. The disorder was orchestrated. Questions were always preceded by a nod from a Muslim leader. A half-educated and volatile Sikh usurped the privileges of the chair by deciding who was to speak.

The confusion was made worse by the delays occasioned by the need for interpreting [as] many of the audience had no English though there had been freely available English classes in the area for at least a decade. I raised my hand to speak several times but was ignored. The atmosphere was highly charged and threatening. I left before the end, bitterly disappointed.

Needless to say, the absenteeism of Asian pupils abroad continues. The authorities have simply given up. And I am left with the ethically indefensible task of complying with a school attendance policy which is determined not, as the law requires, on the basis of individual parental responsibility but by the parent's country of origin a blatant and officially sanctioned policy of racial discrimination.

My disappointment was compounded by a sense of irony. These people, who now so vehemently accused the authorities of denying them a right which, in reality was a privilege no other parents enjoyed, and no other group of immigrants had contemplated claiming these same people enjoyed rights, privileges and aspirations unheard of in their country of origin.

Pakistan is a country which cannot cope with democracy; under martial law since 1977, it is ruled by a military tyrant who, in the opinion of at least half his countrymen, had his predecessor judicially murdered. A country, moreover, which, despite disproportionate western aid because of its important strategic position, remains for most of its people obstinately backward.

Corruption at every level combines with unspeakable treatment not only of criminals, but of those who dare to question Islamic orthodoxy as interpreted by a despot. Even as I write, wounded dissidents are chained to hospital beds awaiting their fate.

Pakistan too, is the heroin capital of the world. (A fact which is now reflected in the drug problems of English cities with Asian populations.) It is not surprising that such a country loses more of its citizens voluntarily to other countries than any state on earth. How could the denizens of such a country so wildly and implacably resent the simple British requirement for all parents to send children to school regularly?

It was this reflection which caused me, perhaps for the first time, to understand why so many fundamentally decent people harbour feelings of resentment. I realised, too, how little the cant term 'racism' explains. In truth, I was affronted by what I had seen in my own school hall.

Again, I recall the reaction to an article I published recently in the *Times Educational Supplement*. I simply attempted to question the conceptual soundness of the ideas which comprise the term 'multi-racial education'. My main argument was that the fashionable way of explaining comparative black pupil failure in British schools as a function of teacher prejudice and an alien curriculum was almost certainly bogus. There is not a scrap of evidence to support such a belief. The roots of black educational failure are, in reality, located in West Indian family structure and values, and the work of misguided radical teachers whose motives are basically political.

Within days, the *Caribbean Times* carried a long letter from a group of black activists known as 'The Haringay[4] Black Pressure Group on Education'. This letter confirmed my belief that much of the pressure for a multi-racial curriculum comes from the vehement, radical left of black organisations. Its tone is strident, its contents poorly argued, its style sub-standard; but the main thrust of its argument accords well with official policy edicts now being imposed on the schools by several local education authorities a process which is certain to be accelerated when the impending Swarm Committee report is published.

The basic intention of the authors of the letter is to intimidate. It is also defamatory, and highly likely to damage me professionally. But redress would be difficult, since no one has had the courage to sign the letter. How do you sue a collective? Amongst other things I am accused of the sins of being white and middle class. Inevitably I am a 'blatant racist'. I should be immediately sacked and a public investigation carried out into how I run my school. I am even accused of trying to deprive negroes of their welfare benefits.

The totalitarian nature of the writers' mentalities may be judged by the following quotation: 'All teachers, especially those like Mr Honeyford, should be compelled to attend massive [sic] in-service training courses to bring them up to date with modern education theory, and practice, and to purge them of their racist outlook and ideology. Teachers who refuse to adapt their teaching and go on in-service training courses should be redeployed or retired off [sic] early. School books with a racist content ... should be scrapped. Racist teachers should be dismissed.'

Of such libellous and mindless bombast is the rhetoric of multi-racialising composed. Of course it might be objected that such a mentality is not representative. That the Haringay[4] Black teachers are simply the disreputable, unacceptable face of the race industry, of which the Commission for Racial Equality is the acceptable front.

But such extremism is becoming the norm. I was recently told by an educational mandarin that, unless I attended a 'racism awareness workshop' arranged by the local authority, I would be deprived of the right to be involved in the appointment of staff to my school.

Consider, too, the following extract from Black Britain by Chris Mullard: 'Already we have started to rebel, to kick out against our jailers ... As more black Britons leave school disgruntled, as more black immigrants discard their yoke of humility, the ultimate confrontation will become clearer ... Blacks will fight with pressure, leaflets, campaigns, demonstrations, fists and scorching resentment which, when peaceful means fail, will explode into street fighting, urban guerrilla warfare, looting, burning and rioting.'

Now the writer of that is not some insignificant devotee of Marcuse spitting out his hatred of the white establishment. He is, in fact, a lecturer in education in the University of London. As such he is accorded expert status. He is influential in the training of teachers, and his views are respected by local education authorities.

More recently, I published a simple report on my contact with Asian parents in a typical school week. The piece contained many positive references to Asian values. But I was immediately and intemperately attacked by a dedicated multi-racialist who publicly accused me of being prejudiced, of fabricating the evidence, and of using phrases which 'must give cause for concern'; and my 'strategy' (whatever that means) was condemned as being 'ignorant and counter productive'.

It is typical of the response to honest discussion of those teachers who have eagerly embraced the career enhancing possibilities of the new multi-racial orthodoxy in schools. Such people never proceed through rational argument, but rather by the tactic of impugning others' good will. At no point in all this sound and fury does the plight of those white children who constitute the 'Ethnic minority' in a growing number of inner-city schools merit even a mention. Yet their educational 'disadvantage' is now confirmed.

It is no more than common sense that if a school contains a disproportionate number of children for whom English is a second language (true of all Asian children, even those born here), or children from homes where educational ambition and the values to support it are completely absent (i.e. the vast majority of West Indian homes, a disproportionate number of which are fatherless) then academic standards are bound to suffer.

This intuition is supported by the findings of the Department of Education and Science Assessment of Performance Unit on primary school English; and there is suggestive evidence in the National Council for Educational Standards' report Standards in English Schools. The absence of concern for the rights of this group of parents is due to three factors: they are overwhelmingly lower working class with little ability to articulate their social and educational anxieties; they have, so far, failed to produce a pressure group generating appropriate propaganda; and unlike non-white children they have no government to plead their cause.

These experiences I here report are the tip of an iceberg. Yet they seem to me important since they point up the real educational consequences of the general acceptance of the notion that multi-racial inner cities are not only inevitable but, in some sense, desirable.

Specifically, they raise for policy makers and public opinion the question of how the following unique factors now operating in our inner cities can be reconciled to produce that integrated harmonious society we all affect to cherish:

- A growing number of Asians whose aim is to preserve as intact as possible the values and attitudes of the Indian subcontinent within a framework of British social and political privilege, i.e. to produce Asian ghettoes.

- An influential group of black intellectuals of aggressive disposition, who know little of the British traditions of understatement, civilised discourse and respect for reason.

- A small but growing group of dispossessed, indigenous parents whose schools are, as a direct result of the multiracial dimension, failing their children.

- The presence in the state education service of a growing number of teachers and advisers who, quite correctly, perceive the professional advantage of supporting the notion of multi-racial curriculum urged by the authorities, and of making colour and race significant, high profile issues in the classroom.

- The successful creation by the race relations lobby of a dubious, officially approved argot which functions to maintain a whole set of questionable beliefs and attitudes about education and race attitudes which have more to do with professional opportunism than the educational progress of ethnic minority children.

I suspect that these elements, far from helping to produce harmony, are, in reality, operating to produce a sense of fragmentation and discord. And I am no longer convinced that the British genius for compromise, for muddling through, and for good natured tolerance will be sufficient to resolve the inevitable tensions.[3]

But this was too uncomfortable, not least to the parents of the 90%[2] or so of the school roll of Asian ethnicity, and so:

It was the piece in The Salisbury Review, however, that led to his downfall. The then mayor of Bradford, Mohammed Ajeeb, called for Honeyford's dismissal, because the headmaster had shown 'an inclination to demonstrate prejudice against certain sections of our community'.

Honeyford was suspended in April 1985, but reinstated five months later after an appeal to the High Court. Some parents formed an action group and kept their children away from school, and in December 1985 Honeyford accepted a financial settlement and took early retirement. Drummond Middle School was eventually burned down in an arson attack. It has since been rebuilt and has been renamed Iqra Community Primary School, though it is still known locally as 'the Drummond'.[5]

And in retrospect, first,

... The local education authority responded and Ray Honeyford was dismissed.[6]

That, as we know, was not the end of the story. Honeyford's articles were written before the rise of radical Islam, and were concerned with the more general question of national identity. He was sounding a warning that was bound to be ignored, given the profoundly anti-patriotic character of the educational establishment of the time. Honeyford was defending a social order founded on secular law and national loyalty, rather than religion. The nation, its land, its law, its language and its culture are things we share. Religion is a thing that divides us. The activists who were attempting to take over Honeyford's school were aware of this, and wanted their children to identify themselves as Muslims living in Britain, rather than as British people who happen to be Muslims. The idea that their children might be integrated into our kafir society was anathema to them, and they saw the school to which they were legally obliged to send their children as a thing to be either subverted or destroyed.[7]

And secondly,

Each day brings a fresh surprise and Sunday evening was a special treat. I remembered the name 'Honeyford' but such is the speed of events, I couldn't recall when or where I had heard it. Angela Honeyford is the widow of the great Ray, who died two years ago. He died too late to see his prescient forecast – that multiculturalism in education makes no sense – accepted by all the leading and respected political parties. Ray was the first-class headmaster of a school in Bradford. In 1984, he spoke out against the Asian community who were determined to ensure that their children, whilst enjoying British social and political privileges, were to be educated with the values of the Indian sub-continent intact.

Honeyford saw that, if we are to preserve the future of our country, we have to integrate our recently arrived minorities through a shared school curriculum and a secular rule of law that protects women and girls from the kind of abuse that he saw daily. There was a predictable explosion of outrage with placards denouncing Ray Honeyford as 'Ray-cist'. He was forced to resign. The educational establishment lost one of its most humane and public-spirited representatives. He continued to protest against the educational establishment's plans to remove all signs of patriotism from our schools and erase the memory of England from the cultural record.

Ray was heroic and a gentle man who was prepared to pay the price of truthfulness at a time of lies. It's a privilege to be the guest of this man's widow.[8]

And lastly, and most recently

I'll leave the last word on this yawning cultural chasm to Noshaba Hussain, middle-aged former headmistress of Springfield Primary, one of the Trojan Horse[9] schools in Birmingham. A nine-year-old pupil had asked why she wasn't wearing a headscarf, declaring 'Only slags don't cover their heads.' 'This attitude is not acceptable in state schools in Britain,' observed Ms Hussain. Well indeed. As Ray Honeyford was so maligned for telling us just 32 years ago.[10]

Notes: *H is for Ray Honeyford*

1. Ray Honeyford was born in 1934. His father, by reason of war wounds, was only able to work intermittently and his mother was the daughter of Irish immigrants. Half of his eleven siblings died in childhood. Ray failed his 11-plus and he left school to work to support the family. He went to evening classes to train as a teacher.

Multiracial myths? is reproduced in Appendix VI by kind permission of the *Times Educational Supplement*.

2. Honeyford's obituary in the *Independent* stated that 'more than 90 per cent of pupils were Asian'.

The article referred to in the next note included

Looking [back at 1984] I define the intake at Bradford's Drummond Middle School where Honeyford was headmaster, as 95% "Asian" even though nearly all of them came from Muslim families share of the Punjab and Kashmir ...

3. This article – *Education and Race – an Alternative View* – is reproduced by kind permission of the *Salisbury Review*.

The so called Trojan Horse letter (*see* F is for fifth column) resulted in inter alia an Ofsted inspection. It was followed in June 2014 by *Was the 1980's Bradford headteacher who criticised multiculturalism right?* in the *Guardian* by Ian Jack. The article began:

> A culture of fear and intimidation has developed inside some of Birmingham's state funded schools says Ofsted's chief inspector, Michael Wilshaw. "Islamic extremism" wants to rule the roost (my quote marks are there not to imply irony or scepticism, but simply because nobody seems sure of what extremism is). Ofsted's report finds that in Park View School the sexes are segregated inside the classroom, their sports events are scheduled for different days and that a madrassa curriculum denies evolutionary theory and omits reproduction from biology classes. One teacher has handed out a worksheet stating that women must always obey their husbands, and another has been using school facilities to copy Osma bin Laden DVD's.

4. It is the London Borough of HaringEy and the HaringEy Black Pressure Group on Education but the article seems to have been written as HaringAy.

5. Part of the obituary in *The Daily Telegraph*, following Mr Honeyford's death on 5 February 2012.

As to the school now being the Iqra Community Primary School, the Ofsted 2010 report noted: 'All of the pupils come from minority ethnic groups and the vast majority are in early stages of learning English. The incidence of pupils arriving new to the school and the country has increased recently, with many of them in the very early stages of learning English.'

6. The obituary in the *Independent* by Martin Childs had it that Honeyford was 'abused, suspended, reinstated and eventually hounded out of education'.

7. *Ray Honeyford was right* by Roger Scruton, *The Spectator*, July 2014.

8. Tom Benyon, OBE, MP for Abingdon (in succession to Airey Neave) 1979–1983. (This is from his *random thoughts* etc. while walking from Ambleside to Oxford during July 2014 to raise money for ZANE.)

9. *See* F is for fifth column. 10. *An inconvenient truth* by James Delingpole, *The Spectator,* April 2016.

And **H** is for 'honour killings'

Such as

- of Shafilea Ahmed of Warrington, who was suffocated by her parents Iftikhar and Faranza;

- of Uzma Naurin and Saif Rehman married in Manchester and murdered in Gujarat;

- of Mahmood Ahmad of Watford, of whom all that was ever found was a thumb after he had been kidnapped, tortured, killed and cut up by his in-laws, Mohammed Riaz and Sharif Mohammed, with the knowledge of their sister, Sabra Sultana, and the assistance of Faisal Chowdhury, Arnold Yousaf and Amirzada Hussain;

- Surjit Athwal was lured to India by her husband, Sukhdave, and mother-in-law to be murdered, possibly by his brother because she wanted a divorce. Sukhdave and his mother, aged seventy at the time of sentencing, were both sentenced to life;

- Benaz Mahmod was killed by Mohammed Ali and Omar Hussain on the orders of her father, Mahmod Mahmod.

The Metropolitan Police reported that, in the year to April 2011, there were 443 cases of honour violence or forced marriage in London, which was more than double that in 2007–8. A separate survey of all police forces estimated that there were nearly 3,600 reported cases of honour attacks in 2010.

The study by the Iranian and Kurdish Women's Rights Organisation found a 47% rise in cases of honour violence in a year. Jasvinder Sanghera of Karma Nirvana, a victim support group, put the real figure at four times as many. (Pakistan's Human Rights Commission has said that 943 women were killed in 2011 for damaging the family name.)

Who knows what was the reason but Shazad Khan killed his wife, Sabia Rani, at their home in Leeds in 2006. He had systematically beaten her over months so that when she died she had fifteen broken ribs and bruising over 85% of her body. She (was) married (to) Khan, her cousin, in 2002 when she was just a teenager. She came to this country in 2005, speaking no English. Khan's mother, two sisters, Nazia and Uzma, and a brother-in-law were convicted of allowing the death of a vulnerable adult under the Domestic Violence Crime and Victims Act 2004. At the murder trial, Uzma, a science teacher, claimed her sister-in-law's injuries were caused by spirits and black magic.

And such is not just in this country. In Canada, Mohammad Shafia, his second wife, Tooba Yahya, and their son, Hamed, were jailed for life for murdering Mohammad's daughters, Sahar, Zainab and Geeti, and their stepmother, Yahya, for what Mohammad deemed to be inappropriate behaviour. The sentencing judge said:

> It is difficult to conceive of a more despicable, more heinous, more honourless crime. The apparent reason behind these cold-blooded shameful murders was that the four completely innocent victims offended your completely twisted concept of honour, a notion of honour that is founded upon the domination and control of women.

And **H** is for housing

> Immigration is one of the many factors contributing to more demand for housing and higher house prices. We note the forecasts that, if current rates of net immigration persist, 20 years hence house prices would be over 10% higher than what they would be if there were zero net immigration. Housing matters alone should not dictate immigration policy but they should be an important consideration when assessing the economic impacts of immigration on the resident population in the UK.[1]

> Since the war, the average worker has been able to afford a decent house deposit after about four years of saving. Now it's 10 years.[2]

> The average first-time buyer deposit in 2015 was £32,927, compared with £29,094 in 2014 and 88pc higher than the average deposit in 2007 at £17,499.[3]

> Rent and house prices are rising drastically faster than wages, too. The average cost of housing for 20-somethings has jumped from 22 per cent of salary in 1993 to 35 per cent of salary in 2012, analysis of ONS data shows.

> Over the same period, first-time buyer house price to 20-something earnings ratios has more than doubled, rising from 3.10 in 1993 to 6.09 in 2012.

> The latest ONS statistics show that the average first-time buyer house has now reached 7.5 times the average salary, with new homeowners spending £14,000 more on a home than a year ago – showing how fast the hurdle of home ownership is rising.

> And in the year to November 2013, rents rose again – more than twice as fast as wages – according to LSL Property Group figures[4]

The average tenant is now forking out 28 per cent of their salary on rent, just below the maximum affordable level, set by the Joseph Rowntree Foundation. Housing costs have become so extreme that under-thirties living alone have experienced a 17 per cent drop in income after housing costs since 2008. Those young adults still living with parents (about a quarter of us) saw their disposable incomes drop by 8 per cent.[5]

The percentage of mean rent to income in London increased between 2004 and 2014 from 24.4% to 34.4% [6]

The average weekly social rent as percentage of 10th percentile gross weekly salary rose from 56 per cent in 2002 to 73% in 2014.[7]

It is not just house prices that are out of control, increasing again despite being already dangerously over-valued. An even more pressing crisis is that rents are shooting up, tightening the screws on the growing minority of Britons who rely on private landlords.[8]

The housing challenge facing government is not complicated: too many people, too few homes. When you have more buyers than sellers, guess what? The price goes up and up until the elastic snaps. The trouble is, few ministers will address part one of the problem –population growth – because it necessitates being honest about immigration and the impact it is having not just on numbers in the country but on tomorrow's birth rates.

Nothing terrifies Westminster MPs more than the suggestion of being 'racist'. This is craven, head-in-the-sand politics. Only last week, the European Union issued a report showing that the United Kingdom has the fastest-growing population. According to Eurostat, official numbers living in the UK (not including illegals) grew by 392,000 in 2012, 38 per cent of which was accounted for by net migration. The Office for National Statistics puts the figure slightly higher at 420,000 and 39 per cent respectively. For context, Nottingham's population is about 300,000.[9]

The boom runs on two types of fuel. The first is a rush of cash. Mortgage rates are low, and banks are keen to make loans on property. Money has flooded in from abroad, as fancy flats are snapped up by foreigners whose governments are less friendly than Britain's…

The second problem is bigger: a long-standing mismatch between supply and demand. Since 2004 Britain's working-age population has risen by nearly 4m, the number of homes by just 1.8m. New supply is stagnant despite high prices. Dream conditions for house builders (debt is cheap, as are labourers) should be creating a building boom. Yet the puny 135,000 houses completed in 2012–13 was the lowest number since records began in 1969. In ten years the construction industry has shrunk by more than 12%.[10]

The average floor space for a dwelling in the UK as a whole is currently 85 sq metres, whilst new-builds average only 76 sq metres – putting Britain at the bottom of a league table of 15 countries including Ireland, Portugal and Italy: (comparison of average dwelling sizes floor space in newly built homes – UK 76; Ireland 87.7; Germany 109.2; Netherlands 115.5 and Denmark 137).[11]

The 1920s houses averaged 1,647 square feet compared with a Lilliputian new-build of 2014 which contains only 925 square feet of living space: the equivalent of two double bedrooms has vanished into thin air.[12]

Today, new homes in the UK are the smallest in Europe – the average British newbuild is 76 sq m, compared with 137 sq m in Denmark – and shrinking.[13]

As house prices go up, they are led to believe that as a society we are richer and yet if no new assets are produced, clearly we are no richer at all……

For this you cannot blame Mr and Mrs Average, whether driven by greed or fear. This is the result of a massive failure of public policy: tight control of building land and massive subsidies to home-ownership, combined with a lax immigration policy. I am not saying that each of these is necessarily wrong but the combination of the three has been catastrophic – wasting resources, distorting the economy, leading to misery and frustration for millions of people and diverting their energies into the zero-sum game of climbing the housing ladder.[14]

It is therefore shocking that just 63.3 per cent of English households now own their own home, down from 70.9 per cent in 2003 and back to levels last seen three decades ago …

The UK is now well below the European Union average: across the 28 member states, 70 per cent of households are owner-occupiers. This is an extraordinary reversal which goes to the heart of David Cameron's vision for as aspirational meritocracy.[15]

By 2001, [the ownership ratio] had reached an all-time high, with 69pc of the population owning the roof over their heads.

Since then, however, something strange has happened. For the last decade and a half it has been ratcheting down relentlessly year after year. We are now down to just 64.8pc … What is surprising is how low that is compared with the rest of Europe.

… Not only do we not own our homes, they are also too small … Even the Greeks have bigger houses than us and are more likely to own them as well (the ownership ratio is 74pc …)

As Thatcher quite rightly recognised three decades ago, owning property is the bedrock of liberal market democracy.[16]

The Bank of England seems to have delayed thoughts of a rate rise. They seem a bit more relaxed about the general strength of bank balance sheets. This should mean more lending for decent property projects and other business ventures. All the time the UK invites in more than 600,000 new people each year, there will be extra demand not just for homes but also for commercial property, in places with good job creation.[17]

And yet beyond the M25 (and, in the case of Ealing, Tower Hamlets, Lambeth – well within it) everyone knows the truth; that for reasons which are, when you examine them, perfectly logical, incomers get social housing ahead of the indigenous population ... For Labour to give priority in social housing to local people who have lived in the area a long time means to scythe away the policy of the last 25 years, where council flats were given on the basis of imminent need rather than longevity of existence on the waiting list ... the policy [of enabling local authorities to provide homes for people who have lived in the area for a long while] goes against the government's own equal rights legislation which insists that local authorities must give priority to the utterly homeless – i.e., people who have just arrived here from a foreign country, rather than those indigenous people who have a place to live already, albeit somewhere which is cramped and unsuitable.[18]

In 2011 Migration Watch UK found that 17% of those born in the UK live in social housing but that 29% of those from Nigeria did – and correspondingly Iran 33% Jamaica 35% Ghana 39% Portugal 40% Bangladesh 41% Turkey 49% and Somalia 80%.

The chairman, then Sir Andrew Green, commented:

The impact of immigration on the availability of social housing for British people has been airbrushed out for too long.[19]

His view foreshadowed that of the Home Office namely in the 2013 Research Report (as to which also *see* note 3 to E is for European Union) namely:

Secondary effects of high migrant demand at the bottom end of the private rental market were reported as poor quality, overcrowded accommodation, inflated rents, unregistered houses of multiple occupation, exploitation by unscrupulous landlords, waste management and pest control issues that quickly spread, and, in a well-reported area in West London, a growing number of beds in sheds.

The pressure on our primary schools is just one consequence of Britain's rapidly growing population.

Others are higher housing costs, transport congestion, dangerous pollution levels and an overstretched NHS. It is surely time to consider whether a stable population would serve us better.[20]

Notes: *H is for housing*

1. Paragraph 172 of the House of Lords Report, April 2008.

2. *George Osborne is a debt addict – and so is the entire Western world* by Fraser Nelson, *The Daily Telegraph*, December 2014.

3. Isabelle Fraser, *The Daily Telegraph*, January 2016.

4. *Rethinking the pension* by Katie Morley, *Investors Chronicle*, January 2014.

5. *How about some help for Generation Rent* by Katie Morley, the *Financial Times*, July 2014.

6. *Living Costs & Food Survey, Expenditure & Food Survey, National Food Survey.*

7. ONS *Housing Summary measures analysis*, August 2015.

8. *Rent controls are madness, we need to build more homes* by Allister Heath, *The Daily Telegraph*, June 2013.

9 *Help to buy is nothing but an election ploy* by Jeff Randall, *The Daily Telegraph*, November 2013.

10. *A very British binge, The Economist,* May 2014.

11. *Rabbit-hutch Britain: Growing health concerns as UK sets record for smallest properties in Europe* by Johnathan Brown, the *Independent,* June 2014.

12. *Modern housing is not fit for purpose. It's eroding our privacy, and suffocating the life out of Britain* by Janet Street-Porter, the *Independent*, August 2014.

13. *The architectural amnesia beneath the mega-basement fad* by Judith Flanders, the *Financial Times*, December 2015.

14. *Bubbling up – the greatest source of investment delusion known to man* by Roger Bootle, *The Daily Telegraph*, March 2013.

15. *The real ticking time bomb for the Tories is home ownership* by Allister Heath, *The Daily Telegraph*, October 2015.

16. *In spite of Britain's love affair with property, too few of us own homes* by Matthew Lynn, *The Daily Telegraph*, December 2015.17. *Expect the central banks to get it wrong* by John Redwood (MP for Wokingham since 1987) the *Financial Times*, December 2015.

18. *Labour's U-turn on social housing for non-immigrants is welcome but too late* by Rod Liddle, *The Spectator*, July 2009.

19. Andrew Green, *Migration Watch*, August 2011.

20. Simon Ross, Chief Executive Population Matters, letter to a newspaper, April 2016.

And **H** is for human rights

We have neither the space nor the wealth[1] to be the world's refuge.

In 2011/12, 177 foreigners who had been convicted successfully 'used' the Human Rights Act 1998 to avoid deportation. One who was unsuccessful was Lincoln Farquharson. He was arrested five times between March 2006 and April 2011 for alleged offences including violent assault and rape; three juries failed to reach a verdict. He appealed against deportation on the basis of Article 8[2] but the tribunal found he was violent and a threat to women.

The Human Rights Act made human rights paramount so that 'primary legislation and subordinate legislation must be read and given effect in a way which is compatible with the Convention rights',[3] and so even though an alien's presence in this country is not conducive to the public good, his human rights would be infringed by his deportation and he can avoid deportation.

Peculiarly (or perhaps merely coincidentally), the family of Article 8 claimants always seem to want to remain here rather than to accompany the criminal to his home country even where at least one member of his family is also from that country. Alfred Gareth Suckoo came here in 2002. Seven years later he was convicted of supplying crack cocaine and heroin:

> There were four defendants ... They were all from Jamaica, none were drug addicts. Thus this was an offence operated through greed for profit and easy money ... It was a conspiracy that had lasted a little over 60 days ... It would seem that the basis for the conspiracy was that there would be telephone contact made for the supply of drugs ... Between 15 May 2008 and 16 July 2008 some 12,934 phone calls ... It seemed to the judge that the conspirators were working on average a sixteen-hour day supplying class-A drugs to the streets of London ... The judge was

unable to determine with accuracy the hierarchy although his suspicions leant more towards Suckoo as the control. Such a view was not reflected in the sentence as all were dealt with equally of five years and five months.

As he had been sentenced to a term in excess of one year, Suckoo was notified that he was subject to deportation proceedings. He appealed, basically 'on' Article 8. The appeal was allowed but the Home Office appealed on the basis that the tribunal had failed to consider adequately the public interest in Suckoo's deportation.

The Upper Tribunal noted that the Home Office's counsel 'most fairly accepts that it would not be reasonable to expect family members to relocate to Jamaica, notwithstanding [Mrs Suckoo] is of Jamaican origin'.

The appeal finding was that deportation, in the family circumstances, would be disproportionate and in breach of fundamental human rights.[4]

And *see* E is for examples perhaps encapsulating where we are, H is for Abu Hamza, Q is for Abu Qatada, and W is for what is to be done? plus:

- Mustafa Abdi was born in Somalia in 1975; he arrived here in 1995 and was refused asylum but granted exceptional leave to remain here until 2000. In 1998, he was sentenced to eight years for rape and indecency with a child. During his imprisonment, his deportation was ordered but the only carrier willing to take enforced returns to Somalia withdrew. A challenge to his detention was refused as he could have returned voluntarily. He was released in 2007 but detained again a year later after breaching his bail conditions. The European Court of Human Rights has held he is entitled to compensation as regular reviews as required by law were not carried out.

- Hesham Mohammed Ali arrived here from Iraq in 2000, probably by way of people smugglers. A later claim to asylum was rejected. In 2005, he was convicted of possessing class-A and class-C drugs and fined. In 2006, he was convicted of possessing class-A drugs with intent to supply and was sentenced to four years. With that being for more than one year he was liable to be deported. He appealed on the grounds that his tattoos would render him liable to being harmed in Iraq and that he was engaged to a Briton. He has two children, one by an Irish woman and another by one from Liverpool; he has no contact with either woman or child. His appeal was allowed.

- Sani Adil Ali came to this country from Darfur in 2003 and was given refugee status two years later. Within months he had raped a twelve-year-old. He was jailed. Upon being released in 2008 it was ordered that he be deported, against which he made a successful appeal to the Upper Tribunal Immigration and Asylum Chamber under Article 3 of the European Convention on Human Rights.

- 'BM' was put under a control order in 2009 and in 2012 under a Terrorism Prevention and Investigations Measures – a 'TPIM'. (It is said that he was part of the group that included one of those convicted of the Ministry of Sound and Bluewater (shopping centre) plots (*see* T is for terrorism) and that two of his brothers were killed by drones in Pakistan.) Upon a review, the judge concluded BM was 'likely to pursue terror-related activity if not subject to a TPIM … Thus I am satisfied that there is reason to believe he has been, is and will continue to be involved in terror-related activity and that a TPIM is necessary.' When it expired at the start of 2014, he was granted anonymity on the basis that disclosure would, allegedly, infringe his human rights.

- Harnault Hospice Kassi was born in 1975 in Ivory Coast. He arrived here in 2002 and two years later married a Belgian and was granted residency on the basis of her being an EU national; five months later a Frenchwoman[4] gave birth to his child in France. He married her in 2010 and two months later she gave birth to their second child, this time in the UK. His marriage has since ended.

In 2008, Kassi began working for Royal Mail as a van driver for high-value items. In 2011, he was arrested and charged with six others; in 2012, he pleaded guilty and was sentenced to two years and nine months; he was released after eighteen months. Because he had 'done' more than a year, his deportation was ordered. Kassi appealed – his right to family life under Article 8 of the European Convention on Human Rights would be breached. The Tribunal agreed with him; the Home Secretary appealed, inter alia on the basis that the tribunal 'had failed to engage with the severity of his offending'. The Upper Tribunal – Immigration and Asylum – dismissed her appeal because it found that Kassi presenting a low risk of re-offending was 'significant', 'he would be unlikely to fall under the bad influence of others in the future' and that he was 'socially and culturally integrated'.

- Keno ('Blood') Forbes was convicted in 2009 of possessing class-A drugs; he went on from there to be convicted in 2011 on eleven counts of supplying same – he used to commute from Stevenage to Islington –

and was jailed for three years and given a ten year anti-social behaviour order banning him from the area. He successfully appealed against a deportation order because such would damage his relationship with his wife and children.

- TH came here in 2007 from Bangladesh on a spouse's visa. The couple had a daughter. TH was sentenced to five years for stabbing the girl so as to prevent the father having her. Upon release, because TH had been sentenced to more than a year, the Home Office automatically began the deportation process. TH claimed that being deported would breach her human rights as she would be unable to see her daughter – who she can see for one hour three times a year – and thereby avoided being deported.

- Deron Peart has been here illegally from 1998. He was jailed in 2007 for a drugs offence; earlier he had been convicted of knifepoint robbery. At the end of 2007, he was ordered to be deported but did not go, and fathered a child. The Immigration and Asylum Tribunal rejected his attempt to overturn the deportation order but the Court of Appeal held that the Tribunal had not fully considered the significance of the family relationships situation.

- Sanel Sahbaz came here in 1993 as ten-year-old from Bosnia Herzegovina as a dependent of his refugee father; he is (still) a citizen of that country. He had been convicted of common assault, handling stolen goods, theft, public order offences and assaulting the police before, in 2008, armed with a chair leg, he broke his victim's arm and finger, three weeks later broke another's leg and, thirdly, while on bail for both incidents, pushed his landlord to the floor and kicked him repeatedly, refused to stop and then stamped on the victim's head. Sahbaz pleaded guilty to causing actual bodily harm and was jailed for four years with an extended licence period. He was notified that he was liable for deportation. His first appeal was rejected. His further appeal, to the Upper Tribunal, was allowed at least in part, under Article 8[2] because of his family (life) here, namely his parents, brother and cousin, despite having extended family in Bosnia plus accommodation there.

- When Sheik Raed Salah, having been banned from entering the country, was mistakenly allowed in (as the notice went to the wrong terminal at Heathrow), he was able to appeal successfully against his deportation on human rights grounds.

- Jumaa Kater Saleh from the Darfur region of Sudan got here in 2004, hidden in a lorry. The next year he claimed asylum, which was refused as the claim was 'vague, unsubstantiated and lacking in detail', but as he was then only sixteen he was allowed to stay until when he would be eighteen. He was not then deported. In May 2007, he was arrested on suspicion of having committed sexual offences. In February 2008, he was convicted, with others, of sexual activity with a thirteen-year-old who was 'clearly disturbed and vulnerable ... far from mature for [her] age' and sentenced to four years. Because that was for more than two years, he was eligible for automatic deportation at the end of his sentence. But he won an appeal against deportation because he was a member of a tribe that had been subject to 'intolerable treatment'. Because it is only permitted to hold someone in detention while there is a 'realistic prospect' of being deported, his detention was unlawful and he was entitled to compensation for the 'unreasonable delays'.

- On 21 February 2008, a jury found all of Adil Aboulkadir, Jumaa Saleh, Mohammed Abdullahi Jimale, Dawt Akal Kefle and Maher Zeregergis guilty of sexual activity with one or more of three children, Aboulkadir also of rape of one of those girls.

  Each of the [five] was a refugee from the Sudan who had claimed asylum in the United Kingdom [in or about 2005]. Two ... spoke Tigrnya, two spoke Arabic and one Sudanese Arabic.[6]

Aboulkadir is now about thirty-eight years old, the others about ten years younger; the girls were born between October 1992 and December 1993.

Aboulkadir was sentenced to imprisonment for public protection with a minimum of four years, the other four to determinate sentences of four years each.

Appeals were dismissed in May 2009.

Aboulkadir's four year term (certain) ended in May 2012. His case was referred to the Parole Board in August 2011 but the first hearing was not listed until the end of 2012 and the hearing was deferred for an interpreter; with further postponements, the hearing did not take place until September 2013. A year before then, Aboulkadir was cleared for release but moved to an immigration centre for deportation, which he is contesting.

Despite forensic evidence that his semen was found in the vagina of one of the girls, Aboulkadir is seeking a referral by the Criminal Cases Review Commission to the Criminal Appeal Court.

In early 2014 it was adjudged that Aboulkadir's human rights were 'arguably' violated by the Parole Board's failure to consider his release as soon as his minimum prison term expired; a full hearing is to follow.

Notes: *H is for human rights*

1. EV, a Filipino care-home worker, and her husband sought to remain in this country so that their children could be educated here. On appeal from rejection of that application, Lord Justice Lawton, in June 2014, said:

> I cannot see that the desirability of being educated at public expense in the UK can outweigh the benefit to the children of remaining with their parents.

> Just as we cannot provide medical treatment for the world, so we cannot educate the world.

And he observed that the immigration judge weighed the best interests of the children without explicitly considering 'the cost to the public purse in providing education to these children'.

2. The Human Rights Act 1998 brought into British law* the rights and freedoms guaranteed by the United Nations' *Universal Declaration of Human Rights* of 1948 and the *Convention for the Protection of Human Rights and Fundamental Freedoms* agreed by the Council of Europe in 1950, the latter providing for recourse to the European Commission and Court of Human Rights. The Convention's rights and freedoms are:

> Article 2 right to life

> 3 Prohibition of torture – 'No one shall be subjected to torture or to inhuman or degrading treatment or punishment'

> 4 Prohibition of slavery and forced labour

> 5 Right to liberty and security

> 6 Right to a fair trial

> 7 No punishment without law

> 8 Right to respect for private and family life namely:

> > '1. Everyone has the right to respect for his private and family life, his home and his correspondence.

> > 2. There shall be no interference by a public authority with the exercise of this right except such as is in accordance with the law and is necessary in a democratic society in the interests of national security,

public safety or the economic well-being of the country, for the prevention of disorder or crime, for the protection of health or morals, or for the protection of the rights and freedoms of others.'

9 Freedom of thought, conscience and religion

10 Freedom of expression

11 Freedom of assembly and association

12 Right to marry

14 Prohibition of discrimination

16 Restrictions on political activity of aliens

17 Prohibition of abuse of rights

18 Limitation on use of restriction on rights

Plus by the Convention's first protocol – Protection of property; Right to education and Right to free elections

* 'Brought into British law' is the standard way to justify the legislation but for the most part is factually incorrect. Magna Carta (of 1215) and the 1689 Bill of Rights did not so much create as state the existing (common) law. This is shown by the judicial decision in 1772 when the slave James Somersett was set free despite his 'owner' having the due bill of sale. The reasoning was that a person enslaved somewhere else, became free as soon as he arrived here because the common law (and likewise statute) did not provide for slavery.

3. Section 3 of the Act. The Convention is the *Convention for the Protection of Human Rights and Fundamental Freedoms*, agreed by the Council of Europe at Rome on 4 November 1950.

4. The facts and the quoted words are taken from the report of the Upper Tribunal (Immigration and Asylum Chamber) Appeal Number DA/00578/2012.

5. Ivory Coast, or Côte d'Ivoire, was a French colony, and French is the official language.

6. The report of the appeal hearing from Maidstone Crown Court [2009] EWCA Crim 956. The legal aid bill, for the five, prompted exposingislam.blogspot.co.uk to the headline *Muslim Paedophiles rape UK taxpayers.*

I is for identity

> I understand why people feel so strongly about these issues. They touch on some of our deepest concerns about the security and identity of our country.[1]

> Overwhelmingly, this increase in immigration has been in England which, within the past 15 years has become the most densely populated country in Europe. England is being fundamentally changed. All too many schools report that English is not the first language for the vast majority of students. Yesterday's statistics show that, over time, the increase in population will to an even greater degree be down to those coming here and their offspring. We have failed fully to integrate many of our newcomers: this shift will further tilt the balance away from a cohesive national identity.[2]

> These developments, plus the change in society brought about by mass immigration, have led to a sense of lost identity, aggravated by a feeling that the political elites are detached and irrelevant to the things that people really care about.[3]

(And *see* F is for fifth column and F is for fissiparous and N is for nation.)

Notes: I is for identity

1. Beverley Hughes; part of her resignation letter. She was MP for Stretford and Ormston 1997/2010, Minister of State for Immigration, Citizenship and Counter-terrorism between 2002 and her resignation on 1 April 2004.

I thought the story/reason was as follows – in late 2002 a Foreign Office official stationed in Romania wrote to the Immigration and Nationality Directorate that Britain's entry controls were being completely undermined by an organised scam. In the spring of 2003, Bob Ainsworth, the government deputy chief whip, wrote to the minister, drawing her attention to apparently fraudulent visa applications from Bucharest to which he had been alerted by the consul there, such as by a self-employed roof tiler who only had one leg. A year later, the minister told the House of Commons that she had no knowledge of the problem. She then caused a review to be made of the Department's correspondence and thereby saw Mr Ainsworth's letter.

But for at least a fuller account *see The Great Immigration Scandal* by Steve Moxon, the civil servant who let the cat out of the bag, (first) published in

2004 by Imprint Academic.

2. *Cowardice on immigration has allowed the BNP to flourish* by Frank Field and Nicholas Soames, *The Daily Telegraph*, October 2009.

3. *Europe's politicians must embrace competition or face slide into obscurity* by Roger Bootle, *The Daily Telegraph*, May 2014.

The 'developments' he referred to were the 'European social model', an 'excessively generous' welfare state, disdain of material success, loss of empire and the scars of war.

And I is for integration

In 1968,

> The other dangerous delusion from which those who are wilfully or otherwise blind to realities suffer, is summed up in the word 'integration'. To be integrated into a population means to become for all practical purposes indistinguishable from its other members.

> Now, at all times where there are marked physical differences, especially of colour, integration is difficult though, over a period, not impossible. There are amongst the Commonwealth immigrants who have come to live here in the last fifteen years or so, many thousands whose wish and purpose is to be integrated and whose every thought and endeavour is bent in that direction.

> But to imagine that such a thing enters the heads of a great and growing majority of immigrants and their descendants is a ludicrous misconception, and a dangerous one.

> We are on the verge here of a change. Hitherto it has been force of circumstance and of background which has rendered the very idea of integration inaccessible to the greater part of the immigrant population – that they never conceived or intended such a thing, and that their numbers and physical concentration meant the pressures towards integration which normally bear upon any small minority did not operate.

> Now we are seeing the growth of positive forces acting against integration, of vested interests in the preservation and sharpening of racial and religious differences, with a view to the exercise of actual domination, first over fellow-immigrants and then over the rest of the population. The cloud no bigger than a man's hand, that can so rapidly overcast the sky, has been visible recently in Wolverhampton and has shown signs of spreading quickly. The words I am about to use, verbatim, as they appeared in the local press on 17 February are not mine, but

those of a Labour Member of Parliament who is a Minister in the present Government.

'The Sikh community's campaign to maintain customs inappropriate in Britain is much to be regretted. Working in Britain, particularly in the public services, they should be prepared to accept the terms and conditions of their employment. To claim special communal rights (or should one say rites?) leads to dangerous fragmentation within society. This communalism is a canker: whether practised by one colour or another it is to be strongly condemned.'

All credit to John Stonehouse for having had the insight to perceive that, and the courage to say it.[1]

[In 2004] All of this without considering the too many Pakistani and Afghan and Jordanian and Palestinian and Sudanese and Senegalese and Maghrebin immigrants who live in Britain on residence permits. Two million, as things stand today. Over 700,000 in the capital only, and all of them people who have not the slightest intention to integrate.[2]

[In 2009] According to the *London Times*, the number of Muslims in the UK climbed by half a million between 2004 and 2008 alone – a rate of growth ten times that of the rest of that country's population.

Yet instead of encouraging these immigrants to integrate and become part of their new societies, Western Europe's governments have allowed them to form self-segregating parallel societies run more or less according to sharia. Many of the residents of these patriarchal enclaves subsist on government benefits, speak the language of their adopted country poorly or not at all, despise pluralistic democracy, look forward to Europe's incorporation into the House of Islam, and support – at least in spirit – terrorism against the West. A 2006 *Sunday Telegraph* poll, for example, showed that 40 per cent of British Muslims wanted sharia in Britain, 14 per cent approved of attacks on Danish embassies in retribution for the famous Mohammed cartoons, 13 per cent supported violence against those who insulted Islam, and 20 per cent sympathized with the July 2005 London bombers.[3]

[In 2012] Analysis of reports and surveys on integration related questions from the time (Royal Commission, 1949; Scarman, 1981; Swann, 1985; Runnymede, 2000) indicates there are, or were, three crucial questions at the heart of concerns:

1. "Are they like us?"

2. "Could they be made to be more like us?"

3. "Can we live together?"

To illustrate the point, the 1949 The Royal Commission on Population expressed a desire to ensure that future cohorts of immigrants should be of 'good human stock and not prevented by their religion or race from intermarrying with the host population and becoming merged in it' (Royal Commission 1949). This is now a dated point of view, but it nevertheless serves to focus attention on two of the three questions of integration: 'Are they like us?' and 'Could they be made to be more like us?'[4]

[In 2011] Under the doctrine of state multiculturalism, we have encouraged different cultures to live separate lives, apart from each other and apart from the mainstream.[5]

[In 2014] That's why, when there have been significant numbers of new people arriving in neighbourhoods ... perhaps not able to speak the same language as those living there ... on occasions not really wanting or even willing to integrate ... that has created a kind of discomfort and disjointedness in some neighbourhoods.[5.1]

[In 2013] Let's not jump to that conclusion [as to people from the A2 countries] about immigration. The bigger problem that is caused in our cities is caused by immigrants from the Third World who have no intention of integrating here. They are people who left their country, came here and are trying to recreate their country in our country.[6]

'[In 2011] I am a consultant neurosurgeon working in the East Midlands. In my clinics I see an increasing number of patients who need an interpreter, provided at taxpayers' expense and costing about £40. Yesterday, I saw a patient and her husband who have lived in Britain since before the Sixties and yet still require a taxpayer-funded Hindi interpreter.

Just how long is it considered reasonable for people who come here to enjoy all the benefits of British society before they are expected to make the most rudimentary effort to join it?[7]

[In 2013] I applaud the fact that new projects will be put in place to help non-English speakers learn the language (report, November 2013). I volunteer in two English classes, one for literacy (which is attended by both English speakers and non-English speakers and which is free) and another for speakers of other languages, which is paid for by the students, who often study in order to receive a permanent British visa.

This course concentrates on real-life situations such as doctors' appointments. More than half of the students are women from Arab or Asian countries who have children attending British schools who are no doubt fluent in English. Some have been here for more than 10 years and still have minimal knowledge of the English language. These women largely remain within their own communities and maintain their own cultures and traditions. Any project put in place to enable them to integrate can only be a good idea.[8]

Imagine if in the next ten years, the entire population of Glasgow moved out of the city. Some 600,000 residents – all gone. 'You'd sort of notice, wouldn't you?' Yet that's how many white British citizens have moved out of London between 2001 and 2011, says Graeme Archer. As a result of 'white flight', white Britons now account for less than half the capital's population. It's a profound change, yet no one seems ready to examine it. The BBC's home editor simply notes that rising property prices have enabled lucky Londoners to relocate to the coast. Is it really as simple as that? The proportion of white Britons in Barking and Dagenham has plummeted from 80% to under 50% – they can't all be after sea air. Isn't it worth pointing out that the mayor of Tower Hamlets was elected with the support of a deeply unpleasant Islamist group; or that in east London there has been a rising number of 'increasingly violent' attacks on gay people? Even to raise such issues is to invite charges of racism. But it isn't racist. By all means let's celebrate the benefits brought by demographic change, but let's not shy away from discussing the problems it brings, as well.[9]

Of the 8.17 million people in London, one million are Muslim, with the majority of them young families. That is not in reality, a great number.[10] But because so many Muslims increasingly insist on emphasising their separateness, it feels as if they have taken over; my female neighbours flap past in full niqab, some so heavily veiled that I can't see their eyes. I've made an effort to communicate by smiling deliberately at the ones I thought I was seeing regularly, but this didn't lead to conversation because they never look at me in the face.[11]

Jyllands-Posten, the Danish newspaper that sparked controversy by printing cartoons of the prophet Mohammed in 2005, wrote in an editorial entitled 'The Swedish Lie': 'The problem is not [the government needing to spend money] but cultural. It stems from an abysmal difference between the mentality that created the rich and well-functioning Sweden, and the foreign mentality exhibited by the aggressive section of young immigrants.[12]

News that Germany will accept a record 800,000 asylum seekers this year is alarming. It is dangerous for liberal European countries to admit too many immigrants with an entirely different way of life too quickly.

Political correctness has prevented a proper debate about immigration, but multiculturalism has clearly failed. France and Britain, in particular, have admitted large numbers of people who have refused to assimilate. This has led to alienation and mutual mistrust illustrated by events in Tower Hamlets, Rotherham and Paris.

> If we continue to ignore these realities, we are sowing the wind and the whirlwind will surely follow.[13]

> Traditionally, in Muslim countries, a new wife moves in with her husband's family – never the opposite. Among European Muslims this custom has been entirely overthrown. Nowadays, when a transnational marriage between Muslim cousins takes place the spouse that migrates is invariably the non-European spouse, whose first residence after migrating is, as a rule, his or her in-laws' home. These marriages – which in Norway have acquired the name 'fetching marriages' – accomplish two things. They enable more and more members of an extended Muslim family to emigrate to Europe and enjoy Western prosperity. And they put the brakes on – or even reverse – whatever progress the European-born spouse might have made toward becoming Westernized. In other words, the disease of integration is prevented by injecting into the European branch of the family a powerful booster shot of 'traditional values' – that is, hostility to pluralism, tolerance, democracy, and sexual equality. These inoculations have proved extraordinarily effective.[14]

It may be that the reason why Muslims 'increasingly insist on emphasising their separateness' is the admonition in the Koran 'O believers, take not Jews and Christians as friends ....'[15]

And on the basis of another verse of the Koran, Muslims consider non-Muslims, the *kuffar*, as like animals[16] and it is pursuant to a verse of the Koran that ISIS decapitates its enemies.[17]

All of which is presumably why an imam in Birmingham has said:

> No one loves the kuffar. No one loves the kuffar, not a single person here from the Muslims loves the kuffar, whether those kuffar are from the UK or the US. We love the people of Islam and we hate the people of kuffar. We hate the kuffar.[18]

The stated reason for the niqab, etc., is religious but the Koran's admonishment re dress is directed to both genders namely 'Children of Adam'.[19] Thus such covering is not religious but cultural: those so covered are merely maintaining their Pakistani, Saudi, Yemeni etc. culture, notwithstanding living in this country and seeking to become British citizens.

> It is commendable that the European Court of Human Rights has upheld the French ban on wearing the burqa in public.[20] It is significant that this funded test case was brought against the French government by a Pakistani-origin citizen who claimed the burqa ban violated (in telling sequence) her religious, cultural and personal rights. This is untrue. There is no Koranic mandate for female facial masks; it is not culturally

common for Pakistani women to conceal their faces; and no one, including women, has an unqualified right to dress as one pleases in public. For too long the British establishment has been hoodwinked by Muslim zealots that the burqa/niqab is intrinsic to Islam. It is nothing of the sort: it is pre-Islamic, non-Koranic and ipso facto un-Muslim.

For this reason alone, all right-thinking people should reject this imported Saudi fad on compelling religious, social, sexist, security and health grounds. If Muslim women are banned from hiding their faces in Mecca or when they perform their daily prayers, why is this archaic tribal rag given any legitimacy in contemporary Britain?

The UK should outlaw this Wahhabi-Salafi-inspired trend. This Saudi-financed campaign is just another salvo in the battle for the hearts and minds of British Muslims. If Britain's liberal and human rights industry fails to counter this, we will all live to regret it.[21]

The Muslim Council defends rather than condemns criminal acts by Muslims. When the so-called lyrical terrorist, Samina Malik,[22] was tried for writing poems such as *How to behead* and having literature as to how to make bombs, the Council complained she was being prosecuted for thought crime. And when there was a major police operation to arrest those who it was thought had conspired to behead a British soldier, the Council complained the country was a police state for Muslims.[23]

Oldham College is a successful further education college. It is also a beacon for its racially divided town, a place where whites and Asians study in almost equal numbers. Yet as I wait in its hall on a visit in May, I notice that all the students are socialising within their own racial groups. In one corner some Asians, including two young women wearing hijabs, huddle over a laptop. Nearby three less modestly dressed white girls share a joke. They are physically close yet seem not to notice each other.[24]

Today parts of the Arab world have become a more permissive environment for al-Qaeda. This is the completion of a cycle: al-Qaeda first moved to Afghanistan in the 1990s due to pressure in their Arab countries of origin. They moved on to Pakistan after the fall of the Taliban. And now some are heading home to the Arab world again. And a small number of British would-be jihadis are also making their way to Arab countries to seek training and opportunities for militant activity, as they do in Somalia and Yemen. Some will return to the UK and pose a threat here. This is a new and worrying development and could get worse as events unfold. In back rooms and in cars and on the streets of this country there is no shortage of individuals talking about wanting to mount terrorist attacks here.[25]

It would seem that the failure of aliens to integrate was ever thus: in the 1930s, a visitor to Kovno, now Kaunas, in Lithuania reported: 'Walking the … streets you had the impression that it was a completely Jewish city.'[26]

The Permanent Secretary himself, John Gieve,[27] put the number of fully-fledged Al-Qaeda activists as 15,000; these made especially dangerous by being ensconced with hundreds of thousands of passive supporters …

What surprised everyone even more than that integration had halted was that it was not so much the result of 'chain migration' of non-English-speaking and culturally non-acclimatised relatives, but due to second or third generation Muslim immigrants becoming increasingly alienated from mainstream British culture; far more so than their parents and grandparents. As John Snow wrote in *The Sunday Times*:

'Today's young British Muslims are less liberal and more devout than their parents. Their beliefs render many of them determined not just to be different but also to be separate from the rest of the nation.'

This turns on its head the standard model of assimilation that, unlike the first generation, second and third generation immigrants do not have one foot in the old country and are therefore fully able to assimilate. …

It would seem therefore that Muslim integration is as intractable as the much-derided 'alarmist' opinion … has maintained … The problem is both religious and cultural. This is of course not remotely surprising for most of us. Only the political classes, blinded by their politically-motivated contempt for ordinary people and lauding of the foreigner and the non-white, could not have foreseen such an obvious outcome of uncontrolled immigration. [28]

Charles Moore's article[29] emphasises the failure to integrate different cultures in cities and towns across the country.

The rapid growth of immigration meant that neither the host country nor the incoming population could ever hope to assimilate their cultures. Therefore, we have a collection of disparate communities, based largely on religious and ethnic lines.

Human nature compels people, from whatever background, to seek safety and comfort by existing within a community with which they are familiar. That arrangement has assisted more radical elements within communities to impose their will, sometimes outside the law, both within their neighbourhoods and more widely around the country.

The vision, championed mainly by Labour and Liberal politicians, whereby everyone lives in harmony irrespective of their background is clearly not the case.[30]

- *See* Lorraine Mbulawa under A is for African, E is for euphemism and L is for Loyzells Road.

- The 7 July 2005 bombers and the would-be ammonium nitrate bombers were all born in this country.

- Umar Farouk Abdulmatallab,[31] the underpants bomber, had been a student at University College London.

- Taimur Abdulwahab al-Abdaly, 'the Stockholm bomber' – Iraqi-born but a Swedish citizen, had been at Bedfordshire University, living in Luton (from where the 7th July[32] bombers assembled before travelling together to London).

- Rebecca Douglas (non-indigenous) killed Julie Sherriff from Sierra Leone with the comb the victim was wearing: a witness described the sound of the blow as being like 'when you kill a goat back home'. (While her victim was in a coma, Douglas texted of going to the hospital to suffocate her.)

- Sara Ege lived in India until 2000, when she was married to Yousaf Ali Ege in Cardiff, whom she had never met. Twelve years later she was convicted of beating her seven-year-old son Yaseen so much that he died, and then attempting to hide what she had done by burning his body. The cause of this violence was the boy's failure to learn the Koran by heart. Having in police interviews 'confessed' when she said she was told to kill the boy by the devil, she subsequently alleged she was forced to make up this story by her husband, Yousef Ali Ege (a postman), and his parents.

- Mohammed Emwazi came here aged six and attended Westminster University but probably went on to become 'Jihadi John'.[33]

- Mike Freer, the MP for Finchley and Golders Green, has related how he was threatened by Muslims against Crusades, who forced their way into a mosque where he was meeting constituents.

- Shabaaz Hussain, a one-time teaching assistant, is serving five years and three months for donating money to fund terrorism and having extremist material in his possession.

- Abdul Kalam came to this country from Bangladesh when he was four. That must have been at least fifty years ago (so before 'the rivers of blood' speech of Enoch Powell) because with his wife Jahamara, who came here as his bride, in an arranged marriage, their eldest child Rugi is now thirty-three: there are also Ripon, Nazira, Nadiya, Mohammed-Abdul and finally Shamima who was born in 1993. In 2004, Nazira fled back here from an arranged marriage in Bangladesh. In 2012, Shamima's youngest brother and her two sisters were convicted of actual bodily harm – slapping and punching Shamima and hacking off her hair – and honour-based domestic violence – because she was consorting with a man indigenous to this country. (The Kalam family do not live in Derby or Rochdale or Wellington or Luton but in Basingstoke.)

- Zahoor Iqbal was born in Pakistan but, with his family, arrived here before his first birthday. Despite having lived here as good as all his life, plotted with Parviz Khan to kidnap and behead a British soldier.

- Khalique Miah, employed by Tesco and who had been on the supermarket's fast-track management programme, imprisoned his wife and assaulted her because she wore clothing indigenous to this country; he was sentenced to eighteen months.

- Rashi Rauf was a one-year-old when his family moved from Kashmir to Birmingham. Twenty years later, so having spent all his formative years in this country, he returned to Pakistan, where five years later he was arrested as a suspect in the conspiracy to put liquid bombs on aircraft (later, he may have escaped from custody and subsequently been killed by a drone).

- Mohammed Atif Siddique was born here but was sentenced to eight years under the Terrorism Acts for Islamist terrorism offences.

- Forty Sikhs locked themselves in a temple near Kembrey Park, Swindon, so as to prevent the wedding of Susan Momi, a Sikh, and Kenny Lawrence, a Christian.

- Umran Javed, born in 1979 and who twenty-eight years later, while living in Birmingham, told a crowd to 'Bomb, bomb Denmark; bomb, bomb USA'. When sentenced to (six reduced upon appeal to) four years for soliciting murder, he cursed the court, cursed the judge and cursed the jury. That term in jail did not reform him; now living in Derby, he has been convicted of possessing material likely to be useful to terrorism. (He appears to have been a member of al-Muhajiroun, whose members probably include Abu Hamza (aka Hook), (*see* H is for Abu Hamza) and Abu Izzadeen, as to whom (*see* A is for African, for Asian and alien).

- Tilak Bahadur Tamang, who despite having been a Gurkha officer, assaulted his wife; when the magistrates asked why he had not had a place on the Integrated Domestic Abuse Programme, they were told, 'his cultural outlook does not fit'.

- Mohammed Yousaf and his wife, Parviaz, and their daughter, Tania, were murdered in Pakistan in 2010. Mr and Mrs Yousaf had been in this country for over thirty years. They married off their children by arranged marriages to Pakistanis. After and because one such marriage came apart, when they went 'back' for the arranged marriage of another of their children, they were gunned down and Tania's grandmother was subsequently battered to death, apparently as part of the same 'dispute'.

Notes: *I* is for integration

1. Enoch Powell 1912/98.

2. *La Forza della Ragione/The Force of Reason* by Oriana Fallaci published by Rizzoli International in 2004.

3. *Heirs to Fortuyn?* by Bruce Bawer, *City Journal*, Spring 2009.

The following two paragraphs are from *Tristes Tropiques* by Claude Levi-Strauss, first published, in French, in 1955:

> On the aesthetic level, Islamic puritanism, abandoning the attempt to abolish sensuality, has been content to reduce it to its minor manifestations: scents, lacework, embroidery and gardens. On the moral level, the same ambiguity is noticeable: there is a display of toleration, accompanied by an obviously compulsive kind of proselytizing. The truth is that contact with non-Moslems distresses Moslems. Their provincial way of life survives, but under constant threat from other lifestyles freer and more flexible than their own, and which may affect it through the mere fact of propinquity.

> This great religion is based not so much on revealed truth as on an inability to establish links with the outside world. In contrast to the universal kindliness of Buddhism, or the Christian desire for dialogue, Moslem intolerance takes an unconscious form among those who are guilty of it; although they do not always seek to make others share their truth by brutal coercion, they are nevertheless (and this is more serious) incapable of tolerating the existence of others as others. The only means they have of protecting themselves against doubt and humiliation is the 'negativisation' of others, considered as witnesses to a different faith and a different way of life. Islamic fraternity is the opposite of an unadmitted

rejection of infidels; it cannot acknowledge itself to be such a rejection, since this would be tantamount to recognising that infidels existed in their own right.

And in Jean Raspail's introduction to the 1985 edition of *The Camp of the Saints* originally published in 1973 – (*see* note 1 of R is for racist/racism) he wrote:

To be sure, a mighty vanguard is already here, and expresses its intention to stay even as it refuses to assimilate; in twenty years they will make up to thirty percent, strongly motivated foreigners, in the bosom of a people that once was French.

4. *The Impacts of Immigration on Social Cohesion and Integration – The Final Report to the Migration Advisory Committee*, January 2012, by Shamit Saggar, Will Somerville, Rob Ford and Maria Sobolewska.

The paper found that the level of strong agreement with 'minorities should maintain own customs and traditions' was *c.*19% among white Britons but nearer half among Indians, Pakistanis and Bangladeshis.

5. David Cameron to the Munich Security Conference, February 2011.

5.1. David Cameron, April 2014.

6. Lord Tebbit, September 2013.

7. Richard Ashpole FRCS, letter to a newspaper, December 2011.

8. S.M. Freedman letter to a newspaper, November 2013.

But from another letter to a newspaper, from Ruth Dowding in January 2016

Almost 30 years ago, I worked at a school in the Home Counties with a growing Muslim presence. It was decided that it would be helpful if the mothers spoke English, so after-school classes were arranged. However, no one came because, we were told, the women did not have suitable male escorts, their husbands being at work.

There are signs that this attitude persists, which could affect David Cameron's plans to encourage Muslim women to speak English.

9. Graeme Archer in *The Daily Telegraph* as reported/precised by *The Week*.

10. One million is not 'a great number'. Of 8.17m it is (over) 12%. (*See* the part of H is for hegemony to which there is note 29.)

11. *I feel like a stranger where I live* by Jane Kelly, *The Daily Telegraph*, January 2013, she is also consulting editor of the *Salisbury Review*. (It is a pity that Kelly's neighbours haven't read the part of L is for language to

which there is note 4.)

12. From an item in the *Financial Times* entitled *Sweden's politicians square up over immigration debate*, June 2013.

13. Gregory Shenkman, letter to a newspaper, August 2015.

14. *While Europe Slept: How radical Islam is Destroying the West from Within* by Bruce Bawer, 2006, published by Doubleday.

And, from *Our PM has led the fight of people smuggling – he musn't waver now* by Fraser Nelson, *The Daily Telegraph*, April 2016.

> The Swedes have found a phenomenon of "anchor children" being sent ahead by their families, so as to stand a better chance of settling.

The article continued

> And by no means all of them are necessarily children: when the Danes did tests recently (with dental checks and collarbone X-rays) they found three quarters of them were adults.

15. Chapter 5:56. Also 3:28 –

> Let not the believers take for friends or helpers, unbelievers rather than believers. [Alternatively] Let not [Muslims] take the [non-Muslims] for friends.

16. Chapter 25:45:

> Hast thou seen him who has taken his caprice to be his god?
> Wilt thou be a Guardian over them?
> Or deemest thou that most of them hear or understand?
> They are but as the cattle; nay, they are further astray from the way.

Muslims consider non-Muslims as, at best, inferior.

To Muslims innovation anyway in matters of religion is forbidden – 'Indeed the most detestable of things to Allah are the innovations' and so the revered ascetic Al-Fudayl ibn 'Iyaad said:

> Whoever sits with a person of innovation, then beware of him and whoever sits with a person of innovation has not been given wisdom. I love there was fort of iron between me and a person of innovation. That I eat with a Jew or Christian is more beloved to me than I eat with a person of innovation.

According to the Muslim Council of Britain's *Towards Greater Understanding: Meeting the Needs of Muslim Pupils in State Schools*:

As most Muslims do not usually shake hands with a member of the opposite sex, staff need to be aware that some pupils and parents may exhibit reluctance or even refuse to do this, for example, at prize-giving ceremonies. This should not be interpreted as offensive, as it is not intended to be so.

Tarik Hassane was born in this country of a Saudi father and Moroccan mother. He was jailed for plotting to shoot policeman at Shepherds Bush Police Station and sodiers at a neighbouring Territorial Army base. He wrote 'Living among the disbelievers in their country is a major sin and hirja [emigration] from these countries is wajib [obligatory]'. (Hassane acquired the guns from two Negroes.)

17. Chapter 8:12:

When thy Lord was revealing to the angels
I am with you; so confirm the believers.
I shall cast unto the unbelievers' hearts terror;
so smite above the necks, and smite every finger of them.

An alternative translation....

Allah revealed his will to the angels, saying 'I shall be with you. Give courage to the believers. I shall cast terror into the hearts of the infidels. Strike off their heads, maim them in every limb'.

This is to be compared with the (relevant) (Christian) beatitudes:

Blessed are the meek
for they will inherit the earth
Blessed are the merciful
for they will be shown mercy
Blessed are the peacemakers
for they will be called the sons of God
Blessed are those who are persecuted because of righteousness
for theirs is the kingdom of God

18. This was Abu-Usamah at Thahabi, an imam at Green Lane Mosque. It is presumably the same throughout the *ummah*; certainly it is in Sweden.

I am indebted to Gatestone Institute for the following – *The Islamization of Sweden* by Ingrid Cariqvist translated by Maria Calender – Sheik Muhammad Saalih al-Munajjid issued the following fatwa:

Allah, may He be exalted, has instructed His believing slaves to love one another and to take one other as friends, and He has instructed them to hate His enemies and regard them with enmity for the sake of Allah. He has stated that friendship can only be among the believers and enmity is to be between them and the kaafirs; disavowing them is one of the basic principles of their faith and is part of perfecting their religious commitment. There are very many verses, hadeeths and comments of the early generation to that effect.

In 2007 *Undercover Mosque*, showed preachers at Green Lane Mosque declaring

Whoever changes his religion from Al Islam to anything else – kill him in the Islamic state.

By the age of 10, it becomes an obligation on us to force her [young girls] to wear hijab, and if she doesn't wear hijab, we hit her.

Take that homosexual and throw him off the mountain.

And Abu Usamah asking

If I were to call homosexuals perverted, dirty, filthy, dogs who should be murdered, that is my freedom of speech isn't it?

19. Chapter 7:5.

20. In fact, it was the full-face niqab.

21. Letter to *The Times* from Dr T. Hargery, imam, Muslim Educational Centre of Oxford, July 2014. The letter was included in *The Week* – 'Pick of the week's correspondence' – which also included a précis of an article by Mary Dejevsky in the *Independent*, namely, with two parts quoted in full from the original:

It's widely derided as being too liberal on human rights and too soft on villains. So it was a surprise, says Mary Dejevsky, when the European Court of Human Rights last week upheld the right of France to ban the wearing of the face veil (or niqab) in public. More surprising still, its judgment rested on implicit understanding of what it means to be European.

The court was 'able to understand the view that individuals might not wish to see, in places open to all, practices or attitudes which would fundamentally call into question the possibility of open interpersonal relationships, which, by virtue of an established consensus, formed an indispensable element of community life within the society in question'.

A judgment of such generality opens the door for Britain and other EU states to follow suit. And I, for one, hope it does.

It does not seem unreasonable to expect those who choose to settle in Britain to observe the prevailing social norms, whether that is not throwing your rubbish from your balcony, being married to one wife at a time, not having your daughters 'cut' – or not covering your face.

Yes, it's divisive, but equally divisive is our 'live and let live' policy which has led, in some places, to Muslim vigilantes threatening women who walk about in Western dress. This is an area where we should be 'a little more like the French'.

Mary Dejevsky also pointed out that the (French) ban was not the first – 'Belgium enacted such a law three years ago, some cities in Spain and Italy have their own laws' and also the Swiss canton of Ticino.

22. Born in Southall in 1984. Worked for WH Smith at Heathrow and passed on information about security to Sohail Quershi, who pleaded guilty to charges under the Terrorism Acts. (*See* B is for the benefit and burden of (im)migration).

23. Parviz Khan admitted charges and was jailed for life. Zahoor Iqbal, Mohammed Irfan, Hamid Elasmar and Basiru Gassama admitting related offences.

24. David Goodhart (author of *The British Dream: Successes and Failures of Post-War Immigration*), *Prospect*, June 2013.

According to Goodhart:

Almost half of Caribbean men are in a relationship outside their ethnic group: for such women the percentage is 34. The rate for Chinese women is 39% and men at 17%; for black African men the rate is 25% and for women 18%. For South Asians the figures are strikingly lower ... Indian men at 8% and women at 7%. Pakistanis were at 6.8% for men and about 5% for women, and Bangladeshis lower still.

25. Johnathan Evans of MI5.

26. Polish Jewish visitor, before 1939.

27. Permanent Secretary to the Home Office, 2001–05, a deputy governor of the Bank of England, 2006–09, during which time the new Home Secretary, John Reid, described at least part of his department as 'not fit for purpose'.

28. *The Great Immigration Scandal* by Steve Moxon; from the Afterword of the second edition; published by Imprint Academic in 2006.

29. *A weak establishment is letting Islamists threaten British freedoms* by Charles Moore, *The Daily Telegraph*, April 2014.

30. Rob Mason, letter to a newspaper, April 2014.

31. He tried to bring down a flight from Amsterdam to Detroit on Christmas Day 2009 by way of explosives hidden in his underpants. There was only a partial detonation – burning Abdulmatallab's groin – only partial because he had been wearing the pants too long and the explosive had deteriorated.

32. Seven July 2005 when fifty-two were murdered.

33. Born in Kuwait, grew up and schooled in London. Possibly responsible for beheading several hostages in Syria for ISIS.

And **I** is for internment and for the Isle of Man

At the beginning of World War II, with war against fascism, fascists were interned on the Isle of Man or imprisoned together with many of the Austrians, Germans and Italians in this country. Now with war against Islamic extremism, logically, many of the Muslims in this country should be interned.

It would seem that Muslims perceive the war has happened, at least in Denmark:

> And why do people keep trying to silence such defenders of free speech in Denmark, Holland and across Europe? [Lars Hedegaard] paraphrases the historian Bernard Lewis: The leaders of the Ummah [Islamic nation] now evidently believe, or want to demonstrate, that sharia law has already gained force in places like Denmark. In other words, it has supplanted our constitution in their minds. Of course it didn't used to be that way, it used to be the way that you could draw Mohammed or paint him or say whatever you wanted in the Dar al-Harb ['The Land of War' as opposed to the Land of Islam'] because this was outside what Islam considered to be its territory. Now they are implicitly claiming that we are under sharia law.[1]

For the rest of the world, the revolution continues:

> It must by now be obvious that the objective of the Islamic Jihad is to eliminate the rule of an un-Islamic system, and establish in its place an Islamic system of state rule. Islam does not intend to confine this rule to a single state or to a handful of countries. The aim of Islam is to bring about a universal revolution. Although in the initial stages, it is incumbent upon members of the Party of Islam to carry out a revolution in the state system of the countries to which they belong, their ultimate objective is none other than a world revolution. No revolutionary ideology which champions the principles of the welfare of humanity as a whole – as opposed to upholding national interests – can restrict its aims and objectives to within the limits of a particular country or nation.[2]

*Notes: **I** is for internment and for the Isle of Man.*

1. *I may be killed if I write this* by Douglas Murray, *The Spectator*, February 2013. Lars Hedegaard had to leave his home and go under police protection in early 2013 after a would-be assassin came to his door dressed as a postman and, in Hedegaard's words, 'looking like a typical Muslim immigrant'. A few years ago, Kurt Westergaard (the Danish cartoonist) was almost killed by a Somali who broke into his house with an axe; the Danish politician Pia Kjaersgaard went under police guard.

Later in 2013, Fixoozeh Bazrafkan, of Iranian parents but a Danish citizen, was fined for being racist, in writing that Muslim men abuse and murder their daughters and adding, 'the Koran is more immoral, deplorable and crazy than manuals of the two other global religions combined'.

See K is for Mohammed Sidique Khan: he said he was at war.

2. From chapter 3 of *Jihad in Islam* by Abul A'la Mawdudi: (*see* paragraph 7.26 of the Clarke Report).

And **I** is for invasion

> They're not refugees, this is an invasion. They come here with cries of 'Allahu Akbar'. They want to take over.[1]

If successful and the invaders don't 'go native', namely integrate, invasion leads on to the invaded being subjected to the invader and so, in no particular order:

First, there is a requirement for ethnic mix:

- Male TV nurses are 'only black or gay'.

  For years, female nurses have been portrayed on screen as the battle-axe or saucy temptress, as typified by characters in the *Carry On* films. But researchers now claim that male nurses are being depicted unfairly. Some feature in scenes for the sake of sex equality and having black, Asian or other minority male characters to deliver the right ethnic mix in the programme "they claim"...[2]

Second, advertisements and public notices 'have to' meet an ethnic quota, and so:

- Dorset & Somerset's leaflet of *Courses for Adults* had four pictures of (presumably) learners – a man probably bird watching (one of the courses), a woman studying, a person painting (another of the courses) and two bescarved brown women not obviously on any of the courses.

- The two faces on an ATM screen of one bank have both been non-indigenous; the Post Office's advert as to providing euros had a white/black couple on the beach; Boots's advert for sexual incapability had a white/black couple in the bedroom.

- A (government) advertisement for maths teachers had a non-indigenous teacher with five pupils of whom three were non-indigenous; an advertisement for D&T teachers had an indigenous teacher and three of her four pupils were non-indigenous.

- The National Gallery's website for group visits had a picture of three people, a man, probably of African heritage, and two women, both of whom are wearing a hijab, despite Islamic disapproval of human beings being depicted.

Third, the invader imposes his culture on the invaded, so halal meat becomes the norm and all that is available to the invaded,[3] the invader requires segregated swimming and teaching, the invader seeks to have his legal system be at least what applies to him:

- 40% of Muslims want sharia law in 'their' areas.[4]

- On just one day[5] it was reported:

    o two fourteen-year-old (Muslim) boys at Mount Carmel Roman Catholic High School in Accrington, Lancashire, were excluded for refusing to shave;[6]

    o two Muslims won compensation from Tesco because managers at the distribution centre at Crick, Northamptonshire, kept the prayer room locked when not in use and had to be asked for the key;

    o Muslims in Glasgow were refusing to have an anti-flu nasal spray because it contained gelatine.

Subsequently, first there were reports that school exams would be rescheduled to avoid Ramadan[7] and that meat in meals provided to the armed forces is to be 'halal' and secondly that a cardiothoracic surgeon was calling for NHS staff to have religious and cultural sensitivity training, namely:

> Unfortunately, as religious and cultural awareness is not currently an essential part of training and development for health care professionals, many remain innocently unaware of its importance to some groups in society.

It can be a source of frustration for clinical staff when patients do not seem to be co-operating but, in the case of Muslim patients for example, it could be something as simple as someone trying to pass them food in their left hand, which they wash with, instead of their right. Muslim patients are also required to wash before and after eating and if bed-bound, may need a portable hand wash facility which again, can seem odd or unnecessary to those who are not familiar with such processes.

It is not widely known Muslims are not allowed to shake hands with a member of the opposite sex, that intoxicating drugs are not permissible or that not all male family members are allowed to visit a female relative without her hijab[8] on. These are all situations that could cause issues between staff and patients, but they could be easily avoided with some basic training or information to help guide staff – and that goes for any religion or culture which involves sensitive traditions or rituals.

The surgeon in question was Aiman Altzetani. A search does not state his ethnicity but the foreign language he can speak is Arabic. He could be seen on the Twitter page of @UHS_Jobs, under the headline '*Mr Aiman Alzetani provides a fascinating view on cultural awareness in relation to healthcare*', doing what looks like a PowerPoint presentation with the screen being labelled *Priorities of Sharia'h – Life, Faith, Sanity, Wealth, Family Lineage.*[9]

Fourth, deference to the invader, indeed the sensibilities of the invader and such community, and so:

- following the disappearance of two teenage girls from Blackpool – Charlene Downes and Paige Chivers – investigations were 'hampered by concerns about upsetting community cohesion';[10]

- following the arrest of Pakistani students as part of Operation Pathway, part of the briefing to the prime minister for Operation Pathway (*see* P is for Pathway and Pakistan) was 'Community Impact, Engagement, Reassurance';[11]

- the government, both central and local, has imposed diversity as a requirement, as a condition, of doing business with it. Professional bodies require diversity policies as a condition of practising and so we have 'SRA planning surprise diversity swoops';[12]

The Solicitors Regulation Authority requires firms (of solicitors) to have 'a written equality and diversity policy', which 'details the firm's arrangements for workforce diversity monitoring'.

The SRA's 'director of inclusion' is Mehrunnisa Lalani – an invader is part of the enforcement of the rule of the invaded by the invader.

But the SRA complains that the hierarchy and top management structures 'do not reflect diversity characteristics among their members'.[12]

Fifth, sensitivity to the wishes (if not the requirements) of the invader, so:

- actors can no longer black up; the Coconut Dancers are suspect; the *Black and White Minstrel Show* went; unavailable is the 'N' word and so gone is the colour nigger brown, 'eeny meny miny mo, catch a nigger by his toe' and golliwog. Captain Guy Gibson's black labrador can no longer be called 'Nigger'. Likewise, the expressions 'work like a black'[13] and 'paddy wagon' and jokes with bananas or monkeys are 'out';

- Bill Jeffrey, a seventy-two-year-old councillor for Peterlee, Co. Durham, was investigated by the County Council's Standards Committee after using the expression 'nigger in the woodpile'. He explained, 'It was a phrase used many years ago amongst the working classes but it isn't acceptable in this day and age. I wish I'd never said it but a fellow of my generation has grown up with certain phrases';

- David Lowe, who had been a radio presenter for thirty years, was sacked by Radio Devon for meeting the outbreak of summer by playing *The Sun has got His Hat On, Hip, Hip Hooray!*;[14]

- Wardie Primary School in Edinburgh has a mural painted in 1936 of scenes from *Alice in Wonderland*, which include a golliwog. After a complaint was made, the head wrote to the parents:

We do recognise some people may find the representation of a golliwog in the mural to be offensive, but at the same time it is important to recognise that this is a historic piece of artwork which has been in our school for over 75 years. Its historic nature has been recognised by the fact that the school recently received heritage lottery funding to restore it and many parents supported our efforts to restore it. After a complaint was made to the police about the mural I met our community police officer earlier this week I have now been informed that they do not intend to take any further action. Following discussions with council officers, we have decided that we won't cover up the mural but instead continue to use it as an educational resource for the school and explore how things that may have been acceptable many years ago are no longer seen in the same way in the present day.

And the council stated – 'While we understand the offensiveness of the image, it is in no way indicative of the attitudes of either the school or council. Our equalities policies and approaches are robustly multicultural and anti-racist, promoting diversity and good relationships among pupils.'

Sixth, reverse discrimination: the (indigenous) people of this country are discriminated against in favour of 'BME' candidates. Cordella Bart-Stewart, a founder of Black Solicitors Network and an immigration judge, complained about the lack of minority ethnics in the judiciary and called for regulators to consider quotas[12] – 'there is a fear of being perceived as racist'.[10]

- a cross that had been on a wall in St Ann's Hospice in Cheshire since it opened in 1971 was removed because of 'our inclusive values';
- Christmas is objectionable to the invader;[15]

Seventh, our language is subjected to that of the invader, so the BBC, notwithstanding that its first B is for British, produces Rastamouse (for broadcasting in this country).

Eighth, the invaders consider areas where they are, at least, in significant numbers, only their norms of behaviour, only their culture, should be allowed.

- *the Truth about Saturday Night.*[16]

  Get a white chair and a white desk and put the white kid in a white corner with a white teacher and keep him away from the others. If that fails, get rid of the white kid. It's what the community want you to do.[17]

  Both the Tower Hamlets police borough commander and the Quilliam Foundation, the anti-extremist think tank, are wrong to minimise the threats to the Whitechapel pharmacy assistant as just the work of a 'small minority' of 'Talibanesque thugs'. The issue is much more serious than that.

  I know the young woman and the pharmacy concerned, which is located in a Muslim-majority residential area under the shadow of the East London Mosque. The intimidation comes from the burqa-wearing women, as well as bearded men, who live in the vicinity and come to the pharmacy for their prescriptions. They are normal, local residents – the Mr and Mrs Smiths of the neighbourhood – who have made it clear that their part of England is now part of Islam and that the non-Muslim young woman must wear Muslim clothing.

218

> It is especially ominous that the police borough commander should play down the matter. He of all people needs to recognise that this is standard Tower Hamlets Islam doing its normal hardline outreach work. The consequences of this are very distressing for the young woman in the chemist's shop. In the long run they are an equally disturbing threat to the liberty of the rest of us.[18]

- after Paul Weston of Liberty GB, on the steps of Winchester Guildhall, had read out the part of Winston Churchill's book *The River War* which is set out below under 1899 of *W is for we were warned*, Mohammed Rafiq, leader of the Ramadan Foundation, said:

> Of course there should be freedom of speech, but with freedom of speech comes responsibility. If someone was to deliver this message in the centre of Bradford for example where there is a large Muslim population, then it could be seen as a deliberate act of incitement.

- Sunny Islam patrolled his part of east London and raped women, including a fifteen-year-old, so as to 'teach her a lesson' for being out at night.[19]

- Dog waste disposal bins have had attached the following 'notice':

> Do not walk your dog here!
> Muslims do not like dogs.
> This is an islamic area now.

The invasion is exemplified by the constituency of

And **I** is for (the constituency of) Ilford South

In 1953, the electoral rolls for roads such as Cavendish Gardens and Mayfair Avenue (in the ward of Cranbrook) had Anderson, Brown, Hepworth, Gee, Pearson, Neill and Sheppard, but by at least 2003 they had been replaced by Afsar, Anwar, Arjan, Hunjan, Khan, Malik and Patel. And yet,

> Of all London Boroughs, Redbridge [of which Ilford is part] has [only] the sixth highest number[20] (85,014) of people whose stated country of birth is outside of the EU (including Accession states) countries. Redbridge ranked ninth highest in England and Wales.

> In total, 103,073 (37%) people in Redbridge were born outside of the United Kingdom.[21]

Notes: *I* is for invasion and for Ilford South

1. Laszlo Kiss-Rigo, bishop of Szeged-Csanad, Hungary.

Part of the race memory of Hungarians is that Buda(pest) was ruled by the Ottomans from the siege in 1541 for 150 years. And a little further afield, Muslims besieged Vienna in 1529 and 1683 and Corfu in 1537, 1571 and 1716; and that Constantinople was besieged twice in (just) the century following Mohammed's death in 632 and apart from any other time, twice in the century before they took it in 1453.

2. The heading to and part of a newspaper item, September 2013.

3. Nando's planned to open an outlet in Blackburn. The Halal Food Authority allows the stunning of chickens and so its spokesman said:

> The Halal Food Authority certify 'recoverable' stunning. This means that following a stun at low amperage the bird is fully alive at the time of slaughter, therefore fully complying with guidelines for halal laid out in the Koran and in hadith. HFA certified birds are never unconscious before slaughter.

But the Lancashire Council of Mosques disagreed. Salim Mulla, chairman of the LCM's Halal Committee, and one-time mayor of Blackburn with Darwen, said:

> I have been in touch by phone with [Nando's head of customer engagement] and told him unless their chicken meets our guidelines we will not consider it to be halal. In that case we shall urge all East Lancashire Muslims to boycott it which will make it very difficult for the new Blackburn restaurant to trade successfully. No young Muslims will go there. The HFA permits stunning before slaughter which we believe is un-Islamic. Only restaurants and suppliers certified by the Halal Monitoring Committee are currently acceptable to the LCM. (*AsianImage: The voice of the Asian community*, May 2015.)

4. ICM poll: *see* note 24 to A is for African, Asian and alien.

5. 4 October 2013.

6. Mohammed Liaquat went to Mount Carmel Roman Catholic High School in Accrington and launched a racist tirade against white members of the staff because two pupils there, not his sons, had been banned from lessons for refusing to shave. After being released from arrest, Liaquat went to St Oswald's RC Primary School and behaved in rather the same way. Upon being asked to leave, Liaquat barged the headteacher Jeff Brown. After a three-day trial, Liaquat was found guilty of racially aggravated behaviour

and assault and sentenced to twenty-seven months' imprisonment and banned from contact with the staff at, and going within 100 yards of, Mount Carmel, St Oswald's and St Peter's Primary in Accrington and Rosehill Special School in Burnley.

However, notwithstanding the school's dress code, which dated back to before any of Liaquat's children were teenagers, the governors of Mount Carmel rescinded the boys' ban provided they carried out the hafiz programme at the local mosque, albeit, as pointed out by the headmaster, there is nothing in the Koran requiring males not to shave.

7. The item *Exam dates could be moved for Ramadan* in *The Daily Telegraph* by Javier Espinoza and Ben Riley-Smith explained why since the last coincidence of Ramadan and exams the sheer weight of increased numbers, had, this time brought up a call for exams to be moved, namely 'According to the [2011] census, there are 2.71 million Muslims in England and Wales – making up 4.8 per cent of the population. In the Eighties [when Ramadan was last at the same time of the year] there were between 300,000 and 550,000.' (*See* P is for progression.)

But (letter to a newspaper from Mike West):

> A muddle headed suggestion has been made to alter school exam dates to accommodate Ramadan (report January 7).
>
> You mention that fasting in Ramadan does not apply to children. Even if they choose to fast, it is not the lack of food that will make exams difficult but more likely the lack of sleep due to late-night iftar and early morning sohur banquets by family members.

8. Turkish women did not stop being Muslims when, in the 1920s, Ataturk forbade the wearing of headscarves by civil servants; girls in France do not stop being Muslim when they take off their head covering upon entering their school, pursuant to the 2004 law.

Towards Greater Understanding: Meeting the Needs of Muslim Pupils in State Schools by the Muslim Council of Britain under 'Dress codes in schools: features of good practice' includes:

> Muslim girls who choose to wear the headscarf during all school lessons and activities are permitted to do so, including during physical education.

Note the word 'choose'.

The point, that wearing a headscarf is merely cultural, is reinforced by an issue in December 2015 of the *Catholic Herald* the front cover/page of which had President Putin of Russia with a group of Christian women wearing (white) hijabs.

9. *The People's Daily Morning Star* of 3 June 2014. UHS is, presumably, University Hospital Southampton.

10. Retired Detective Superintendent M. Gradwell: *see* D is for Derby.

11. Although the arrests were in Lancashire, the MPs for Perry Bar, Birmingham and Glasgow Central wrote to the then Home Secretary:

> Incidents such as this do irreparable damage to the vital race relations work that is being done and has been done by the Government and leaders of ethnic minority communities, both at home in this country and abroad ... An important strand of counter-terrorism must be about winning the hearts and minds as well as the confidence of Britain's Muslim community.

That two members of the UK Parliament should be so concerned about foreign nationals is telling but the explanation must be that the two MPs, Khalid Mahmood and Mohammad Sarwar, were both born in Pakistan.

12. *The Law Society Gazette*, 1st September 2012.

According to Baron Ouseley of Peckham Rye (born in Guyana in 1945 and came here eleven years later), April 2013:

> In its response to the workforce review, completed in November last year but circulated to members of the equality and diversity committee last week, the SRA acknowledges that progress had been slow, particularly in appointing BME candidates to senior positions.

And following the publication of the BSN's 2014 Diversity League Table:

> We are in a situation where, at the very least, we have to look at targets being set by the regulators in terms of seeing change.

13. Or in literature as in 'I think he ought to keep some of it. He's a good lawyer and works like a black' – *Friends at Court* by Henry Cecil, first published 1956.

14. He did not know that lines include:

> He's been tannin' niggers out in Timbuktu
> Now he's coming back to do the same to you.

15. Paragraphs 4.35 and 4.36 of the Clarke Report:

> Christmas was banned by governors at Nansen Primary in December 2013. The staff and children had prepared their usual nativity play, the

school was decorated with trees, presents were bought, and the post box was in place for the usual posting of cards. However, the headteacher was severely reprimanded for making such arrangements and allowing the school to celebrate the feast. She argued with the governors and eventually they told her that the nativity could take place without a baby Jesus, but that everything else must go. Parents attended the nativity play as usual and the whole school came together. Neither staff nor parents think that words such as 'Christmas' should be banned within the school.

Also in 2013 the governors of Oldknow agreed that celebrations for Christmas, Diwali and Easter would not take place, and that the focus would be on teaching. A governor objected to an afternoon of Christmas celebrations. There were no trees to be ordered and no parties and the Birmingham City Mission speaker was cancelled despite complaints from parents. The school was closed for two days to celebrate Eid.

16. www.youtube.com/watch?v=zqNYjximCko.

17. Muslim parent at Anderton Park School, Birmingham, to staff there – paragraph 4.42 of the Clarke Report.

18. Alan Craig of London E7, letter to *The Sunday Times*, April 2011, and reproduced by *The Week*. Additionally, this is to be found, apart from anywhere else, on the internet site *Islamophobia Watch Documenting Anti-Muslim bigotry*.

In early 2011, posters went up across Tower Hamlets stating the area to be a gay-free zone and stating 'Verily Allah is severe in punishment'. The police had clear CCTV evidence of the perpetrators but would not release them because, in the words of a homosexual activist, 'The police told us no one was allowed to talk publicly about this because they did not want to upset the Muslim community.' Soon after the CCTV photos were eventually published, the perpetrator was identified namely Mohammed Hasnath. He was fined: he was already on bail for defacing advertisements featuring women. A year later he was jailed for terrorism offences.

19. Coincidentally, Sunny Islam's defence counsel, the prosecuting counsel and the judge were all women but perhaps Mr Islam would not have been concerned with that as (while in court) their heads were covered – by wigs.

20. The London boroughs with greater immigration were Newham, Brent and Ealing; and outside of London were Slough, Luton, Leicester and Birmingham.

21. Redbridge Home Page.

J is for joke

First of all funny (or at least telling):

Welcome to a brand new edition of *Asylum*.

Today's programme features another chance to take part in our exciting competition. Hijack an airliner and win a council house! We've already given away hundreds of millions of pounds and thousands of dream homes, courtesy of our sponsor the British taxpayer. And don't forget we're now the fastest-growing game on the planet.

Anyone can play, provided they don't already hold a valid British passport, and you only need one word of English: Asylum.

Prizes include all-expenses paid accommodation, cash benefits starting at £180 a week and a chance to earn thousands more begging, mugging and accosting drivers at traffic lights. This competition is open to everyone buying a ticket or stowing away on one of our partner airlines, ferry companies or Eurostar.

No application ever refused reasonable or unreasonable. All you have to do is destroy all your papers and remember the magic password: Asylum.

A few years ago 140 members of the Taliban family from Afghanistan were flown Goat Class from Kabul to our international gateway at Stansted where local law enforcement officers were on hand to fast track them to their luxury £200 a night rooms in the fabulous four star Hilton Hotel. They join tens of thousands of other lucky winners already staying in hotels all over Britain.

Our most popular destinations also include the White Cliffs of Dover and the world famous Toddington services area in historic Bedfordshire.

If you still don't understand the rules, don't forget there's no need to phone a friend or ask the audience, just apply for legal aid. Hundreds of lawyers, social workers and counsellors are waiting to help. It won't cost you a penny so play today. It could change your life forever.

Iraqi terrorists, Afghan dissidents, Albanian gangsters, pro Pinochet activists, anti-Pinochet activists, Kosovan drug smugglers, Tamil tigers, bogus Bosnians, Rwandan murderers, Somali guerrillas ... Come On Down.

Get along to the airport, get along to the lorry park, get along to the ferry terminal. Don't stop in Germany or France. Go straight to Britain and you are guaranteed to be one of tens of thousands of lucky winners in the softest game on earth.[1]

And

I cross ocean, poor and broke. Take bus, see employment folk.
Nice man treat me good in there. Say I need to see welfare.
Welfare say, You come no more, we send cash right to your door.
Welfare cheques – they make you wealthy! NHS – it keep you healthy.
By and by, I got plenty money. Thanks to you, you British dummy!
Write to friends in motherland. Tell them 'come fast as you can'.
They come in turbans and Ford trucks. And buy big house with welfare bucks!
They come here, we all live together. More welfare cheques, it gets better!
Fourteen families, they moving in, but neighbour's patience wearing thin.
Finally British guy moves away. Now I buy his house, then I say.
Find more immigrants to rent. And in the yard I put a tent.
Everything is good and soon we own the neighbourhood.
We have hobby, it's called breeding. Welfare pays for baby feeding.
Kids need dentist? Wives need pills? We get free! We got no bills!
British crazy! They work all year, to keep the welfare running here.
We think UK darn good place. Too darn good for British race!
If they no like us, they can scram. Got lots of room in Afghanistan![2]

Secondly sick (or at least telling) is the story told by the first seven paragraphs of a decision of the Court of Appeal and its decision:[3]

1. YM was born in Uganda on 24 June 1984. He came to the UK with his mother and siblings in 1991 when he was aged six. He obtained indefinite leave to remain in the UK in 2001 when he was 16. His mother and siblings have obtained British nationality, but YM has not. This is because he started to commit crimes when he was 14, his age when he was convicted of robbery. He was subsequently convicted of assault occasioning actual bodily harm when he was 15, of three assaults on constables, committed when he was 18, and of aggravated burglary when he was 19. For this last offence he was sentenced in Croydon Crown Court on 5 September 2003 to 3 years 6 months in a Youth Offender Institution ('YOI'). On 11 November 2004 YM was warned in a letter from the Secretary of State for the Home Office ('SSHD') that a serious view was taken of the aggravated burglary offence and that he was at risk of being deported if he should 'come to adverse notice in the future'.

2. Whilst in detention in the YOI, YM began seriously to practise Islam, the religion to which he was born. On the day of his release, 18 March 2005, YM married J, a British citizen, in an Islamic marriage ceremony. They have remained married and have 3 children, who were born, respectively, in December 2005 (IS), October 2009 (AQ) and 25 December 2011 (IL). J, who converted to Islam before marrying YM, is a trained midwife who works part-time.

3. After YM's release on licence in 2005 he used to attend Croydon Mosque and that led him to go to meetings at the house of a man called Hamid, who subsequently YM admitted was a fanatical Islamist. These encounters resulted in YM attending two terrorist training camps in the New Forest in 2006. He was arrested in September 2006 and charged on two counts of offences under section 8(2)(a) of the Terrorism Act 2006. Broadly speaking this sub-section makes it an offence for anyone to attend a place, in the UK or elsewhere, where he has instruction or training in (for short) activities that can be used for terrorist purposes or in the use of weapons, where instruction or training is wholly or partly for purposes connected with terrorism. Under section 8(2)(a) it has to be proved that the offender knew or believed that instruction or training is being provided at the particular place 'wholly or partly for purposes connected with the commission or preparation of acts or terrorism or Convention offences'. YM pleaded guilty to the two counts and on 26 February 2008, in the Crown Court at Woolwich, Pitchers J sentenced YM to 3 years 5 months' imprisonment on each count, the sentences to run concurrently. Because YM had been in custody since his arrest, he was actually released on licence in June 2008.

4. Meanwhile on 22 May 2008 YM was served with a deportation notice by the SSHD which stated that, as a result of his convictions and sentences for the terrorist offences, the SSHD deemed it to be conducive to the public good to make a deportation order against him pursuant to sections 3(5)(a) and 5(1) of the Immigration Act 1971 as amended. A letter dated 23 June 2008 set out the SSHD's reasons. It stated that 'it was not accepted' that the decision to deport would give rise to any interference with the family life of YM within the terms of Article 8 of the European Convention on Human Rights (ECHR) or, if there was any such interference, it 'could be justified in the circumstances' of his case.

5. YM appealed the deportation decision and on 1 July 2009 the Asylum and Immigration Tribunal (AIT) allowed his appeal both on human rights grounds under Article 8 and on immigration grounds under paragraph 364 of the Immigration Rules (HC 395) as amended. In August 2009 YM was warned for having contacted a co-defendant to the terrorist charges. (Non-contact was a condition of YM's licence). In December 2009 YM was recalled to prison at the same time as being arrested on suspicion

of handling stolen goods. Those charges were not pursued and in January 2010 YM was released on licence again. Then on 5 October 2011 he was given a caution as a result of a 'road rage' incident. In June 2012 YM was arrested on a charge of fraud in connection with an application for motor insurance. He subsequently pleaded guilty and was sentenced to a 12-month community supervision order and disqualified from driving for 12 months.

6. The SSHD appealed the AIT's decision and on 22 June 2011 the Upper Tribunal (UT) set aside the determination of the AIT for error of law and directed that the UT should re-make the decision. At the re-determination hearing on 22 February 2013 the UT heard oral evidence from YM, his wife J, YM's mother and also J's mother. It had before it written evidence from various witnesses in support of YM's case. It also had expert written evidence from Professor Silke, someone the UT described as 'having considerable expertise' on terrorism generally and terrorist psychology in particular, and Professor Allen, an expert on East African and Ugandan affairs and professor at the London School of Economics. Lastly, the UT had reports from independent social workers who had twice visited YM, J and their family to observe and comment upon the family relationships and possible consequences if YM were to be deported.

7. The UT promulgated its decision on 2 May 2013 and allowed SSHD's appeal. In summary, it rejected arguments advanced by [YM's counsel] that there was a real risk that YM's rights under Article 3 of the ECHR would be breached if he were to be returned to Uganda. The UT also rejected the argument that, with regard to YM's Article 8 rights, the case should be dealt with on the basis of the revised Immigration Rules that had come into force on 9 July 2012. However, the UT also found that YM could not have satisfied their terms even if they were applicable. Further, whilst the UT accepted that the deportation of YM would interfere with his Article 8 rights, it concluded that there were very serious reasons justifying deportation despite YM's long residence in the UK and the impact deportation would have on his family life. The UT was satisfied that 'the decision to deport [YM] is necessary and proportionate to a legitimate aim within Article 8(2).' The effect was that, in re-making the AIT's decision, it dismissed YM's appeal based on Article 3 and Article 8 grounds 'as well as on humanitarian protection and immigration grounds'. Therefore the SSHD's decision to deport was upheld.

But YM appealed (again). The Court of Appeal allowed the appeal on the Article 8 ground but dismissed it on the Article 3 ground,[4] the former aspect to be remitted to a differently constituted UT in order to re-find the relevant facts and apply them (to the new rules). Thus, in short:

- May 2008: notice from SSHD that YM be deported
- July 2009: the AIT allowed YM's appeal
- SSHD appealed and, in June 2011, the UT set aside the AIT's determination
- May 2013: the UT allowed SSHD's appeal
- YM appealed to the Court of Appeal, who in part rejected the appeal and in part sent the case back to the UT.

And all even though YM is evidently a violent criminal and turned to terrorism after being warned he was at risk of being deported if he should 'come to adverse notice'.

Notes: *J is for joke*

1. Joke on emailsphere.

That a claim for asylum is usually the fall-back claim if an ordinary request for entry is refused is shown by the UK Border Agency reporting, in the spring of 2011, that some 450,000 asylum seekers had gone missing. (The number seeking asylum from Tunisia increased with the departure of President Ali).

It is not just this country where 'it is tried on'. In 2011, Denmark had 3,400 asylum applications of which only about one third were granted. Denmark found that the number of Somali asylum seekers increased as the security situation improved – 35 in 2010, 18 in 2011 and 900 in 2012. Following a joint Danish–Norwegian visit to Mogadishu in October 2012, it was decided that the security situation had so improved that Somali asylum seekers should be sent back.

Cases of claiming asylum as an excuse for entry, and/or to remain, include:

- an Afghani who arrived in Dover in 2008 claiming to be fifteen, was dispersed to Cardiff and there threatened to take the daughter of the family who was fostering him to Iran: at the start of 2011 he was adjudged, then, to be over twenty.
- Mehmet Baybasin, having in the 1990s claimed political asylum from Turkey, is serving thirty years for conspiracy to import tonnes of cocaine.

- Mohamed Bouzalim claimed asylum on the basis of being an Afghani whose father had been killed by the Taliban, but was in fact from Morocco.

- Teresa Matos was born in Angola and was granted asylum in 2004. Six years later she was imprisoned for attempting to smuggle cocaine into this country; she was sentenced with Raul Beia, Abdul Banda and Dean Langley.

- Amina Muse sought asylum on the grounds of having been gang raped in Somalia and her family home looted by militia, but in fact, at such time, had been living in Sweden; she was jailed for a 'professionally planned' benefit fraud.

- Ubax Said entered this country in the mid-1990s as a child and was given exceptional leave to remain. In 2000, she borrowed a child for seeing the Home Office when she claimed she had been smuggled into the country as Iyan Artan. She was sentenced to imprisonment for false accounting, obtaining a money transfer by deception, fraudulently obtaining a tax credit and obtaining leave to remain in the country.

2. Joke going around the emailsphere.

And apart from anything else there is *Brand New Leather Jacket* to which the chorus is:

> Oh I've got a brand new leather jacket and a brand new mobile phone.
> The Brits they live in cardboard boxes while we get furnished homes.
> Legal aid, driving licences, central heating and free pills,
> Oh we get all the benefits and you get all the bills.

3. *YM (Uganda) v. The Secretary of State for the Home Department* [2014] EWCA Civ 1292 (The first seven of the 66 paragraph judgment of the Court of Appeal.)

4. YM argued that the treatment he would get in Uganda, would be in breach of Article 3. For the wording of the Articles *see* note 1 to H is for human rights.

K is for Mohammad Sidique Khan

... of Pakistani heritage from Beeston, Leeds, who, with Hasib Hussain, also of Pakistani origin and from Leeds, Germaine Lindsay, born in the West Indies and from Aylesbury, and Shehzad Tanweer, again of Pakistani origin and from Leeds, murdered fifty-two people on London Transport on 5 July 2005. London had previously been reconnoitred by Waheed Ali, Sadeo Saleem and Mohammed Shakilir.

Before going out on such killings, Khan left a 'testament' which includes:

> We are at war ... I am a soldier.

> I and thousands like me are forsaking everything for what we believe. Our driving motivation doesn't come from tangible commodities that this world has to offer. Our religion is Islam, obedience to the one true God, Allah and follow in the footsteps of the final prophet and messenger Muhammad.

Presumably he was (also) heeding the direction of the Koran to

> Fight those who do not believe in God, and the last Day
> and do not forbid what God and his Messenger
> have forbidden – such men as practise not the
> religion of truth, being of those who have been given
> the Book – until they pay tribute out of hand
> and have been humbled.[1]

Such direction (and others[2]) of the Koran is presumably why

> Essentially, Islamism is a doctrine which provides a reason to hate and kill everyone who does not subscribe to it. Start with the people in the frontline of your malice – Jews, Christians in the Arab world, the professional soldiers of infidel countries. Progress to those who transgress your morality – 'loose' women who do not cover their faces, homosexuals, people who drink alcohol. And then end up with anyone who does not submit to the will of Allah, as interpreted by your pop-up theologians. Isil is the apotheosis of this – a would be state based upon the annihilation of all diversity. The most beastly atrocities are, in its collective mind, the best proof of its purity ...

> What brings it all home, literally, is immigration. Even if it is true, as it probably is, that the great majority of Muslims are as peace-loving and decent as any other group of people, you have the simple problem of numbers. If a million Muslims are reaching Germany this year, and even

if only 1 per cent subscribe to the doctrines of ISIL, that means 10,000 people dedicated to killing their hosts and assailing the society that accommodates them.

And such is the power of Islamist grievance culture and their infiltration of social media, charities, community groups, mosques and public-policy forums, that 1 per cent would be a conservative estimate. The grim fact is that we have within our midst thousands of people whose lives are devoted to doing our society harm and hundreds of thousands more who are susceptible to the lies they tell. Yet still our policies amplify their voices and swell their numbers.[3]

Notes: *K is for Mohammad Sidique Khan*

1. Chapter 9:29 of the Koran.

2. For example chapters 3:27, 5:56 and 8:21.

3. *How many more people have to die before we stop appeasing Islamists? Why aren't we standing up to the enemy within?* Charles Moore, *The Daily Telegraph*, November 2015.

L is for language

> We have room for but one language in this country and that is the English language.[1]

> It seems like we're straying away from [previous waves of immigrants adopting English] now and people want to return to the culture of the country they came from. When people come to a country to improve their lot, they should assimilate into that country.[2]

> No one would expect or indeed want British Muslims, or any other group, to lay aside their faith, traditions or heritage. But they must not forget that for the child to prosper in Britain and to reach his or her full potential, he or she will also have to have fluent command of English.[3]

> It is not difficult to see the benefits to integration of even a basic level of English language skills. It must be beneficial for a newly arrived partner to be able to go into a shop and buy groceries or other necessaries, to say 'hello' to the neighbours, to navigate public transport, to interact at a simple level with bureaucrats and health care professionals. Integration is a two-way process. It must be beneficial for others to see that the people living in our midst and intending to stay here are able and willing to join in and play a part in everyday social interactions, rather than keeping themselves separate and apart.[4]

Gladstone Primary School in Peterborough, for the spring term of 2013, had not one pupil whose first language was English.

Early in 2014, as part of Operation Erle, a joint enquiry between Cambridgeshire Police and Peterborough City's children services, four Roma – Zdeno Mirga, Renato Balog, Jan Kandrac and an unnamed fourteen-year-old, plus Iraqi Kurd Hassan Abdulla, were all jailed for raping and selling girls aged between twelve and fourteen. Having been told that the cost of translators for the two-month trial was £40,000, Judge John Bevan QC commented:

> The fact is that the defendants all came to this country with their families between 5 and 10 years ago and the majority are still teenagers. The acquisition of a new language is not difficult if you put your mind to it. They have not attempted to learn the language of the country of their choice … The combination of the crimes you have committed and your attitude to these crimes both in this country and this court bring discredit on all of you in the dock and does a disservice to your fellow Roma who want to work hard in this country, improve themselves and make a positive contribution.

232

City of Leeds School, where natives are in a minority, is reported to be going to teach English as a foreign language.

> Around half of our children are new to the country, within four years. It is generally thought it takes five years to properly learn a language and that is when you have total immersion. A lot of our children don't have that because it is not being spoken at home.[5]

The Race Equality Policy of Bethnal Green Academy[6] includes:

> 5.4 Guidelines for working with pupils who have English as an additional language
>
> - We recognise and value multi-lingualism.
>
> - The language and learning needs of multi-lingual pupils are clearly defined and appropriate support identified and used. The school will reflect and develop pupils' and communities' languages and cultural backgrounds through resources and displays throughout the school. For example, multilingual signs[7], notices and students' writing.
>
> - We will explore a broad range of other media, for example computer software, the internet, audio and videotapes, films, songs, games etc, to support the maintenance and development of home/community language skills and cultural heritage.
>
> - We will seek to provide community languages and dual language texts, both fiction and non-fiction, in order to facilitate access for students who are developing literacy in their own language.
>
> - We will draw on the skills of parents and local communities in producing resources.
>
> - We will seek to provide high quality interpretation and translation across all areas of the school's work as appropriate.

Notes: *L is for language*

1. Theodore Roosevelt (president of the United States of America 1901/09), in 1919 to the American Defense Society. The sentence was followed by 'For we intend to see that the crucible turns out people as Americans, of American nationality, and not as dwellers in a polyglot boarding-house.'

2. A town councillor of Jackson, New York, USA.

3. John Patten in 1989 while Minister of State for Home Affairs 1987/92 and then Secretary of State for Education 1992/94.

4. Lady Hale, deputy president of the Supreme Court, in the applications of Ali and Bibi to join their respective spouses here, from Yemen and Pakistan, despite not speaking English (*2015 UKSC 68*).

5. Georgiana Sale, the headteacher, March 2014. She commented that an adverse Ofsted report – failure to reach national averages in English – was unfair when so many pupils were new to the language: the school did achieve national targets in both science and maths. She also said that one of the largest groups of non-indigenous were Czech Roma, of whom 'many … are not only new to English but they are not even literate in their own language. In some cases we are the first people to put a pen in their hand.'

6. *See* O is for obscenity.

7. The signage must be enormous – because the school roll is '47% … of Bangladeshi heritage, 20% are of African/Caribbean heritage and the remaining 33% is comprised of 18 different ethnic groups'.

And **L** is for law

… the increase thereof – for instance Prohibition of Female Circumcision Act 1985; Female Genital Mutilation Act 2003; the Forced Marriage Act 2007; increased planning law because of increased population density; licensing of houses in multiple occupation because of increased population density; minimum wage because of immigrants forcing down wage levels (*see* E is for the economics of immigration); anti-discrimination and race relations legislation:

> … there are now more than 35 Acts of Parliament, 52 Statutory Instruments, 13 Codes of Practice, 3 Codes of Guidance and 16 European Commission Directives that deal with discrimination, animosities and hatred. Together, various Public Order Acts and related laws make it illegal to hate anyone because of their race, colour, ethnic origin, nationality, national origin, religion, lack of religion, sex, sexual orientation, gender identity, disability or age.[1]

*Notes: **L** is for law*

1. *The Diversity Illusion: What We Got Wrong about Immigration and How to Solve It*, by Ed West, Gibson Square Books.

The same point/numbers is made by Jon Gower Davies in his commentary entitled *Immigrants Come From Somewhere (Else)* to Trevor Phillips' *Race and Faith: The Deafening Silence*.

And **L** is for the losers by immigration

- School children whose classmates do not have English as their first language.

- Parents who cannot get their children into the school of their choice.

- (Young) adults who cannot buy their homes because immigration and the increase in numbers/demand for housing has pushed up prices: (*see* H is for housing).

- The lowest paid, whose pay rates are pushed down by immigrant labour: (*see* E is for the economics of immigration).

- All of us by cost (*see* C is for cost), increase in crime (*see* C is for crime), reduction of social capital and reduction of social cohesion.

- All of us through increase in insurance premiums and water bills (*see* P is for population).

And **L** is for Loyzells Road in Birmingham

… which is predominately black (African) on one side and predominately brown (Asian) on the other, the parents in the latter telling their daughters they can date whomsoever they like so long as he is not BMW, namely he is not black, or Muslim or white – in a country which is (or was) white, immigrants tell their daughters not to have anything to do with the male part of the local/indigenous population.

And **L** is for Luton

According to the 2011 census the population of Luton was then

White: English/Welsh/Scottish/N. Irish /British were a minority, namely 44.6%.

Asian/Asian British: Indian and Asian/Asian British: Pakistani and Asian/Asian British Bangladeshi and Asian/Asian British: Chinese and Asian /Asian British: Other Asian

together made up 29.27% and 24.6% were Muslim, compared with 4.8% nationally, an increase over the preceding decade of 85.4%.

Such is the reputation of Luton (*see* F is for fissiparous and for fifth column) that is synonymous with Muslim behaviour, so:

You know how, in C of E sermons, the vicar is at pains to make his sermons as locally relevant and as secular as possible? Well, Islamic sermons are the exact opposite of that. Though [the one I inadvertently tuned into while driving through Birmingham] had been recorded in a Cape Town Mosque it could have come from anywhere in the *ummah*,[1] from Islamabad to Jeddah to Luton. The preacher would illustrate his points by regularly breaking into fluent, chanted excerpts from the Koran or the Hadith, and he spoke with the absolute conviction of a man who is relaying directly the word of God to the ignorant masses.[2]

Whether or not the following is typical of Luton, certainly that is where:

• Troops returned from Iraq were jeered and spat at.

• Mohammed Sharfaraz Ahmed of Maidenhall Road, Umar Arshad of Crawley Road, Zahid Iqbal of Bishopsgate Road and Syed Farhan Hussain of Comel Close, all described as British, pleaded guilty, nearly a year after being arrested, on charges of terrorism. They had identified the Territorial Army base in Marsh Road as a would-be target. They had written material including *44 ways to support jihad, 21 techniques of silent killing*, the al-Qaeda manual, *The book of jihad, The explosives course 2* and al-Qaeda's magazine *Inspire* with an item entitled *How to make a bomb in the kitchen of your mom*. Having had a quarter reduction for pleading guilty, the four were sentenced to terms of between eleven years and three months and five years and three months.

• Nasserdine Menni, an Algerian, while living in Luton provided funds to the (Iraqi-born) Stockholm bomber:

in the knowledge or with reasonable cause to suspect that those sums of money would or might be used for the purposes of terrorism … You have been convicted of seven charges, including four charges of fraud, one contravention of Section 24A(1)(a) of the Immigration Act 1971, involving the use of false particulars in support of an asylum claim and one contravention of Section 25(1)(b) of the Identity Cards Act 2006, involving your possession of an immigrant status document which was improperly obtained.[3]

- Late in the evening of Friday, 22 November 2013, two sisters aged thirty-two and twenty-two were in their flat (in Luton). One of them went to a neighbouring flat to ask that the music be turned down. At the party was Imran Ghafoor of Newhouse Crescent, Watford. Sometime later, he went to the sisters' flat, forced his way in and then 'literally forced drugs into their mouths'[4] before sexually assaulting them. Later that night, a neighbour saw the sisters were in a stupified and confused state: she called an ambulance. Medical examination found traces of cocaine and Viagra. Three days later, Ghafoor was arrested. He denied having done anything wrong, saying the drugs were the women's. Ghafoor was found guilty of, inter alia, assault and administering a substance, and was sentenced to sixteen years.[5]

- Runa Khan, of Maple Road West has six children.

  She has said 'the UK was the last place I would want to live in. The majority of people with my mindset are actually behind bars because they don't want to stay in Britain.'

  She has posted an image of a suicide vest tagged with the words 'sacrificing your life to benefit Islam'.

  She wrote: 'I pictured the future while I was zipping up [her son's] jacket, in sha Allah I'll be tying the shahada bandana round his forehead and hand him his rifle and send him out to play the big boys game.'

  She has posted on social media: 'Sisters, if you love your sons, husbands and brothers, prove it by sending them to fight for Allah.'

  And she has forwarded details of a route into Syria.

And (yet), throughout her time in court, she was allowed to wear a burqa.[6]

The reporter Stacey Dooley grew up and went to school – Stopsley – in Luton. In 2013, she returned to investigate what had happened to her home town. She accompanied a march on which there were placards such as 'British Police terrorise Muslims', 'Stop terrorising Muslims', 'British

Police go to hell' and 'UK go to hell'. She visited Bury Park, where 30,000 Muslims live and which both indigenous and non-indigenous describe as foreign.[7]

Notes: *L is for Luton*

1. Islamic nation.

2. *The Islamic sermon that taught me what's happened to Birmingham* by James Delingpole, *The Spectator*, November 2014.

3. From the judgment of Lord Matthews in *HMA v. Menni.*

4. The prosecuting counsel, David Harounoff.

5. Sources include *Luton on Sunday, Watford Observer* and *Fahreneit211.*

6. Khan was sentenced to five years and three months for promoting terrorism. She appealed, on the basis that the sentence was too harsh: the Court of Appeal dismissed her appeal.

Others who have appeared in court so covered include:

- Abu Hamza's daughter-in-law – *see* H is for Abu Hamza.

- Alaa Esayad, although she took it off for the street. Despite her father fleeing Iraq in 1999, she became known as the 'Twitter terrorist' after – posting more than 45,000 messages such as (a translation of one of which is) 'They take it skilfully, when the boy starts school, let him like Kalashnikov, raise him on pictures of weapons so that he likes them instead of clinging to the Play Station machine'; – writing poems such as *Mother of the Martyr*; – posting the advice of a Muslim scholar to 'strike the English and their followers and every Muslim in the world must fight them and kill them wherever they are'.

7. www.youtube.com/watch?v=SgKM1wVOpn.

M is for madness

Those whom the gods wish to destroy, they first make mad. We must be mad, literally mad, as a nation to be permitting the annual inflow of some 50,000 dependents, who are for the most part the material of the future growth of the immigrant-descended population. It is like watching a nation busily engaged in heaping up its own funeral pyre. So insane are we that we actually permit unmarried persons to immigrate for the purpose of founding a family with spouses and fiancés whom they have never seen.[1]

If low-paid Brits work more, even now, they can lose so much in welfare that they are just 15p better off for every extra pound earned. Who would work with an 85 per cent tax rate? Iain Duncan Smith's universal credit, now being slowly rolled out, would cut this to 65 per cent. It's still an outrageously high sum, although David Cameron seems to have stopped being outraged by it. This is, in effect the tax rate on the poor. And it's perhaps the most widely ignored scandal in the British economy. For as long as this rate is so crushingly high, we'll have to keep importing workers – with the attendant pressure on school places, the NHS and housing. It is economic madness.[2]

If not madness, it must be at least stupid to employ aliens to have any hand in control of entry into this country, to guard our borders:

- Khurram Shahzad, a visa officer employed in our High Commission in Islamabad, was arrested by the Pakistani authorities on suspicion of selling sponsorship letters.

- Violet Savizon, an immigration officer, and Samuel Shoyeju, an agency entry clearance officer, were both sacked for giving indefinite leave to remain in this country to Nigerians, presumably in return for payment.

- Benjamin Orororo obtained £50,000 from asylum seekers for assisting with them obtaining leave to stay in this country. He was sentenced to five years. (His wife also works (worked?) for the Border Agency.)

It must be mad to provide the keys to this country by authorising aliens to conduct marriages:

- Rev. Cannon Dr John Magumba, from Uganda, purported to effect at least twenty-eight marriages between Nigerian men and female citizens of the European Union, in the process pocketing more than £8,000 of marriage fees that were never passed on to the parish.

Then there is the madness of compensation for illegal immigrants who are held in custody pending deportation, such as 'Joseph Meir', who, having committed more than twenty offences, delayed his repatriation by hiding his place of origin.

If not mad it must at least be stupid only to start the deportation process after a foreign criminal has served his sentence (*see* E is for examples perhaps encapsulating where we are and H is for human rights).

- Aziz Lamari, an Algerian, arrived in this country in July 2009 and was arrested within days whereupon he applied for asylum. He was moved to Liverpool but absconded. In July, he was arrested in Cambridgeshire. He absconded again and was arrested in Holland, where he was sent back here for his asylum claim to be dealt with, but absconded again and in October failed to turn up for an asylum interview. In 2010, he was convicted twice for offences of exposure and also robbery, and jailed. Upon completion of his time, he was detained for deportation; that continued despite it being clear that deportation could not be effected within a reasonable period and so he was entitled to compensation. (He eventually returned to Algeria.)

And there is the madness of extraditing non-indigenous criminals to this country – Eildon Habilaj arrived in this country in 1998 on 'the back of a lorry', saying he was Bekim Ademi, a refugee from Kosovo, and claiming asylum. That was granted in 2001 and later British citizenship. He used that to obtain a job with the Serious Organised Crime Agency but his details came up on its database. After his true identity came to light he was sentenced to eighteen months but he fled; now his extradition from his home in Albania is being considered.

There is the madness of obstructing illegal visitors from leaving:

- Ayouba-Ali Sihame came here as part of the Comoros 2012 Olympic team. She absconded and procured a fake French passport but was stopped at the Channel, arrested and jailed for eight months. To avoid deportation upon completion of her sentence she applied for asylum.

There is the madness of automatically providing citizenship, notwithstanding no connection with this country other than being born here:

A child born in the United Kingdom is granted British citizenship if either its mother or father is a British citizen or settled in the United Kingdom ... All individuals born in the UK to someone legally resident in the country are British at birth ... The provisions granting citizenship by birth to children of legal residents ensure that all migrants resident in the country for more than four years, if the apply for permanent residency, will secure for their children British citizenship. Those who are not residents but later naturalise have an entitlement to claim citizenship for their children under 18. For those that become residents but not citizens after their children are born, British citizenship will automatically be conferred on them at 10 years of age.[3]

Notes: *M is for madness*

1. Enoch Powell.

2. *We have to wean the country off the drug of immigration* by Fraser Nelson, *The Daily Telegraph*, July 2013.

3. *Citizenship and Immigration in Post-war Britain* by Randall Hansen, published in 2000 by Oxford University Press.

And **M** is for marriage

First, arranged and/or forced marriage:

In July 2011, it was predicted by the Forced Marriage Unit that more than 350 girls would be missing when the following term started. The report of this prediction continued that the Forced Marriage Unit (FMU) had received 738 calls so far that year and that 'Pakistani' families were involved in 56.2% of cases.

According to the Crown Prosecution Service there are 10,000 forced marriages a year in the UK along with about the same number of 'honour crimes'.

Hundreds of adults with severe learning difficulties are being forced into marriage with spouses brought to Britain from overseas, a major government-funded study has found.

Academics say their research has revealed that 56 cases reported to the Forced Marriage Unit (FMU) last year are the 'tip of the iceberg'...

Professionals are sometimes afraid to act because they fear being seen as culturally insensitive or racist ...

Rachel Clawson, an academic at the University of Nottingham, worked with the Ann Craft Trust to carry out the research for ministers. She found that only about one in eight cases had been referred to the FMU. 'I do absolutely believe that [the 56 known cases] are the tip of the iceberg,' she said.

... Men travelling to the UK often left their wife as soon as they had a visa.

[An example is] one young man who had profound learning disabilities and needed help with feeding, personal care and dressing. His father brought over a woman from India and the wedding took place in a Hindu temple. The family are desperate for him to have a child and have been looking at IVF.

Another case was Rena, whose mother came under pressure from her local community to allow a marriage to help a man obtain a visa. The mother now regretted it as her daughter was being assaulted on a regular basis, had a miscarriage and was having her benefits taken by her husband and sent abroad. Despite her regrets, the mother had encouraged her daughter to remain in the marriage for the sake of 'family honour'.

In a third case a woman from the Midlands described how her learning disabled brother was pressurised into a marriage but the wife disappeared as soon as she had a visa.[1]

Rotherham is poor. There is little economic hope. The youth unemployment rate among the 8,000-strong Kashmiri community is twice that for white school leavers. So-called arranged – in truth compulsory – marriages with cousins from Kashmir brought in new immigrants with no English from backgrounds of peasant poverty where women had no status or rights.[2]

- TK came here in 2009 as a student. Two years later, shortly before his appeal against deportation, he began a relationship with SY, who was in care with an IQ of 49, probably so as to show he had a family life here. He was told by police that he would be committing an offence if he tried to marry her because of her lack of capacity but an Islamic ceremony of marriage took place. TK was subsequently deported and the so-called marriage was declared invalid.

- A mentally disabled man was taken by his parents to the Indian subcontinent to marry a Punjabi. Sandwell Metropolitan Borough Council sought the court's directions. The judge, after noting the man did not have the capacity to marry, told the woman that 'if [you] were to have any form of sexual intimacy with him, he would be the victim of a criminal act' and said:

I have been told that within the area of this particular local authority there are a number of incapacitated adults who have been the subject of arranged or forced marriages and that it is important to send a strong signal to the Muslim and Sikh communities ... that arranged marriages, where one party is mentally incapacitated, simply will not be tolerated.[3]

Second, bogus/sham marriage:

We allow anyone living here to marry here and so EU nationals can provide spousal status and thereby a claim to the right to residence to people from non-EU countries.

The Home Office has estimated that about 4,000 to 10,000 applications to stay in the UK in 2013 were made on the basis of a sham marriage although it has said that this broad estimate should be approached with caution. When asked his view on the 4,000 to 10,000 estimate, John Vine [The Independent Chief Inspector of Borders and Immigration] said, 'the Home Office does not really know' the scale of the problem and 'the fact that we are estimating in the first place says it all'. Furthermore, Mr Vine got the impression from talking to the Home Office staff that the issue was 'more widespread' than the figures suggested'.[4.1]

... In effect, somebody who is married to an EEA national acquires the Treaty rights, the same Treaty rights of the EEA national, and can reside indefinitely in the UK and can bring their descendants, their children or dependent children or grandchildren or, indeed their dependent parents or grandparents.[4.2]

The problem is exacerbated by 'The fact that the burden is on the Home Office to show that a marriage was a sham when entered into ...'.[4.2]

Examples of the use of EU citizens, usually female, by non-EU citizens, usually male, to obtain residence through 'marriage' include:

- Nadeza Mirgova from Eastern Europe and Olarotimi Ojugbele from Nigeria

- Helena Puchalska from Poland and Asif Ali from Pakistan

- Marcela Tancosova from Slovakia and Choudry Kanwal from Pakistan

- Monika Slepcikova, a Czech and Unchenna Peter Ezimorah from Nigeria

- Katalin Ottlyk from Hungary and Sufyan Shahzad from Pakistan (who were both sentenced to twenty months in prison, she to an additional four months for using a false identification card).

The con can be on an 'industrial' scale:

- Trevfick Souleiman, solicitor, with assistants Zafer Altinbas, Cenk Guclu and Furrah Kosimov, flew in brides on a 'conveyor belt' from various EU countries for would-be immigrants. Souleiman was sentenced to ten years, Cuclu and Kosimov to nine years and Altinbas to six years and nine months. Kosimov was sentenced in his absence, having fled the country while on bail; perhaps Souleiman's wife who works[ed?] for the CPS will also leave. The men are all Turkish Cypriots; their crime came to light when a consignment of drugs of Albanian Behar and Elton Dika was intercepted and it was discovered that such drug money was going through the books of Souleiman's firm.

- Mohammed Tanin from Bangladesh and Maria Marques from Portugal entered into a sham marriage before bringing in four foreigners to marry his friends at £2,000 each. The 'bride purchasers', all Bangladeshi, three of whom were here on student visas, were merely cautioned. Tanin was sentenced to four years and Marques to two.

- In Rotherham (or thereabouts), Khalda Ahmed, Nikola Horvathova, Veronica Horvathova, Eva Holubova, Aftab Hussain, Talib Hussain, Michaela Lengelova, Peter Pohlodko, Veronika Pohlodkova, Zanna Holubova, Louise Kelly, Farah Khan, Sabina Khan, Kristin Popikva, Tariq Mehmood, Yasser Nasser, Mohammed Ramzan, Svetlana Krausova, Nadia Qureshi and Rahina Zaman conspired to have Eastern European women living in the UK 'marry' Pakistanis so that they could enter the UK. Forged documents were found in the attic of Mohammed Ramzan and his wife Musserat Bi; she was cleared of conspiracy. Mehmood and Horvathova are on the run.

- In Bolton, Maria Loureiro, Portuguese, with Ilias Neki, whose filings at Companies House state him to be British, arranged for Indians legally here but whose visa had or was shortly to expire to 'marry' women flown in from Portugal for the purpose namely of such Indians marrying an EU citizen and thereby having the right to live here. Loureiro was jailed for forty-five months and Neki to thirty-two, while the Indians – Bhavesh Bapodora, Faisal Chand, Yunusbhai Duka, Sajuddin Mansuri, Safvan Minja, Amjadhusen Patel, Mehulkumar Patel, and Inayathussain Tailor – were also jailed.

- Shrewsbury Registry Office noticed that would-be couples could not communicate. The arranger of the would-be marriages was Zaffar Abbas, 'a British national' of Walsall, once a 'licensed immigration adviser' who used that expertise to plan and organise scam marriages –

marrying EU nationals to other aliens with a view to the latter thereby being allowed to stay in the country. Co-conspirator was Davinder Singh (a Slovakian by marriage who married off his pregnant wife to his cousin). As well as those two there were also jailed Marcella Brotac, from Romania (but) resident in James Turner Street, Birmingham,[7] who 'married' Harjeet Singh, Vladimir Gazi from Slovakia, Ivars Mizans from Latvia and Gurpreet Kaur from India.

The con can be conducted by Britons – the Reverend Alex Brown presided over 360 marriages at the Church of St Peter and St Paul in St Leonards-on-Sea in the four years to July 2009, usually between Africans and EU citizens. When, in 2010, sentencing him plus Michael Adelasoye[6] and Vladmyr Buchak[8] each to four years for conspiring to breach immigration laws, Judge Richard Hayward said:

> None of you have pleaded guilty. You have expressed no remorse. I confess I was hoping to hear from counsel for Adelasoye and Buchak that they were helping you for altruistic reasons. I have heard no such mitigation [...] The participants were perfectly willing but this conspiracy involved the exploitation of two vulnerable groups. The Eastern Europeans had come to the UK for a better life but found themselves in poor accommodation and in hard and low-paid jobs. They were vulnerable to being exploited and they agreed to marry for money, although evidence suggests none of them received the full amount promised.

Later, Brown was also sentenced for not publishing marriage banns and Larisa Kuznecova pleaded guilty to being part of the scam.

In November 2014, Muhammad 'Jimmy' Amir, a national of Pakistan, but living in Blackburn, was sentenced to four years for marriage fraud. With Diana Fernandes Moreira-Miguel (from Portugal), he used Portuguese women to be brides for Pakistani students whose student visas were expiring (or had expired). She was one of the brides. She was sentenced to fifteen months (but with the time on remand, she was allowed to return to Portugal to care for her daughter). The students – Mohammed Mudasser, Ali Mobeen, Ashraf Muhammed and Asrar Zeeshan Shafqat (all living in Manchester) – were each sentenced to a year.

Not in the Home Office press release but, for example in the *Lancashire Telegraph*, it was stated that several other Pakistani grooms and Portuguese brides returned home without being prosecuted. The Immigration and Security Minister commented:

This case sends a clear message to the criminals who think they can cheat our immigration laws. Our dedicated investigative teams will catch you and you will be imprisoned.

Last year, we intervened in more than 1,300 sham marriages – more than double that of the previous year. We are building a system that is fair to British citizens, but leaves no room for those who flout the rules.

The new Immigration Act is also making it even tougher for the fraudsters by extending the marriage and civil partnership notice period – giving officers and registrars longer to investigate suspicious marriages.

Thirdly – if one of the million plus persons here of Asian origin wants to get married, or his parents want him to get married, there is no reason why the bride should not be found here rather than further delaying integration by the import of further alien input preventing assimilation, by allowing in women with no connection to this country apart from being betrothed to someone who lives here. If such non-indigenous person has to marry someone from 'his' village, he should go and live there rather than bring her here; and, correspondingly, if the person here to be married is female and the prospective spouse is abroad.

It can be no part of any policy that existing families should be kept divided; but there are two directions in which families can be reunited, and if our former and present immigration laws have brought about the division of families, albeit voluntarily or semi-voluntarily, we ought to be prepared to arrange for them to be re-united in their countries of origin. In short, suspension of immigration and encouragement of re-immigration hang together, logically and humanely as two aspects of the same approach.[9]

Notes: *M is for marriage*

1. Anushka Asthana, *The Times*, July 2012.

2. *Our wilful blindness let the children down by* Denis MacShane, *The Tablet*, September 2014.

3. Mr Justice Holman.

4. Paragraph 15 of House of Commons' Home Affairs Committee – *The Work of the Immigration Directorates* (October–December 2013), July 2014.

4.1. Paragraph 8.

4.2. Paragraph 2.

5. Reports, such as at *themuslimissue.wordpress.com*, refer to 2,000 such marriages.

6. Adelasoye came from Nigeria. He was a church pastor and a solicitor. In 2011, he was sentenced to additional time because in 2007 he had falsely represented his salary to two building societies and written his own reference.

7. *See* what has note 30 to it of H is for hegemony.

8. From Ukraine.

9. Enoch Powell.

Readers who speak French, are referred to *L'immigration par escroquerie sentimentale* by Marie-Annick Delaunay. She dedicated the book 'aux dizaines de milliers de femmes et d'hommes, victimes silencieuses des lois de l'immigration et des pratiques frauduleuses d'individuls sans scrupules, avec la complicite des gouvernements successifs'.

And **M** is for Michael Michaels

Michaels, who despite being a British citizen and a crown servant, thought of Israel first when in the 1960s he passed nuclear technology to his first loyalty: his middle initial was I, standing for Israel. More recently Daniel James, who was born in Iran and became a British citizen in 1986, served in the Territorial Army for eighteen years, but spied for Iran.

And **M** is for Mirpur

About 70% of the 1.2 million persons living in this country who are, or whose ancestry is, Pakistani, come from Mirpur.[1]

> Yet in retrospect this Gastarbeiter period in the 1950s and 1960s, when everyone still thought the immigration was temporary, seems like a golden age of integration. The Mipuris worked alongside whites, often with other immigrants such as Poles and Ukrainians. They joined trade unions, went to pubs and sometimes had relationships with white women.

> Then the story changes in the three towns [Bradford, Burnley and Oldham] in roughly the same way. For various reasons, including changes in immigration laws, the Mipuris realised they were staying put in Britain, and over came their families and the imams. The era of segregation began. Looking back, this was the time when the authorities

– local and national – should have offered a clearer path to full citizenship and integration. Some limited attempts to disperse the expanded immigrant population were made, and Bradford persisted with a school bussing scheme for several years. But by the early 1980s the textile industry had all but vanished and it had been largely accepted that the different races would live, and therefore go to school, within their own groups.

This was endorsed by the emerging ideology of multiculturalism. At the soft end this meant responding to reasonable requests of the minority population for, say, halal meat in schools. But as Graham Mahony[2] now admits, 'we went too far, we were making it up as we went along'. Segregation or what Mahony calls 'internal colonisation' was, in effect, encouraged.[3]

The vast majority of convicted child-sex offenders in the UK are single white men. However, with this specific model of offending[4] there is a widespread perception that the majority of perpetrators are of Asian, British Asian or Muslim origin. This would certainly seem to be the case from the major grooming prosecutions which have gone to court so far, but in fact both CEOP[5] and the Office of the Children's Commissioner have found serious inconsistencies with recording of ethnicities and gender of both victims and perpetrators across UK forces. Given the number of child sexual exploitation cases which have so far failed to make it to court, for the reasons discussed, this highly unsatisfactory situation means that it is extremely difficult to form an evidence-based opinion on the true nature of what is still a largely hidden crime. Nevertheless, the perception, that grooming perpetrators are largely of Asian, British Asian or Muslim origin, colours the attitudes of those working in the field, as well as the media and the wider public. Ann Cryer, the former MP for Keighley, who raised concerns about localised grooming in her constituency as long ago as 2003, faced a backlash when she described the offenders as Asian and pointed to the fact that most of them came from the Mirpur district of Kashmir (a description which she still stands by). She suggested that underlying cultural attitudes might be a factor in the offending. As Andrew Norfolk[6] told us:

'The far right leapt on the story, predictably, and [Ann Cryer] was accused of demonising all Muslims. I think that it almost acted as a brake for several years on anybody seriously looking at whether there was any truth in what she was saying but, as the years passed, I noticed cases cropping up from time to time across Yorkshire and Lancashire with a very similar pattern.'[7]

Notes: M is for Mirpur

1. Mirpur is almost on the border of the two parts of Kashmir administered by Pakistan and India.

In about 1960, the UK provided some financial assistance towards a dam – the Mangla Dam – and offered work permits to some of those thereby displaced. Today there are of the order of three quarters of a million people in this country who, or whose parents, came from Mirpur – about 70% of the persons here of Pakistani origin/heritage.

2. Head of race relations in Bradford in the mid-1980s.

3. David Goodhart (author of *The British Dream: Successes and Failures of Post-War Immigration*), *Prospect*, June 2013. (And *see* W is for we were warned, for the letter from Denis to Bill as to Bradford being colonised.)

4. Localised grooming 'is a model of child sexual exploitation in which a group of abusers target vulnerable children, including, but not confined to, those who are looked after by a local authority' – paragraph 8 of the report detailed by note 7.

5. Child Exploitation and Online Protection Centre.

6. Correspondent of *The Times, see* D is for Derby.

7. Paragraph 108 of *Child Sexual Exploitation and the Response to Localised Grooming* of The House of Commons' Home Affairs Committee, published June 2013.

David Winnick, MP for Croydon South, 1966–70, and Walsall North from 1979, proposed that in line 13 after 'perception' there be inserted 'which we believe to be false'. He was outvoted – he was alone.

And **M** is for misfeasance in public office[1]

The Labour Party's manifesto for the 1997 general election, as to immigration, was (under the section headed 'Real rights for citizens' and out of forty-seven pages of one print):

> Every country must have firm control over immigration and Britain is no exception. All applications, however, should be dealt with speedily and fairly. There are, rightly, criteria for those who want to enter this country to join husband or wife. We will ensure that these are properly enforced. We will, however, reform the system in current use to remove the

arbitrary and unfair results that can follow from the existing 'primary purpose rule'. There will be a streamlined system of appeals for visitors denied a visa.

The system for dealing with asylum seekers is expensive and slow – there are many undecided cases dating back beyond 1993. We will ensure swift and fair decisions on whether someone can stay or go, control unscrupulous immigration advisors and crack down on fraudulent use of birth certificates.

That year net inward immigration was 48,000.

The manifesto for the 2001 general election was silent as to immigration.

In 2004, following the resignation of Beverley Hughes,[2] the then prime minister, Tony Blair, said he would take 'a close interest' in immigration.

In 2004, net inward immigration was 245,000.

The manifesto for the 2005 general election, as to immigration (and asylum), is three pages of, in one print, 112: those three are Appendix II.

In 2005, net inward migration was 206,000.

On a small and crowded island, boosting the population from 60 million to 70 million by 2030, almost entirely as a result of immigration, as official figures forecast is a serious matter ...

Did the Government take a decision in 1997 that the British population was not growing rapidly enough and that, for the long-term betterment of the country, it had to be boosted by roughly one sixth in just over 30 years?

If so, it passed everyone by. It was never debated by Parliament or put to the people in a general election. When there was an attempt to raise the issue in the 2001 election campaign, the Government cynically played the race card to close the debate down.[3]

It is almost impossible to exaggerate what a revolution Britain has undergone in the past dozen years, a demographic change not just unprecedented in our history, but in almost any country's. This island was quite fantastically undiverse until recently – before the Second World War between 70 and 75 per cent of British DNA had been British for 13,000 years,[4] and later migrations made a negligible impact, with even the largest and most culturally influential, the Anglo-Saxon invasion, comprising only about 4 per cent of British DNA. Last year a quarter of births in England were to foreign mothers.

But what Labour has done is not only borderline treason, it's also very, very stupid, and against their own interests. Multi and bi-racial societies do not vote along class lines, as the monocultural British always have done: they tend to vote along tribal lines. Look at the Deep South, Northern Ireland and Lebanon and ask yourself – where are their multicultural Centre-Left socialist parties? Labour has gained a multi-cultural following but, as we saw at the Euro elections, lost much of its traditional power base to the previously laughable British National Party, now the new tribal party of working-class white Britons. Labour's great gift to the British people is the poisonous legacy of tribal politics.[5]

The migrants' desire to get into Britain is only half the story of why so many are here. The other half is the explanation of why the government decided to let so many migrants into Britain. For the past 12 years, Labour has been convinced that allowing high levels of immigration should be a policy priority, and it has taken steps to ensure that it is relatively easy for migrants to get permanent, legally recognised residence here. Why has Labour done that?

In 1997 Tony Blair and his Cabinet had several reasons for wishing to increase the number of immigrants into Britain. One was that they perceived an electoral advantage. The outcome of elections in an increasing number of constituencies was, and is, dictated in large part by the votes from relatively recent immigrants. People who have moved here from, say, the Indian subcontinent understandably hated the rules that prevented their families joining them in Britain.

The most onerous of those rules was known as 'the primary purpose rule', which was imposed by the Conservatives in 1993. It required that someone wishing to follow his or her spouse into Britain to prove the 'the marriage was not entered into primarily to obtain permission to the UK'. Proving a negative, as the rule obliged a candidate to do, was extremely difficult, and large numbers of spouses were refused entry into Britain as a result.

Labour abolished the rule soon after the election in 1997. The move was extremely popular in immigrant communities, because it made it far easier for families to move here. Immigration by spouses has increased by 50 per cent since the primary purpose rule was abolished. More than 40,000 people were granted citizenship here on the basis of marriage in 2008 alone.[6]

… but equally there is no question that Labour in power took a number of key decisions that contributed to the sharp increase.

… Between 1997 and 2003 there were four significant ones.

First, there was the abolition of the so-called primary purpose rule, which had the effect of significantly raising the inflow of foreign spouses.[7] (This was a payback to Labour's loyal South Asian voters, who particularly resented the rule and how it was applied.)[8]

That is why, in the notorious words of one of his advisers, Blair was so desperate to 'rub the Right's nose in diversity', Border controls were abolished, visas were dished out like confetti and the enforcement of the dogma of multiculturalism became the central ethos of the state.[9]

The revelations get worse. "there was a reluctance …in government", he wrote, "to discuss what increased immigration would mean, above all for Labour's core white working class vote". The social outcomes that ministers cared about were those affecting the immigrants. This, Neather explains, shone out in a report published in 2001 after these confidential deliberations.

Knowingly to impose a transformative policy without truthfulness on the government's side or informed consent on the people's side was simple fascism – and to do so with silly propaganda about multiculturalism and unjust sneers about racism has made these injustices only more bitter. Under these circumstances.

Labour's obvious gerrymandering by mass immigration – black and ethnic minority people are very likely to vote Labour – is perhaps the least of its crimes. There are lots of such practical things that could be done to ensure immigration is controlled in future. But the first thing to do is to expose the patronising lies, the seigneurial arrogance and the criminally foolish social engineering of the Blair-Brown regime; it does not deserve the name of Labour government.[10]

A few weeks ago I visited my 92-year-old aunt in Birmingham. A Gloucestershire farmer's daughter, in the war years she waited on the tables of the Army High Command. She married my uncle, a sergeant in the Parachute Regiment and raised her family after the end of the war.

Little of this will be known to her new neighbours, many of whom do not speak her language and are not aware of her or of our history. She is one of a handful of the old working-class people left in an area of roughly two miles almost entirely populated by arrivals from the Muslim areas of Asia.

They are mostly decent, friendly folk, but where for her is the enriching multicultural experience dreamt of by Tony Blair?

We also visited another of our childhood haunts to find the memorial plaque in the church commemorating my wife's great uncles killed in the First World War. The congregation of lovely, middle-aged [people] from the West Indies had little idea of the war, or the reason for our visit. The plaque had been destroyed some years since. There was no one to care.

Decisions made for Labour's short-term gain will cause long-term and cultural pain.[11]

[What was revealed by the 2011 Census] is not so much a wakeup call, it is almost time for the firing squad for politicians who have allowed this to happen.[12]

And so over the course of Labour's three terms in office, we had net migration of 3.6 million into the country, four times higher than over the previous 13 years. That this was a deliberate policy is beyond doubt – as MigrationWatch UK put it this week, Labour loosened immigration controls and imposed no transitional controls on the new A8 member of the European Union – and all of this done with little or no discussion and certainly without public consent. Nor was this receptiveness, this eagerness for immigration stated in any one of the party's three general election manifestos (for 1997, 2001 or 2005).[13]

In May 2014, Daniel Hannan[14] wrote *Look who's not voting Tory* (*The Daily Telegraph*), which included:

Look at how people from different backgrounds voted in the last general election. Labour enjoyed colossal leads among every ethnic minority community. Even Indians, who are significantly less anti-Tory than other non-white groups, were four times as likely to vote for Gordon Brown as for David Cameron.

Although the source was not given, Mr Hannan stated that in 2010 the respective percentages of votes were:

	Tory	**Labour**
White	37	31
Indian	24	61
Pakistani	11	60
Bangladeshi	72[15]	18[15]
Black African	6	87
Black Caribbean	9	78

Notes: M is for misfeasance in public office

1. The doing or attempt to do, by act or omission, something for which there is no authority (usually) for perceived political or personal gain.

2. *See* note 1 as to I is for identity.

3. *Official: immigration doesn't benefit Britain* by Philip Johnston, *The Daily Telegraph*, March 2008. More of the article is in the part of E is for economics, to which note 11 applies.

4. Alternatively, 'In 2001 DNA tests showed that most of the people living in south England share DNA with pure-blooded Celts. It was an astonishing revelation. More than 2,000 years after the Romans invaded, our pre-Roman landscape is still inhabited by descendants of the ancient Britons who first shaped the contours of Hambledon Hill.' *What the Romans didn't have to do for us – create our countryside* by Harry Mount, *The Daily Telegraph*, August 2014.

And 'The English of 1927 were more than 90 per cent the descendants of the English of 927, which makes it entirely untrue to talk of "a nation of immigrants".' – Ed West, (*see* next note; he drew on *History of England* by G.M. Trevelyan 1926).

5. *Labour's secret plan to lure immigrants was borderline treason – and plain stupid* by Ed West, *The Daily Telegraph*, February 2010.

6. *All you need to know about immigration in Britain today* by Alasdair Palmer, *The Daily Telegraph*, March 2009.

(Bribery is defined as promise, offer or give something usually money to procure services or gain influence especially illegally; any persuasion or lure.)

7/8. *The British Dream: Successes and Failures of Post-War Immigration* by David Goodhart: 'The number of wives who came in under the more liberal regime rose steadily from about 14,000 a year to 24,000 between 1997 and 2007.'

The quoted words are from chapter 5, which is entitled *The Second Great Arrival 1997–Today* followed by the section *Labour's Greatest Legacy*.

In July 2007 in a debate in the House of Commons on immigration which he had initiated, Nicholas Soames MP for Mid Sussex apparently put the figure rather higher – "At the same time [the Government's] decision in June 1997 to abolish the primary purpose rule has led to the number of spouses admitted to Britain doubling from 20,000 to 40,000 a year."

9. *Jim Callaghan, 'our worst PM', was nothing of the sort* by Leo McKistry, *The Daily Telegraph* March 2013. Blair's adviser [and speech writer] was Andrew Neather.

10. *Labour migration policy was criminal social engineering* by Minette Marrin, *The Sunday Times*, November 2009.

"He" as in "he wrote" was Andrew Neather who by 2009 was comment editor of the *London Evening Standard*.

11. Mike Dalton, letter to a newspaper, July 2012.

12. Frank Field, MP for Birkenhead since 1979; Minister for Welfare Reform 1997/8 and, since 2010, the Coalition's 'poverty czar'.

In 2005, Mr Field flew this kite:

> Let us rewind the cameras to before the last election. The parties are about to issue their manifestos. What would have been the reaction if Tony Blair had included the following passage in Labour's manifesto?
>
> 'We intend to pursue an open borders policy. We will welcome all comers from the new EU accession countries. We intend to allow unlimited access to our labour market even if other European countries refuse to open their borders. We know that this policy will depress wages, make it more difficult for students to find holiday jobs while ensuring it is impossible to move one million people from incapacity benefit into work and persuade an additional 600,000 single parents to take jobs. Yet we believe the gains outweigh the losses.'
>
> There would have been uproar.

13. *Jihadi John, Cage and the fools who gave it money* by Rod Liddle, *The Spectator,* March 2015.

14. Member of the European Parliament for South East England since 1999.

15. This is how it was published but the two figures have surely been reversed.

And **M** is for mistake

> One spectacular mistake in which I participated [not alone] was in lifting the transitional restrictions on the Eastern European states like Poland and Hungary which joined the EU in mid-2004. Other existing EU members, notably France and Germany, decided to stick to the general rule which prevented migrants from these new states from working here until 2011. But we thought that it would be good for Britain if these folk could come and work here from 2004.
>
> Thorough research by the Home Office suggested that the impact of this benevolence would in any event be relatively small, at between 5,000 and 13,000 immigrants per year up to 2010. Events proved these

forecasts worthless. Net migration reached close to a quarter of a million at its peak in 2010. Lots of red faces, mine included.[1]

Notes: *M is for mistake*

1. Jack Straw, MP for Blackburn since 1979, Home Secretary 1997/05; November 2013.

A mistake that was lesser in number but in fact of far greater and longer consequence was Jack Straw's prediction as to the abolition of the primary purpose rule –

> There will be about 10, 000 immigrants a year coming from India and Pakistan.In fact, *see* M is for misfeasance in public office, anyway in 2008 "more than 40,000 were granted citizenship here."

And **M** is for the Moynihan Report

In 1965, US Senator Daniel Moynihan pointed out that nearly a quarter of black children were born to unmarried women and warned that the collapse of the married family spelt continued inequality for African Americans. He was execrated. By 1980, the proportion of black children born to unmarried women had risen to 56% and by 2008 to more than 70%.[1]

> in today's Britain 59 per cent of Caribbean and 44 per cent of African children grow up fatherless.[2]

> It is also significant that families from West Africa are more likely to have two parents than British Caribbean families. According to the Runnymeade Trust, 59 per cent of black Caribbean children grow up in single parent families, as opposed to 44 per cent of black African children. Family stability is a major factor in school success.[3]

Notes: *M is for the Moynihan Report*

1. *The Negro Family: The Case for National Action* (also known as the Moynihan Report).

2. *Dark Albion: A Requiem for the English* by David Abbott published by Sparrow Books in 2013.

3. *Don't act white, act migrant* by Tony Sewell, *Deccan Chronicle*, August 2015.

And **M** is for multiculturalism

Fleeing from what is one's own.[1]

Multiculturalism rests on the supposition – or better, the dishonest pretence – that all cultures are equal in all respects and that no fundamental conflict can arise between the customs, mores and philosophical outlook of two different cultures.[2]

Yet Blunkett was right in other respects. Though the rioting youths could speak English, the brides they would bring back from Pakistan would not – and, furthermore, never would. Many women I have encountered as patients who came to Britain from Pakistan 30 years ago, at age 16 or 18, still know little English – but not necessarily from any unwillingness to learn. Their husbands actively prevented them from learning the language, to make sure that they would stay enclosed in a ghetto and not get any ideas above their station. The same rioting youths who protested at British society's failure to accept them as equal citizens have themselves sought to reproduce the unequal social patterns of rural Pakistan, half a world away, because it suited them to do so.

Multiculturalism encourages this stance. If all cultures are equal, and none has the right to impose its standards on any other, what is wrong with the immigrant ghettos that have emerged, where the population (that is to say, the male population) enjoys, de facto, extraterritorial rights? If it is the custom of their ancestral culture to keep girls out of school and force them into marriages that they do not want and to confiscate the passports that the British government issues them for their personal use, what can a multiculturalist object to without asserting the superiority of his own values?[2.1]

Of course the tendency had been to say 'Let's adopt the multicultural concept and live happily side by side, and be happy to be living with each other.' But this concept has failed and failed utterly.[3]

[Russia] will not accept Western-style political correctness and multiculturalism that have been taken to the point of absurdity.[4]

We have a culture in which the quickest route to public sympathy is to be a victim. So it does pay to be a victim … and I think to be a victim is to be part of the culture that is the absolute opposite of the culture of responsibility …

The real danger in a multicultural society is that every ethnic group and religious group becomes a pressure group, putting our people's interest instead of the national interest. [Lessons for such a discrete group] are – number one, don't try to impose your views on the majority population. Number two, you have to be what I call bilingual, you know you are

Jewish and you're English … because it forces you to realise that actually society and life is complicated. It mustn't and can't be simplified. Number three, there are times when it's uncomfortable, when you realize there is such a thing as anti-Semitism. [Being] a minority isn't always fun.[5]

Rochdale, Rotherham, Derby, Oxford. The towns change, but the pattern is always the same. Gangs of men, mainly of Pakistani Muslim heritage, lure white girls as young as 10 with gifts and displays of affection. Next, the girl is raped as a way of 'breaking her in'. Once the child's spirit is subdued, and her mind is fogged with drugs, she is sold for sex to multiple men at £200 a time. If the girl tries to break away, a gang member might threaten to behead her or firebomb her home. Mohammed Karrar, who was found guilty, last week in the Oxford sex-grooming case this week, took a scalding hairpin and branded M on one girl's bottom so she would know she was his property. Later, the gang gave the same girl a DIY abortion. She was 12 years old. And this, all this, is happening in Britain now.

In a particularly warped twist, the pimp will teach his victim that her parents are racist towards Asians, which is why they disapprove of their relationship – absolutely nothing, of course, to do with him being a violent, controlling thug. Gang members have grown wise to the wimpish ways of Western society. They exploit the fact that police, newly trained in 'cultural sensitivity', are terrified of being accused of racism. So the pimps operate with impunity until, years later, the slave girls find the courage to testify in court against their masters …

Back in January, there was a profoundly disturbing case at Nottingham Crown Court. Adil Rashid, who had 'raped' an underage girl, was spared a prison term after the judge heard that the naïve 18-year-old attended an Islamic faith school where he was taught that women are worthless. Rashid told psychologists he had no idea that having sex with a willing 13-year-old was against the law; besides, his education had taught him to believe that 'women are no more worthy than a lollipop that has been dropped on the ground'.

If the fresh-faced Rashid had picked up that view in a madrassa in Karachi it would be profoundly depressing, though not surprising. But the school he attended was in Birmingham, for heaven's sake! Although it cannot be named for 'legal reasons', the school is voluntary-aided – mainly funded by the taxpayer. At this hugely popular Islamic school, where a majority of pupils are from a Pakistani background, boys and girls are taught in separate classes: a segregation policy no normal comprehensive could get away with.

Rashid's barrister said; 'the school he attended, it is not going too far to say, can be described as a closed community'. So, the defence against a rape charge by a young Muslim living in the twenty-first century Britain was not just ignorance of the law (which should be no defence at all). It was that the law and, indeed, the values of the wider country, were irrelevant in his Islamic school, even though it was a state institution funded by citizens who would go straight to jail if, for instance, they tried to have sex with a child.

The fact that the judge accepted Rashid's defence shows what a god-awful mess this country has got itself into over multiculturalism.[6]

Multiculturalism is a fundamentally incoherent doctrine, invented to conceal the serious conflicts which have arisen when peoples from vastly different cultures, with different values, are forced to live together.[7]

Yet, in spite of this history of Ottoman dominance, some critics of Western behaviour portray the Orient as if it were the constant victim of Western imperialism. Current Islamic militant groups have adopted this false view. This false view, accompanied with memories of past Islamic and Ottoman power, has given rise to a new problem in European societies, one that did not present itself to our six writers.[8] This stems from the increasing number of Islamic immigrants to European countries, some of whom are not fully integrated in their host societies or do not show inclination to become assimilated, do not define their identity other than by their religion, may not accept the legitimacy of non-Islamic values, and have memories of past Islamic glories. It is not irrelevant that the name 'Muhammad' has been the most popular name for boys in some Western countries in recent years. In host countries questions have arisen of whether sharia law should be given legal authority, or whether existing law should be changed to satisfy the cultural traditions of immigrants. In some British cities sharia courts have been functioning, making decisions on issues of divorce and to a lesser degree on issues of property, inheritance, and physical injury. It is still an open question whether these decisions can be considered officially part of the British legal system. This problem is compounded by the approval in some European countries of the controversial concept of multiculturalism, which aims at preserving cultural and ethical diversity in a society, and perhaps treating differences in culture as unimportant, but which, in practice, may hinder integration of minority groups and may make discussion of them more difficult.[9]

Multiculturalism leads to parallel societies and therefore remains a 'life lie' or a sham.[10]

It is shameful that both 'Jihadi John' and his new replacement ... are British, and a product of our education system.

Multiculturalism and the encouragement of parallel cultures simply do not work. It is time to acknowledge this.[11]

Notes: *M is for multiculturalism*

1. Cardinal Ratzinger (later Pope Benedict).

2. *Not With a Bang But a Whimper* by Theodore Dalrymple, published by Monday Books in 2009.

2.1. Ditto. The two immediately preceding paragraphs were:

> The then Home Secretary, David Blunkett [2001 to 2004], for example, suddenly announced that immigrants should learn English. Blunkett made this heterodox suggestion in response to riotous clashes in northern England between white youths and Muslim youths of Pakistani descent. Liberals predictably decried his comments as tactless at best and proto-fascist at worst. Didn't they give succour to the vicious xenophobic elements in British society, perhaps even portending a new dark age of intolerance?

> In fact, Blunkett's remarks were both on and off the mark. Doubtless all of the rioting Muslim youths spoke English. Hardly any British-born young men and women of South Asian descent do not speak it – though some, given the undemanding British school system, speak it poorly. So it is not true, as Blunkett implied, that a failure to learn English was to blame for the rioters' aggrieved sense of being unequal citizens in British society.

3. Chancellor Angela Merkel of Germany – 2010.

4. President Vladimir Putin of Russia (reported by *The Tablet*, November 2013).

5. Chief Rabbi Johnathan Sacks, upon his retirement in 2013. *Multiculturalism has had its day and it's time to move on, The Times.*

6. *Oxford grooming gang: We will regret ignoring Asian thugs who target white girls* by Allison Pearson, *The Daily Telegraph*, May 2013.

7. *'Easy meat': Multiculturalism, Islam and Child Sex Slavery* by Peter McLoughlin, published 2014 by the Law and Freedom Foundation, which also includes:

> Modern multiculturalism has been a short-sighted and cowardly doctrine, designed to suppress the conflicts in value systems of different cultures. It has meant that for 20 to 50 years, there has been mounting pressure (driven by a metropolitan elite who mostly live in middle-class, monocultural, Anglophone enclaves) to suppress any signs of the cultural conflict between the host culture and some antagonistic minority cultures.

8. The six are: Montesquieu 1689–1755, Edmund Burke 1729/97, Alexis de

Tocqueville 1805/59, James Mill 1773–1836, John Stuart Mill 1806/73, Karl Marx 1818/83 and Max Weber 1864–1920.

9. *Orientalism and Islam* by Michael Curtis, Cambridge University Press, 2009.

10. Chancellor Angela Merkel of Germany, December 2015.

11. Letter to a newspaper from Philip Congdon, January 2016. The two 'Jihadi Johns' he referred to were presumably first (alleged to be) Mohammed Emwazi, born in Kuwait but came here when he was nine, and secondly (thought to be) Siddhartha Dhar (aka Abu Rumassayah), born and raised here.

And **M** is for myopia

The reason why midwifery and maternity services are overstretched and primary school places are in such short supply is the babies and children of immigrants.[1]

Why we have a housing shortage is not that 'at the end of the day our fundamental problem is we just don't build enough new houses'[2] but that millions of housing units have become occupied by immigrants.

An example of this myopia, not as to those three shortages, but as to jobs, is apparent in the following letter to the *Financial Times* in May 2014:

> Most young people would have read the news that the economy is approaching pre-crash levels of growth with bewilderment. For many, times are still hard, money is tight and former social norms – such as home ownership or starting a family – seem as far off as ever.
>
> The chancellor talked up the new growth figures as vindication of his policies. While rising gross domestic product shouldn't be belittled, in reality the fruits of growth are being enjoyed [by] a narrow baby boomer-dominated sector of society. For the rest, particularly the estimated 583,000 people (around 2 per cent of the UK workforce) on zero-hours contracts, sufficient work is scarce and the cost of living too high. This isn't a true 'recovery'.
>
> The issues threatening the UK's long-term health require more radical measures. Build more homes to lower prices (and rents), thus reducing personal debt of the young. Add engineering, IT and management disciplines to school curriculums and higher education, to equip young Brits with the skills for tomorrow's labour market. And give businesses financial incentives, such as corporation tax breaks, for hiring under-25s

and taking on apprentices.[3]

(Thus) not a word about most new jobs going to immigrants, the excess supply of labour provided by immigration forcing down labour rates: (*see* B is for betrayal and E is for economics).

But, nearly two years later, the following letter to the *Guardian*, albeit as to the national living wage and membership of the EU, lists many of the downsides to immigration, and points out the myopia:

> The new "national living wage" will increase the pull factor of the UK of migrants from poorer EU countries. Already the national minimum wage, equivalent to £1,200pcm, is more that double the average wage of £500pcm in Poland. The unrestricted supply of cheap labour will mean less job security and poorer terms and conditions for low paid workers. Any reduction in inward migration likely to be achieved by restrictions on tax credits – even if introduced – is likely to be cancelled out, placing ever more unmanageable strain on public services, especially the NHS, given that it is one of the few healthcare systems in Europe where anyone with a right to be here can get all treatment free (another reason the UK is such a draw for migrants).
>
> Unrestricted freedom of movement benefits mainly our better-off pensioners who want to retire to sunnier climes. It's not beneficial if you are a low-paid workers vying for a job in a low-wage economy. The working conditions of the low-paid, our NHS, public services, affordability and access to housing are all things most adversely affected by continued membership of the EU, and yet Labour, the Lib Dems and the centre-left are its most enthusiastic supporters. The myopia is truly staggering.[4]

Notes: *M is for myopia*

1. In 2001, live births in England and Wales numbered 594,634; in 2012; the number was 729,674.

2. Nick Clegg – during an interview with Ivan Davies for the *Today* programme, 16 September 2013 – at the party conference in Glasgow.

3. Letter to the *Financial Times* from George Baggaley, director, The Next Generation Party. This was after it was announced that in the first quarter of 2014 the economy had grown by 0.9 per cent albeit that the economy was still 0.6 per cent smaller than before the crash. Three months later much was made of that the economy, in the second quarter of the year, became larger than in the first quarter of 2008. But per capita it was not.

There are various ways of measuring GDP and, anyway, figures are adjusted/updated but:

- If in the first quarter of 2008, GDP was £392,786m and six years later, the first quarter of 2014, it was less by 0.6%, namely £390,429m, but during that period the population increased (from 60m) by one million, output per head was less, not by 0.6%, but by 2.2%.

- If in the second quarter of 2014, the economy regained the level of output during the first quarter of 2008, using the same amount of immigration (despite a further quarter during which immigration was running at over 100,000 a year) output per head was less by 1.6%.

And the figures in those examples do not take account of the costs of immigration, not least the loss of social capital and cohesion (*see* C is for the cost of immigration).

4. From L. Langrick.

N is for nation

The abolition of border controls has resulted in Britain losing its historic identity and indeed voters believe that their identity is being stolen. The reason for balanced migration is a belief that we can still by reason change what our destiny is about. Are we actually going to have border controls? Are we going to limit the numbers of people coming here so that we can integrate them? Or are we as a nation lost?[1]

One definition of a country is a set of people all subject to the same obligations and all enjoying the same rights. Accommodating sharia law makes a mockery of that noble principle. It sacrifices the priceless idea of legal equality on the high altar of 'cultural sensitivity' effectively sanctioning lower-grade legal status for those people who are considered different. This is the very antithesis of a good legal system.[2]

Notes: N is for nation

1. Frank Field, MP for Birkenhead since 1979 and now chairman of the Work and Pensions Select Committee. (*See* M is for misfeasance in public office – note 12).

2. Charlie Klendijan, secretary of the Lawyers' Secular Society.

And N is for newspeak[1]

The name 'Managed Migration' is, I presume, unintentionally comic and could be straight out of 1984, being a classic 'Newspeak' term that George Orwell might have dreamed up. Overwhelming levels of migration and the inadequate management thrown at it, clearly required a name to try to contradict the reality.[2]

Notes: N is for newspeak

1. With apologies to George Orwell (1903/48) the author of *1984*. His name was a pseudonym: he was actually Eric Arthur Blair, which leads beautifully to Tony Blair's part in the immediately next chapter of N is for nonsense.

2. *The Great Immigration Scandal* by Steve Moxon, published in 2004 by Imprint Academic (and *see* I is for identity).

And **N** is for nonsense

… as in Britain, according to Tony Blair,[1] is a young country. But:

- 'In the name of God, go!'[2] was said to Parliament 300 years before he was born.

- 'I know I have the body of a week and feeble woman, but I have the heart and stomach of a king, and a king of England too'[3] was said by the then queen 345 years before he was born.

- 'Gentlemen of England abed tonight shall call themselves accursed they were not here'[4] was written of a battle 538 years before he was born.

- Durham Cathedral, in the constituency adjacent to Mr Blair's, was built over a thousand years ago.

- Boadicea – the 'large' statue at Hyde Park Corner and the smaller one beside the Palace of Westminster of a woman driving a chariot – died fighting the invader, two thousand years ago.

Australia is a young country, anyway for the 99% or so who date their arrival or that of their forbears to post 1788. The other 1% know what is the outcome of aliens swarming, and then swamping, namely well-nigh obliteration. And it was very much the same for the original inhabitants of the Americas.

Notes: N is for nonsense

1. MP for Sedgefield 1983–2007, prime minister 1997–2007.

2. Oliver Cromwell to the Rump Parliament. His preceding words were:

> It is high time for me to put an end to your sitting in this place, which you have dishonoured by your contempt of all virtue, and defiled by your practice of every vice; ye are a factious crew, and enemies to all good government; ye are a pack of mercenary wretches, and would like Esau sell your country for a mess of pottage, and like Judas betray your God for a few pieces of money.

> Is there a single virtue now remaining amongst you? Is there one vice you do not possess? Ye have no more religion than my horse; gold is your God; which of you have not barter'd your conscience for bribes? Is there a man amongst you that has the least care for the good of the Commonwealth?

Ye sordid prostitutes have you not defil'd this sacred place, and turn'd the Lord's temple into a den of thieves, by your immoral principles and wicked practices? Ye are grown intolerably odious to the whole nation; you were deputed here by the people to get grievances redress'd, are yourselves gone! So! Take away that shining bauble there, and lock up the doors.

3. Queen Elizabeth I, allegedly, to the troops assembled at Tilbury against the Armada, in 1588, the full speech being:

My loving people, we have been persuaded by some that are careful for our safety to take heed how we commit ourselves to armed multitudes, for fear of treachery. But I assure you I do not desire to live to distrust my faithful and loving people. Let tyrants fear. I have always so behaved myself that, under God, I have placed my chiefest strength and a safeguard in the loyal hearts and goodwill of my subjects: and therefore I am come amongst you, as you see, resolved, in the midst and heat of the battle, to live and die amongst you all, to lay down for my God, and for my kingdom, and for my people, my honour and my blood, even in the dust. I know I have the body of a weak and feeble woman, but I have the heart and stomach of a king, and of a king of England too, and think foul scorn that Parma or Spain or any prince of Europe should dare to invade the borders of my realm; to which, rather than any dishonour shall grow by me, I myself will take up arms, I myself will be your general, judge and rewarder of every one of your virtues in the field. I know already for your forwardness you have deserved rewards and crowns; and we do assure you, in the word of a prince, they shall be duly paid to you.

4. Battle of Agincourt 1415.

O is for obscenity

Lord Alli of Norbury told the House of Lords, in discussing whether to suspend Lord Bhatia of Hampton, Lord Paul of Marylebone and Baroness Uddin of Bethnal Green for fiddling their expenses, 'It cannot have escaped your attention that the only three members of the House who were referred to the Committee for Privileges and Conduct and subsequently investigated under these procedures are all Asian.'[1]

The Pakistani community mobbed 'Asian' members of the bar for prosecuting Shabir Ahmed (a Rochdale Pakistani, *see* D is for Derby), alleging his prosecution was racist.

(Nigerian) supporters of James Ibori disrupted his trial (here). He moved here from Nigeria in the 1980s, got his hands in the till while working in a Wickes outlet in Ruislip and was then convicted of handling a stolen credit card before moving back to Nigeria to become a regional governor, where he became immune from prosecution (there) for embezzlement/theft. He, his wife, his mistress and three others were jailed.

The parents of Amira Abase[2] (a pupil at Bethnal Green Academy[3]) complained that the police and security services had placed a 'heavy burden' on their daughter and should have done more to stop her travelling to Syria to join ISIS but assuredly they taught her that 'O believers, take not Jews and Christians as friends'[4] is a translation of the word of God and her father Hussen, rather than taking her to see the Natural History Museum in Kensington, or the *Cutty Sark* at Greenwich, or the Geffrye Museum (of the home) in neighbouring Shoreditch being free to do so because of being unemployed, took her on a march[5] with Michael Abedowale[6] and Anjem Choudary,[7] organised by Muslims against Crusades,[8] where there were banners proclaiming 'Islam will dominate the world' and 'The followers of Mohammed will conquer America' and the flags of Israel and the USA were burnt to shouts of 'Allahu Akbar' and 'Burn, burn USA'.

Notes: O is for obscenity

1. I believe Lord Alli's point was not that Asians were dishonest but that only Asian members of the House were being castigated.

Bhatia had not acted in good faith. Paul couldn't understand what was meant by 'main residence' and was said to have been 'grossly irresponsible and negligent' but had not been dishonest.

Uddin claimed for travelling to a flat in Maidstone, albeit having social housing in Tower Hamlets (*see* U is for Uddin and V is for vote rigging).

2. With Shamina Begum and Kadiza Sultana, all aged fifteen or sixteen, they flew (February 2015) to Istanbul and then got a bus to the border with Syria so as, it is thought, to join ISIS.

3. Bethnal Green Academy has a nine-page Race Equality Policy, one sentence of which is:

> We have a rich mix of ethnic groups, cultures and languages: 47% of our pupils are of Bangladeshi heritage; 20% are of African/Caribbean heritage and the remaining 33% is comprised of 18 different ethnic groups.

4. Chapter 5:56 of the Koran.

5. From the Central London Mosque in NW8 to the USA embassy in Grosvenor Square in W1 on Friday, 14 September 2013.

6. *See* note 37 to A is for African, Asian and alien.

7. *See* note 5 to B is for benefit and burden of immigration.

8. Probably a reincarnation of al-Muhajiroun (and/or Islam4UK). In 2002, al-Muhajiroun called the perpetrators of the 9/11 attacks on the World Trade Center in New York 'The Magnificent 19'. The group was proscribed under the Terrorism Act 2000 on 14 January 2010.

And **O** is for obeisance and obsequious

I suspect that the part of Hell to which I will be sent will be quiet like Alton Towers. So I couldn't care less about the inconvenience caused to its normal users by an Islamic day out. What's really interesting here is the whole idea that Muslims require a theme park to be run under special rules for them to be happy there.

No other religion would ask for this, I think. It's a metaphor for Islam's view of our entire society that it has to change to suit them, rather than the other way round. I can't blame them for trying. But why do we give in? How long before non-Muslim women are compelled to dress like bats to enter certain parts of British cities?[1]

Cultural sensitivities were also given as a possible reason why allegations sometimes were not investigated. It was suggested by one local political party that the police and ROs had been reluctant to get involved where there were perceived to be concerns about respecting cultural sensitivities in relation to some South Asian communities.[2]

I'd be so alarmed by the situation I'd do everything possible to suggest it was under control. It's up to politicians to play mood music, in a crisis, and up to the people to understand that there's little else governments can do. The last thing they can say is that we face a threat to which we can see no end because it's based on a fundamental clash of cultures. On the IRA we told the truth, on the Islamic problem, we lie. That itself is a terrorist victory.[3]

The briefing note for the prime minister as to Operation Pathway (*see* below for P is for Pakistan and Operation Pathway), which was as to a 'suspected AQ driven attack', felt it necessary to include 'Community Impact, Engagement and Reassurance'.

On 5 February 2011 David Cameron gave a speech to the Munich Security Conference – 'the Munich Speech' which included:

Under the doctrine of state multiculturalism, we have encouraged different cultures to live separate lives, apart from each other and the mainstream. We have failed to provide a vision of a society to which they feel they want to belong. We have even tolerated these segregated communities behaving in ways that run counter to our values.

It so happened that, that same day, the English Defence League held a march in Luton. The coincidence produced:

The prime minister's comments were unhelpful. On a day when extremist groups of varying persuasions were descending on Luton, his words were open to misinterpretation at best, and at worst were potentially inflammatory.[4]

[and that his speech was] 'ill timed' and 'ill judged'.[5]

In 2014 the Law Society[6] published a practice note to 'assist [solicitors] with the intricacies of sharia law succession rules, which is the code of law derived from the Quran and from the teachings and example of Mohammed' until it was pointed out that such succession rules were contrary to English law.[6.1]

Yvette Cooper[7] complained that the mobile adverts *In the UK illegally? Go home or face arrest* were 'divisive'.

In comment on the appointment of Peter Clarke, head of Counter Terrorism Command 2002–8, to investigate the Trojan Horse letter,[8] the chief constable of the West Midlands, Chris Sims, said the appointment was 'desperately unfortunate' and Fr Oliver Coss, vice chair of one of the subject schools, said such appointment was a 'disaster for community cohesion'. (Mr Clarke's conclusion was that whether or not the letter was genuine, Islamist infiltration with a radical intent was a reality.)

Even though senior officers of Birmingham City Council's education department knew of Trojan Horse-style practices years[9] before the letter's arrival in late 2013, a briefing note to the leader of the council about the letter stated, 'The motivation was seen as an attempt to raise community tension and defusing this threat was seen as more important than speculating on the origins of the letter.'[10]

Notes: *O is for obeisance and obsequious*

1. I cannot vouch for the truth etc. of this item – I saw it in a newsletter from VOMIT (acronym for *victims of masonic ill treatment*) according to which it was within *Rewriting the rules...it's Islam's idea of fun* by Peter Hitchens (the author of *The Abolition of Britain*) in the *Mail on Sunday* 16 July 2006

2. *Electoral Fraud in the UK*, The Electoral Commission, May 2013, paragraph 3.62.

3. *Time to Emigrate?* by George Walden MP for Buckingham, 1983–97, Minister for Higher Education, 1985–87.

4. Nick Lowles, director of *Hope Not Hate*. (As to Luton *see* L is for Luton.)

5. Jack Straw MP and one-time Home Secretary.

6. The professional body to support and represent solicitors.

6.1 The Inheritance (*Provision for Family and Dependents*) Act 1975 and the Equality Act 2010.

7. MP for Normanton, Pontefract and Castleford since 1997, shadow Home Secretary, married to Ed Balls, the then shadow Chancellor of the Exchequer.

8. *See* F is for fifth column.

9. The Department for Education's *Review into Possible Warnings to DfE Relating to Extremism in Birmingham Schools* of January 2016 found that during the 20 year review period 'between 1994 and December 2013' there were six such warnings. The first and fourth of those were

> 1994 – The Department was contacted by Revd John Ray [chair of the governors of one of what would be a Trojan Horse school and see the

Introduction] who raised concerns with ministers about extremist infiltration of Birmingham schools. Departmental records show that senior leaders [actually heads] in three schools in Birmingham wrote to education Ministers in 1994….expressing concerns about the extremist group Hizb-ut-Tahir gaining an influence over schools in the city.

2010 – Post-election, a DfE Minister and officials met Birmingham headteacher, Tim Boyes, on two occasions in 2010. The then Secretary of State was not aware of these meetings at the time. At both of these meetings, there was a discussion about the challenges that political Islam posed for schools in Birmingham. The discussions covered similar issues to those raised in the Trojan Horse letter.

Following publication of the Review, Mr Boyes said

It's farcical that central government can dodge responsibility when it wants to, that ministers feel that such stark warnings can be ignored and neither immediate action nor policy change needs to take place.

10. Pages 6 and 9 of the Clarke Report.

And **O** is for oxymoron

… British Asian, British Muslim, British Pakistani, Irish travellers wanting a (permanent) home (in Britain) and 'Unity through diversity'.

The effort to keep our citizenship divided against itself by the use of the hyphen and along the lines of national origin is certain to breed a spirit of bitterness and prejudice and dislike between great bodies of our citizens. If some citizens band together as German-Americans or Irish-Americans then after a while others are certain to band together as English-Americans or Scandinavian-Americans and every such banding together, every attempt to make for political purposes a German-American alliance or a Scandinavian-American alliance, means down at the bottom, an effort against the interest of straight out American citizenship, an effort to bring into our nation the bitter Old World rivalries and jealousies and hatreds.[1]

In the first place, we should insist that if the immigrant who comes here in good faith becomes an American and assimilates himself to us, he should be treated on an exact equality with everyone else, for it is an outrage to discriminate against any such man because of creed, or birthplace, or origin. But this is predicated upon the person's becoming in every facet an American, and nothing but an American. There can be no divided allegiance here. Any man who says he is an American, but something else also, isn't an American at all. We have room for but one flag, the American flag … We have room for but one language here, and

271

that is the English language ... and we have room for but one sole loyalty, and that is loyalty to the American people.[2]

Notes: O is for oxymoron

1. Theodore Roosevelt (president of the United States of America, 1901–09) in 1916 in a Memorial Day speech in St Louis.

2. (Part of) Theodore Roosevelt's letter to the American Defense Society in 1919.

P is for Pakistan and Operation Pathway

On 8 April 2009, Metropolitan Police Assistant Commissioner Bob Quick, when going to No. 10 Downing Street, inadvertently disclosed the following:

Secret Briefing Note – Operation PATHWAY

General Overview

This is a Security service-led investigation into suspected AQ-driven attack planning within the UK.

11 x Subjects

10 x student visas from Pakistan

1 x UK-born British national

Community Impact, Engagement, Reassurance

Media strategy

As the result of Mr Quick's error, twelve were arrested later that day – five in Manchester, five in Liverpool and two in Clitheroe in Lancashire. One was released without being taken to a police station. After fourteen days the police released them all, save Abdul Wahab Khan and Abid Naseer, but the others, save the British national, so eight, were immediately served with deportation notices. The eight eventually returned to Pakistan on condition that deportation charges were dropped or because their visas were curtailed. From there, four appealed to SIAC but it found:

- Naseer's explanation for an email was 'utterly implausible' and 'We are satisfied that Naseer was an al-Qaeda operative who posed and still poses a serious threat to national security ... he should be deported'.

- 'Wahab was a committed Islamist extremist and ... he and Rehman were knowing participants in Naseer's plans'.

- 'Faraz's case is, in principle, indistinguishable from Wahab's ...'

- and that Ahmed Faraz Khan and Abid Naseer had been planning terrorism but should not be returned to Pakistan because of the risk of torture or execution.

In fact, Khan, having been released on bail (with conditions), returned to Pakistan of his own accord. And at the start of 2012, Naseer was extradited to the USA, where three years later he was convicted of conspiring to attack the Arndale Centre in Manchester.[1]

Notes: *P is for Pakistan and Operation Pathway*

1. Sir Peter Fahy, who was the chief constable of Manchester Police at the time, explained that he had not been able to convince the Crown Prosecution Service that there was a good enough chance, on the evidence then available, of securing a conviction; it had been necessary, in order to protect the public, to nip the conspiracy in the bud rather than to wait for further evidence. Further evidence was obtained in 2011 from Osama bin Laden's compound in Abbottabad in Pakistan.

And **P** is for Poland

Since the beginning of 2004, with this country allowing unfettered immigration from the EU's A8 states, the number of Polish born people in this country has multiplied by about ten times … from 60,711 according the 2001 census.

> The head of the national organisation of Poles in this country has told me that it is now impossible to get a Polish plumber in Warsaw. There are now so many in western Europe that when someone calls for a plumber in Warsaw, they end up with a Romanian, Bulgarian or Ukrainian.[1]

> [Poland's] fertility rate at 1.3 children per woman … the fertility rate of Poles in Britain … is at the replacement rate of 2.1, higher than for the rest of the local population.

> The number of 19 to 24-year-olds in Poland is expected to fall by an astounding 27% between 2012 and 2020 … And over the next 40 years the entire working population is likely to contract by more than 20% …[2]

Notes: *P is for Poland*

1. Damian Green MP for Ashford – in the debate in the House of Commons in July 2007.

2. *The Economist*, June 2014.

While in London for the 2016 Conference on Syria, President Buhari of Nigeria said, '[Nigerians] can remain at home, where their services are required to rebuild the country.'

And **P** is for population

In 1991, the population of England and Wales was 50,748,000, of which 93% was white including white Irish and white other; in 2001, the respective figures were 52,841,000 and 91%, and in 2011, 56,076,000 and 86%.[1]

> Since the late 1980s, when net migration to the UK was close to zero or even negative for some years, immigration has been steadily rising ... evident in [table below] ... based on figures from the British Labour Force Survey ... over the past 15 years the native population has barely increased, remaining relatively stable at around 52 million.[2]

The immigrant population, on the other hand, has grown substantially over that period, from about 4.8 million in 1995 to around 9 million in 2011, an increase from 8.4% to 14.7% of the general population, in just seventeen years.[3]

Fiscal year	natives	EU	Non-EU
1995	52,172,016	885,367	3,920,502
1997	52,024,832	953,449	4,178,270
2000	52,167,122	1,054,930	4,509,258
2004	52,384,909	1,282,428	5,010,460
2007	52,054,165	2,271,159	5,436,642
2011	52,360,031	2,847,289	6,146,430

And so over those seventeen years:

- immigrants increased from 9.21% to 17.17% of the whole;

- EU immigrants increased from 1.69% to 5.43% of the whole;

- non-EU immigrants increased from 7.5% to 11.73% of the whole.

> The 2011 census ....show the largest growth in population in England and Wales (by 3.7 million) in any 10-year period since records began in 1810, with one principal cause being a rise in immigration.[4]

Born in Bradford (by Bradford Royal Infirmary) found that 85% of the babies born to a third-and-more-generation Asian, had at least one parent who had been born there.

Between 2001 and 2010, the population of Bradford grew by 11%.

Bradford has the largest proportion of people of Pakistani ethnic origin in the country. Over the decade from 2001 the people of Pakistani origin increased from 14.5% to 20.4%. The rate of *Pakistanisation* is likely to increase – because 22% of the population is less than fifteen years old.

And nationally there are more ethnic-minority pupils in primary than in secondary schools – in state-funded primary schools, 30.4% of pupils are from minority ethnic origins; in state-funded secondary schools, the proportion is 26.6%. These proportions have increased from 29.5% and 25.3% respectively since January 2014.

In state-funded secondary schools, 26.6% of pupils were classified as being of minority ethnic origin, an increase from 25.3% in 2014. In 2009, less than 20% of pupils in state-funded secondary schools were from minority ethnic backgrounds, so in six years the proportion of pupils in secondary schools from such backgrounds has increased by more than 30% as the increased numbers in primary schools flow through into secondary schools. The ethnic groups with the largest changes in absolute numbers between 2014 and 2015 were: White British (down 41,900), Asian (up 13,600), any other white background and mixed (up 7,100).[5]

The increase in population density has and is leading to boundary disputes, building on 'on our green and pleasant land', building on flood plains with the obvious result, congestion, conversion of houses into flats, housing estates with little or no connection to any other settlement; and so with no infrastructure, services or employment; and therefore making the residents car dependent; (residential) cul-de-sacs off main roads, loss of gardens, overcrowding, loss of open space and playing fields; and so obesity, loss of identity through towns and villages being too quickly and too greatly increased in size, reduced living space,[6] replacement of existing dwellings by high-density housing, infilling/squeezing a new dwelling between existing ones.

The Campaign to Protect Rural England (CPRE) wants to protect the precious English countryside (Letters, July 13) yet at the same time states that we urgently need more affordable homes.

The 2011 census gave the population of England and Wales as 56.1 million, an increase of 7.1 per cent from 2001. The Office for National Statistics says that, on current trends, the increase from 2011 to 2021 will be 4.5 million. The additional housing to meet population growth of over 1,000 extra people every day is only part of the picture. We need corresponding growth in energy and power supplies, schools, hospitals, transport, shops, etc.

If rising population is accepted as an unalterable given, the countryside is doomed. The CPRE needs to work in collaboration with organisations such as Population Matters in order to achieve a sustainable future for the countryside.[7]

The increase of population under some of the projections is very large. Under the ONS high migration projection (net migration 225,000 p.a.) population increases by 29.2 million over the period. This is equivalent to adding a city almost the size of Birmingham to the UK population every two and a half years for the next 75 years. Note that the assumed rate of net migration under this projection is less than the average of 236,000 p.a. for UK net migration during the period 2001–2014 and is well below the latest figure of 330,000 for the year ending March 2015.[8]

Notes: *P* is for population

1. *The Dynamics of Diversity: Evidence from the 2011 Census*. ESRC Centre on Dynamics of Ethnicity (CoDE), University of Manchester, December 2012.

2. So the population was steady but from *Is fertility really a problem? Population, aging, dependency, and consumption* by Ronald Lee and Andrew Mason, *Science*, October 2014:

> Immigration is often suggested to help reduce the population ageing that results from low fertility. Immigration does lead to a younger population in the short term, but it has a muted effect in the long term. Immigrants are relatively young on average when they arrive, but over time their age distribution tends to become similar to or older than the age distribution of the receiving population. This occurs because the immigrant populations age and because fertility rates typically converge towards the fertility rate of the receiving population. A summary of the literature concluded: 'a steady stream of migrants almost always makes a population younger in the short-term but older in the long-term'. Net immigration also raises the population growth rate, which imposes capital costs ... that must be balanced against possible benefits from age structure.

The introduction to the article concluded with:

> Although low fertility will indeed challenge government programs and very low fertility undermines living standards, we find that moderately low

fertility and population decline favour the broader material standard of living.

3. *The Fiscal Effects of Immigration to the UK* by Christian Dustmann and Tommaso Frattini of the Centre for Research and Analysis of Migration, November 2013. The authors defined as immigrants all foreign individuals and their children under sixteen years of age, regardless of their country of birth, and as natives everyone who was at least sixteen and was UK-born, regardless of where their parents were born.

4. A search for this brought up *What hope for the faith school?* by Peter Stanford, *The Daily Telegraph* July 2012 which included 'Thirty years ago, its 400 pupils were all Catholics, many of them first or second-generation Irish. Now all but 10 per cent are Muslims, yet their parents are apparently happy for them to sit through lessons taught by a largely Christian staff and taken from a Catholic syllabus that includes subjects such as the Pope, the Virgin Mary, the Mass and Jesus.'

5. Department for Education statistical first release, January 2015.

6. The average new British home is now 76 square metres compared to 109 in Germany: (*see* H is for housing).

7. Peter Graystone, Staffs, letter to a newspaper, July 2013.

8. *The Costs and Benefits of Large-Scale Immigration* by Professor Robert Rowthorn, published by Civitas, December 2015.

Elsewhere in his book, Professor Rowthorn likens the population increase, under the ONS high-migration scenario, to a Letchworth Garden City 'every month for the next seventy-five years simply to keep up with the growth of population. This takes no account of the additional homes required to eliminate the existing housing shortage.'

David Cameron's 'tens of thousands' (*see* D is for disingenuous) was in January 2010. He became prime minister in May of that year. In the six calendar years 2010 to 2015, immigration (net of emigration) was at least 1,500,000 (*see* D is for disingenuous for the ONS figures as to migration). One sixth of that is 250,000; the ONS high-migration scenario is (only) 225,000 – so a new Letchworth Garden City would be required more often than once every month.

And **P** is for progression – compound and exponential

In 1951, there were 1.9 million people in England and Wales who had been born abroad, 4.3% of the total. In 2011, those two figures had increased to 7.5 million and 13% respectively.[1]

In 2001, 20% of births were to foreign-born mothers; a decade later such share had increased to 25%.

Between 2008 and 2012, the birth rate in England and Wales of UK-born mothers rose by 0.5% while that of foreign mothers rose by 10.7%.

In 1951, there were 111,000 people here who had been born in India. In 2011, there were 694,000.[1]

> In 2001 the census recorded 373,933 black Africans in London; in 2011 that figure had gone up by 51% to 573,931. Clustered in Greenwich, Lambeth and Southwark – none of them all that close to Smithfield – West Africans now outnumber Afro-Caribbeans in these boroughs.[2]

According to the University of Manchester's *Dynamics of Diversity: Evidence from the 2011 Census*, the non-white share of the population of England and Wales was 7% in 1991, 9% in 2001 and 17% in 2011. And the 'ethnic minority group population of England & Wales' increased between 2001 and 2011 as follows (percentage change from 2001 shown in brackets):

Indian   1,412,958 (+34%)
Pakistani   1,124,511 (+55%)
African   989,628 (+100%)
Caribbean   594,825 (+4%)
Bangladeshi   447,201 (+56%)
Chinese   393,141 (+69%)

Mixed
White Caribbean   426,715 (+78%)
White-African   165,974 (+106%)
White-Asian   341,727 (+78%)
Mixed Other   289,984 (+83%)

Other Asian   835,720 (+238%)
Other Black   280,437 (+186%)
Arab   230,600 (no figure available)
Other   333,096 (+46%)

The Greater London Authority's 2011 Census Snapshot: Ethnic Diversity Indices has:

Key Findings

- The 2011 Census found that nearly 11 million residents in England and Wales are from an ethnic group other than White British comprising some 19.5 per cent of the total population.

- Greater London is home to 4.5 million non-White British residents; accounting for 41 per cent of the all non-White British residents in England and Wales. This is disproportionately higher as Londoners comprise 14.5 per cent of the national population.

- London local authorities are some of the highest ranked nationally in terms of proportions of ethnic minority populations as a percentage of the total population. For instance, in both Newham and Brent over 80 per cent of the resident population is non-White British (83 per cent and 82 per cent) respectively).

- In national rankings of ethnic diversity indices 26 of the top 30 local authorities are London boroughs, with four outside London (Slough, Luton, Leicester and Birmingham).

- Although Greater London may not be the most diversity area in the country according to diversity index values, it comprises local authorities that are undoubtedly the most diverse.

- Greater London has a diversity index score of 4.26 which is only slightly lower than Slough (5.21). ... Greater London is certainly more diverse than any other conurbation, however, Slough could arguably claim to be the most diverse area. Greater London, without doubt, comprises some of the most diverse local authorities in the country.

And there are two factoids that suggest there is a potential long-term 'divergence' problem to be addressed. The first, from Eric Kaufmann's[3] work on the 2011 census, finds that 41 per cent of the non-white population (some 4.1 million people) live in wards where white Britons are a minority, in some cases a small minority. That figure was just 25 per cent in 2001.

The second, from the work of Simon Burgess,[4] finds that more than half of ethnic-minority pupils in England are in schools where white British children are a minority. That rises to 60 per cent for those in Year One (and 90 per cent in Year One in London).[5]

Moving to one particular part of Greater London, namely Redbridge:

2.0 Demographic Analysis

Redbridge's population in mid-2008 was estimated to be 263,200, making Redbridge 9th largest borough in London.

The population increased by 10.5% between the 2001 Census and mid-2008. The Redbridge population is projected to grow to more than 300,000 people by 2028(ONS).

Redbridge is a young Borough, with 21.4% of its population under the age of 16 in mid-2008. It has a higher proportion of children than London (19.2%) and outer London (20.1%).

Just over half of population change in Redbridge in 2008 was accounted for by natural change (births and deaths). The remaining 49% was account for by net migration.

3.0 Diversity in Redbridge

It is estimated that in the proportion of residents from White ethnic groups declined from 63.5% in 2001 to 51.9% in 2009.[6]

Although the proportion of Redbridge residents who were born in England decreased by 12 percentage points between 2011 and 2001 censuses it was in line with the London average (61.1%).

India (7.6%) was the most common birthplace outside the UK for Redbridge residents.

Of all London Boroughs, Redbridge has the sixth highest number (85,014) of people whose stated country of birth is outside of the EU (including Accession states) countries. Redbridge ranked ninth highest in England and Wales.

In total, 103,073 (37%) people in Redbridge were born outside of the United Kingdom.[7]

In the ten years from 2001 to 2011, the 'English/Welsh/Scottish/Northern Irish/British' population of Wiltshire increased by 6% while 'Other Asian' increased by 874%.

In 2014, without the source/authority being given, the following figures were stated to be those of the five largest ethnic minorities:

Indian   1,412,958
Pakistani   1,124,511
black African   989,628
black Caribbean   594,825
Bangladeshi   447,201

a total, for just those five source of immigration, of 4,569,123.[8]

It is to be noted that none of those five sources are in the EU so immigration from there is additional, and so:

The same, alas, was true for the opposition. During the televised leadership debates in the 2010 election campaign, Nick Clegg challenged David Cameron to say whether he was 'right or wrong that 80 per cent of people who come here come from the European Union'. The Lib Dem leader was wrong, laughably so: the real figure was 35 per cent (as anyone who had vaguely studied the subject would know). But worse, neither Cameron nor Gordon Brown was able to correct him. This short exchange summed up the situation perfectly: Britain's immigration policy was set by a party that knew little, fighting rivals who knew less.[9]

But one avenue into Europe has remained wide open – because it cannot be closed without compromising the rights of natives. Half of ethnically Turkish German citizens seek their spouses in Turkey, according to the interior ministry. For years, about 25,000 people a year, two-thirds of them women, have successfully applied at consulates in Turkey to form families in Germany.

That means, since the mid-1980s, half a million imported spouses – fresh nuclei around whom brothers, sisters, parents, and children can later make their own legal claims to immigrate under family reunification criteria. 'Chain migration', as it is called, ensures exponential growth of minority populations, even if the borders are completely closed to illegal immigration. The Turkish population in Germany multiplies not once in a life cycle but twice – at childbirth and at marriage.

The situation is similar in every country in Europe. In France, the number of foreign spouses rose from 23,000 in 1990 to more than 60,000 in 2004 and family-related immigration now accounts for 78 per cent of permanent legal immigration. In Denmark, the vast majority of first-, second-, and third- generation Turks and Pakistanis take their spouses from the home country: some studies have shown the rate for Turks to be over 90 percent. In the Bradford District Race Review, published after Britain was hit by a wave of race riots in the summer of 2001, Sir Herman (later Lord) Ouseley warned that '50% of the marriages that take place in the Asian community result in an intake of new residents who are unable to communicate in the English language, which limits their participation in mainstream social and educational activities'. Fully 60 percent of Pakistani and Bangladeshi marriages are to spouses born abroad, a major factor in the roughly 50 per cent growth of the Pakistani population of Manchester, Birmingham and Bradford over the 1990s. Six decades into the mass immigration from the Indian subcontinent, three-quarters of Bengali children aged 0–4 have mothers born in Bangladesh.[10]

The 'curry industry' claims that as south-east Asian cooks grow old, replacements must come from south-east Asia rather than be home-trained, despite the *c.*three million[11] from, India, Pakistan and Bangladesh already here.

> As the history of America showed, migration has a tendency to accelerate because diasporas tend to draw more people after them. Collier[12] adds that rising incomes in poor countries lead to still more acceleration, not less, since the very poorest cannot afford the price of a people-smuggler's fee, let alone an airfare. The slave trade excepted, the people who flocked to the United States were not the poorest of the global poor from parts of Asia and Africa. They were the moderately poor urban masses of Europe. Likewise, today it is generally the people who have already migrated from village to city, and scraped together some savings who come to Britain. Even rising educational standards accelerate migration by allowing more people to surmount any educational hurdles in the path of migrants, Collier argues.[13]

That one immigrant tends to be followed by others is illustrated by:

- the 'man on a homemade raft'. Asif Hussainkhil was rescued by French coastguards two miles off Sangatte near Calais. He was trying to 'sail' across the channel on a raft constructed of six pieces of timber, three buoys and a sail of an old bedsheet. He said he left Afghanistan in 2000 and, having had several jobs on the way, got to Calais in March 2014; he had already made several attempts to get across the Channel and explained, 'I want to join my uncle and cousins.'

- ZAT, IAF, KAM, AAM, MAT, MAJ and LAM all 'claim to be Syrian nationals'. The latter three are related to the former four. The latter three had been granted refugee status and were here. The former four were in 'the jungle' outside Calais; they were able to use Article 8 ECHR/Human Rights Act – right to family life – to require to be allowed to join the latter three (here).[14]

> The relationship is not additive but multiplicative: a wide gap [in economic levels] but a small diaspora, and a small gap and a large diaspora, will both only generate a trickle of migration. Big flows depend upon a wide gap interacting with a large diaspora and an inadequate level of income in the countries of origin.[15]

> In state-funded primary schools, 30.4 per cent of pupils were classified as being of minority ethnic origin – an increase from 29.5 per cent in January 2014. Minority ethnic pupils make up 71 per cent of the increase in the number of pupils in state-funded primary schools (with White British the remainder). The ethnic groups with the largest increases in absolute numbers from January 2014 to January 2015 were: White British (up 22,400), any other White background (up 22,700), mixed (up 11,900), Asian (up 11,300) and Chinese (up 1,100).[16]

Over the last five decades, the Muslim population of the UK has on average doubled every 10 years.[17]

The actual numbers of Muslims and their percentage of the population, for England and Wales, have been something like:

1961   50,000 of 46,104,548 = 0.11%
1971   226,000 = 0.46%
1981   553,000 = 1.11%
1991   between 950,000 of 50,748,000 = 1.86% and 1,250,000 of 50,748,000 = 1.46%
2001   between 1,500,000 of 52,841,000 = 2.83% and 1,600,000 of 52,841,000 = 3.07%
2011   2,700,000 of 56,017,000 = 4.81% (the increase over the decade from 2001 being at least 68.75%).

That growth must increase as the Muslim percentage of the population that is under five is twice the average: half of Muslims are under twenty-five and a third are under fifteen.

And yet Muslims are probably the most alien (*see* A is for African, Asian and alien, and especially the last section thereof, F is for fissiparous, K is for Khan and T is for terrorism and I is for integration) but in fact the least likely to integrate.

In one place, the London Borough of Redbridge, the number of Muslims increased between 2001 and 2011 from 28,487 to 64,999, an increase of 228%, and as a percentage of the residents of the borough, almost doubled, from 11.9% to 23.3%.[18]

Notes: *P is for progression – compound and exponential*

1. Office for National Statistics.

'The United Kingdom began the post-war years with a non-white population of some 30,000 people; it approaches the end of the century with over 3 million, whose origins extend from Africa, the Pacific Rim, the Caribbean, and the Indian Subcontinent' – *Citizenship and Immigration in Post-war Britain*, Randall Hansen, published 2000.

2. *Smithfield Meat Hook* (hence the significance of proximity to Smithfield), *The Economist*, January 2013.

3. The author of *Shall the Religious Inherit the Earth? Demography and Politics in the Twenty-First Century*.

4. Professor of Economics, Director of Centre for Market and Public Organisation.

5. *When it comes to integrating immigrants, friendship is the key*, January 2016, David Goodhart (the author of *The British Dream*).

6. *Redbridge Today: A Portrait of the Borough*, May 2008.

7. Redbridge home page.

8. Daniel Hannan, MEP for South East England. His figures were in an article that included, 'Britain is undergoing unprecedented demographic change. In 1950 white people were close to 100 per cent of the population; in 2050 they will be 65 per cent.'

Hannan's source would appear to be University of Manchester's *Dynamics of Diversity: Evidence from the 2011 Census* (*see* what follows to what has note 2 to it).

9. *Leaving the EU wouldn't solve Britain's immigration problem* by Fraser Nelson, *The Daily Telegraph*, October 2014.

10. *Reflections on the Revolution in Europe* by Christopher Caldwell, published in 2009 by Allen Lane.

11. *See* what has note 8 to it.

12. 'Collier' is Professor Collier: (*see* note 15).

13. *Let immigrants in. Then send them home* by Matt Ridley, *The Times*, November 2013.

14. The quote is taken from the report of Upper Tribunal Immigration and Asylum Chamber Judicial Review Decision of 21 January 2016 – JR/15401 and 5/2015N. The facts are complicated but, at least in part, this is the finding that was made: all seven were minors (save one who is vulnerable) when the application was made, hence the anonymity.

15. *Exodus Immigration and Multiculturalism in the 21st Century* by Professor Paul Collier.

16. Department for Education Statistical First Release, January 2015.

17. *'Easy Meat': Multiculturalism, Islam and Child Sex Slavery* by Peter McLoughlin.

18. Redbridge home page.

And **P** is for prostitute[1]

The Russians, quite correctly, view Cyprus, as a convenient backdoor to the European Union – and they are not alone. The Chinese have also started arriving, encouraged by what they regard as an incredibly low bar to immigration.

Forget all those tricky visa forms, for anyone prepared to spend £300,000 on a property in Cyprus there is the bonus of eligibility for permanent residency. Once this is achieved, the owner is entitled to move anywhere within the EU. For the price of a shoebox in Shanghai, Cyprus is offering a gold-card travel pass and much more besides.[2]

In the last year, the number of foreigners entering the country on Tier 1 visas – only available to those who have more than £1 million to invest in the UK – jumped by 78 per cent. One of the perks of this visa is that you're eligible for fast-track residency status, with indefinite leave to remain after just two years. Best of all, a significant percentage of your 'investment' can be in the London housing market. Which might explain why more than 60 per cent of all sales above £2 million in the capital are currently going to overseas buyers.[3]

At present, migrants who invest substantial sums in gilts or in British registered companies can apply for permanent residence. A million pounds gets them leave to remain after five years; £5m reduces the waiting time to three years and £10m to two. They need not speak English and can bring their families. Between 2009 and 2013 Britain flogged 1,628 such visas, about half to Chinese and Russians. The market is heating up: 560 went last year.[4]

In October 2014, it was announced that the amount required (for fast-track settlement here) was being doubled to £2 million.

The UK is not the only country to sell such a favour; for instance, Cyprus and Malta. And Bulgaria is a lot cheaper and easier.

(And) once someone from outside of the EU has citizenship, or even the right to residency, in an EU country, under the EU's free movement of people he can move within and live anywhere within the EU (*see* E is for European Union).

Notes: P is for prostitute

1. The verb, as opposed to the noun, and so to sell oneself especially for an unworthy cause.

2. *Cash-strapped Cyprus plots Russian exit from austerity* by Jeff Randall, *The Daily Telegraph*, October 2012.

3. *Money Walks* by Toby Young in *The Spectator*, June 2013.

4. No country for poor men in *The Economist*, March 2014.

The item presumably resulted from a report released on 25 February 2014 by (the Home Office's) Migration Advisory Committee, which pointed out that, as interest is paid on the gilts, visas are in effect being given away:

> The present system, it seems, is designed to minimise the gains to UK residents and maximise the gains to migrants. Indeed we pay them for making the application. They get interest on their loan, the gilts.

In fact, the one-sidedness of the deal is worse: buying somewhere to live qualifies as investment and the gain on that investment can be free of capital gains tax.

The paragraph which followed what is quoted of *The Economist* was:

> This system is deeply flawed. The minimum investment level has not gone up since 1994. Because the value of an investment must remain above £1m until residency is granted, most applicants pile into low-risk gilts, for which buyers are already plentiful. Investors are likely to sell those gilts when they obtain settlement. Rich foreigners, who prize London's schools and England's legal system, are benefiting more than the country that hosts them, thinks the committee.

And **P** is for puzzle

Who said each of the following?

First:

> The great majority of the immigrants now coming in are dependents, and most of these are women and children, who have all or most of their reproductive life before them. In other words, the race problem of the future is something we are still engaged in building up by this continued immigration.[1]

Second:

> Immigration and settlement largely by coloured persons into a relatively small number of concentrated areas would aggravate social problems.[2]

Third:

> ... there is surely no question about the net rate of intake at which we should be aiming. It is a maximum of nil. The natural increase of the million or more already within our shores will face us, and still more our children, with intractable problems enough. In the name of sanity and common sense we ought not avoidably to add to it.[3]

Fourth:

> It is almost incredible that under our law a person who has made good his entry into this country unlawfully cannot be sent home when the malpractice comes to light. The people of other countries, Commonwealth countries no less than others, have no hesitation whatever in expelling those who break the law to cross their frontiers. They must think that, to use a famous phrase, we are 'stark, staring bonkers' to offer illegal entrants a prize for breaking the law ...[4]

Fifth:

> It is easy – indeed unavoidable ... to laugh, but pity the country where immigrants or the children of immigrants have no desire to ape its culture.[5]

Notes: *P is for puzzle*

1. Enoch Powell.

2. James Callaghan.

3. Enoch Powell.

4. Enoch Powell.

5. Charles Moore.

Q is for quacks

Foreign-trained doctors are up to four times more likely to be suspended or struck off than those trained in the UK.

- On average, 1 in 1,000 of UK-trained doctors are struck off, 1 in 250 of those trained in India and 1 in 350 of those trained in Pakistan.

- The British Association of Physicians of Indian Origin (BAPIO) complains that their members are discriminated against by the General Medical Council (GMC) (*see* U is for unintended consequences).

- It is similar with solicitors … when ethnic-minority practices are intervened by the Law Society and/or ethnic solicitors are struck off, their fellow non-indigenous allege racism.

- Taking in doctors from the undeveloped/poor parts of the world purloins the investment of their home countries.

- *See* Appendix IV for cases of foreign doctors who have failed, medically or otherwise.

And Q is for questions

1. Eight years ago in a respectable street in Wolverhampton a house was sold to a negro. Now only one white (a woman old age pensioner) lives there. This is her story. She lost her husband and both her sons in the war. So she turned her seven-roomed house, her only asset, into a boarding house. She worked hard and did well, paid off her mortgage and began to put something aside for her old age. Then the immigrants moved in. With growing fear, she saw one house after another taken over. The quiet street became a place of noise and confusion. Regretfully, her white tenants moved out.

   The day after the last one left, she was awakened at 7 a.m. by two negroes who wanted to use her phone to contact their employer. When she refused, as she would have refused any stranger at such an hour, she was abused and feared she would have been attacked but for the chain on her door. Immigrant families have tried to rent rooms in her house, but she has always refused. Her little store of money went and, after paying her rates, she has less than £2 per week. She went to apply for a rate reduction and was seen by a young girl, who on hearing she had a seven-roomed house, suggested she should let part of it. When she said the only people she could get were negroes, the girl said, 'racial prejudice won't get you anywhere in this country'. So she went home.

The telephone is her lifeline. Her family pay the bill, and help her out as best they can. Immigrants have offered to buy her house – at a price which the prospective landlord would be able to recover from his tenants in weeks, or at most a few months. She is becoming afraid to go out. Windows are broken. She finds excreta pushed through her letterbox. When she goes out to the shops, she is followed by children, charming, wide-grinning piccaninnies. They cannot speak English, but one word they know. 'Racialist,' they chant. When the new Race Relations Bill is passed, this woman is convinced she will go to prison. And is she so wrong? I begin to wonder.[1]

2. How can an immigrant, whose face is covered, either assimilate or integrate?

3. Is multiculturalism reconcilable with assimilation and integration?

4. Why aren't British citizens who plot to kill a member of HM armed forces prosecuted for treason?[2]

5. When, in September 2007, Gordon Brown, then prime minister, promised 'British jobs for British workers':

- was it because he anticipated that in the next general election Labour would obtain 68% of the ethnic-minority vote?

- was he being prescient because, in the following year, the number of foreign workers rose by 175,000 and the number of British workers fell by 46,000?

- was it because of the 2.5 million extra persons in employment since 1997, three quarters were foreigners?

6. When we are told that we are bound by European Treaty to submit to unrestricted access from anywhere else within the European Union, is that deceitful, dishonest, disingenuous, honest, ignorant or merely being happy with immigration?

7. Why in any debate about planning law and the preservation of our countryside is the fact of immigration never mentioned?

8. Why is immigration not recognised as a reason for the cost and shortage of housing, overloading of midwifery services and the shortage of primary school places? If not myopia, is it stupidity or something more cognitive? If the latter, what is such thinking?

How many "white british" have housing which does not meet the Parker Morris standard?

9. Why were any of those immigrants named in this book, who have committed an offence for which they were imprisoned, still in this country?

10. Why were Magalie Bamu and Eric Bikubi (*see* A is for African, Asian and alien) being from the Congo, or Seydou Diarrassouba from the Ivory Coast, or Derrick Kinsasi and his brother from the Congo (*see* E is for examples perhaps encapsulating where we are) ever allowed into this country (when those countries were never part of the British Empire and/or Commonwealth but part of the francophone world)?

11. Why don't we immediately expel any citizen of another country who commits an offence to obtain entry to this country or who while here breaks the law, such criminal to be accompanied by spouse/partner/ cohabitee and issue, and such expulsion to be effected immediately upon conviction and without appeal?

12. How much child benefit was paid in 2012/13 for children from an A2 country? And likewise for each of the following three years?

12.1 How much child benefit was paid in each of those four years for children in an A2 country?

13. What was the cost in 2010/11 and each of the following years of each of
i) Lord Carlile's 'large resources and eternal vigilance?'[3]

ii) legal aid for would be immigrants?

iii) having in prison those convicted of terrorism?

iv) having in prison criminals who are not UK citizens?

v) repatriation of deportees?

vi) the 'Somali community'?[4]

vii) of 'immigration law' meaning the Asylum and Immigration Tribunal (first tier and appeal) and applications on human right grounds by would-be aliens either to come here or to stay?[5]

13.1 Should the cost of any one of the seven items be deducted from the percentage of GNP, which is the requirement for what is to be provided in foreign aid? And if so which?

14. How much of the cost of housing benefit (£24 thousand million in 2013/14) is attributable to immigrants?

14.1 And how much of the balance is attributable to immigration pushing up the cost of housing for the indigenous?

15. What in each of 2010/11 and the following years was the total of capital expenditure that was produced by immigration?

16. What in each of 2010/11 and the following years was the amount of remittances 'home' to first of all, each of the A8 countries, secondly the A2 countries, thirdly India, fourthly Pakistan and fifthly the various countries in Africa?

16.1 What proportion of our balance of payments deficit in each of 2010/11 and the following years was the sum of those remittances?

17. Are 'Asian restaurants' more likely than businesses owned by indigenous people to have illegal entrants as part of the workforce?[6]

18. Out of the budget of which government department or quango is there the payment for translation for the NHS?

18.1 What was the cost in 2010/11 and in each of the following years of The NHS Equality and Diversity Council?

19. Who was the officer of the Rotherham Safeguarding Children Board who wrote of what was to be its report into grooming of (white) girls:

> Although the alleged perpetrators are of Asian origin and the victims are white, this is the factuality of these cases alone; nothing more can be drawn from that. It is imperative that suggestions/allusions of a wider cultural phenomenon are avoided. These assertions are without foundation.[7]

19.1 Is he still in post? And if not, why not?

19.2 Who were the members of the board who acted on that view?

20. Will all the imams in Blackburn, Blackpool, Birmingham, Derby, Dewsbury, Leicester, Manchester, Oxford, Rochdale and Rotherham condemn *malak ul-yameen*?[8] And, if so, in what terms?

21. You have girls being abused and raped and yet the most senior officers are refusing to comment on it. [First] on what other subject would you get that? [Secondly] how many young girls have been abused and raped because of the reluctance of the authorities to say exactly what is happening?[9]

22. Why did trading standards officers visit the home of Ilyas and Tallat Ashar in Eccles?[10]

22.1 How did the Border Agency allow into this country:

- Ilyas and Tallat Ashar's ten/twelve-year-old domestic – on the passport of a twenty-year-old, and apparently several times?

- Rebecca Muwonge (*see* E is for examples perhaps encapsulating where we are) in 1996 when she was thirty, on the passport of her eighteen-year-old niece?

23. What was the thinking behind or the motive for commentators arguing that the 2011 rioters were not predominately of an ethnic minority or not predominately motivated by racism?

24. If immigration is such 'a good thing' economically, why after so much immigration:

i) is the gap between government expenditure and income so great?

ii) is the national debt so high?

iii) is the trade gap so big?

iv) are there so many 'economically inactive'?

v) are there so many NEETs?

vi) is there so much unemployment?

vii) are 'hundreds of thousands' turning to food banks?[11]

viii) is 'The plain fact is that, unless taxes rise or great swathes of public spending cease to exist, Britain is broke'?[12]

ix) were six million people in Britain paid less than the National Living Wage?[13]

x) has our current account deficit reached 7 per cent of GDP, the worst (save in and as the result of war) since 1772?

25. At the end of 2013, both output and productivity were 15 percentage points lower than they would have been had the economy grown since 2007 at its long-term trend rate: so what did immigration achieve in those five years?

26. If acquisition of English, and in this country, is so conducive to future trade, how does Switzerland, with only an eighth of this country's population, sell more to India than this country?[14]

27. If we need immigration to man the NHS, why after so much immigration is our under-fives mortality rate at 5.38 per thousand births the highest in

Europe, our (female) life expectancy at 82.6 the lowest in Europe and survival rates for breast, bowel and cervical cancer the second worst in the developed world?

28. What is ethnic origin of John Brown and Rhodes Levin,[15] who were given life-time immunity from prosecution for the murder of PC Keith Blakelock notwithstanding that they both admitted kicking him?

29.   The city is booming from record population growth. But as you are forced to stand on the train tomorrow, to search fruitlessly for a place at a nursery school or somewhere to live or rent, how happy or wealthy does that make you feel?[16]

30. If there is global warming and sea levels are rising, so England is getting smaller, and it is agreed that flood plains should be what is implicit in such term, should there be any immigration at all?

31. How many Pakistani spouses[17] were there in each of the calendar years since the beginning of 1994?

32.   Call me Alex,' he said, assuming that his Polish name would be too hard to pronounce. We were looking for a reliable builder to construct a patio and he had been recommended by a neighbour. Alex was the operation's frontman: educated, polite and with impeccable English. A few days later, he brought along one of his team who worked for twelve hours on a baking hot Sunday digging and laying the foundations, completing the task the following day and clearing the site of all the mess. And the cost? With labour and materials, it was less than half the price we had been quoted by a British counterpart.

32.1   So what would you do? Hire the British worker who needs to charge more because his overheads include a mortgage to pay and a family to look after; or opt for the cheaper, but equally proficient Pole living with four or five other men in rented accommodation who is in this country for just six months while his wife and children are at home in Cracow?

32.2   Before we start criticising Tesco and Next for hiring cheap workers from Eastern Europe, as Labour's Chris Bryant has done, should we not examine the beam that is in our own eye? The fact is that a good deal of immigration from Poland and other former Soviet bloc countries that joined the EU in 2004 has been sustained by the middle classes looking to improve their homes, and retailers, bars and hotels anxious to keep down their wage bills.

32.3   Mr Bryant, Labour's immigration spokesman, walked into a fusillade of criticism for the speech he made at the Institute for Public Policy Research (IPPR) think tank yesterday, even before he delivered it. Yet his central claim – that Eastern European nationals are undercutting the pay of British workers – was hardly revelatory. Who did not know this? Well, presumably Labour didn't. Despite the fact that 80% of newly created jobs were going to foreign workers, for most of their thirteen years in office Labour ministers insisted that immigrants were simply filling vacancies the British did not want.

Yet one reason they did not want them – a point Mr Bryant studiously ignored yesterday – is that benefit payments are high enough to let Britons stay at home rather than compete with the incomers for low-paid jobs. Why, otherwise, is the carwash at the superstore near where I live in south London staffed entirely by Eastern Europeans when within a mile radius there must be hundreds of young people out of work? Even if a jobless local youngster wanted to work there he would have a tough job breaking into the closed shop of Poles and Latvians who recruit from among their own community here in the UK or back home.

A study by Migration Watch UK several years ago found that a combination of benefits and immigrant labour willing to work for low wages was creating 'an underclass of discouraged British workers'. The higher the level of immigration in an area, the harder it was for the unemployed to come off Jobseeker's Allowance. A single person under 25 on the minimum wage was only £10 a day better off than a non-working person. By contrast, a Pole on the minimum wage in Britain was picking up four to five times what they would earn at home and by living in multi-occupancy accommodation could send considerable sums back to their families. And why wouldn't they?[18]

33.   'The employment minister says it is "inevitable" that Britain will have to import some foreign workers to do skilled jobs. What is wrong with training more British people in the skills of which we are short?'[19]

34. If Joe Public described something as hideously black/Jewish/ Muslim he would, if not prosecuted, at least be excoriated, so why did Greg Dyke,[20] if anything, get approval when he said the BBC was 'hideously white'?

35. In respect of the 'White Pride' march in Manchester on 22 August 2015, Councillor Sue Murphy, deputy leader of the council, said, 'Manchester is a diverse and inclusive city and we would much prefer that this event was not happening here at all. But we would encourage everyone to ignore it just as

they would treat any other in our thriving city centre.' What would she have said about a 'Black Pride'[21] march?

36. Was the consequence of the Equality Act 2010, as set out in U is for unintended consequences, in fact, intended?

37. Did you know that 'the UK received 583,000 migrants in the year to June 2014, 0.9% of the population' (so 1 in 111 of the population migrated here in that one year)?[22]

38. In 2010/11 and in each of the following tax years, how much was paid to the inhabitants of postal code WF12 (Savile Town, Dewsbury) in welfare payments, and in each of those years how much was paid by such people in taxes?

39.   Do they believe in universal human rights – including women and people of other faiths? Do they believe in equality of law for all? Do they believe in democracy and the right of people to elect their own government? Do they encourage integration or separatism?[23]

40. What is the benefit, to either the indigenous or to the immigrant, of having here those to whom the culture and way of life of the indigenous is anathema?[24]

41. What has Bradford Council done pursuant to the Trojan Horse letter being apparently addressed to someone in Bradford?[25]

42. Is it appropriate for a school in this country to have as (part of) its name a word of a foreign language?

42.1 Is it appropriate for a secular school to have as (part of) its name the first word, in Arabic, of the Koran?[26]

43.   Finally, we need to look with objectivity at the attitudes common in countries to which we open our borders. We have to ask whether a society in which sharia law, and all that it entails, is supported by the majority, can fit easily in to a secular Western democracy. We have to ask what problems this brings, and more importantly, we must prioritise the best interests of the people in Britain. The question that must be answered, but is not yet being asked is this: is it in the best interests of the people of Britain (particularly women) to open our borders to countries which stone rape victims, and kill people for blasphemy? I would submit that it is not, as Rotherham and elsewhere have shown.[27]

Notes: Q is for questions

1. This is part of Enoch Powell's so-called 'rivers of blood' speech of April 1968. He said he told this story from 'just one' of the 'many letters' that he said he had received from his constituents.

2. In 2008, Parviz Khan and to varying degrees Hamid Elasmar, Basiru Gassama, Mahmood Irfan, Zahoor Iqbal and Amjad Mahmood plotted to kidnap and behead a British soldier. Mr Justice Henriques in sentencing Khan to life with a minimum of fourteen years said, 'This was not only a plot to kill a soldier but to undermine the morale of the British army and inhibit recruitment.'

And in 2013, Michael Adebolajo and Michael Adebowale killed Fusilier Lee Rigby outside Woolwich Barracks, because he was a member of HM armed forces.

3. *See* C is for cost of immigration.

4. 80% of the Somalis in this country live in social, i.e. subsidised housing.

5. The appeal to the Supreme Court in *R (on the application of Lumba) v. Secretary of State for the Home Department (co-heard with Mighty)* occupied nine judges and the report is seventy-three pages long.

Other examples of 'immigration law' include Abu Hamza's attempt to stay in this country and his daughter-in-law's fight to stay here rather than return to her native Morocco; plus the applications of Ali and Bibi (*see* L is for language, E is for examples of cases encapsulating where we are, P is for Pakistan and Operation Pathway, and S is for students as to the case of HU).

6. The blog *Liars, Buggers and Thieves* has the following items:

Labour Councillor Balbir Sandhu – illegal immigrants

Border police raided a clothing factory owned by a leading city politician yesterday, leading to the arrest of five illegal immigrants. The officers were acting on a tip-off when they targeted the A Star clothing factory belonging to Normanton Ward councillor Balbir Sandhu. (Monday, 14 January 2013)

Conservative Councillor – Illegal Immigrants

A councillor fined £15,000 after three illegal immigrants were arrested working in his Chinese restaurant earlier this year has appealed.

The Canton Restaurant, run by Cllr Patrick Chung and his family in Hatter Street, Bury St Edmunds, was just one of four takeaways raided by border and immigration officials in August, when a total of 10 workers were arrested. (Friday, 21 November, 2008)

In 2010, Mustafa Khan and Mohammed Azeem set up the Madina Superstore in Stockport Road, Levenshulme. A year later, they were fined £15,000 for employing four illegal immigrants and in 2012 there was a fine of £8,750 for a similar crime. But that was followed by a third fine but, following a plea in mitigation from their barrister, of apparently the same ethnicity (being Ahmed Nadim), which included:

> This is a situation where the defendants operate a substantial business in an area where there is a significant immigrant population, who do their shopping there. As a result they are subjected to pressure by people who need work. What the defendants have done is to exhibit inappropriate compassion.

> The two got away with, only, community orders.

7. *See* D is for Derby.

8. Abdurrahman Wahid, president of Indonesia, 1999/2001.

> The Saudi people still believe in the Old Islamic teaching, which is belief in slavery. So a woman who works for them is considered a slave. For some men in Saudi Arabia, sexual relations with a housemaid are not considered as rape, because they believe that such a practice is permitted by their beliefs.

9. Retired Detective Superintendent Mick Gradwell; *see* D is for Derby as to the grooming etc. of (white) girls by (brown) men.

10. They brought a ten-year-old deaf and mute girl into this country. While using the girl for his sexual pleasure and to work for them, Mr and Mrs Ashar and their daughter Faaiza used the girl to obtain social security benefits. (*See* S is for slavery).

11. *Oxfam and Church Action on Poverty*: 2013.

12. *A wake up call for those sick of politics* by Jeremy Paxman, *The Financial Times*, April 2015.

13. KPMG report of the autumn of 2015.

14. 'We import students but we export contacts, networks and reputation': Baroness Hamwee, leader of the Liberal Democrats in the House of Lords, during the second reading of the Immigration Bill, 10 February 2014.

15. Pseudonyms as to two of those who were there when PC Keith Blakelock was hacked to death.

16. This from a review entitled: *An awful warning* by Harriet Sergeant, of *Bending Adversity: Japan and the Art of Survival* by David Pilling about the Japanese response to the economic situation of the last two-plus decades. The preceding part of the paragraph was:

> So what can Japan teach us? Certainly living in Tokyo during its boom years was a lesson to me that economic growth does not necessarily translate into a better quality of life. The majority of Japanese paid a harsh cost for their country's success. We see something similar in London nowadays.

17. 'Pakistani spouses' means persons who were resident in Pakistan until marriage to a person resident in this country but of Pakistani heritage.

18. *From Labour's breathtaking hypocrisy over foreign workers* by Philip Johnston, *The Telegraph*, August 2013.

In 2011, the Migration Advisory Committee concluded that at least 160,000 British workers had missed out on work because of immigration:

> Since 2004, almost a million workers from Poland and other former Soviet bloc countries have come to the UK. Their import has been startling. Figures released this [third] week [of January 2012] show that over the past year the number of British people with jobs has fallen by 100,000 even though nearly 300,000 foreign nationals have found work. In the final years of the last Labour government 90 per cent of new jobs went to overseas workers, mainly from Eastern Europe.

19. Letter to a newspaper from Stanley Eckersley, July 2014. The 'employment minister' was Esther McVey, appointed October 2013 in succession to Mark Harper (who had resigned due to his discovering that his long-term cleaner was an illegal immigrant).

20. At the time, namely 2001, Director General of the BBC. These words were apparently also used by Maurice Glasman, now Baron Glasman, when advisor to Ed Miliband. It is the title of the second chapter of Gavin Cooke's *Britain's Great Immigration Disaster*.

21. The term 'Black Pride' may well have been hijacked by black homosexuals.

22. *Barometer*, February 2015, whose source was ONS/Statistics.

23. David Cameron, February 2011, to the Munich Security Conference ('the Munich Speech'). His immediately preceding words were:

> Some organisations that seek to present themselves as a gateway to the Muslim community are showered with public money despite doing little to combat terrorism. As others have observed, this is like turning to a right-wing white supremacist movement. So let's properly judge these organisations.

24. *See* what of H is for Ray Honeyford has note 7 to it.

25. The letter included '… implementing [Trojan Horse] in Bradford will not be difficult for you' and 'Tahir [Alam] and I will be happy to support your efforts in Bradford'.

26. What was Drummond Middle School, Drummond Road, Bradford (*see* H is for Ray Honeyford) is now Iqra Community Primary School. '*Iqra*' is an Arabic word and is the first word of the Koran.

27. Rotherham: *The Perfect Storm – An Investigation In To Muslim Grooming Gangs* by Anne Marie Waters, December 2015. And see the answer to Why is the apostate to be executed in Islam? On *Islam Question and Answer* at https:/islamqa.info/em/20327.

And Q is for queues

… caused generally by there being more people in the country, and so congestion, but specifically at airports, caused by the so-called liquid bomb plot.

Abdulla Ahmed Ali, Tanvir Hussain and Assad Ali Sarwar conspired, in 2006, to explode homemade bombs fuelled by materials such as hair bleach, substituted for innocuous refreshments, to blow up seven aircraft between the UK and USA/Canada in a two-and-half-hour slot. The materials were stored in a wood in High Wycombe and a flat in Forest Road, East London, with the mixing in a property in Walthamstow.

Subsequently Umar Aslam was convicted of conspiracy to murder but the jury couldn't agree on the charge of conspiring to blow up an aircraft. (Subsequently Ali appealed to the European Court of Human Rights that publicity before trial would have prejudiced the outcome, albeit he left a martyrdom video wherein he described himself as the leader of the 'blessed' operation.)

Umar Islam was convicted of conspiracy to murder; the jury was unable to decide if he knew the plot would target aircraft.

Two juries could not reach a decision as to Ibrahim Savant, Arafat Waheed Khan and Waheed Zaman.

And **Q** is for quod erat demonstrandum

Yet one of Powell's predictions proved to be truer than he could have imagined. In May 2011, the Office for National Statistics announced that Britain's ethnic minority population had risen by 40 per cent in eight years. In England and Wales, 9.1 million people, one in six of the population, were non-white. Officially, London's ethnic population is just over 40 per cent. Empirically, it is well over 50 per cent and in some boroughs over 80 per cent. Were Powell alive today, he might well have said '*Quod erat demonstrandum*'.[1]

Notes: Q is for quod erat demonstrandum

1. This is the final paragraph of Tom Bower's essay entitled *Immigration* in *Enoch at 100*, published by Bitemark Publishing in 2012.

R is for racist/racism

A definition of racist/racism is:

> A belief that one's own racial or ethnic group is superior, or that other such groups represent a threat to one's cultural identity, racial integrity or economic wellbeing; (also) a belief that the members of different racial or ethnic groups possess specific characteristics, abilities, or qualities, which can be compared and evaluated. Hence: prejudice, discrimination, or antagonism directed against people of other ethnic groups (or more widely, of other nationalities), esp. based on such beliefs.
>
> [And a racist is] an advocate or supporter of racism ...

It must be very difficult not to be racist because necessarily implicit in diversity is difference, if not between races, then at least between cultures, and so both those who applaud and those who execrate diversity are racist; and likewise with multiculturalism. Those who believe immigrants should integrate and immigrants who want to maintain their cultural heritage despite living here are both racist as they both 'come from' the belief that immigrants and the indigenous are culturally different.

And so, all, whether white, brown or black, are racist.

> Now, it's a known fact that racism comes in two forms: that practiced by whites – heinous and inexcusable, whatever its motives – and that practiced by blacks – quite justified, whatever its excesses, since it's merely the expression of righteous revenge, and its up to the whites to be patient and understanding.[1]
>
> I do not have any English blood in my veins, a thing I am inordinately proud of. Look at all these English people ... buying up all the houses. Who can stop it? Does that mean I must be a racialist? I think I have to confess I am. It doesn't mean I don't like foreigners. I love them, all colours. I have many Indian friends and even one or two black ones. But I don't want them to settle and create ghettos in my patch of the country.[2]
>
> The British invented racism.[3]
>
> We know what parent power means in London. In practice, it means giving power to small groups of white middle class parents, or if not to capture by one ethnic group as opposed to another, the best organised.[3]
>
> White people love playing divide and rule play. We should not play their game.[3]

Black boys are more interested in hustling, which is a quick way of making a living, rather than commitment to study.[4]

I'm sure people are very cross. They see the area has been hard hit by the EU opening its doors and this area has been swamped a bit [by the Roma influx]. There is no doubt people are upset about it.[5]

The only people who should play for England are English people. If you live in England for five years, it doesn't make you English. It doesn't mean you can play for a country. If I went to Spain and lived there for five years, I'm not going to play for Spain. We are English, we tackle hard and we are tough on the pitch and we are hard to beat. We have great characters. You think of Spain and you think technical but you think of England and you think they are brave and they tackle hard. We have to remember that.[6]

On 26 February 2014, at a Council meeting open to the public, Mr Choudhury lost control of himself: he pointed to a Labour Councillor and former (non-elected) Mayor, Ms Ann Jackson, and shouted, 'Oswald Moseley had his blackshirts, John Biggs had his black cardigans.' This outburst was extraordinary in itself but Mr Rahman made no attempt to ask Mr Choudhury to withdraw the remark or to apologise. In the end, the Council voted to remove Mr Choudhury's right to speak.[7]

Black people and Asian people should not be forced to accept British values or to adopt a British identity. Rather, different peoples should have the right to express their own identities, explore their own identities, formulate their own values, pursue their own lifestyles.[8]

When your country is taken over by 100,000 Germans, you get angry.[9]

We couldn't speak out on Pakistani sex gangs for fear of appearing institutionally racist.[10] The main pressure police have is being called institutionally racist if they highlight a trend like this. There is a fantastic reluctance to be absolutely straight because some people may take such offence.[11]

The police are over cautious because they fear being branded racist.[12]

British jobs for British workers.[13]

That [between 1997 and 2009, 2.9 million more people came to live in Britain than those who left to live abroad is] the biggest influx of people Britain has ever had and it has placed real pressures on communities. Not just pressures on schools, housing and healthcare – though those have been serious – but social pressures, too.[14]

I believe in Britain. It is a great country. The British people are a great people ... I want a Britain that is one nation, with shared values and purpose ....[15]

Worrying about immigration, talking about immigration, thinking about immigration, does not make [the electorate of Doncaster North] bigots.[16]

This building is a fine tribute to the many generations of 'canny' Scottish bankers, who have made – and are still making – such a valuable contribution to the national economy.[17]

We have got to change the behaviour and the culture of the incoming community, the Roma community because there's going to be an explosion otherwise. We all know that.[18]

I have never underestimated the social dislocation that can occur when large numbers of people from abroad settle in a particular area – as happened in east Lancashire.[19]

There is an issue of ethnicity here [of white girls being sexually abused by Asians] which can't be ignored. In terms of group grooming there is an ethnic dimension which typically is of Asian men on white girls ... And this is an issue which has to be faced and addressed within the Asian community. That kind of leads to a sense of denial by them that all this is going on. These are small communities, so people will have a rough idea that people are abusing white girls in this way.[19]

No black person in the UK can be racist. Racism is prejudice plus power. Black people can be prejudiced but not racist.[20]

Anybody who says that the fact that most of the men [the grooming rape gangs] are Asian and most of the children are white is not relevant – that's just fatuous.[21]

You white people train them in sex and drinking so when they come to us they're fully trained.[22]

Pakistani men pass you round like a ball, they're all in a massive circle and put a white girl in the middle.[23]

The fact of the matter is I have to look at the children's cultural and ethnic needs. The children have been in care proceedings before and the judge had previously criticised us for not looking after the children's cultural and ethnic needs, and we have had to really take that into consideration with the placement that they were in.

We have to think about [UKIP's] clear statements on ending multiculturalism. These children are from EU migrant backgrounds and UKIP has very clear statements on ending multiculturalism.

These children are not UK children and we were not aware of the foster parents having strong political views. There are some strong views in the

UKIP party and we have to think of the future of the children.[24]

Victoria [Climbié] was a black child who was murdered by her two black carers. Many of the professionals with whom she came into contact during her life in this country were also black. Therefore, it is tempting to conclude that racism can have had no part to play in her case. But such a conclusion fails to recognise that racism finds expression in many ways other than in the direct application of prejudice.

… As Counsel to the Inquiry perceptively pointed out … 'Race can affect the way people conduct themselves in other ways. Fear of being accused of racism can stop people acting when otherwise they would. Fear of being thought unsympathetic to someone of the same race can change responses'.[25]

Racism is the key word for those committed to the confidence trick that is race. Suppressing free thought has always been around. In the Middle Ages it was the H-word, as in heretic; now it's the R-word for racist. That's how they got Enoch and that's how they've managed to bring Europe to the state it is in today. As I write, there are riots in Sweden, race riots, but the media are not reporting the facts; which are African and Muslim crowds, to a man in Sweden in order to collect generous benefits, are attacking the police after a criminal was shot. In America, as over here, the newspapers and television do not report a person's colour after a crime has been committed, only what kind of baseball cap he was wearing. See what I mean by suppressing free speech?[26]

In fact, Muslims believe we are not just culturally but biologically racist:

British schooling and British society is the home of institutional racism. The result is that Muslim children are unable to develop self-confidence and self-esteem; therefore, most of them leave school with low grades. Racism is deeply rooted in British society. Every native child is born with a gene or virus of racism.[27]

And the indigenous agree

The locals there and elsewhere argue that it is not nice to feel an alien in your own town. They do not wish for a high street in which the English shops have closed down, to be replaced by ones which advertise their wares in a foreign tongue. This is, I suppose, racist of them. Just as it is racist of London East Enders, if there are any left, who look at the Mile End Road – two miles of unrelieved burkas – and feel shoved out, colonised. Or the south Londoners who see shops down Southwark Park Road which resemble the flyblown, half empty caverns from which meat is sold in downtown Mogadishu.[28]

Notes: *R* is for racist/racism

1. *The Camp of the Saints* by Jean Raspail translated by Norman R. Shapiro and published by The Social Contract Press: originally *Le Camp Des Saints* was first published in 1973 by Editions Robert Laffont-Fixot.

2. Sir Iain Noble, Scottish banker, 1935–2010.

3. Diane Abbott, MP for Hackney North and Stoke Newington since 1987. The third of her quoted statements was 'racism' according to fellow MP, Nadhim Zahawi (born in Iraq and the member for Stratford upon Avon since 2010). She responded to the furore as the result of the third quote by "apologising" for "any offence caused ... not to make any generalisations about white people".

4. Adolph Cameron, the head of the Jamaican Teachers' Association.

5. Julie Blacker – a community cohesion officer, Page Hall area of Sheffield.

6. Jack Wilshire, Arsenal/England midfielder. (Athletic Bilbao only has Basque players.)

7. Paragraph 414 of the judgment in *Erlam and others v. Rahman and another (M/350/14 and see* V is for vote rigging).

A poem by Benjamin Zephaniah (born here but of Jamaican ethnicity) begins:

> The coconuts have got the jobs
> The race industry is a growth industry
> We despairing, they careering
> We want more peace, they want more police
> The Uncle Toms are getting paid ...

8. Kenan Malik.

9. Gunnar Sonsteby 1918–2012.

10. The Macpherson Report of 1999 into the defective police performance after the murder of Stephen Lawrence (*see* B is for benefit and burden of immigration) found the police to be "institutionally racist". This was probably inevitable because of the enquiry's definitions –

> A racist incident is any incident which is perceived to be racist by the victim or any other person.

> "Institutional Racism" consists of conduct or the collective failure of an organisation to provide an appropriate and professional service to people because of their colour, culture or ethnic origin. It can be seen or detected

in processes, attitudes and behaviour which amount to discrimination through unwitting prejudice, ignorance, thoughtlessness, and racist stereotyping which disadvantages minority ethnic people.

11. Retired Detective Superintendent Mick Gradwell: *see* D is for Derby.

12. Mohammed Shafiq, director of Lancashire-based Ramadhan Foundation, the aim of which is 'to enhance a better understanding between Muslims and non-Muslims in the West'. He was speaking after nine men of Pakistani origin, living in Rochdale, were convicted of child sexual abuse: *see* D is for Derby.

13. Gordon Brown, MP, Prime Minister 2007–10.

14. David Cameron, Prime Minister 2010–16.

15. Tony Blair's foreword to his party's manifesto for the 1997 general election. David Cameron, was similarly racist when he spoke of 'British values'.

16. Ed Miliband, MP for Doncaster North since 1997 (but according to Gordon Brown, Miliband's boss in the 2010 general election, Gillian Duffy of Rochdale was a bigot as she was worried about immigration).

17. Queen Elizabeth upon the opening of the new RBS headquarters outside Edinburgh on 14 September 2005.

18. David Blunkett, MP for Sheffield Brightside from 1987–2015 (when he got moved to the House of Lords) and, inter alia, Home Secretary 2001–5.

19. Jack Straw, MP for Blackburn from 1979, Home Secretary 1997–2005.

20. Lee Jasper, born in Manchester to a mixed-race mother and Jamaican father; chair of *Black Activists Rising Against Cuts* (BARAC); one-time senior adviser to Ken Livingstone and who subsequently asked, 'Which mayor has seen the number of black youth going to jail in London increase by 100% during his term?'

21. Trevor Phillips, the chairman of the Equality and Human Rights Commission.

In this connection, the Network of Sikh Organisations complained – about the term "Asian grooming/sex gangs" – "It is something that the leaders of the Muslim community, the Pakistani community, need to address".

22. One of the Rochdale CSE gang convicted in 2012: *see* D is for Derby.

23. Victim 'Girl C' of the Rochdale CSE gang convicted in 2012: *see* D is for Derby. Another such victim, or possibly the same one, said, 'Asians pick me up. They get me drunk, they give me drugs, they have sex with me and tell me not to tell anyone. I want to move.'

24. Joyce Thacker, Rotherham Borough Council's Strategic Director of Children and Young People's Services.

In the aftermath of the publication of the Jay Report, Mrs Thacker eventually went but with a payout of £40,000.

The following sentences are probably not in the correct order and certainly not a complete statement of what Mrs Thacker said – after the conviction in 2010 of five 'British-born Pakistanis' of child sexual exploitation (*see* D is for Derby):

> [The victims] were under child protection plans following family breakdowns or other issues with their behaviour.

> When we pieced together a map of what was happening we stepped in very quickly to move these girls to a place of safety outside Rotherham. It started off as a grooming exercise by men who became friendly with the girls, gave them gifts and introduced them to their friends.

> When they got used to being abused it just became a normal way of life for the girls.

> It is akin to self-harm.

> It is very dangerous.

> The girls could have faced death if the men weren't getting what they wanted.

25. Parts of Paragraph 16.1 and 7 of the Laming Report following the death of Victoria Climbié. The chapter's heading was *Working with Diversity* followed by:

> There is some evidence to suggest that one of the consequences of an exclusive focus on 'culture' in work with black children and families is [that] it leaves black and ethnic minority children in potentially dangerous situations, because the assessment has failed to address a child's fundamental care and protection needs.
>
> (Ratna Dutt, director of the Race Equality Unit)

26. Taki Theodoracopulos, *The Spectator* just after rioting in Stockholm and several other Swedish cities with a large immigrant population – the summer of 2013: (and *see* note 2 to D is for diversity). In April 2014 he wrote:

In the meantime, students at New York University tried to shut down a restaurant because its owner, a devout Christian, kept it shut on Sundays. 'He must be a homophobe and a racist' was one sign that can be repeated in these pages – i.e. Christianity now translates into racism and homophobia. Go figure.

So what has happened to us? That's an easy one: egalitarianism and immigration. Once upon a time the Wasp establishment had standards and people tried their best to uphold them. Teachers and priests held us to account. Now they reach way down to the lowest common denominator in order to avoid the R word being slung at them.

27. Ifikhar Ahmad of The London School of Islamics Trust.

28. *Is it racist to want a high street where you can understand the shop signs?* by Rod Liddle, *The Spectator*, December 2013.

And **R** is for the 2011 riots

The apparent spark for the riots was the shooting dead by the police of Mark Duggan just after Kevin Hutchinson-Foster had handed over to him an illegal firearm. Duggan was possibly under surveillance as it was thought he was planning to avenge the murder of his cousin Kelvin Easton (for which no one has been convicted). Hutchinson-Foster has admitted using the gun to pistol-whip a barber a week before Duggan's death and was on probation when he handed the gun to Duggan; he had convictions for possessing crack cocaine and heroin with intent to supply. Duggan, Hutchinson-Foster and Easton are all at least partially non-indigenous.

The longest prison term in connection with the riots, eleven and a half years, was to Gordon Thompson, non-indigenous, for burning (down) the House of Reeves in Croydon.

In Birmingham, Jermaine Lewis, Nicholas Francis, Wayne Collins, Renardo Farrell and Tyrone Laidley petrol-bombed The Barton Arms so as to lure in the police in order to shoot them; those five, all non-indigenous, were convicted of possessing a firearm with intent to endanger life, reckless arson and riot. In connection with the same crime, Amirul Rehman, a minor, was convicted of riot and possessing a firearm.

Nooragha Zadran helped set a police car alight (his one year sentence was suspended because he was suffering from PTSD from his time in Afghanistan).

At or soon after the riots there were conflicting statements:

It wasn't race riots.[1]

These riots were about race. Why ignore the fact?[2]

[The London 2011 riots are] an insurrection of a generation of poor, primarily black people from the Caribbean and from Africa.[3]

This is not about race at all.[4]

A year after the riots:

Indeed, the only official document to present the proper, unvarnished picture is "The Statistical Bulletin of the Ministry of Justice on the Public Disorder of 6th–9th August 2011". And it is incontrovertible: 41% of those charged were white, 50% black or mixed race, 7% Asian and 2% Chinese or other. These figures must be read against the proportion of the various groups in the population as a whole: in London, to which some two thirds of the cases relate, some 12% of the population is black and 69% is white. Whites, in other words were significantly under-represented among the rioters: while blacks were four times over-represented.

Nor are the figures for the riots a fluke, as the Metropolitan Police statistics for 2009–10 show even more extreme disparities: 54% of those proceeded against for street crime were black: for robbery, 59%; and for gun crimes, 67%. This is also where the figures for previous criminality of the rioters come in: 76% of the rioters brought before the courts were previous offenders: those convicted had committed a grand total of 16,000 offences between them and over a third had served time in jail ...

The conclusion is inescapable and painful. Far from being opportunistic, the core of the rioters was formed of an already existing criminal class and that class is disproportionately black[5]

And after the result in January 2014 of the inquest into Duggan's death:

It is also a gross exaggeration to describe the riots as a direct result of Duggan's death. Those who took to the streets of Manchester and Milton Keynes had little idea who he was: they saw, from 24-hour news, that order seemed to have collapsed and that there was a great chance of some profitable criminality. Overwhelmingly, it was former convicts who went off to loot. Of the 3,000 convicted, four fifths had been through the courts before and a quarter had chalked up more than 10 previous offences. This looks less like an act of mass protest – against the treatment of Duggan, or anything else – and more like opportunistic crime.

Known members of criminal gangs were disproportionately represented in the rioters, especially in Leeds and Nottingham. But again, you can look in vain for a racial element. Britain has no equivalent of Los Angeles-style gangs organised by ethnicity: ours almost always tend to reflect the composition of the communities they come from. In its long investigation into the riots, the London School of Economics said that half of those it interviewed were black – but 'those involved did not consider these race riots'.

If a government paves the road towards welfare dependency and petty criminality, it should not be surprised that so many walk down it. If you have millions of people not working – in a country where more than 1,000 people are arriving to work every day – then social ill will follow. Fewer than a third of London's rioters had any kind of job – and this takes us closer to Britain's real problem. It's less grabby than racism, but far more daunting. Our discrimination is economic – a system that is loaded against those trying to work their way out from poverty. There is still all too much to be done in putting this right.[6]

Notes: *R* is for the 2011 riots

1. David Cameron.

2. Katharine Birbalsingh.

3. Darcus Howe from Trinidad.

4. Max Wind-Cowie of Demos.

5. *The 2011 English summer riots revisited* by David Starkey, *The Daily Telegraph*, August 2012.

In early 2015, the *Evening Standard* reported that 1,539 out of the 3,914 charged or cautioned (for misbehaviour during the riots) had since reoffended.

6. *Gangsterism, not racism, was the root of Mark Duggan's shooting* by Fraser Nelson, *The Daily Telegraph*, January 2014. That was immediately after the result of the inquest into Duggan's death.

And **R** is for Roma and Romanians

Romania joined the EU at the start of 2007 and is an A2 country. Romanians, if self-employed, could work here from then; under transitional arrangements they could be employed here from the start of 2014.

Philip Johnston is absolutely right in his criticism of Chris Bryant, the shadow immigration minister, and Labour's hypocrisy on the subject of immigrant workers (*Comment*, August). However, what is most worrying is that the Government is doing nothing to prevent the situation becoming worse.

Theresa May, the Home Secretary, trumpets statistics showing that net immigration is falling, while maintaining that nothing can be done about the majority of economic immigration because we are bound by EU rules.

She also claims that predictions about the scale of the influx of Bulgarians and Romanians from 2004 onwards are grossly exaggerated. Unfortunately, official predictions of the likely impact of opening our borders to the eight Eastern European nations which joined the EU in 2004 were exceeded by 640 per cent: so why should we assume that 2014 will be different? What we need is a pragmatic and practical solution: tell Brussels that we simply cannot allow unrestricted access by EU states.[1]

Romanians appear to use children to beg, to be the source of much of ATM[2] crime and pickpocketing[3]:

- George-Josif Blaj was convicted in Romania of rape in 2009 when he was sixteen. Early in 2013, he throttled a woman until she was unconscious; when she awoke he attacked her again and then raped her. He was convicted of assault, burglary and rape; it was requested that a further burglary be taken into account. He is due to be deported when he has completed his sentence of eleven years (and four on licence). (The victim's MP has asked why the Romanian authorities failed to inform the UK of Blaj's history.)

- Dumitru Dolonescu, having been deported, returned and took the benefit of out-of-date official data to obtain housing benefit and income support (for which he was jailed).

- Marius Gheorge has a sweet tooth or just used stolen sweets as a form of currency. He was first caught living in Shoreham-by-Sea with sweets worth £782 and given a one year conditional discharge. He was next caught in Wrexham with sweets worth £1,100 and was fined £100 plus costs but spared from paying as it was considered that his two days in police custody were sufficient punishment. His defence told the court that he was 'desperate to get back to Romania'. He was next caught in Cobham stealing chewing gum worth £887. And all within eight weeks of arriving here in the spring of 2013.

- Leonid Rotaru skipped bail while under investigation for skimming in Axminster in 2011; he was caught again in Minehead. Under questioning, he gave a false name. He was convicted when his DNA was found inside a device; he was convicted of possessing an article for use in fraud, possessing or controlling a false or improperly obtained identification card.

- Stefan Balint, Jean-Robert Kimelman and Ananda Odagiu tricked tourists into thinking they were policemen. The sentencing of the latter two was delayed as they had convictions in Romania.

- Telus Dumitru, his wife Ramona, her sister Dorina plus Marian Gheorghe, Claudia Radu, Ion Lincan and Ion Stoica flew back and forth to/from Romania; they somehow convinced the court that together they had to repay less than one sixth of the benefits they fraudulently obtained. They had been supplied with forged job references by Abdel Lemsatef and thus obtained NI Numbers.

- Gold campers – Vasile Bararga, Marius Barbu, Iulian Culba, Puiu-danut Paunescu, Ovidiu Gabor, Ioan Gavrilit, Cinstantin Irina, Catalin Paise and Iulian Roman camped in woodland while targeting jewellers so as to get gold and take it home, and of whom the prosecutor said, 'It appears that all came to this country with the sole purpose of committing robberies and taking part in this particular conspiracy. They were not people who had come here to work and got diverted. This is effectively a professional gang who came here to rob.'

- The Rostas family – Marin, Robert, Cornell, Robert, Romulus and Govinder – targeted late-night train passengers between London and Kent for mobile phones and cash. They were described by DC Weekes of British Police as 'career criminals who worked in a coordinated and organised manner. Their aim was to generate as much as possible to pass back to other family members in Romania to buy land and property'.

- Vasile Bogdan, with four convictions at home and after seven years in jail there, carried on in the same way here: he obtained entry to jewellers by dressing as a woman; up to ten members of the gang are still at large. He was sentenced to ten years.

It is similar elsewhere:

The new factor, says Christian Pfeiffer, director of the Criminology Research Institute of Lower Saxony in Hanover, is the eastward expansion of the European Union, with full rights of free movement. Eight countries joined in 2004, followed by Bulgaria and Romania in 2007. Romania and Bulgaria, in particular, have sophisticated crime syndicates with training and scouting networks reaching deep into the nearest rich EU countries, Germany and Austria. Of the suspects in Berlin's trick-robbery cases [in 2012], 75% were non-German; 31% came from

Romania. (Only 24% of suspects in overall German crime cases were foreign.)[4]

Notes: *R is for Roma and Romanians*

1. John Waine, letter to a newspaper, August 2013.

2. 'ATM crime' is stealing cash from 'a hole in the wall' by electronic means but Constantin Alexandroaia used more direct means: he pumped gas into three ATMs and then ignited it. He caused £73,000 of damage and obtained £27,000 in cash. The gang, which included Teofil Bortos and Gregore Paladi, introduced malware into fifty-one ATMs over the spring bank holiday of 2014.

3. Over 40% of pickpockets in central London, who are caught, are Romanians.

4. *Crime in Germany, The Economist*, July 2013.

S is for borders that leak like a sieve

Hakim Benmakhlouf was jailed in 2005 for three and a half years for stealing money, passports and designer handbags. While in prison, he was offered £3,000 under the government's voluntary deportation scheme. He left in July 2007 on Eurostar but returned the next day from Paris. In 2008, he was jailed again after admitting another string of thefts. He was freed from prison in 2009 and flown home. He was again deported in January 2010 but in March was back here. When police tried to arrest him he kicked an officer. At this point the judiciary gave up – there was no point imposing a jail sentence as 'you shouldn't be in the country'.

The reality is that coach transport into London represents an immigration sieve.

There are no effective border controls on those coming into the UK and making their way to Victoria coach station and we are paying the price of that sudden influx of Eastern European rough sleepers – especially Romanians – around Marble Arch.

This is being systematically organised from Romania and those running this cynical racket are the only ones who profit from it. The problem for London is that one of London's most iconic landmarks is being turned into an impromptu campsite just 95 days ahead of the London Olympics.

The risk is that we could get a torrent of people coming here from Eastern Europe in the deluded belief that London can provide a more lucrative living ahead of the Games.[1]

Notes: S is for borders that leak like a sieve

1. Nickie Aiken, Westminster Councillor, spokeswoman for Children, Young People and Community Protection.

See *Romanian beggars "flooding" London* by Katie Hodge, *Independent,* April 2012.

And **S** is for slavery

The common law does not recognise slavery.[1]

> The British slave-owning society produced Wilberforce, the passionate abolitionist. The British not only abolished slavery by statute, they also found the money to compensate the slave owners who had lost the services of their slaves. They did this right through the Caribbean. Even in little Antigua no one lost. The compensation paid varied with the value of the slaves. In Antigua, slaves were valued at £14 per head.[2]

There is nothing in the Koran against slavery. Rather, it states how slaves are to be treated[3] and Mohammed had slaves so there is nothing wrong with slavery. (Muslims believe Mohammed was 'perfect' and so believe it is good to emulate his behaviour – to wear black, to have a beard, to marry a pre-teen girl; and that for a married man to have sexual intercourse with a slave girl is not adultery.)

> These schoolgirls were sacrificed so that the middle-class monocultural elite did not have to entertain the disturbing idea that some cultures think that slavery is legitimate, and that a 50-year-old man having sex with a 9-year-old girl is an act of piety.[4]

Just about the only cases in this country of slavery are by non-indigenous:

- 'travellers', for instance the Connors family;
- Ilyas Ashar and his wife Tallat trafficked into the UK from Pakistan a ten-year-old deaf girl and thereafter treated her as a slave;[5]

Notes: S is for slavery

1. Somersett case of 1772.

2. From the speech in 2014 entitled *Freedom & Democracy* by V.S. Naipul at the Centre for Policy Studies Conference.

The immediately preceding sentence was: 'It is important to remember that where there is a free interplay of ideas the good can often overcome the bad.'

3. *See*, for example, chapter 24:33.

4. *'Easy Meat': Multiculturalism, Islam and Child Sex Slavery* by Peter McLoughlin, published by the Law and Freedom Foundation, 2014.

It is unclear if this reference to a fifty-year-old man and a nine-year-old girl is an allusion to Mohammed and his wife Aisha, their respective ages when he married her, or to today.

According to the Iranian and Kurdish Women's Rights Organisation (IKWRO), at least thirty girls in the London Borough of Islington were forced into marriage in 2010.

> They have to cook for them, wash their clothes, everything. They are still attending schools in Islington, struggling to do their primary school homework, and at the same time being practically raped by a middle-aged man regularly and being abused by their families. So they are a wife, but in a primary school uniform.
> (Dianna Nammi, director of IKWRO)

5. *See* number 22 of Q is for questions. Ashar was convicted of rape and of trafficking for exploitation. His wife and their daughter were convicted of using the girl to obtain welfare benefits. Since Ashar's imprisonment, the girl has been awarded £100,000 damages and/or compensation for unpaid work.

And S is for the story of the Sharmas[1]

Jatinder Kumar Sharma was born in or about 1965, Neelam Sharma in or about 1971 and Rakhi Shahi in or about 1978. Jatinder and Neelam were married in or about 1989. Sometime later, he also purported to marry Rakhi. Those births and marriages were all in India.

Neelam came here as a teacher, as a highly skilled immigrant, and in 2005 applied for leave to remain. Rahki arrived here on a student visa but worked.

Jatinder qualified, in India, as a lawyer and in 2003 came here as a visitor; a year later he was admitted as a solicitor under the qualified lawyers transfer test and in 2005 he obtained leave to remain as Neelam's husband.

Jatinder, Neelam and Shakhi lived together in Southall.

Between October 2006 and May 2008, Jatinder, as a solicitor, made 980 visa applications.Jatinder pleaded guilty to conspiracy to defraud, handling the proceeds of crime, and immigration offences and was sentenced to seven years: Rakhi was convicted and sentenced to eight years, and Neelam to four years.

Five comments: first, the UKBA – 'We know of 1,000 foreign nationals who have come illegally into this country but what we have discovered so far is merely a snapshot. It was an extremely sophisticated scheme.'

Second, the prosecutor – 'Between them they submitted the largest number of fraudulent visa applications ever received by the Home Office from one source, making this the biggest immigration scam ever seen in this country … Applicants with humble backgrounds found themselves in possession of degrees, post-graduate qualifications and diplomas within a matter of months.'

Third, the judge, Richard McGregor-Johnson (who recommended all three defendants be deported at the end of their sentences) – 'Various criticisms have been made of the actions of the agencies responsible for checking those documents. Those criticisms are plainly well founded in my view. The checks were woefully inadequate and frequently non-existent.'

Fourth, the Solicitors Regulation Authority – 'His trial has raised important issues that we are examining to ensure this cannot happen again. Since the SRA was set up three years ago, we have made improvements to the admission process and will continue this work. We have also recently consulted on proposals for a more stringent entry regime for lawyers who qualified abroad and who want to practise in England and Wales.'

(But) fifth, an immigration lawyer – 'It is not, and never should be the SRA's role to investigate the immigration status of lawyers. That kind of scrutiny could damage trust and lead to accusations of institutional racism.'[2]

Notes: *S is for the story of the Sharmas*

1. This was originally under C is for crime, in the section as to crooked lawyers, but on reading a further source it became evident that it could be under E is for examples perhaps encapsulating where we are or M is for marriage or R is for racist/racism (the comment of the immigration lawyer that for the professional regulator to check a foreign lawyer's immigration status would be 'institutional racism') or S is for borders that leak like a sieve. So it became its own item, the story of the Sharmas.

2. Gulay Mehmet.

Now, as employers and letting agents have to check the immigration status of would-be employees/tenants, presumably they also may be accused of being 'institutionally racist'.

And **S** is for Stockholm syndrome

Despite having been betrayed (*see* B is for betrayal) The Workers Educational Association is 'committed to equality and diversity'. And the London Borough of Lewisham[1] has the following equality and diversity statement

> Lewisham is a diverse community made up of many different groups and individuals. We value and celebrate diversity and believe it essential to try to understand the different contributions, perspectives and experience that people in our community have. We believe the diversity of our population and workforce is one of our greatest strengths.

Notes: S is for Stockholm syndrome

1. The *2011 Census Second Release* of December 2012 reported that some of the percentages of Lewisham's residents by ethnic group were

	in 2011	and had been in 2001
White – British	41.5	56.9
Other Asian	4.3	1.5
Black African	11.6	9.0
Black Caribbean	11.2	12.3
Black – Other	4.4	2.1

And **S** is for stupidity

The stupidity of only starting the deportation process when foreign prisoners have completed their prison sentence.

> In September 2012, 547 foreign national offenders were detained by UK Border Agency in prisons following completion of their custodial sentence. A further 919 foreign national offenders were detained beyond the end of their sentence in immigration removal centres.[1]

- Kadian Mighty from Jamaica was jailed for three and a half years for possession of a class-A drug with intent to supply, and Walumba Lumba from the Congo was jailed for four years for wounding with intent; upon completion of sentences in 2006 they were detained for deportation but because the new Home Office presumption of deportation had not been published they sought compensation for unlawful detention. On legal aid, they went all the way to the Supreme Court, where, in 2011, an earlier award of £1 was confirmed. It was last reported that Lumba had left the country and Mighty was on immigration bail.

Notes: *S is for stupidity*

1. Mark Harper, MP for the Forest of Dean since 2005; immigration minister 2012/14. The cost, then, was over £100 per day/night. (He had to resign as it was found that his cleaner was an illegal immigrant.)

And **S** is for students

A Home Office study carried out over the turn of 2011/12 found that 32% of so-called students given visas to enter this country for the purpose of study were not credible students through lacking an adequate level of English or other reasons; 59% of such failures were from Sudan and Nigeria.

In July 2012, UKBA officers found twenty students of almost a dozen different nationalities working in the Tesco.com building in Croydon, in breach of the terms of their visas.

- Abu Hamza (*see* H is for Abu Hamza) came to this country as a student.

- Abdul Rahman came to Britain in 2004, allegedly, to study biotechnology at Dundee University: at one stage he was a sales assistant for Primark. He attended not a single lecture or tutorial before leaving for Manchester; in 2006 he participated in would-be military training in the Lake District and in 2007 was convicted of disseminating terrorist information.

- HU was born in Libya in 1962. He came here as an aeronautical student in 1981. Apart from fourteen months in 1993/4, he has been here ever since, 'is an alcoholic and, largely possibly exclusively, as a consequence of his alcoholism, he has behaved disgracefully and has been convicted of 78 different offences on a total of 52 different occasions.'[1]

On 1 July 2008 [HU] was served with a notice of intention to make him a subject of a deportation order. He appealed successfully against that decision on Article 3 and Article 8 grounds. A further notice of intention to make a deportation order was served on 25 March 2010 and then withdrawn in May 2010. [HU] continued to offend. On 30 November 2012 a decision was made to make [HU] the subject of a deportation order. That was served in 9 January 2013. He applied to have the deportation order revoked. The application to revoke was refused on 9 October 2013 and he appealed that decision relying on Article 3 and Article 8 of the

European Convention on Human Rights.[2]

His appeal was successful before the first-tier tribunal. The Secretary of State appealed – HU could get alcohol in Libya but if caught he would be whipped and that would be treatment contrary to his rights under Article 3.

Notes: *S is for students*

1. From the decision of the Upper Tribunal (Immigration and Asylum Chamber) on *Secretary of State for the Home Department v. H U DA/02122/2013*, promulgated 19 December 2014.

2. Against cruel punishment and a right to private/family life respectively: *see* H is for human rights.

And S is for summation

A reasonable assessment of the evidence of the previous chapters, stripped of the near-overwhelming desire to see it in the light best suited to whatever are one's moral prejudices, is that moderate immigration has predominately favourable economic effects on the indigenous population, and ambiguous social effects. There is a gain from greater cultural variety, offset by the adverse effect of diversity on mutual regard, and the potential weakening of a functional social model by diaspora attached to dysfunctional social models. Sustained rapid migration would be an entirely different matter: both the economic and social effects would most probably be adverse for host populations. The fundamental economic forces of the simple models would kick in: wages would be bid down and public capital spread more thinly. The social benefits to increased variety are most likely subject to diminishing returns, while the social costs of diversity and dysfunctional social models are likely increasing. To think concretely, consider immigration from a low-income country in which the social model is manifestly highly dysfunctional, namely Somalia. For any host society the first ten thousand Somali immigrants are likely to provide a pleasing gain in cultural variety and little else. But immigration that increases a culturally separate Somali diaspora from one million to two million would bring little additional gain in variety, while weakening mutual regard and giving significant weight to a bad social model.[1]

I would argue, therefore, that there are important lessons to be learnt from the Pietersen debacle. We can acknowledge that open borders and the free movement of capital – the key conceptions of neo-liberalism – have brought great prosperity and a certain vitality to Britain over the past quarter century. There is no mainstream political party that would like to risk scaring away Goldman Sachs or Ford Motors.

But the wealth brought by international capital can be intensely damaging. It drives up values of houses so that ordinary working people are priced out of the market. The impact of globalisation, especially through immigration, can make some British citizens feel that they are living in communities that no longer belong to them in a political system that no longer listens to them.[2]

The latest figures show that immigration rose by 84,000 to 636,000 in the year to March [2015] while emigration dropped slightly to 307,000 – leaving net migration at a record 330,000. The Office of National Statistics also confirmed that 8.28 million people now living in Britain were born overseas. Add in the fact that 27% of the babies born in the UK last year had migrant parents, and it is clear that we are "experiencing an unprecedented upheaval in the make-up of a country once united by ties of language, history, creed and patriotism".[3]

Notes: *S is for summation*

1. *Exodus Immigration and Multiculturalism in the 21st Century* by Professor Paul Collier.

2. *The Kevin Pietersen debacle is a morality tale for our times* by Peter Oborne, *The Daily Telegraph*, February 2014.

3. *The Week,* September 2015.

And S is for supine

In her article on immigration, Minette Marrin is correct to argue that numbers matter. If migration continues at the 2004 rate (the latest year for which statistics are available), then by 2051 there will be a net outflow of 5.8 million British-born individuals and a net inflow of 15.8 million foreign-born individuals. Taking into account the children born to immigrants, the combined effect of these flows will be to add another 16 million to the British population by 2051.

Such a rapid transformation of British society through migration is without precedent since the Danish and Anglo-Saxon settlements which took place more than a thousand years ago. It may be that mass immigration is a good thing for Britain, or maybe not.

Either way, we need a serious and informed debate on the issue. Yet only a handful of respectable politicians will even discuss it.[1]

On 23 of April 2015, judgment was given in the case of *Erlam and others v. Rahman and another* – the result of the election petition as to Mr Rahman's 'election' on 22 May 2014 as mayor of (the London Borough of) Tower Hamlets. Mr Rahman was found guilty of corrupt and illegal practices and that therefore his election was avoided. Paragraphs 610 and 611 of the judgment are:

> Nor is this judgment inclined to blame the Metropolitan Police. Policing Tower Hamlets under its current political regime is not an easy task. Many in the police feel that the imputation of 'institutional racism' made by the Macpherson Enquiry, albeit 16 years ago, still dogs the Force and they are conscious that, in Mr Rahman, whose personal control of the Borough is tight, they are dealing with a man whose hair-trigger reaction is to accuse anyone who disagrees with him of racism and/or Islamophobia. In the circumstances it would be unreasonable to expect of the police anything other than an approach of considerable caution.

> In policing the polling stations, their primary concern was not the provisions of the [Representation of the People] 1983 Act: their primary concern was the possible commission of public order offences. Though officers did intervene from time to time to cool things down and to attempt to disperse over-large crowds of supporters, they cannot be criticised for failing to react if such conduct fell short, as usually it did, of a public order offence.

The day after the judgment, the *Jeremy Vine* show on Radio 2 had on the first of the claimants, Mr Erlam. Why had he taken the case? He explained that he had seen intimidation at polling stations, political literature there, voters accompanied into polling booths. He had complained to both the police and the election officials but to no avail. Mr Erlam was followed (apart from music) by Mr Vine saying that Gavin (Colp?) of Basingstoke had contacted the programme, asking why the police hadn't charged Rahman; Mike of Brecon had pointed out that (the satirical magazine) *Private Eye* had been on about Rahman for years but for its pains had been accused of racism. Cassandra Cook, now of Looe, was heard live. Thirty years ago she worked for Tower Hamlets Council and related how, at elections, there were Asians outside voting stations telling people what to do, even taking them into the voting booths, and that if one said anything, one was accused of racism. And that in those days, about thirty years ago, there were quite a lot of white people in Tower Hamlets; the council had paid them to move so that the housing was available to Bangladeshis.

Mr Vine said Hamish from Dundee was asking why only now were the facts coming out and at the instigation of private individuals – it was like

Rotherham ... the authorities did nothing.

John Osborne of Abingdon was also live. He had been a policeman in Tower Hamlets and it had been just as Cassandra had described. His task, on election days, was to go round four polling stations, one after the other, and then round again. Usually there was nothing untoward but one polling station was full of children, some taking old people into the polling booths to show them what to do. He told the election official, who answered, 'What can I do? They don't speak English.'[2] It was much the same at another voting station where he raised the matter with the election official, who replied, 'Oh, we make allowances.' Upon returning to his station, Mr Osborne reported all this to an inspector, who asked if he had informed the election official, and, upon being told yes he had done so, concluded the matter by saying he (Osborne) had done his job.[3]

Notes: *S is for supine*

1. Letter to *The Sunday Times*, from Professor Rowthorn (*see* E is for economics of immigration) August 2006. The letter was included in *The Week – Pick of the week's correspondence.*

2. One does not have to be British, in the sense of being a British citizen, to be entitled to vote (*see* V is for voting).

So fixed is the Electoral Commission on anyone in the country voting that it facilitates what it calls "community languages". Its "EU Referendum voting guides" are available in Arabic, Bengali, Chinese, French, Gaelic, Gujarati, Hindi, Punjabi, Urdu and Scots (but not, for instance, in Geordie).

3. This and indeed the whole of this 'report' of the programme are not from a transcript but merely what I thought I heard – not necessarily absolutely correct but I am sure the gist is a correct account of what was on the programme.

And **S** is for swarm and swamp

[In the fifth century] In a short time swarms of the aforesaid nations came over into the island, and the foreigners began to increase so much, that they became a source of terror to the natives who had invited them.[1]

[In 2002] Whilst they're going through the process, the children will be educated on the site, which will be open. People will be able to come and go but importantly not swamping the local school.[2]

[In 2014] That is still being worked at the moment to see what we can do to prevent whole towns and communities being swamped by huge numbers of migrant workers. In some areas, particularly on the east coast, yes, towns do feel under siege from large numbers of migrant workers and people claiming benefits.[3]

Of course, the diaspora that British migrants established around the world, swamping Native Americans, Maoris and French Canadians, created a rather successful sense of supranational solidarity. Daniel Hannan's new book *How We Invented Freedom and Why It Matters*, published today, tells an extraordinary story about how the values of 'the West' were actually a very peculiar set of Anglosphere traditions – above all, the notion that the State is the servant, not the master, of the individual.[4]

[In 2015] I accept that you have got a swarm of people coming across the Mediterranean, seeking a better life, wanting to come to Britain, because Britain has got jobs, it's got a growing economy, it's an incredible place to live.[5]

The indigenous now account for less than half of their capital city, London[6] and only about one third of the population of the London boroughs of Tower Hamlets,[7] Harrow, Ealing, Brent and Newham. The indigenous are also a minority in Leicester, Luton and Slough. Birmingham, the country's 'second city' is headed the same way, and for at least one part – Small Heath – has arrived. Small Heath, Birmingham, is where are many of the Trojan Horse schools (*see* F is for fifth column). Wikipedia's entry as to Small Heath starts with a picture of 'Green Lane Masjid, formerly Green Lane Public Library and Baths', and at one time continued with:

The total population of the area is approximately 36,898 based on 2007 estimates. The majority are of South Asian origin, mainly of Pakistani (51%) and Bangladeshi (9%) descent, white British ethnicity is 22%. Many residents are also Muslim; there are many mosques in the area, the biggest in Small Heath being the Ghankol Sharif Masjid which incidentally is also one of the largest in the UK. It holds regular Muslim prayers, funeral services and other religious ceremonies. Only 11% of the population in the area were actually born in the West Midlands; the white British population has steadily declined in the whole of Birmingham; since 2001 it has dropped from 65.6% to 53.1% by 2011; less than a half the population considers himself Christian; the Pakistani population is growing in Birmingham at a rate of 1% per year, while the population of Pakistanis in Small Heath is growing at rate of 6% per year. Over 45% of the population have arrived within the last 12 months. Ref. Birmingham City Council 2011 census.[8]

Fourteen schools in Small Heath and nearby tell the story.[9]

School	Number on roll	Eligibility for free school meals	Ethnic background	Speak English as a first language
Adderley Primary School	605	56.9%	99.4%	9.7%
Anderton Park Primary School	708	42.9%	99.8%	5.6%
Golden Hillock School	880	68.3%	99.8%	8.4%
Ladypool Primary School	485	52.4%	100%	5.3%
Montgomery Primary Academy	661	39%	100%	Low
Moseley School	1,275	61.4%	99%	16.9%
Nansen Primary School	capacity for 750 but 871 on roll	51.1%	high	Low
Oldknow Academy	601	53.4%	99.3%	5.5%
Park View School	615	72.7%	99.8%	7.5%

Regents Park Community Primary School	542	50%	98.7%	5.1%
Saltley School and Specialist Science College	952	70.1%	96.5%	14.5%
Small Heath School	1,333	58.4%	99.8%	9.0%
Springfield Primary School	673	37%	100%	1.9%
Washwood Heath Academy	1,332	61.2%	99.2%	29.8%

Those fourteen schools in Birmingham are not alone.[10] In 2013, there were 1,755 (primary and secondary) schools where the majority of the children spoke some language other than English, the ten most telling being:

School	Number of children	% who do not speak English as their first language
Sacred Heart Primary; Sandwell	131	99.0
Field Lane Junior Infant and Nursery, Kirklees	230	98.9
Maidenhall Primary, Luton	621	98.9
Ashfield Valley Primary, Rochdale	228	98.9
Purlwell Infant and Nursery, Kirklees	347	98.8
Guru Nanak Academy, Hillingdon	1,323	98.7
Redlands Primary, Tower Hamlets	462	98.6
Keighley St Andrews Primary, Bradford	473	98.6
Heybrook Primary School, Rochdale	544	98.5
Lomeshaye Junior School, Nelson	267	98.5

Part of the London Borough of Redbridge is the constituency of Ilford South. The following information is from *Redbridge Today A Portrait of the Borough,* May 2008:

The constituents' country of birth is:

- United Kingdom 53.4%

- Ireland 0.9%

- European Union Countries as at March 2001 1.9%

- EU's A8 and A2 countries 3.6%

- Other countries 40.2%

And the ethnic group of the constituents is

- White (comprising English/Welsh/Scottish/ Northern Irish/British)

- plus Irish, Gypsy or Irish Traveller and Other White 24.2%

- Asian/Asian British 57.2%

- Black /African/Caribbean/Black British 11.3%

- Mixed/multiple ethnic groups 3.8%

- Other ethnic group 3.4%

Religious identification is as follows:

- 34.9% of the residents are Muslim

- 28% are Christian

- 13.3% are Hindu

- 9.4% are Sikh

Passport ownership: 6.0% of the residents of Redbridge have no passport. Of the remainder of 131,035 residents:

- 93,254, namely 71.2%, of all residents have a UK passport

- 1,324, namely 1%, are of Eire

- 8,916, namely 6.8%, are of EU countries

- 530, namely 4%, are of other European countries

- 3,227, namely 2.5%, are of countries in Africa

- 17,229, namely 13.2%, are of countries in the Middle East and Asia

- 1,522, namely 0.8%, are of countries in the Americas and Oceania

And the household language is:

- all aged sixteen and over who have English as a main language; 56.7%

- at least one but not all people aged sixteen and over have English as a main language; 19.6%

- no one aged 16 and over but at least one person aged 3 to 15 has English as a main language; 5.4%

- no one in the household has English as a main language; 18.2%

Since 1997 the share of our workforce born outside the UK has doubled from 7%. A quarter of those born today in this country are to mothers who were born elsewhere. On average, a Somalian woman living here has 4.2 children (and a decade before it was 6). Romanian women living here typically have 2.9 children but 1.3 if living in Romania. For Czech women, the corresponding figures are 2.9 and 1.25, and for Polish women, 2.1 and 1.3 respectively.

A summation of the episode of *Eastenders* for 24 December 2011 was 'Masood and Zainab try to stop Yusef's plan'.

In late 2013, a newspaper item about the effect of building HS2 on Camden Market quoted three views – those of Armin Sismai (ladieswear trader), Ahrash Akbari-Kahlur (ice-cream seller) and Ibrahim Ayar (clothes stallholder).

Notes: *S is for swarm and swamp*

1. The Venerable Bede (673–735) writing about the fifth century (Christian Classics, Ethereal Library).

In 1978 Margaret Thatcher, then leader of the opposition, warned of the danger of being 'swamped' (*see* W is for we were warned).

2. David Blunkett, in 2002, the then Home Secretary, as to educating the children of asylum seekers in separate centres rather than local schools.

Number 10's spokesman explained that Mr Blunkett 'was not talking about immigration as a whole', that 'What he was doing was reflecting a particular context and a particular issue rather than talking about the overall issue of immigration' and that 'He was simply talking about what happens at ground level.'

But, in 2014 (and out of office), Mr Blunkett agreed with Michael Fallon: *see* note 3.

Diane Abbott MP (*see* R is for racist/racism) commented: 'I thought that David's use of the word "swamping" was unfortunate. We are talking about children here, not raw sewage.'

3. Michael Fallon, MP for Darlington 1983/92 and for Sevenoaks since 1997; defence secretary from 2014.

In 2014, with Angela Merkel (Chancellor of Germany) having said, 'We must not interfere with the fundamental principle of free movement in Europe', Mr Fallon was asked about this, said the Conservative proposals were being worked on and continued as set out. He had to backtrack – 'I misspoke yesterday. I used words I wouldn't normally have used.'

4. *Let Immigrants in. Then send them home* by Matt Ridley, *The Times*, November 2014.

5. David Cameron, as prime minister, July 2015.

6. According to the 2011 census:

Leicester – 45% white British; 28% Asian; 8% African

Luton – 45% white British; 14% Pakistani; 7% Bangladeshi

Slough – 35% white British; 18% Pakistani; 16% Indian

The Evening Standard (and included in *The Week*) reported that, in 2007, one third of the people living in London were born abroad and a further 10,000 foreigners settled in the capital every month.

7. Paragraph 178 of the judgment in *Erlam v. Rahman* (where Rahman's election in 2014 was voided by reason of corrupt and illegal practices) is:

> The 2011 census showed that the Bangladeshi population of Tower Hamlets was 32% of the total, which compares with the figure of 3% for London as a whole and less than 1% for England. The census reported, 'Tower Hamlets has the largest Bangladeshi population in England. Residents describing themselves as "White British" amounted to 31% of the population: black ethnic groups made up 7%'. The conclusion of the census was that 'More than two thirds (69%) of the borough's population belong to minority ethnic groups (i.e. not White British); 55 percent belong to BME (Black and Minority Ethnic) groups and a further 14% from White minority groups.'

8. I could not find this quote when going back to Wikipedia to check the figures. Eventually I did find it in – *The Voice of Reason, 'What made Islamophobic Ukrainian terrorist Lapsyhn do it?* which gave as its source http://en.wikipedia.org/wiki/Small_Heath, Birmingham#Population.

Perhaps the explanation is that the quoted item was there in Wikipedia at some stage but then deleted, perhaps because it was thought to be incorrect. However, its accuracy is shown by the same search coming up in www.birmingham.gov.uk ('Ethnic Groups; Population and Census'), which has:

Birmingham's residents are from a wide range of national, ethnic and religious backgrounds.

The chart below shows that the largest ethnic group in Birmingham was White British with 570,217 (53.1%). This is down from 2001 (65.6%) and lower than the average in England (79.8%).

A chart entitled '2001 Census: Population by Ethnic Group – Birmingham, 2001 and 2011' gives the following information:

Ethnic group	2001	2011
White British	65.6	53.1
Pakistani	10.6	13.5
Other ethnicity	2.3	6.7
Indian	5.7	4.8
Caribbean	4.9	4.4
Mixed	2.9	4.4
Bangladeshi	2.1	4.0
African	0.6	2.8
Chinese	0.5	1.2

Other large groups include Pakistani (144,627, 13.5%) and Indian (64,621, 6.0%) which have grown since 2001, while people defining themselves as Black Caribbean (47,641, 4.4%) have declined.

283,313 Birmingham residents were born outside the UK. Of these around 45% arrived during the last decade.

9. Appendix 5 of the Clarke Report into the Trojan Horse affair.

This is not to belittle the problem for Lebanon of refugees from Syria (and Palestine), but in London, February 2016, for the London Conference on Syria, the Lebanese minister of education, Elias Boa Saab, spoke of the schools that used to have (only) Lebanese children but where the children from Syria had become '80 and 90%' (of the school roll). Here, the influx is such that the foreign element can be 100%.

10. That the Small Heath area of Birmingham is not on its own is shown by Recommendation no. 6 of the Trojan Horse Review Group to the leader of Birmingham City Council:

> To reinvigorate a Birmingham-wide approach to inclusivity, integration, openness and transparency across all schools, taking into account in particular the demographic trends across the city and emerging new communities – including that children and young people from minority ethnic groups now account for 60.6% of all children living in the area, and proportion of children and young people with English as an additional language in Birmingham primary schools is 43% and in secondary schools is 38%. This must include strong and visible support towards empowering all girls in all our schools, and to ensure they are treated with total equality and respect.

T is for terrorism

On 30 March 2004 arrests were effected because of fears that persons of Pakistani heritage were planning to use ammonium nitrate to make bombs. Three years later Omar Khyam, Waheed Mahmood, Jawad Akbar, Salahuddin Amin and Anthony Garcia were convicted of conspiring to cause explosions likely to endanger life (between the start of 2003 and the end of March 2004).

On 7 July 2005 Mohammed Sidique Khan and the three other Muslims (*see* K is for Khan) murdered fifty-two people who were using public transport.

A fortnight later Muktar Said Ibrahim, Osman Hussain, Yassin Hassan Omar and Ramzi Mohammed attempted to repeat that murder and mayhem, at Shepherd's Bush, Warren Street and Oval Tube stations and on a bus in Shoreditch. Their fellow conspirators were, or anyway included, Manfo Asiedu, Is Mail Abduraham, Muhedin Ali, Siraj Ali, Wabbi Mohammed and Adel Yahya, Omar's wife Yeshi Girma, her brother Esayas Girma and sister Mulu Girma, Malu's boyfriend Mohamed Kabashi and Omar's fiancée Fardosa Abdullahi.

Two years later having failed to kill anyone at or outside the Tiger Tiger nightclub, Bilal Abdulla (born in Iraq) and Kafeel Ahmed (born in India) set off from London and, after visiting Mohammed Asha (born in Saudi Arabia) near Stoke-on-Trent, continued back to Scotland, where they attempted to drive a jeep laden with gas cylinders and containers of fuel into the passenger terminal at Glasgow airport. Ahmed died four weeks later of the burns sustained in the attack; Abdullah was sentenced to life imprisonment with a minimum of thirty-two years.

- The so-called liquid bombers (*see* Q is for queues).

- Rajib Karim moved in 2006 from Bangladesh to Newcastle upon Tyne with his 'British' wife Zijarin Raja as they believed their son, then two, would get better treatment for cancer. Karim is now serving thirty years for planning to use the cover of working for British Airways to commit aircraft terrorist crime.

- In 2007, Samina Malik was given a nine-month suspended prison sentence after being convicted of possessing documents likely to be useful to a terrorist; on her computer were her poems including *How to*

Behead and weapons manuals and literature on poisons – hence the sobriquet of 'lyrical terrorist'. The Crown Prosecution Service said, '[Malik] was not prosecuted for writing poetry … was convicted of collecting information of a kind likely to be useful to a person committing or preparing an act of terrorism'. However, her conviction for terrorism was quashed by the Court of Appeal as 'there was scope for the jury to have become confused'.

- In 2009, Houria Chahed Chentouf, born in Tangiers but with Dutch citizenship, was sentenced to two years for trying to bring into the country an explosives manual on a memory stick hidden in her burka: (she planned to move here, with her six children, because she alleged she had suffered religious discrimination in the Netherlands).

This terrorism continues –

- Mohammed Chowdhury, Usman Khan, Nazam Hussain, Omar Latif, Mohibur Rahman, Shah Rahman, Mohammed Shahjahan, Gurukanth Desai and Abdul Miah, all British citizens, from Cardiff, east London or Stoke-on-Trent, were convicted in early 2012 of plotting to cause explosions at one or more of Big Ben, the London Eye, the Stock Exchange and Westminster Abbey. Ruksana Begum, the sister to the last two of those last nine, has a first-class degree in accountancy. Upon marrying, she moved from Cardiff to London, where a month later she was found to have al-Qaeda material on her mobile; she pleaded guilty to having material likely to be useful to someone committing or preparing an act of terrorism. She appeared in court with only her eyes visible.

- Norman Idris Faridi from Kenya downloaded terrorist material including *39 Ways to Serve* and *Proceed with Jihad* and had a video of Abu Hamza on his mobile.

- In March 2013, the Metropolitan Police's deputy assistant commissioner said:

  On average we've probably had about one potential attack planned with an intent similar to July 7 every year. The UK threat as we stand today remains substantial, which means that a terrorist attack remains a strong possibility and could occur without warning.

- On 26 April 2013, Irfan Khalid, Irfan Naseer and Ashik Ali, all from Birmingham, were sentenced to terms of imprisonment ranging from life with a minimum of eighteen years to four years for plotting to repeat the murders on 7 July 2005, recruiting others for terrorism and terrorism fundraising. They had planned 'mass death' and 'carnage in the name of Allah'. They complained that the 7 July murderers had not caused 'enough damage'. With the benefit of Naseer's pharmacy course at Ashton University, they attempted to concoct explosives in Ali's council flat. Associates Naweed Ali, Ishaaq Hussain, Khobaib Hussain and Shadid Khan had already pleaded guilty to travelling to Pakistan for terrorist training.

- On 22 May 2013, Fusilier Lee Rigby was run down and then almost decapitated by two Africans who had converted to Islam.

- In July 2015, Peter Clarke, head of Scotland Yard's Counter Terrorism Command 2002/08, wrote:

Since 2005, terrorists have repeatedly tried to launch attacks in this country. Most have been thwarted. There have been hundreds of convictions for terrorist-related crimes, and arrests are at their highest ever level. At the moment, on average there is one arrest every day for terrorism, and about 120 people are awaiting trial.

And **T** is for translation

Translation of public notices and the like has the following:

...an unintentional adverse impact on integration by reducing the incentive for some migrant communities to learn English ...[1]

Should the state be funding, for example, the teaching of native languages such as Urdu and when not enough ethnic communities in Britain currently speak English?[2]

I agree with Boris Johnson that we should be positive about Labour's errors on immigration, and work towards integration.

We may have absorbed more than our fair share of undesirables, but we have also absorbed hard-working people who enhance our society. Labour's policy of multiculturalism has failed, as we have alternative societies growing in our cities.

Language is the key to addressing this. Instead of spending millions on translation services we need to spend the money on teaching English. Speaking the language should be a prerequisite for those who wish to settle here.[3]

The 'NHS Care Records Service Information form' as to obtaining the NHS care Records Service Guarantee and the leaflet entitled *Your Health Information, Confidentiality and the NHS Care Records Service* is available, apart from in large print, braille, 'Easy Read' picture version and audio, in Bengali, Guajarati, Urdu, Punjabi, Arabic, Turkish, Kurdish, Mandarin, Somali, Polish, French, Albanian, Farsi, Portuguese, Spanish and Russian.

A letter from the NHS *Cancer Screening Programmes* has a notice as to the subject matter in Albanian, Arabic, Bengali, Chinese, Farsi, Guajarati, Hindi, Polish, Portuguese, Punjabi, Somali, Turkish and Urdu. And its 'Patient Agreement to the Investigation or Treatment' has appended to it 'Statement of interpreter (where appropriate)'.

The NHS's *Choose and Book* appointment request offers the chance to make an appointment in Albanian, Arabic, Bengali, Chinese simplified and Chinese traditional, French, Guajarati, Kurdish-Sorani, Polish, Portuguese, Punjabi, Somali, Spanish, Tamil, Turkish and Urdu.

In 2011, the NHS spent more than £11 million on interpreters, an increase over the preceding year of nearly 15%. When asked about this, the Department of Health justified this expenditure with: 'NHS organisations have a duty to make sure patients understand information. We would encourage trusts to be efficient.'

A notice in the premises of a (non-metropolitan) council has a notice in over a dozen languages ranging from Albanian to Vietnamese.[4] And the 'A–Z of Useful Contacts' of a housing association operating in the same area has under T – 'TV Licence, Telecare, Tenancy Agreements, Tenant Handbook, Toilets, Transfers, Translations and Trees'.[5]

Crawley Borough Council was reported to have spent £627 translating a housing newsletter into Urdu for the benefit of one resident (Urdu is the second most likely spoken language in Crawley after English).

> The surgery is multicultural and polyglot. The touchscreen on which you can sign yourself in offers instructions in Russian, Polish, Spanish, French, Arabic, Turkish, Somali – and something I can't identify. Romanian or Bulgarian?[6]

Notes: *T is for translation*

1. Eric Pickles, MP for Brentwood and Ongar from 1992, Communities and Local Government Secretary 2010/15.

2. George Alagiah (who is from Sri Lanka) at the Hay Literary Festival in 2012.

3. Letter to a newspaper from Mick Ferrie.

4. North Dorset District Council.

5. Synergy, now Aster, Housing.

6. Penelope Lively, February 2014, about going to her surgery for an old-age MOT.

U is for Lady Uddin of Bethnal Green

She was born in Bangladesh, was 'enobled' at the behest of Mr Blair, and falsely claimed expenses for travelling between Westminster and her 'home' in Maidstone, where she had a flat but did not live. Despite that flat in Maidstone and a house in Bangladesh, she has social housing in Tower Hamlets: (the Bangladeshi proportion of the borough is about 30%).

> On the last day of evidence this gap was sought to be filled by calling Pola, now Baroness, Uddin. This was not a good idea. She did not succeed in supporting the thesis that the broadcast had caused immediate outrage and her credibility was comprehensively demolished by cross-examination about the six-figure expenses defalcation that had led to her suspension[1] from the House of Lords.[2]

Notes: U is for Lady Uddin

1. According to Steerpike in June 2013 –

> Rogue peers are to be evicted from Parliament under new laws planned by the Lib Dems. Cheats like Baroness Uddin, who had to repay £125,000 in fiddled expenses, will be shown the door, although the miscreants will retain their nominal status as members of the nobility. This, of course, is what most peers want. A posh title to impress the maître d' and no parliamentary chores whatsoever.

But the baroness was subsequently allowed, having repaid the fiddled expenses, to return to the House. In 2014/15, Baroness Uddin claimed expenses in 2014/14 of £37,800.

2. Paragraph 401 of the judgment on the (successful) claim that Mohammed Lutfur Rahman had been elected Mayor of Tower Hamlets in 2014 on the strength of corrupt and illegal practices and so his election was void (M/350/14).

And U is for unintended consequences[1]

Between them, the Royal College of General Practitioners (RCGP) and the General Medical Council (GMC), so as to ensure doctors are fit to practise medicine in the UK, prescribe a Clinical Skills Assessment (CSA).

The Clinical Skills Assessment is designed to assess a doctor's skills in three respects: 1) gathering information from patients; 2) developing a diagnosis; 3) communicating with the patient.[2]

Four attempts, plus, exceptionally, a fifth, are allowed. (Para 6)

All but a handful, at most three per cent, of the doctors who submit to the assessment eventually succeed. Figures … show that between October 2007 and May 2012, 133 out of 11,862 candidates who had undertaken the CSA more than four times still failed. Of that 133, 120 were foreign graduates. (Para 7)

There is a marked difference in the pass rate at first attempt of doctors who have a first degree from a UK medical school and those with a first degree from a foreign medical school and between different groups of doctors, categorised by race in each category. The difference is illustrated by the figures for the year August 2012 to July 2013. There are minor anomalies in the figures supplied which do not materially affect the overall pattern. 87.7 per cent of UK graduates passed at first attempt, but only 52.1 per cent of non-UK graduates. Within the category of UK graduates, 93.5 of those describing themselves as 'white' passed but only 76.4 and 72.7 per cent of those describing themselves as 'South Asian' or 'black' respectively. Within the category of non-UK graduates, 62 per cent of those describing themselves as 'white' passed at first attempt but only 49.6 and 51.6 per cent of those describing themselves as 'South Asian' or 'black' respectively. (Para 8).

The British Association of Physicians of Indian Origin (BAPIO) sought a court declaration that the RCGP, as assessor, and the GMC, as regulator, had failed to fulfil the public sector equality duty (PSED) imposed on them by section 149 of the Equality Act 2010 – a duty imposed on those exercising public functions to eliminate discrimination, to advance equality of opportunity and to foster good relations between those who have a protected characteristic (such as race, colour, ethnic origin) and those who do not.

Thus the Royal College is empowered to encourage the Deaneries to address the fact of underperformance by South Asian and BME candidates … by providing training … (Para 20)

and

If the Royal College were not to consider taking such steps as those, it might well be that it would not … discharge its duty under section 149. (Para 21)

But BAPIO's claim was in regard to the Clinical Skills Assessment itself: BAPIO sought a declaration that it was unlawful, despite the fact that in 2010 the GMC/RCGP had changed the system because the old system was thought to be 'potentially unfair' and between October 2007 and May 2012 procured about eighteen investigations into the discrimination or otherwise of the CSA.

However, the judge stated:

I consider, therefore, and hold that the Royal College was and remains under a continuing duty to have regard to the need to eliminate discrimination and advance equality of opportunity in the exercise of its public functions ... and in setting and administering assessments ... and that it can only discharge that duty by conscientiously applying its mind to that need. (Para 29)

I am satisfied that the CSA does put South Asians ... at a disadvantage when compared with their white colleagues. (Para 40)

Section 19 of the Act provides that a person discriminates against another if the former applies a provision, criterion or practice that is discriminatory against the latter in relation to a protected characteristic and the former cannot show that such discrimination is proportionate to achieving a legitimate aim; so the judge asked, 'Can the Royal College show that the assessments are a proportionate means of achieving a legitimate aim?'

In their report, Professors Esmail and Roberts described the assessment (namely the CSA) as follows:

The CSA is not a culturally neutral examination and nor is it intended to be. It is not and nor should it be just a clinical exam testing clinical knowledge in a very narrow sense. It is designed to ensure that doctors are safe to practise in UK general practice. The cultural norms of what is expected in a consultation will vary from country to country. So for example, a British graduate will have difficulty in practising in a general practice setting in France or India until they become acculturated to that system of care. British graduates have much greater exposure, both personally and through their training, to general practice when compared to the majority of International Medical Graduates who graduate from health systems which are not dominated by primary care as the NHS. Most medical schools in the UK now have well developed programmes for communication skills training, reflective practice and direct exposure of students to General Practice as a discipline. (Para 41)

And so Mr Justice Mitting found the CSA was discriminatory but dismissed BAPIO's claim as such discrimination was proportionate to ensuring that only those suitable to practice medicine could do so.

However, because BAPIO had 'achieved, if not a legal victory, then a moral success' (para 51) and the claim had 'been brought in the public interest' (para 50), the CMC and RCGP were only awarded about one fifth of their costs.

Thus (subject to it being proportionate), the effect of the Equality Act is:

- it is illegal to discriminate against those who do not have English as their first language and/or

- those who do not have English as their first language and/or the cultural empathy and innate understanding of the indigenous, must be given, at very least, assistance to overcome that 'disability' (failing which, it is discriminatory).

'even though there was no basis for contending that the small number who fail do so for any reason apart from their own shortcomings' (para 43).

And so this country's way of doing things, the way that has emerged over decades if not centuries out of shared language, common ways of thinking and customs of the indigenous population, is rendered unlawful because those who do not have English as their mother tongue, those who grew up elsewhere and thereby don't think in quite the same way, are disadvantaged and therefore, according to the Equality Act, are discriminated against.

After the case, RCGP, BAPIO and the British International Doctors Association (BIDA) met and made a joint statement:

> RCGP, BAPIO and BIDA have announced that they will be working in close collaboration to address supporting international medical graduates and Black and Minority Ethnic doctors in relation to training and passing the CSA.

> At a very positive and productive meeting held at the College, the three organisations pledged to work together to determine what support could be offered to identify struggling trainees at an early stage and improve their training experience in order to better prepare them for the CSA and for safe independent practice. The RCGP shared some of their specific skills to support trainees and trainers such as developing e-learning resources for Clinical Skills Assessment preparation (based on sociolinguistic research) and reviewing ways to enhance CSA feedback to candidates. BAPIO and BIDA were both very supportive of these initiatives.

RCGP Chair Dr Maureen Baker said:

> We are very pleased to now be working in partnership with BAPIO, BIDA

and other key stakeholders to look at solutions and find the best way of supporting the small number of trainees who fail the CSA component of the ... licensing exam to give them every chance of passing.

It was very reassuring to have the High Court judgment rule out the claims of discrimination.

As the High Court ruling highlighted, patient safety is the key purpose of the ... exam and the College must have total confidence in those who pass the exam, having clearly demonstrated the appropriate skills and clinical knowledge.

But as an organisation committed to equality and diversity, we have always been, and remain, concerned that international medical graduates do not do as well in the exam as those from UK medical schools. Indeed, we were the first of the Medical Royal Colleges to publicly raise this issue and have commissioned and supported research to understand what is happening and to try and identify what the causes may be.

And Dr Ramesh Mehta president of BAPIO said:

We have had a very fruitful discussion with the RCGP. We are pleased that the Royal College has identified several steps to implement the equality impact assessment. We have discussed the issue of those trainees who have been removed from the training and the possibility of them getting back in to general practice. We are looking forward to working constructively with the Royal College for fairness and professional excellence in the interest of doctors and patients.[3]

It is time to make progress and we welcome the proactive approach of the RCGP to provide much needed relevant support to the international medical graduates and Black and Minority Ethnic doctors in relation to training and passing the [exam].[4]

It is argued that the Equality Act requires the government to consult those who are here illegally, namely breaking the law, before doing anything about it:

RAMFEL[5] is delighted that the Government has finally recognised that it should have consulted and engaged directly with individuals and organisations representing the needs and concerns of immigrants on the UK about the 'Go Home' campaign and the use of vans saying 'Go Home or Face Arrest' on the streets of London.

The Government's failure to do so and the subsequent 'immigration spot checks' have caused much distress to a cross section of communities locally and nationally. The fact that the campaign has also been commented on extensively in the international media, also suggests that this has tarnished the UK's long-standing reputation as a tolerant and welcoming society.

We welcome the Government's commitment to engaging more broadly and taking on board the views of those affected by their policies. We will be making sure that they are true to their word by scrutinising and advocating for 'fairness' across a cross-section of government proposals and policies as they impact on migrant communities.

Rita Chadha, CEO of RAMFEL, the organisation supporting two service user migrants to bring the case, said, 'informed and effective policy is always made when Governments listen to the reaction of communities. Whilst immigration will no doubt remain a hotly contested issue until the next election, we are glad that the Government has finally recognised that fair policy making requires the views of all sections of the community to be heard, including those that it directly impacts upon. We remain vigilant to the possibility of other attacks and policies that increasingly view immigration only as a negative, encourage miscommunication between local communities, and seek to create divisions within British society. Our message to government is "we're watching you".'

RAMFEL is the Refugee and Migrant Forum of East London. We provide free legal advice and a wide range of support to asylum seekers, migrants, refugees, Black, Asian and Minority individuals and communities across London. We have a long history of campaigning on local and national issues relating to equality and immigration matters.

In July 2013, the UK Home Office introduced a campaign called 'Go Home'. The campaign targeted six areas of London with two vans, with large billboards with the message 'Go Home or Face Arrest'. The billboards were allegedly targeting those who were 'illegal' or undocumented in the UK. The following week there was also an intensification of immigration spot checks at major transport hubs in the capital. The Go Home Campaign is part of a Government campaign that has caused a national outcry, and infuriated a cross-section of communities.

RAMFEL has supported two of its services users via Deighton, Pierce, Glynn to issue legal proceedings against the Home Office for a failure to consult and breach of the Equality Act 2010. Whilst the direct legal costs of the action are paid for, we are seeking funding to help with the associated campaigning and public education work needed now up and down the country.[6]

- The production and distribution of advice and information to those directly affected by the 'Go Home' campaign, with clear and easy to understand information on their rights and responsibilities.

- A programme of public education to explain to people the reality of modern day immigration which will include leaflets, adverts in newspapers, videos and documentaries. Production of information and teaching packs for schools. Production of information and resource packs for migrant community organisations to help challenge the 'Go Home' and similar campaigns locally within their own communities.

The Impact. This has been remarked by some as a turning point in the UK immigration story, people have described 'Go Home' as very unBritish.

We have a once in a lifetime opportunity to show that the debate on immigration no longer needs to be neither negative or toxic.[7]

Notes: *U is for unintended consequences*

1. The expression appears to come from the aptly entitled paper (in 1936) *The Unanticipated Consequences of Purposive Social Action.*

This chapter could have been under A is for the abolition of Britain. But that would have trodden on the toes of Peter Hitchens' *The Abolition of Britain*, published by Quartet Books in 1999, which has fifteen chapters (none of which are about immigration).

Thesaurus came up with suitable alternatives such as extinguish, put an end to, terminate and wipe out; and nullify, the last of which would have been appropriate as that would have put it adjacent to N is for nonsense.

However, with a proviso, the Equality Act has the unintended consequence of those alternatives. The proviso is whether the consequence was actually intended, in which case this section should, perhaps, be under M is for misfeasance in public office.

2. Paragraph 3 of Mr Justice Mitting's judgment in *The Queen on the application of BAPIO Action Ltd v. Royal College of General Practitioners, General Medical Council* [2014] EWHC 1416 (Admin); 2014 WL 1220093.

The paragraphs of the judgment that are quoted from are stated at the end of each such quotation.

3. The order is telling.

According to the RCGP's chief examiner, 'Patient safety is … paramount and given that assessment is an imperfect science, the treatment of the measurable error must act in favour of the patients rather than doctors' (paragraph 40 of the judgment).

4. If there is a shortage of doctors with the necessary linguistic and sociological skills, yes, but otherwise why? And at whose cost?

5. At the time, RAMFEL was *Refugee and Migrant Forum of East London* with a strapline of 'A positively pro immigration group, showing, it is no threat to you, your country, your house, family or job'. That changed to *Refugee and Migrant Forum of Essex and London* with a strapline of 'localising equality and globalisation for all communities in London and Essex'.

6. By the time that the would-be claim would have been issued, the government's poster campaign had been stopped or ended.

7. *Go Home Campaign Victory for Migrants: Refugee and Migrant Forum of East London,* Press Release, 12th August 2013, *Action Against Racism and Xenophobia.*

V is for Vietnamese

When the police accidentally found and then lost cannabis in a former nightclub in Merthyr Tydfil, it was four Vietnamese men aged between seventeen and forty-eight who were arrested and charged with producing cannabis.

(And *see* Y is for you couldn't make it up).

And V is for voting

A local authority questionnaire for its Register of Electors includes:

Who can register to vote?

[and under] Nationality

People who are entitled to register to vote:

- British citizens.

- Citizens of the Irish Republic.

- Citizens of other European Union countries. EU citizens will be registered as local government electors only (except citizens of Cyrus, Malta, or The Irish Republic, who can vote in all elections).

- Qualifying Commonwealth citizens. This means commonwealth citizens who: have leave to enter or remain in the UK; or do not require such leave.[1]

Thus, as soon as citizens of the British Commonwealth have an address in this country, they are eligible to vote so that those who are citizens of Bangladesh (but likewise Ghana, India, Jamaica, Nigeria and Pakistan, despite not being citizens of this country but of another), can vote on everything from the effectiveness of our border controls and for those who promise to cancel the primary purpose rule.[2]

Democracy is government by the people or their (duly) elected representatives. Muslims believe that government should be by clerics and law should only be sharia or compatible with sharia, which is presumably why on Muslim marches there are placards such as 'Democracy go to Hell'.[3]

Notes: V is for voting

1. Professor (emeritus) S.F. Bush, University of Manchester, wrote to the letters section of a newspaper, May 2014:

> In his perceptive article on how foreign London has become, Charles Moore mentions that many of the capital's residents are 'not British citizens and therefore cannot vote'.
>
> In fact, all Commonwealth, EU and Irish citizens are permitted to vote in local and European Parliament elections. Commonwealth citizens can vote in British general elections as well, a hangover from the Empire. In London around two million of the 5.5 million electors (36 per cent) are foreigners, a situation without parallel in any other country in the world.
>
> A first step to making London a bit less of a foreign city would be to remove the bias in favour of continued high levels of immigration by restricting voting entitlement to British citizens only, fully accepting this will only be possible in respect of European Union nationals when Britain leaves that organisation.

In fact, the position is more extreme. Pakistan left the Commonwealth in 1972. It rejoined in 1989 (its membership was suspended in 1999 until 2004 and again suspended 2007/08). And so in 1982, in *Multiracial myths?* Raymond Honeyford (*see* H is for Ray Honeyford) could write:

> A large majority of the Asians come from a country which is not even a member of the British Commonwealth. They have exercised their legal right to British citizenship, conferred as a direct result of living in territory formerly part of the British Empire.

The full article is to be found in Appendix VI.

2. *See* M is for misfeasance in public office, and number 41 of W is for what is to be done?

3. *See* Amira Abase under O is for obscene. And the person who it is suggested might to be Jihadi John's successor, Siddhartha Dhar (aka Ubu Rumaysah), was seen with a placard equating democracy with hypocrisy.

In Afghanistan, the Taliban complained that voting was 'unpious' – presumably on the basis of the following explanation in Michel Houellebecq's *Submission* (or, in the original French, *Soumission*, translated by Lorin Stein):

> For [Salafists] France is a land of disbelief – Dar al-Kufr, for the Muslim Brotherhood, France is ready to be absorbed into the Dar al–Islam. More to the point, for the Salafists [akin to ISIS] all authority comes from God.

To them the very idea of popular representation is sacrilege. They'd never dream of founding or supporting, a political party.

And V is for vote rigging

The following are some of the 714 paragraphs of the Birmingham election case:[1]

684. If one takes as a working hypothesis that the Labour Party organisation is bent on postal vote fraud to rig elections, one would expect three things.

685. Firstly, one would expect that, in safe Labour Wards, nobody would bother with fraud. Thus the number of postal votes would not mushroom between 2003 and 2004. Is this what we find? In general it is. Safe Labour Wards like Erdington show a very small increase – 620 postal votes in 2003 and 907 in 2004, an increase of 46%.

686. Secondly, one would expect that, in safe Conservative Wards, nobody would bother with fraud. If a safe Conservative Ward suddenly swung to Labour (in the middle of a Parliamentary term to boot) then the public would smell a rat. Again, is this found? It is. Take Bourneville which I understand to be true-blue Conservative territory: in 2003, 692 postal votes and in 2004, 1083 postal votes (an increase of 56%).

687. Finally, in the marginal Wards (particularly those with a high Asian population), one would expect the mushroom effect. A good example is Washwood Heath.....Before the 2004 election the Ward was split between Liberal Democrat and Labour and in 2003 the Liberal Democrat candidate had won. It was almost a carbon copy of nearby Aston, mirroring the victory of Mr Ayoub Khan in 2003. Washwood Heath had a high Asian population – adjacent to Bordesley Green it had, until 2002, a PJP councillor.

688. What do we find in Washwood Heath? In 2003 there were 329 postal votes and 478 in 2003. In 2004 no fewer than 5583 applications were made for postal votes – an increase of 1,068%.

689. Lozells and East Handsworth is the adjacent Ward to Aston. The boundary changes from the former Ward of Handsworth had brought in some of the pre-2004 Aston Ward. In the light of the 2003 result in Aston, Lozells and East Handsworth could fairly be regarded as a problematical Ward. The pattern is the same here as for Aston, Bordesley Green and Washwood Heath. In 2003 the postal votes for Handsworth were 328 but in 2004 they were 3898 (an increase of 1,088%).

690. Sparkwood (pre-June 2004 split between Labour and Liberal Democrat) showing an increase from 1300 to 4483 (245%).

691. The pattern certainly seems to be there. Marginal, particularly Asian, Wards were the target of postal vote fraud. The conclusion appears inescapable that Bordesley Green and Aston were not related incidents but part of a Birmingham-wide campaign by the Labour Party to try, by the use of bogus postal votes, to counter the adverse effect of the Iraq war on its electoral fortunes.

692. To conclude this section, however, I must make it abundantly clear that there is not the slightest evidence before me to show that the frauds of the Labour Party in Birmingham were known to or approved by the national Labour Party.

693. Patently, most of the protagonists in these Petitions are members of the Muslim Asian community. Is this relevant?

694.The way in which it is certainly not relevant is in showing any community disposition to fraud or misconduct. To suggest that Muslim Asians are prone to frauds of this kind whereas other communities are not would be racist and moreover would not be justified by any evidence before this court. I am aware that there are those on the fringes of politics who may seek to use this judgment for racist ends. There is no warrant for anyone to do so and I hope they will not.

695. There are, however, two ways in which the ethnic makeup of the communities in Bordesley Green[2] and Aston is relevant, one minor and one major.

696. The minor factor lies in the structures of the Muslim Asian community. There is no doubt that this community retains, where others have lost, an ingrained respect for those in the community who are in positions of trust and responsibility. In normal circumstances this is wholly admirable, but it only works if those who are in such positions are worthy of the trust placed in them. It is clear that some community leaders in Birmingham must have abused the respect and trust of the community to persuade voters who were confused or had poor understanding of the process to hand over unused postal vote packages or to entrust party canvassers with completed votes.

697. The major relevance of the Asian factor is the Iraq war. It was the Iraq war which turned many Muslim Labour supporters away from voting Labour, in some cases towards voting for the Liberal Democrats or other parties who opposed the war, such as the PJP. The principal purpose of the campaign of electoral fraud waged by the Labour Party was to target precisely those formerly safe Labour Wards with large Muslim populations where the fraud would redress the balance.

698. The reason why the frauds were most blatant in Muslim Asian Wards was precisely because the voters were Muslim. They could no longer be trusted to vote the straight Labour ticket, so bogus votes had to be cast instead.

699. It seems inevitable that the considerations set out above must have applied in other electoral areas of England with large Muslim populations and it would be surprising if similar incidents did not occur in future elections in such areas.

And so it proved to be:

- In 2009, Mahboob Khan, Eshaq Khan, Gulnawaz Khan, Basharat Khan, Altaf Khan and Arshad Raja were jailed for, or in connection with, a postal vote scam in Slough. This came to light when it was pointed out that, at a number of properties, up to nineteen names, all Asian, had been registered.

- In 2010 Mohammed Rafiq, Jamshed Khan, Mohammed Sultan, Alyas Khan and Reis Khan (aged between seventy and forty) were jailed for using fraudulent postal vote applications in a bid to get Haroon Rashid elected in 2005 for Bradford West.

- In the London Borough of Tower Hamlets, it was found that almost half of the signatories to a petition were 'invalid', with entire pages of names and addresses in the same handwriting and with thousands of names not on the electoral register.

In May 2013 the Electoral Commission stated:

There are strongly held views, based in particular on reported first-hand experience by some campaigners and elected representatives in particular, that electoral fraud is more likely to be committed by or in support of candidates standing for election in areas which are largely or predominately populated by some South Asian communities, specifically those with roots in parts of Pakistan or Bangladesh. These concerns reflect issues also highlighted by a small number of previous studies of political and electoral participation.

These studies have suggested that extended family and community networks may have been mobilised to secure the support of large numbers of electors in some areas, effectively constituting a 'block vote' – although this does not necessarily involve electoral fraud. They also argue that the wider availability of postal voting in Great Britain since 2001 may have increased the risk of electoral fraud associated with this approach, as the greater safeguards of secrecy provided in polling stations are removed.

Evidence from police data and prosecutions does show that people from these communities are represented among those accused of electoral fraud and also among those convicted of fraud. But white British people and people from other communities are also represented, and it would be a mistake for any Returning Officer or police force to think that electoral fraud only happens within these specific communities. Our analysis over a number of years has enabled us to identify particular police forces and local authorities where allegations of electoral fraud have been most frequent and we will continue to target our monitoring activities in these areas.[3]

And in its final report (of January 2014), the Electoral Commission identified sixteen local authority areas 'where there appears to be a greater risk of alleged electoral fraud being reported', and continued:

These areas are also often home to communities with a diverse range of nationalities and ethnic backgrounds. We have heard some strongly held views, based in particular on reported first-hand experience by some campaigners and elected representatives, that electoral fraud is more likely to be committed by or in support of candidates standing for election in areas which are largely or predominately populated by some South Asian communities, specifically those with roots in parts of Pakistan or Bangladesh.[4]

[Electoral fraud] is predominately within the Asian community.[5]

Voter fraud is endemic in Bangladeshi and Pakistani communities. Because it is our culture.[6]

Lutfur Mohammed Rahman[7] was born in what is now Bangladesh in 1965. He was elected mayor of Tower Hamlets in 2010.

In November 2014, the local government secretary took control of Tower Hamlets and sent in commissioners after finding an administration that was 'at best dysfunctional, at worst riddled with cronyism and corruption'.

In 2015, it was adjudged that Rahman's (re)election in 2014 had been 'avoided by … corrupt or illegal practices … also to have been avoided on the ground of general corruption …' apart from undue spiritual influence by having 101 local imams equate being a good Muslim as voting for Rahman (*see* Appendix V for paragraph 549 of the judgment which set out their proclamation, and also note 33 to A is for African, Asian and alien for various paragraphs from the judgment).

In November 2015, Rahman declared himself bankrupt and two months later Chief Master Marsh found that 'Both Mr Rahman and his broker must have been aware they were providing misleading information', adding that

Rahman's wife, Ayesha Farid, was 'a thoroughly unsatisfactory and unreliable witness'.

Notes: V is for vote rigging

1. Election petition *Aston M/307/04, Bordesley Green* M/309/04 – which was reported at [2005] All ER (D) 15 with Appeal at [2005] EWHC 2365).

Bordesley Green is described by Wikipedia as

> The area is an ethnically diverse community with ethnic minorities consisting of 71.1% of the population compared to 29.6% for Birmingham overall. 33.5% of the population was born outside of the United Kingdom, much higher than the city average of 16.5% and the national average of 9.3%. 62.2% of the population was of Asian origin, of which 50.5% were British Pakistanis. The proportion of Asian people in Birmingham is much lower at 19.5% and the proportion of Pakistani people is 10.6%. White British people represented 25.7% of the ward's population. There is a wide variety of languages spoken within the area such as Punjabi, Urdu, Mirpuri, Bengali, Pushto and Arabic with English being the most widely spoken language.

2. It has been alleged that Abdelhamid Abaaoud, a resident of Belgium and one of those who planned the murders in Paris during the evening of 13 November 2015, had visited Bordesley Green and/or been in communication with persons resident there. Certainly, pictures of places in Birmingham were on his mobile.

3. *Electoral fraud in the UK: Evidence and issues paper,* May 2013 – paragraphs 3.104 to 3.106

4. *Electoral fraud in the UK: Final report and recommendations*, January 2014 – paragraph 3.4.

5. Lady Warsi, born in this country but whose parents came from Mirpur (*see* M is for Mirpur) speaking about the 2010 general election.

6. Azmal Hussein. (He was one of the four who took the action against Rahman for 'subverting democracy', running a 'den of iniquity' and 'systematically stealing votes').

(For further reading *see Elections, Voting and Electoral Fraud: An exploratory study focusing on British Pakistanis and Bangladeshis* by Valdeep Gill and Fatima Hussain of NatCen Social Research, January 2015, and *Understanding electoral fraud vulnerability in Pakistani and Bangladeshi origin communities in England prepared for the Electoral*

Commission by Maria Sobolewska, Stuart Wilks-Heeg, Eleanor Hill and Magda Borkowska of the Centre on Dynamics of Ethnicity, the Universities of Manchester and Liverpool, January 2015).

7. Mr Rahman provided a court reference for Zamal Uddin, as to whom *see* note 6 to C is for community, and a reference for Mahee Jalil, who went on to be imprisoned for money laundering.

W is for welfare

The 1942 Beveridge Report[1] recommended:

> Benefit in return for contributions, rather than free allowances from the state, is what the people of Britain desire.

> ... social security must be achieved by co-operation between the State and the individual. The State should offer security for service and contribution.

In 2014, the shadow secretary of state for work and pensions said:

> The social security system was created so that you paid in when in work and drew on support if you were out of work, ill or old.

> And as Ed Miliband set out in June, we want to go further to make sure our system is based on what you have paid in over time, meaning that those who have lived and worked here for years get more than those who have only recently joined the workforce.

> ... rebuilding the 'something for nothing' principle that is at the heart of our welfare system, but that too many people feel has been eroded over time.

> So we want to change Jobseeker's Allowance so that someone who has been working for many years gets more help if they lose their job than someone who has been working for a short time or not at all.

> ... a step on the route to creating a benefit system that is fair and decent, and rewards those who do the right thing. And as I've said before, to make sure that the system is fair and seen to be fair we must clamp down on the scandal of child benefit being sent abroad. It's not right that people are able to claim child benefits for children who don't live in this country. The Government should be negotiating now to bear down on this abuse of our system and to ensure people who come to the UK come to contribute and not just to claim benefits.[2]

Notes: *W is for welfare*

1. William Beveridge, *Social Insurance and Allied Services* (aka the Beveridge Report).

2. Rachel Reeves (MP for Leeds West since 2010), August 2014, speaking – *The Choice on Social Security* – to a meeting of the Labour Party in the constituency of Pudsey.

And W is for we were warned

[In 1899] How dreadful are the curses which Mohammedanism lays on its votaries! Besides the fanatical frenzy, which is as dangerous in a man as hydrophobia in a dog, there is this fearful fatalistic apathy. The effects are apparent in many countries. Improvident habits, slovenly systems of agriculture, sluggish methods of commerce, and insecurity of property exist wherever the followers of the Prophet rule or live. A degraded sensualism deprives this life of its grace and refinement; the next of its dignity and sanctity. The fact that in Mohammedan law every woman must belong to some man as his absolute property – either as a child, a wife, or a concubine – must delay the final extinction of slavery until the faith of Islam has ceased to be a great power among men. Thousands become the brave and loyal soldiers of the Queen: all know how to die but the influence of the religion paralyses the social development of those who follow it. No stronger retrograde force exists in the world. Far from being moribund, Mohammedanism is a militant and proselytising faith. It has already spread throughout Central Africa, raising fearless warriors at every step; and were it not that Christianity is sheltered in the strong arms of science – the science against which it had vainly struggled – the civilisation of modern Europe might fall, as fell the civilisation of ancient Rome.[1]

[In 1918] ... the Arab appealed to my imagination. It is the old, old civilisation, which has defined itself clear of household gods, and half the trappings which ours hastens to assume. The gospel of bareness is a good one, and it involves apparently a sort of moral bareness too. They think for the moment, and endeavour to slip through life without turning corners or climbing hills. In part it is a mental and moral fatigue, a race trained out, and to avoid difficulties they have to jettison so much that we think honourable and grave: and yet without in any way sharing their point of view, I think I can understand it enough to look at myself and other foreigners from their direction, and without condemning it, I know I am a stranger to them, and always will be; but I cannot believe them worse, any more than I could change to their ways.[2]

[In 1938] How courteous is the Japanese
He always says 'Excuse it please'
He climbs into his neighbor's garden
And smiles and says 'I beg your pardon'
He bows and grins a friendly grin
And calls his hungry family in
He grins and bows a friendly bow
'So sorry, this my garden now'.[3]

[In 1948] The British people fortunately enjoy a profound unity without uniformity in their way of life and are blessed by the absence of a colour racial problem. An influx of coloured people domiciled here is likely to impair the harmony, strength and cohesion of our public and social life and cause discord and unhappiness among all concerned.[4]

[In 1968] In fifteen or twenty years, on present trends, there will be in this country three and a half million Commonwealth immigrants and their descendants. That is not my figure. That is the official figure given to Parliament by the spokesman of the Registrar General's office.

There is no comparable figure for the year 2000: but it must be in the region of 5–7 million, approaching one-tenth of the whole population, and approaching that of greater London. Of course, it will not be evenly distributed from Margate to Aberystwyth and from Penzance to Aberdeen. Whole areas, towns and parts of towns across England will be occupied largely and wholly by different sections of the immigrant and immigrant-descended population.[5]

[In 1974] One day, millions of men will leave the southern hemisphere to go to the northern hemisphere. And they will not go there as friends. Because they will go there to conquer it; and they will conquer it with their sons. The wombs of our women will give us victory.[6]

[In 1978] If we went on as we are then, by the end of the century, there would be four million people of the new Commonwealth or Pakistan here. Now, that is an awful lot and I think that means people are rather afraid that this country might be rather swamped by people with a different culture and, you know, the British character has done so much for democracy, for law and done so much throughout the world that if there is any fear that it might be swamped people are going to react and be rather hostile to those coming in. So if you want good race relations, you have got to allay peoples' fears on numbers.[7]

[In 1981] The banquet was very much what you would expect, a touch of the old Raj, curry and turbans, only enlivened by a frightful shouting match between M. and the Gandhi woman, both at it like a pair of fishwives. All the Indians are up in arms about Whitelaw's latest scheme to stem the immigrant tide. On that leg of the trip the drink laws still hadn't begun to bite, and owing to jetlag I may have been over-enthusiastic about putting my oar in. I told our dusky hostess that in view of recent events in Brixton we just couldn't afford to let in a whole lot more of her compatriots. All industrious, charming little fellows, etc., but put them in South London and in no time at all they'd be bunging bricks at the Constabulary like some country coconut shy. Not that I can say I blame them.

Whereupon, Bill, solids hit the punkah. Gandhi woman rises to her feet, eyes blazing, pointing out that all her mob are quiet as mice, running newspaper shops and colonising Bradford. Brixton lot an inferior breed altogether, mad as coots, high on drugs, etc., and wouldn't let them into her sub-continent in a million years, etc.[8]

In 1982 there was published *Multiracial myths* by Ray Honeyford, headmaster of Drummond Middle School, Bradford (*see* Appendix VI) and two years later there was published his *Education and Race – an Alternative View* (*see* H is for Ray Honeyford).

[In 1999] Thanks to your democratic laws we will invade you. Thanks to our religious laws we will dominate you.[9]

[In 2001] Ils se multiplient comme les rats.[10]

[In 2007] Those for whom this country has always been a model of tolerance and freedom cannot but have cause for deep concern about the seemingly reckless pace and scale on which immigration has recently been allowed to proceed, if not actively encouraged. As a result of it, the country may possibly have already reached a tipping point beyond which it can no longer be said to contain a single nation. Should that point have been reached, then, ironically in the course of Britain having become a nation of immigrants, it would have ceased to be a nation. Once such a point is reached, political disintegration may be predicted to be not long in following.[11]

But despite these warnings: in 2016, as the result of the school seeking funding for puzzles and jigsaws that require communication in English for the children, it came out that Annette Street Primary School in Govan Hill, Glasgow has no Scottish pupils – all 222 children are either from Slovakia or Romania or the children of Asian families. The headteacher, Mrs Taylor, was reported as saying –

Families originally came from Slovakia. They settled and then started communicating with families back home and word got out for others to come.

And now the same thing is happening with our Romanian families. Most come from the same area, Arad,[12] and word got back to their extended families that if you go to Glasgow go to Annette Street.

So the children who have been here for a while act as interpreters for the children who are new.

A lot of the children have never been to school in their home countries.

Notes: *W is for we were warned*

1. *The River War*, Winston Churchill.

Sir James Porter was the ambassador to the Sublime Porte of the Ottoman Empire from 1746 to 1762 and came to the following conclusion:

> The Turks hold all who are not of their belief and embrace not the doctrines of their Prophet, to be objects of divine vengeance, and consequently of their detestation, and against whom they are to exercise violence, fraud, and rapine. ... Muhammetans are ever ready to demonstrate their zeal by spurning and ill-treating the persons, plundering the property, and even destroying the very existence of those who profess a different religion – such behaviour being – 'most meritorious in the sight of God and his Prophet'.

In October 1915 – a *Reuters* correspondent reported:

> Women and children were taken out of town [Zile, about 300 km east of Ankara] in ox-carts and exposed on the open plain to hunger and cold for many days and nights until it was thought the women were sufficiently desperate to accept conversion to Islam in order to save their lives. They were told their husbands were dead, and that if they accepted the true faith they could return home with their children. Without exception, the women refused. The Turkish commander then ordered the children to be put into carts, and had the mothers bayoneted by the gendarmes before the children's eyes.

About one hundred years later, president and formerly prime minister Recep Erdogan of Turkey said that Germany's attempts to force its Turkish gasarbeiters, originally temporary guest workers but now permanent residents, to learn German was "a crime against humanity" such Turks should be allowed their own Turkish speaking schools and "Assimilation is a violation of human rights" all this despite Erdogan imprisoning journalists.

2. Letter from T.E. Lawrence (of Arabia).

3. Ogden Nash, 1902–1971.

4. Eleven Labour MPs writing to the then prime minister, Clement Attlee.

5. Enoch Powell, 1912–1998. Powell was right: the 2011census reported that "white British" were a minority in two thirds of London boroughs.

6. Allegedly said by Houari Boumedienne, 1932–78, in April 1974, in his speech to the United Nations General Assembly while chairman of the Revolutionary Council of Algeria: 'allegedly' because an official record of the speech does not seem to be available; certainly there are slightly different

versions (*see*, for instance, the blog *Islam versus Europe: Where Islam Spreads, Freedom Dies.*)

7. Margaret Thatcher Prime Minister, 1979/92. If anything, her prognosis was an understatement of what has happened: (*see* P is for progression).

Thirty-seven years later, David Cameron used the same 'S' word: (*see* S is for swarm and swamp).

8. On 24 April 1981, on the way back from India, Denis Thatcher (or rather Richard Ingrams and John Wells) 'wrote' thus to his friend Bill. (*The Other Half* published by Private Eye Productions).

As he had previously admitted, Denis seems to have been confused – 'India, or it may have been Pakistan' – which may be the explanation for that, according to Bradford District Council, in Bradford, rather than Brixton, in 2007 'the second largest ethnic group is composed of people with an Asian heritage (20%). Just over three quarters of the Asian population has a Pakistani background and people of an Indian origin make up most of the remainder of the Asian population (14%).'

9. This was reported by Germano Bernardini, the Archbishop of Izmir (in Turkey). He was relating how to the Second Synod of European Bishops in 1999, 'during an official meeting on Islamic-Christian dialogue an authorative Muslim figure' had said these words 'to the Christians ... calmly and confidently'.

I have not been able to confirm the identity of the 'authorative Muslim figure' but it may have been Anwar Sadat, President of Egypt from 1971 to (his assassination by Islamists in) 1981 (and so if the words were those of Sadat, this warning must have been before 1981; perhaps at the time of Boumedienne's warning in 1974).

10. *La Forza della Ragione*, Oriana Fallaci 1929–2006.

In the English edition – *The Force of Reason* – (published by Rizzoli International, 2004), the quoted words were within:

In our subjugated Europe the Islamic fertility is such a taboo that nobody ever dares to speak about it. If you try, you go straight to court for racism and xenophobia and blasphemy. (Among the charges moved against me at the trial in Paris there was the following sentence of mine: 'Ils se multiplient comme les rats'. They breed like rats. A little brutal I agree, but indisputably accurate). The fact is that no trial, no liberticide law, will ever be able to negate what they themselves boast. In the last half century Muslims have increased by 235 percent (Christians only by 47 percent).

Fallaci translated herself into English and reported that certain critics had found the result to contain "the oddities of Fallaci's English". Those with cradle English would probably say 'they breed like rabbits'.

Fallaci was also the authoress of, inter alia, *The Rage and the Pride*, which (almost) concluded with:

> Woe betide those who invade [my country, Italy]. Whoever the invaders are. Because whether they be the French of Napoleon or the Austrians of Franz Joseph or the Germans of Hitler or the Moslems of Osama bin Laden, for me it is exactly the same. Whether they come with troops and cannons or with children and boats, idem.

11. From the conclusion to *A Nation of Immigrants?* by David Conway published by Civitas 2007.

12. Arad is in the west of Romania, near the border with Hungary.

And **W** is for what is to be done?

With the existing number of aliens already here because of one or more of

- first, having come here from somewhere else in the European Union, particularly an A2 country or A8 country

- second, those from elsewhere being given permission to enter

- third, those who were given permission after arriving here

- fourth, natural increase (of those three)

- fifth, family reunion

- sixth, those who are here illegally

either dispose of the present stable door and allow in anybody/everybody, namely there is an open door, or (possibilities include)[1]

1. A complete stop to the provision of British citizenship to aliens no matter the length of time he/she has lived here and/or being married to a British citizen.

2. Amend the Housing Act so that inspections can be made without notice.[2]

3. Amend the Immigration Acts so that

- rather than a foreign national prisoner being liable to deportation upon completion of his sentence of imprisonment, he will be deported come what may or is deported, automatically, upon being sentenced to any term of imprisonment (even if suspended);

- any alien found using a 'bed in a shed'[2] or sleeping rough is immediately deported together with the owner and/or manager of such 'shed' if he is also an alien.

4. Amend all 'indefinite leave to remain' permissions to stay in this country to a limited period, say two years, with national insurance and NHS accessibility being cancelled, automatically, from the end of such period.

5. Automatic refusal of entry to anybody, not obviously a tourist, without a visa, any such person there and then being put on a return flight/boat without appeal (and without any chance to 'disappear into the community').

5.1 Anybody who arrives hidden in a lorry, stowed away on a ship or hidden in an aircraft to be expelled, without more ado.

6. Automatic and immediate expulsion of any unsuccessful applicant for asylum without any possibility of appeal.

6.1 Clear the backlog of asylum applications by a blanket refusal.

6.2 Cancel subsistence payments from those seeking asylum. (Apply the monies thereby saved in effecting repatriation.)

7. Automatic and immediate expulsion of any non-indigenous person who committed an offence to get here or to get into the country.

8. Automatic and immediate expulsion of a non-indigenous person who is convicted of an offence for which prison is a possible outcome, whatever his/her age, whatever the system of governance of his/her place of origin, whether or not he has family here and without waiting for any term of imprisonment to be served.

9. Automatic and immediate expulsion of any non-citizen who works without a permit, together with the employer if he is also not a citizen.

10. Automatic and immediate expulsion of any female who has had FGM wherever and whenever it was effected, along with both her parents and together with her husband and those who effected the procedure or abetted in procuring it.

11. Automatic and immediate expulsion of all (non-indigenous) persons involved in bogus marriages.

12. Automatic and immediate expulsion of both sets of parents of the parties to a forced marriage.

13. Automatic and immediate expulsion of all parties to a polygamous marriage.

14. Automatic and immediate expulsion of all those engaged in international sex traffic/trade, both the traffickers and traffickees, whatever his/her age and however ill-treated he/she might be might have been or might be upon his/her return home.

15. Automatic and immediate expulsion of any (foreign) student who does not attend/pursue his/her course.

16. Automatic refusal of entry to those seeking to enter this country without prior authority, whether or not accompanied by a minor, without any appeal process.

17. Cancellation of the Seasonal Agricultural Workers Scheme. (If, despite the millions of unemployed people in this country, this scheme really is necessary, then exit from this country of such foreign workers at the end of the season to be secured by requiring say half of the earnings to be retained until after such worker has left this country.)

18. Cancel the grant of asylum upon a regime change of the individual's former home.

19. Clear the Border Agency's backlog of applicants to live in this country by a blanket refusal.

20. Deny publicly funded services (education, health and legal aid) and welfare payments (child benefit, disability payment, housing benefit, working tax credit and unemployment benefit) to those who by reason of non-European apparel and/or lack of the English language, evidence separatedness and/or inability or unwillingness to integrate.[3]

21. Stop encouragement of diversity and/or multiculturalism.

22. Stop the public funding of translating.

23. Deport all persons (who are not British by birth) who at any time and anywhere committed an offence by act or omission, which under English law is punishable by imprisonment, notwithstanding the length of time he has been here, any treaty to which this country is a party, any convention or protocol to which this country is a signatory, any asylum granted to such person, any permission whether temporary or permanent to reside in this

country and notwithstanding that such person is now serving a term of imprisonment.

24. Enforce the illegality of polygamy by DNA testing of men, women and children.

24.1 Equate polygamy with bigamy.

24.2 Expel polygamists and their issue.

25. Extend the definition of incest to include first and second cousins.[4]

26. Immediate expulsion from this country of anyone found to be here without authorisation or whose timed permission has expired, without any appeal process and notwithstanding having or claiming to have a family here.

27. Immediate expulsion from this country of any would-be immigrant who has been here for two years and who cannot speak English adequately.

28. Limit the Human Rights Act to British citizens (by birth).

28.1 Revoke the Human Rights Act.

28.2 Withdraw from the 1950 European Convention on Human Rights.

29. Limit the provision of publicly funded benefits and services to British citizens by birth and, where such is now being provided to others, withdraw such benefits after notice of, say, six months.

30. The Home Secretary to declare that the wearing of the niqab in public or the public advocacy of the introduction of sharia law will be considered as non-conducive to the public good.[5]

30.1 Declare that any indefinite leave to remain in the UK (or a shorter period) will be cancelled for anyone who wears the niqab in any public place or advocates the introduction of sharia law.

31. Outlaw the covering of the face in any public place and empower any police constable, whether male or female, to remove and dispose of such covering.[6]

32. Outlaw pupils/students wearing the hijab on educational premises.

32.1 Extend this ban to all females (of whatever age) on educational premises.

33. Offer all non-indigenous who are in prison immediate release upon leaving the country (never to return) but provided they are accompanied

with spouse and all children.

34. Introduce 'Two strikes – two convictions for a crime for which jail is a possibility – and you are out' of the country.

35. Make aid conditional upon the would-be recipient country receiving back (from this country) persons of its ethnicity.

36. Postpone the availability of British citizenship for those born elsewhere until the applicant has lived here for two decades of adult life and provides compelling evidence of assimilation and mastery of the English language by all members of his/her family.[7]

37. Publication of all briefing papers, contributions, minutes of meetings and responses towards *Research, Development and Statistics Occasional Paper No. 67 – Migration: an economic and social analysis* together with all drafts/editions thereof.

38. Publicise the name of the school in Birmingham where Adil Rashid was educated.[8]

38.1 Close such school.

39. Realise that immigrants from Africa and Asia outnumber those from the EU by about two to one.[9]

40. Recognise and take into account in any application for entry that those who live in Australia, or Canada or New Zealand are likely to be related to us and to share our heritage and history and culture and that we have very little if anything in common with those from, for example, Angola, Cameroon, Nigeria and Zimbabwe.

41. Reinstate the Primary Purpose Rule.

42. Remove all public funding from the race industry.

43. Require all those who do not require a visa to enter the country to prove they do not have any criminal convictions (failing which to be refused entry).

44. Require all those having a public sector equality duty (under the Equality Act 2010) to forbid female employees from covering their heads while on the premises of such an employer.[10]

45. Require those here but not British citizens who have a child born here to register such child with the diplomatic mission of the country of origin of the mother and to exclude such mother and child from any state-funded benefits.

46. Require all those from other than an EU country who arrived here since say the end of 1999 not to work here without a work permit.

47. Require surety for any would-be student that he will leave this country.

48. Restrict voting to those with British citizenship.[11]

49. Revoke asylum (and any right to be in the country) upon the grantee becoming involved in any political activity, whether here or elsewhere.

50. Revoke or at least amend the equalities legislation so that the culture, ethos, language, philosophy and traditions of this country have primacy.

51. Revert to the requirements to vote by post that prevailed before 1997.[12]

52. Sequester any aeroplane/vehicle/vessel by which a person arrives in this country without a passport.[13]

53. Stop non-indigenous persons from having the right, having married his cousin (or anyone else) from his 'village' (or anywhere else in his country of origin) to bring her here because she is his spouse.[14]

54. Stop the automatic provision of British citizenship to those born here if neither of the parents was, at that time, a British citizen, and postdate this change to those so born since the end of 1999.

54.1. Withdraw British citizenship from those born here since, say, the end of 1999, neither of whose parents was at the time of that birth a British citizen.

55. Unequivocal refusal of entry for any unaccompanied minor (who does not have a British passport).

56. Stop the conducting in this country of marriages where neither party is a UK citizen.

56.1 Void all marriages effected in this country since, say, the end of 1999 where neither of the parties was, at the time, a British citizen.

57. Withdraw publicly funded services – such as education, healthcare and social security benefits – from those given leave, of whatever length of time, to be in this country.

58. Withdraw from the United Nations conventions relating to the Status of Refugees and the Rights of the Child.

59. Withdraw from the International Covenant on Civil and Political Rights or at least restrict the UK's agreements thereunder to British citizens.

60. Withhold any accreditation or award as to education and/or training until the student has left the country.

And as to the European Union:

61.1 Exercise all opt-outs as to the free movement of people within the Union and, failing there be any such treaty opt-out, give notice that national identity and/or national security requires such steps to be taken.[15]

61.2 Give notice that the European Union Asylum Qualification Directive will not be observed/complied with.

61.3 (Unilaterally) change the requirement that an EU citizen has to have been given a two year sentence before there is a presumption of deportation, to conviction for any offence for which imprisonment is possible.

61.4 Give notice that the free movement of workers within the EU will no longer apply to those from A8 and/or A2 countries and that such persons already here will have to have work permits, which failing they will have to leave within, say, six months.

61.5 Limit publicly financed benefits/services to what the applicant would get in his home country.[16]

61.6 Require all those from any country of the EU who have arrived here since, say, the end of 2003 to be self-supporting or to have work permits.

61.7 Require any person who wishes to reside in this country to produce evidence that he does not have any criminal convictions, failing which to refuse him entry or deport him.

61.8 Write to the (five) EU presidents along the following lines:

Dear Presidents,

For present purposes, I accept that what follows, without derogation, will be in breach of treaty obligations and indeed may be the consequence of decisions of what at the time was the government of this country, but where we are now, in this country, with the free movement of people throughout the EU, is untenable. What I am referring to is – the population is being displaced, there is a housing crisis, midwifery provision is overloaded, schools are overflowing, infrastructure is overloaded, welfare funds are being depleted and misallocated, employment is being disrupted, social cohesion is being destroyed and wage levels are being forced down.

366

The degree of each, but even more so when added together, is such that this country has no alternative but to take unilateral action. And so I am informing you, whether or not the necessary derogations are granted, that

- from three months after the date of this letter, no national of an A2 country shall have access to (this country's) publicly funded education, health or housing or welfare benefits;

- from four months from now, no national of an A2 country will be allowed to work here without a work permit. (Steps will be taken to prevent avoidance of this measure through employment by a corporation, and correspondingly by an agency and a person from an A2 country presenting as from another member of the EU);

- within six months from now, all A2 nationals shall have to leave.

It is likely that some, if not all, of these steps will be extended to the A8 states. And it may be that such steps will also be extended (to a greater or lesser extent) to all the remaining states of the European Union.

I am sorry to take this action but for the reasons listed above, Her Majesty's government has decided it must be taken.

I realise this letter is missing detail; that has still to be worked out but as lives will be disrupted I am letting you know the decision immediately and indeed this letter will be published when you should receive it.

I am copying this letter, directly, to the government of each/all of the European Union member states.

Movement of people within the European Union is only part of the impossible position this country finds itself in: there is also immigration from elsewhere. If it is any consolation, I can assure you that, in respect of such other immigration, the steps to be taken by Her Majesty's government will be at least as robust.

Yours sincerely,

61.9 Withdraw from the European Union.[17]

Notes: *W is for what is to be done?*

1. The list is just a list of possibilities and so individual ones may, at least in part, either conflict or duplicate.

2. Local authorities find it difficult to stop 'beds in sheds' as the current

requirement for twenty-four hours' notice enables the bed users to go before the inspector calls.

3. *See* I is for integration, and particularly note 21 thereto.

4. *Born in Bradford* found that cousin marriage has been so prevalent in Pakistani society that the level of genetic defects is hardly less in the issue of second cousin parents than with the issue of first cousin parents

5. *See* C is for non-conducive.

6. Something similar was done in France … for reasons of *laïcité*, which Christopher Caldwell in *Reflections on the Revolution in Europe* explains 'is difficult to translate. It differs from the Anglo-American tradition in that it seeks less to neutralize public authorities in matters of religion than to neutralize religious bodies in matters of public life.'

Britain could never debate the burka like France by Agnes Poirier, *The Times*, June 2009

> the burka and all ostentatious religious signs have already been banned in state-run schools since 2004. And in hospitals or municipal offices, anywhere where people interact as equal citizens, staff are not allowed to wear hijabs or burka, and patients and members will be told to unveil.

Manuel Valls, now prime minister of France and previously Minister of the Interior, but before that mayor of Evry, went so far as to ban mothers who were accompanying their child on a school outing from wearing a hijab. As prime minister, he may want to go further – according to Google he was asked, in April 2016

> Are you in favour of a law to ban the veil at university? [and replied]

> It should be done, but there are constitutional rules that make this a difficult prohibition. We must be uncompromising on the rules of secularism in higher education.

However the original was

> Maintenez-vous l'idée que le voile est un asservissement pour la femme? [and replied]

> Oui, dès lors qu'il est revendiqué politiquement de manière militante. On ne peut pas faire comme si c'était un objet de mode ou de consommation comme un autre.

In the UK, such ban would be so as to procure assimilation and integration. Jack Straw, MP for Blackburn 1979/2015, Home Secretary 1997/01, and

Foreign Secretary 2001/06, described such face covering as 'a visible statement of separation and difference'.

7. 'Just because a man is born in a stable, it doesn't make him a horse' – Duke of Wellington, about 1800.

'Since his parents are Scottish it follows he must be Scottish, even if he was born in England. If a cat had kittens in an oven would you call them biscuits?' – part of a letter to a newspaper from Dr Robert Hanson, May 2014.

8. *See* the part of M is for multiculturalism to which note 6 applies.

9. The following is from *Nigel Farage keeps on about EU migration, but non-EU migration is the greater problem* by Melanie McDonagh, *The Spectator,* March 2014.

> Look, I do realise that freedom of movement within the EU is a problem, though nothing like what it'd be if the main parties had their way and Turkey joins, because it is a virtually unlimited pool of labour. Nonetheless, in terms of numbers and the capacity to integrate, it is immigration from outside the EU which poses the real problem. Of the 532,000 people who came to Britain in the year to last September, 244,000 of them were non-EU citizens. That's less than 269,000 the year before but still nearly half, and it was about half the previous year's total too. And of the 3.8 million people – net, not gross – who came to Britain under Labour, no fewer than 70 per cent were from outside the EU. The notion that immigration is a problem of EU membership just isn't true.

And the following from *Slam the door on the migrants' grans, Dave. It'll cheer you right up* by Rod Liddle, *The Sunday Times*, August 2015.

> But that's only a small fraction of our immigration problem. There's the migration from Europe with which to contend and, granted, that is a problem that will become soluble only when we have renegotiated our membership of the European Union or got the hell out. We can wait a year for that.
>
> More pressing is the immigration from the Indian subcontinent. You can come here to live if you can show that you are related to someone living here now. Grandparent, sister, brother, grandchild – it doesn't matter, the border is open for you. And that is the biggest slice of our immigration problem. So cheer yourself up Dave. Call a halt to it. If they miss their relations, encourage them to catch up with each other in Sylhet or Karachi, maybe permanently.

10. *See* U is for unintended consequences.

11. *See* V is for vote rigging.
From *We are too respectful of other "cultures"* by Libby Purves, *The Times*, November 2013:

> The prosecutor said, 'The systems to deal with fraud are not working well, they are not working badly. The fact is there are no real systems. Until there are, fraud will continue unabated. The system for voting would disgrace a banana republic.'

> In 2012 the London Borough of Tower Hamlets, with Bangladeshis comprising over 30 per cent of the population, was ordered to clear up its electoral register after it was found 550 people in 64 properties, an average of three per bedroom, were registered to vote, and a non-existent voter was removed from the list of voters registered to vote from the home of the mayor, Lutfur Rahman.

> Britain, is in global terms, remarkably strict about bribes. Before the lazy convenience of postal votes, we were strict about electoral fraud too: you had to stand alone in a shielded booth with a pencil on a string. Since postal voting there has been a conviction (in Slough) for downright fraud, and wide anecdotal evidence of community patriarchs using their habitual know-best dominance to collect up family votes rather than let their wives, sisters, in-laws and 18-year-olds make up their minds privately. Baroness Warsi noted this in 2010, to much tutting.

12. Three paragraphs from the report of the Birmingham election case (*see* V is for vote rigging) in 2005 are:

> 714. In this judgment I have set out at length what has clearly been shown to be the weakness of the current law relating to postal votes. As some parts of this judgment may be seen as critical of the Government, I wish to make it clear that the responsibility for the present unsatisfactory situation must be shared. All political parties welcomed and supported postal voting on demand. Until very recently, none has treated electoral fraud as representing a problem. Apart from the Electoral Commission, whose role I have described above, the only voices raised against the laxity of the system have been in the media, in particular The Times newspaper, and the tendency of politicians of all Parties has been to dismiss these warnings as scaremongering.

> 715. In the course of preparing my judgment, my attention was drawn to what I am told is an official Government statement about postal voting which I hope I quote correctly:

> There are no proposals to change the rules governing election procedures for the next election, including those for postal voting. The systems already in place to deal with the allegations of electoral fraud

are clearly working.

> 716. Anybody who has sat through the case I have just tried and listened to evidence of electoral fraud that would disgrace a banana republic would find this statement surprising. To assert that "The systems already in place to deal with allegations of electoral fraud are clearly working" indicates a state not simply of complacency but of denial.

13. This is to prevent the abuse of a passenger disposing of his passport during the journey to this country.

Hardial Singh avoided being deported back to India. He had twice been convicted of burglary. Because his passport had been mislaid and the India High Commission or the Home Office, or both, delayed so long in issuing a passport, his continued detention (pending deportation) became unlawful.

In 2012, Amada Bizimana avoided deportation because Burundi would not accept that he came from there; likewise, DRC and Tanzania. There was some doubt as to whether he was giving genuine answers (during his interview with Burundi officials for travel documents) while being detained pending deportation.

14. See the part of I is for integration to which note 14 applies – as to 'fetching' marriages.

15. Article 48 of the Treaty of Rome provides that free movement of workers is subject to the following proviso – 'subject to limitations justified on grounds of public policy, public security or public health …'

Gintas Burinskas arrived here from Lithuania after serving a ten year sentence for rape. Within two months he had raped again, in Northampton (the sentence of seven years in prison and three on licence did 'not adequately protect the public' and so was increased to life with a minimum of six years).

16. The point is illustrated by *Better for Britain to be a Scrooge than a sucker* by Philip Johnson, *The Daily Telegraph*, December 2015.

> Why do we continue to pay benefit for the upkeep of thousands of foreign children living abroad? Most EU countries do not make transfers for offspring living outside their territory because entitlement is based on residency, Britain, however, pays for 34,000 children living elsewhere in the EU at a cost of £30 million annually. Even if we are compelled to do so under EU non-discrimination rules, why is the benefit set at UK rates? It is supposed to defray the additional costs of bringing up a family so it should surely be paid at a level appropriate to the country in which the child lives. Invariably, this is a far lower sum than it is here.

17. The first three of the five paragraphs of Article 50 of the Treaty of Lisbon are:

1. Any Member State may decide to withdraw from the Union in accordance with its own constitutional requirements.

2. A Member State which decides to withdraw shall notify the European Council of its intention. In the light of the guidelines provided by the European Council, the Union shall negotiate and conclude an agreement with that State, setting out the arrangements for its withdrawal, taking account of the framework for its future relationship with the Union. It shall be concluded on behalf of the Union by the Council, acting by a qualified majority, after obtaining the consent of the European Parliament.

3. The Treaties shall cease to apply to the State in question from the date of entry into force of the withdrawal agreement or, failing that, two years after the notification referred to in paragraph 2, unless the European Council, in agreement with the Member State concerned, unanimously decides to extend this period.

X is for a vote in favour of any of those sixty-plus possibilities of W is for what's to be done.

Y is for Yarlswood

A reception or holding centre burnt down by would-be immigrants so as to prevent or delay or obstruct their expulsion from this country.

And Y is for you couldn't make it up

When, in May 2014, the police raided a house in Marlborough Avenue, Goole, they found ninety-six cannabis plants and nineteen-year-old Byn Nguyen hiding behind some bins. His fingerprints were found on two cups and a can of Red Bull.

At the trial six months later, Byn Nguyen having been in custody since being apprehended, the judge decided/directed the jury:

> The Crown's case is that there were three fingerprints found at the scene. They are inviting you to infer by their presence [that he] was involved in cannabis production.
>
> Mere presence at the scene of a crime is not enough.
>
> If you or I had been to this house and sat down and had a cup of tea with those people who were running this, our conduct may be reprehensible but it would not mean we were guilty of drug production.
>
> He says he only stayed there the night. This case, to use the vernacular, stinks. The fact he has a nasty smell does not imply guilt.
>
> You the jury may have reached the view, as I have, that he was probably involved. It is highly [probable that] he did. But probable is not a crime.
>
> I have formed the view that there is just not enough evidence to prove [guilt].[1]

And said to Byn Nguyen:

> You are an illegal immigrant. You should not be in the UK. I have no idea how you got here. That is for the Home Office to sort out. I think it highly likely that you will be deported and not allowed back in the UK or any other European state. For you, it is a pyrrhic victory as you will be sent back to Vietnam.[1]

And the judge ordered:

> He will have to be reported to the Home Office. I am going to release him very shortly indeed. I would like the Home Office to know of this immediately, otherwise I think he will evaporate into what is described as the black economy.[1]

However, nobody came to collect Byn Nguyen. And so just two hours after leaving the dock, he was given £50 to get himself by train to Solihull.[2] He disappeared; he did not report to the Home Office.

A G4S security guard said,

> This is not the first time. We are fed up with it, frankly. We had an illegal immigrant we released from Grimsby Crown Court last Friday. We rang up the Home Office and they said, 'There is nobody here. It's 3 pm. Tell him to come and see us on Monday.' So we just let him go from the cells. It's a complete farce.

The Home Office said: 'We do not comment on individual cases.'

And Ann Widdecombe[3] said: 'You just could not make this up.'

Notes: Y is for you couldn't make it up

1. I haven't got a transcript, just various newspaper reports. At very least the sequence of the sentences may be wrong.

2. There is an 'immigration centre' in Birmingham and he had said he had a friend there.

3. MP 1987–2010, Maidstone/Maidstone and The Weald; inter alia, Minister of State for Prisons 1995–97; shadow Home Secretary 1999–2001.

And **Y** is for you haven't seen the half of it yet

Between 2001 and 2011, Bradford's population increased by 11%; the white British population reduced (from 76.1% to 63.9%), and

> 22.0% of the population is between 0 and 14 years of age. Only two other local authorities have a larger percentage – Slough and the London Borough of Barking and Dagenham.

> Bradford has the largest proportion of people of Pakistani ethnic origin (20.4%) in England, an increase of nearly 6% since the 2001 census (14.5%).[1]

The House of Lords Report contained the government actuary's statement that the population of England and Wales in 2006 was 53.8 million, with the projection that in 2031 it would be 63.7 million; an increase of 18.4%.

The 2011 census stated the then population of England and Wales to be 56,075,912: it was subsequently reported that such number was likely, with illegal and undeclared persons, to be another half million.

65% of babies born in London in 2010 had at least one foreign-born parent.

In 2011, of the babies born in England and Wales, one in four, so 25%, were to foreign-born mothers.

> More than one in four babies born in England and Wales are from mothers who arrived in Britain from other countries. In 2014 there were 695,000 births of which 188,000 [so 27%] were born to foreign mothers, the majority from Poland, Pakistan and India. That rate has doubled since Tony Blair launched his 1997 open door immigration policy ... In the census of 2001, just 16 per cent of births were to foreign-born mothers.[2]

Almost one in eight people now resident in Britain was born abroad.

The average Muslim woman throughout the EU has 3.5 children (as opposed to 1.4 by other women).

England needs 410 new primary schools so as to take the increasing number of pupils.

(*See* the first item under both P is for puzzle and Q is for *quod erat demonstrandum*).

Notes: *Y is for you haven't seen the half of it yet*

1. City of Bradford Metropolitan District Council.

2. *What's truly "nasty" is the meltdown in our maternity care* by Allison Pearson, *The Daily Telegraph*, October 2015.

Z is for zero-sum game

Foreign competition, both in the form of immigration and imported goods and services, has been a big constraint on wage growth. This, in turn, has limited the incentive for efficiency gain. Cheap labour has become a substitute for investment in plant, machinery, training and research and development.

When the last administration boasted of the umpteenth successive quarter of successive growth, it neglected to say that this was largely the result of population growth. Income per head was becoming progressively becalmed.

Britain is an open economy that certainly needs to be in the market for top international talent. Yet high levels of low-end immigration have been, at best, a zero-sum game and, by holding back necessary investment in the future, possibly quite a negative economic influence.[1]

The evidence – from the OECD, the House of Lords' Economic Affairs Committee and many academics – shows that while there are benefits of selective and controlled immigration, at best the net economic and fiscal effect of high immigration is close to zero.[2]

Notes: Z is for zero-sum game

1. *Mass immigration has made Britain a less competitive economy* by Jeremy Warner, *The Daily Telegraph*, September 2013.

2. Theresa May, when Home Secretary to the 2015 Conservative Party Conference 2015.

Abbreviations and acronyms

A8 (countries) = the eight states that joined the European Union on 1 May 2004, namely Czech Republic, Estonia, Hungary, Latvia, Lithuania, Poland, Slovakia and Slovenia, and whose citizens had free movement to, and employment in, the UK and two other EU states immediately from accession.

A2 (countries) = the two countries that joined the EU on 1 January 2007, namely Bulgaria and Romania, but whose citizens were entirely free to work throughout the EU from the start of 2014.

BME or BAME = black and minority ethnic.

EU = European Union.

ITEM Club = Independent Treasury Economic Model (an Independent economic forecasting group).

NIESR = National Institute of Economic and Social Research.

MP = Member of Parliament.

OBR = Office of Budget Responsibility.

The Clarke Report = the report by Peter Clarke CVO OBE QPM (head of Counter Terrorism Command at Scotland Yard 2002/08) entitled *Report into Allegations Concerning Birmingham Schools Arising from the 'Trojan Horse' letter*, July 2014:

> By 15 April [2014] events had moved on to the point where the Secretary of State for Education appointed [him] as the Education Commissioner for Birmingham, with a remit to investigate what had happened in the schools of concern; to gather and scrutinise evidence …

The Casey Report = the report by Louise Casey CB entitled *Report of Inspection of Rotherham Metropolitan Borough Council* to the House of Commons of February 2015.

The Jay Report = the report by Professor Alexis Jay OBE entitled *Independent Inquiry into Child Sexual Exploitation in Rotherham 1997– 2013*, August 2014. This was commissioned in October 2013 by Rotherham Metropolitan Borough Council.

The Kershaw Report = *Report of Ian Kershaw of Northern Education for*

Birmingham City Council in Respect of Issues Arising as a Result of Concerns Raised in a Letter Dated 27 November 2013, Known as the Trojan Horse letter.

The House of Lords Report = the Report of the House of Lords' Select Committee on Economic Affairs entitled *The Economic Impact of Immigration* published 1 April 2008. And a paragraph thereof is particularised by [paragraph…]

The Research Report = Research Report 72 of July 2013 entitled *Social and Public Service Impacts of International Migration at the Local Level* by Jon Simmons, Head of Migration and Border Analysis, Home Office, with Sarah Poppleton, Kate Hitchcock, Kitty Lymperopoulou and Rebecca Gillespie.

SIAC = Special Immigration Appeals Commission.

Author's notes

I understand that English and Arabic alphabets do not correspond and so, in English, it is either, or neither, Muslim or Moslem. However, the former seems to be the standard alternative. Similarly, in English, there is no one/correct way to spell either Mohammed or sharia. Similarly, with ISIS and ISIS (or Daesh) and *malak ul yameen.*

The translation of the Koran which I have used is by Arthur J. Arberry, Oxford University Press.

I have not changed the spelling of what is quoted, so for example 'colour' is spelt 'color' (when it is American).

Where there is a list or a series, I have tried to impose a sequence – but either alphabetical or chronological. The problem of grooming of (usually indigenous) girls by gangs of non-indigenous first became widely known following convictions in Derby, but it was foreshadowed years before, according to a policeman who was there, in Blackburn. Derby is followed, alphabetically but not necessarily chronologically, by Ipswich, Oxford, Rochdale, Rotherham and Telford.

COPYRIGHT

I refer to the introduction.

What is original may not be clear. *Unity through Diversity* (*see* O is for oxymoron) was in a newspaper article in 2008 by Sam Leith. It sounds orwellian but while perhaps not as old, it predates Mr Leith's article. In 1999, it was the theme of the presidential address to the British Psychological Society – *Unity through Diversity: an achievable goal*, in which the president, Ingrid Lunt, 'outlined her belief in the Society's ability to draw strength from the many facets of the discipline of psychology' (*The Psychologist*, vol. 12, no. 10).

'Unity through Diversity' is the strapline of the African Code (which must be somewhat tarnished by the antipathy of many Libyans to Qaddafi's 'African' mercenaries).

'United in diversity' is the motto of the European Union.

When quoting what was said, I have tried, while not quoting the entirety, to be sure that at least the import of what was being said is correctly portrayed. A prime example of this is what Ed Miliband said (*see* note 30 to B is for betrayal).

BIBLIOGRAPHY

At the beginning of this book I listed the newspapers and periodicals which I quote from. I also quote from the papers and reports for which there is an abbreviation (as above) plus the following:

The Economic and Fiscal Impact of Immigration – A cross-departmental submission to the House of Lords' Select Committee on Economic Affairs by the Home Office in partnership with the Department for Work and Pensions, October 2007.

Immigration and the Labour Market: Theory, Evidence and Policy by Will Somerville and Madeleine Sumption of the Migration Policy Institute, March 2009.

The Impacts of Migration on Social Cohesion and Integration by Shamit Saggar, Will Somerville, Rob Ford and Maria Sobolewska to the Migration Advisory Committee, January 2012.

Electoral fraud in the UK, both *Evidence and issues paper* of May 2013 and *Final Report and recommendations* of January 2014 plus *Elections voting and electoral fraud* by Valdeep Gill, Natalie Jago and Fatima Husain at NatCen Social Research.

Serious Case Review into CSE in Oxfordshire from the experiences of Children A, B, C, D, E, and F by Alan Bedford 2015.

And together with the following books:

The Other Half by Richard Ingrams and John Wells published by Private Eye Productions/Pressdram in 1981.

The Lives of Enoch Powell by Patrick Cosgrave, published by The Bodley Head in 1989.

The Great Immigration Scandal by Steve Moxon, published by Imprint Academic in 2004.

The Rage and the Pride and *The Force of Reason* by Oriana Fallaci, published by Rizzoli International in 2001 and 2006 respectively.

While Europe Slept: How Radical Islam is Destroying the West from Within by Bruce Bawer, published by Doubleday in 2006.

L'immigration par escroquerie sentimentale by Marie-Annick Delaunay, published by Tatamis in 2006.

Not with a Bang but a Whimper: The Politics & Culture of Decline by Theodore Dalrymple, published by Monday Books in 2009.

Orientalism and Islam by Michael Curtis, published by Cambridge University Press in 2009.

Jilted Generation: How Britain has Bankrupted its Youth by Ed Howker and Shiv Malik, published by Icon Books in 2010.

The Pinch: How the baby boomers took their children's future – and why they should give it back by David Willetts, published by Atlantic Books in 2010.

Guilty Men by Peter Oborne and Frances Weaver, with a foreword by Peter Jay, published by the Centre for Policy Studies in 2011.

The Islamic Republic of Dewsbury by Danny Lockwood, published by The Press News in 2011.

Enoch at 100 edited by Lord Howard of Rising, published by Biteback Publishing in 2012.

Europe's Unfinished Currency by Thomas Mayer, published by Anthem Press in 2012.

The British Dream: Successes and Failures of Post-War Immigration by David Goodhart, published by Atlantic Books in 2013.

The Diversity Illusion by Ed West, published by Gibson Square in 2013.

Exodus Immigration and Multiculturalism in the 21st Century by Paul Collier, published by Allen Lane in 2013.

'Easy Meat': Multiculturalism, Islam and Child Sex Slavery by Peter McLoughlin, published by the Law and Freedom Foundation in 2014.

Heaven's Door: Immigration Policy and the American Economy, *Immigration Economics* and *Immigration Economics* by George J. Borjas, published, respectively, by Princetown University Press in 1999 and Harvard University Press in 2014.

The Costs and Benefits of Large-scale Immigration by Robert Rowthorn, and *Race and Faith: The Deafening Silence* by Trevor Phillips published by Civitas: Institute for the Study of Civil Society in 2015 and 2016 respectively.

This book had pretty well been written before *This is London: Life and Death in the World City*, by Ben Judah, was published by Picador in early 2016. Obviously it is London centric but the following four items are from it

> Every week two thousand migrants unload at Victoria Coach Station. This is where tens of thousands of migrants arrive every year, the equivalent of a whole city, the size of Basildon or Bath.

> The English don't want to live in this borough anymore ... The white British population is now around 18 per cent. South Asians make up 33 per cent. The black population, roughly 19 per cent. Between 2001 and 2011 the white British population of Brent tumbled: losing almost 30 per cent.

> The Teacher is Nigerian [... He] has promised to tell me what the schoolchildren are like in Plaistow, where almost 80 per cent speak English as a second language and less than 10 per cent are white British.

> In 2005 and 2006 the police conducted 802 skunk raids in London and found over two-thirds run by Vietnamese gangs. The locations: suburban houses, railway lines and wreckers' yards.

Appendix I

This appendix was to have been examples of, for the most part, egregious crime by immigrants. There were over twenty pages, with individuals and types from A8/A2 rapists through bent coppers, crash for cash con artists, crooked lawyers, lover murderers, muggers, postmen to welfare thieves. Despite those different types, the Appendix got rather tedious so here instead is what was to be T is for three tales of today in three cities.

First. Rachel Kenehan (born *c*.1979) took a degree at the London School of Economics. She went on to teach sociology and psychology at the London Metropolitan University and to study for a PhD in criminology at the University of Essex. In 2012, she met Pierre Lewis (born *c*.1992) of Castlenau, Barnes, through a prisoner-mentoring scheme while he was in prison. After his release, she financed him in the supply and transport of class-A drugs to Southampton.

Jahmel Jones (born *c*.1991) of Brixton sold crack cocaine and heroin in the St Mary's area of the city of Southampton.

Isaac Boateng (born *c*.1981 of Cloudesdale Road, Tooting) with Lewis and Jemmikai Orlebar-Forbes (born *c*.1982, of Mill Farm Crescent, Hounslow) fell out with Jones. Boateng, Lewis and Orlebar-Forbes travelled from London to Southampton, where on 20 April 2013 Orlebar-Forbes shot Jones twice, once in the head: he died in hospital three days later. Kenehan texted Lewis: 'be smart, act normal … don't disappear, that'll look weird'. The three got a taxi to Basingstoke. Kenehan picked them up from there and took them back to her flat in Hewlett Road, Tower Hamlets, where they stayed for three days. Lewis's trainers were found there; they had been 'wiped' with white spirit.

The three admitted two counts of conspiracy to supply class-A drugs but denied murder. All three were convicted and sentenced to life, with Pierre Lewis to a minimum of twenty-nine years, Isaac Boateng thirty years and Jemmikai Orlebar-Forbes thirty-one years.

Kenehan was convicted of assisting offenders, conspiracy to supply class-A drugs and with perverting the course of justice.

After the trial, Jones's mother said,

> Though nothing will bring Jahmel back I am pleased we now have justice for his family. Jahmel had his life taken from him – it is wrong ... Jahmel was a loving son, dad and cousin. We are all still feeling the loss of Jahmel. His brother, sister, grandmother, cousins, aunts and uncles, friends and neighbours truly miss him,

but not a word about the harm to the citizens of St Mary's and the rest of Southampton.

Second.[1] Omar Abdi (59) came from Somalia to Scotland in 1990. His son Mohammed (25) attended Drummond Community High School, Edinburgh. Mr Abdi became a lecturer in Arabic and Somali, and an imam at Edinburgh Central Mosque. In the spring of 2013, some of the family moved to Birmingham but father and son stayed on in a flat in Buchanan Street.

On 3 May 2013, the flat was raided by police who found (illegal) drugs. Mohammed was arrested, and charged with possession and supply and in connection with the proceeds of crime.

Mr Abdi (senior) was 'shocked' and 'I asked [Mohammed] about the drugs and he said it belonged to his friend' and warned him, 'I told him anyone involved in this either ended up in jail or being murdered.'

And so it came to pass.

At some point during the night of 25/26 May 2013, Mohammed evaded a trap, but early in the morning of the 26th, with one or more of Abdulrakim Abdulrahman, Mohamed Farah and Mohammed El-Helili, he was seen in a Ford Focus by one or more of Hussein Ali (26), Cadil Huseen (23) and Mohamud Mohamud (30) plus Ahmed Ahmed (28), Liban Ahmed (30), Said Fadal (32) and Said Tarabi (27), who were in either a VW Sharan (registration number FT62 TFX) and/or a Ford Fiesta. A report has them coming up from Birmingham to see Mohammed or rather 'to see to' him as in one or other car they had a 'spray and pray' Mac-10 and a converted revolver: mobile phone records and CCTV 'have' the cars coming from London to Glasgow and onto Edinburgh. The two cars did a U-ey and chased the Focus. It forced the Fiesta to pull in, and the Sharan crashed. Mohammed ran at it with a baseball bat but was cut down by the Mac-10. Five shots were taken before it jammed; it was found in undergrowth. The revolver, which had been fired four times, was found in one of the two vehicles. Mohamud was caught at the scene. Huseen hid in a garden shed and then fled to London, where he was detained on 4 June 2013. Ali got all the way to Kenya but gave up when extradition proceedings started.

The seven 'visitors' from Birmingham or further south pleaded not guilty, until the fourth week of the trial when the first three changed their pleas (whereupon the Crown accepted the not guilty plea of the other four 'visitors').

The deceased's father, who coincidentally was in Birmingham when his son was killed, said,

> Nothing will bring my son back but I am relieved to know the persons who committed this terrible crime will no longer be able to hurt anyone and I hope no other family will have to suffer as we have. I would like to thank wholeheartedly the various communities across Edinburgh who were affected by this tragic death and went on to provide vital support for the police investigation.

but there was not a word of contrition for the harm done by his son's drug purveying.

Note to second story

The story was put together from *BBC News* and newspaper reports including the *Somaliland Sun* and *The Express*, which latter on 14 June 2014 (*Edinburgh machine-gun killers jailed for life*, by Rod Mills), included the following:

At the High Court in Glasgow, Lord Turnbull said they were engaged in a 'wholly corrupt lifestyle' and were prepared to 'engage in violence of an extreme nature'.

He added, 'This is a level of criminality seldom seen in our country and mercifully so.'

Commenting on the killers' Somali background, Lord Turnbull said, 'It is very disappointing to realise that you abused the opportunity of a new life free from the violence and oppression which your parents sought to escape.'

Mohamud and Ali showed little emotion as they were taken down. Huseen smiled and gave a thumbs-up.

In the run-up to the murder, a Somalian crime network with London connections was operating in Edinburgh and Glasgow. Huseen and Ali were involved in large-scale drug dealing with Mohamud, a close associate. There were claims Huseen and Ali earned £15,000 a week and downed £100 bottles of vodka and brandy in nightclubs.

Mr Abdi had been close to the group but had set up a rival gang. His move sparked tit-for-tat incidents leading up to the fatal shooting in Duddingston on May 26 last year.

Two days earlier, a friend of Huseen and Ali sent a message to an associate of Mr Abdi warning: 'The guns are coming out.'

The groups clashed after a high-speed car chase through Edinburgh. Five shots were fired from the machine-gun, three hitting Mr Abdi. Mr Abdi's friend, Mohammed El-Halil, recalled 'flashes' before finding the victim in a pool of blood. He told the jury that Mr Abdi had just gone past his car 'with a big smile on his face'.

Mohamud was caught at the scene. Huseen and Ali both fled but were tracked down later.

Police Scotland said the investigation cost £323,486 and was the most expensive since the start of the single force.

Third. Mohammed Yasser ('Yasa') Afzal was a minicab controller for E20 on Stratford Broadway, and Nargis Riaz, the daughter of a Muslim cleric, was reading law at City University. They became intimate and on his phone there were photos of them together. She became frightened that he would post them online and to her parents.

In February 2014, Gulam Chowdhury was released from an immigration detention centre where he had got religion. Within days of his release, he became reacquainted with Riaz and in the following month they exchanged about 8,000 messages, which included:

From him to her:

I am willing to burn in hell for you, I swear

I am going to sort this out and sort it proper. I will use the flame from my ancestors to burn the world of this scum ... no one will hurt Nargis and live ... A killing would be justified according to Islam [because of the words 'Cut the neck of the man who eyed up his wife']

Don't worry little angel, it's me who's the psycho not you

And from her to him:

How would I live with myself knowing I got you to do the ultimate?

And Chowdhury texted Muhammad Khan:

I was going to get a black boy to steal Yasa's phone and make it look like a jacking.

At 8 pm on 24 March 2014, a hooded man leapt over the counter where Yasa worked and stabbed him twenty times. Riaz appeared from the back of the premises. The next day her phone was restored to its factory settings.

Chowdhury and Riaz were tried for Yasa's murder and Khan for assisting an offender. Chowdhury was convicted; the jury could not reach a decision as to Riaz; Khan was acquitted. A year later a second jury acquitted Riaz.

Appendix II

The Labour Party's manifesto of 2005 as to immigration

Migration: The facts

Over seven million people entered the UK from outside the EU in 2003 of whom 180,000 came here to work and over 300,000 to study, with the rest coming here as business visitors and tourists. People from overseas spent almost £12 billion in the UK, and overseas students alone are worth £5 billion a year to our economy. At a time when we have over 600,000 vacancies in the UK job market, skilled migrants are contributing 10–15% of our economy's growth.

Since 1997, the time taken to process an initial asylum application has been reduced from twenty months to two months in over 80% of cases. The number of asylum applications has been cut by two thirds since 2002. The backlog of claims has been cut from over 50,000 at the end of 1996 to just over 10,000. There are 550 UK Immigration Officers posted in France and Belgium to check passports of people boarding boats and trains, and Airline Liaison Officers and overseas entry clearance staff are helping to stop over 1,000 people improperly entering the UK.

Building a strong and diverse country

For centuries Britain has been a home for people from the rest of Europe and further afield. Immigration has been good for Britain. We want to keep it that way.

Our philosophy is simple: if you are ready to work hard and there is work for you to do, then you are welcome here. We need controls that work and a crackdown on abuse to ensure that we have a robust and fair immigration system fit for the twenty-first century that is in the interests of Britain.

A points system for immigration

We need skilled workers. So we will establish a points system for those seeking to migrate here. More skills mean more points and more chance of being allowed to come here.

We will ensure that only skilled workers are allowed to settle long-term in the UK with English language tests for everyone who wants to stay permanently and an end to chain migration.

Where there has been evidence of abuse from particular countries, the immigration service will be able to ask for financial bonds to guarantee that migrants return home. We will continue to improve the quality and speed of immigration and asylum decisions. Appeal rights for non-family immigration cases will be removed and we will introduce civil penalties on employers of up to £2,000 for each illegal immigrant they employ here.

Strong and secure borders

While the Tories would halve investment in our immigration services, we would invest in the latest technology to keep our borders strong and secure.

By 2008, those needing a visa to enter the UK will be fingerprinted. We will issue ID cards to all visitors planning to say for more than three months. Over the next five years we will implement a new electronic borders system that will track visitors entering or leaving the UK.

Across the world there is a drive to increase the security of identity documents and we cannot be left behind. From next year we are introducing biometric 'ePassports'. It makes sense to provide citizens with an equally secure identity card to protect them at home from identity theft and clamp down on illegal working and fraudulent use of public services. We will introduce ID cards, including biometric data like fingerprints, backed up by a national register and rolling out initially on a voluntary basis as people renew their passports.

Fair rules

We can and should honour our obligations to victims of persecution without allowing abuse of the asylum system. We will:

- Fast-track all unfounded asylum seekers with electronic tagging where necessary and more use of detention as we expand the number of detention places available.

- Remove failed applicants. We have more than doubled the number of failed asylum seekers we remove from the UK compared to 1996. By finger printing every visa applicant and prosecuting those who deliberately destroy their documents we will speed up the time taken to redocument and remove people and will take action against those countries that refuse to cooperate. By the end of 2005, our aim is for removals of failed asylum seekers to exceed new unfounded claims.

Tough action to combat international terrorism

We know that there are people already in the country and who seek to enter the United Kingdom who want to attack our way of life. Our liberties are prized but so is our security.

Police and other law enforcement agencies now have the powers they need to ban terrorist organisations, to clamp down on their fundraising and to hold suspects for extended questioning while charges are brought. Over 700 arrests have been made since 2001. Wherever possible, suspects should be prosecuted through the courts in the normal way. So we will introduce new laws to help catch and convict those involved in helping to plan terrorist activity or who glorify or condone acts of terror. But we also need to disrupt and prevent terrorist activity. New control orders will enable police and security agencies to keep track on those who they suspect of planning terrorist outrages including bans on who that can contact or meet, electronic tagging and curfew orders, and for those who present the highest risk, a requirement to stay permanently at home.

We will continue to improve coordination between enforcement agencies and cooperation with other countries so that every effort is made to defeat the terrorists.

The Labour Party's manifesto of 2010 as to immigration

The choice for 2010

Labour's goals for 2010 are clear. Overall crime down, the number of offenders brought to justice up, with a neighbourhood policing team in every community to crack down on crime and disorder and a modern criminal justice system fit for the twenty-first century. And to reduce threats from overseas: secure borders backed up by ID cards and a crackdown on abuse of our immigration system. The Conservative threat is equally clear. Savage cuts to our border controls, 'fantasy island' asylum policies and a return to the days of broken promises on police numbers and crime investment.

Appendix III

The Conservative Party's manifesto of 2010 as to immigration

Attract the brightest and best to our country

Immigration has enriched our nation over the years and we want to attract the brightest and the best people who can make a real difference to our economic growth. But immigration today is too high and needs to be reduced. We do not need to attract people to do jobs that could be carried out by British citizens, given the right training and support. So we will take steps to take net migration back to the levels of the 1990s – tens of thousands a year, not hundreds of thousands.

To help achieve this goal, we will introduce a number of measures, such as:

- setting an annual limit on the number of non-EU economic migrants admitted into the UK to live and work;

- limiting access only to those who will bring the most value to the British economy; and,

- applying transitional controls as a matter of course in the future for all new EU Member States.

In addition, we will promote integration into British society, as we believe that everyone coming to this country must be ready to embrace our core values and become a part of their local community. So there will be an English language test for anyone coming here to get married.

We want to encourage students to come to our universities and colleges, but our student visa system has become the biggest weakness in our border controls. A Conservative government will strengthen the system of granting student visas so that it is less open to abuse. We want to make it easier for reputable universities and colleges to accept applications, while putting extra scrutiny on new institutions looking to accept foreign students or existing institutions not registered with Companies House. In addition, we will:

- insist foreign students at new or unregistered institutions pay a bond in order to study in this country, to be repaid after the student has left the country at the end of their studies;

- ensure foreign students can prove that they have the financial means to support themselves in the UK; and,

- require that students must usually leave the country and reapply if they want to switch to another course or apply for a work permit.

The Conservative Party's manifesto of 2015 as to immigration

Controlled immigration that benefits Britain

Our commitment to you:

Our plan to control immigration will put you, your family and the British people first. We will reduce the number of people coming to our country with tough new welfare conditions and robust enforcement. We will:

- keep our ambition of delivering annual net migration in the tens of thousands, not the hundreds of thousands

- control migration from the European Union, by reforming welfare rules

- clamp down on illegal immigration and abuse of the Minimum Wage

- enhance our border security and strengthen the enforcement of immigration rules

- develop a fund to ease pressure on local areas and public services.

Conservatives believe in controlled immigration, not mass immigration. Immigration brings real benefits to Britain – to our economy, our culture and our national life. We will always be a party that is open, outward looking and welcoming to people from all around the world. We also know that immigration must be controlled. When immigration is out of control, it puts pressure on schools, hospitals and transport; and it can cause social pressures if communities find it hard to integrate.

We must work to control immigration and put Britain first

Between 1997 and 2009, under the last Labour Government, we had the largest influx of people Britain had ever seen. Their open borders policy, combined with their failure to reform welfare, meant that for years over 90% of employment growth in this country was accounted for by foreign nationals – even though there were 1.4 million people who spent most of the 2000s living on out-of-work benefits. For the past five years, we have been working to turn around the situation we inherited.

Since 2010, we have stripped more than 850 bogus colleges of their rights to sponsor foreign students; installed proper exit checks at our borders; cracked down on illegal working and sham marriages; made it harder for people to live in the UK illegally, by restricting their access to bank accounts, driving licences and private housing; and reduced the number of appeal routes to stop people clogging up our courts with spurious attempts to remain in the country. All of this has made a difference. Immigration from outside the EU has come down since 2010.

Non-EU migration cut by 13 per cent – and economic migration from outside the EU capped

We have seen many more people from the EU coming to Britain than originally anticipated, principally because our economy has been growing so much more rapidly and creating more jobs than other EU countries. As a result, our action has not been enough to cut annual net migration to the tens of thousands. That ambition remains the right one. But it is clearly going to take more time, more work and more difficult long-term decisions to achieve. Continuing this vital work will be our priority over the next five years.

We will negotiate new rules with the EU, so that people will have to be earning for a number of years before they can claim benefits, including the tax credits that top up low wages. Instead of something-for-nothing, we will build a system based on the principle of something-for-something. We will then put these changes to the British people in a straight in–out referendum on our membership of the European Union by the end of 2017. At the same time, we will continue to strengthen our borders, improve the enforcement of our immigration laws and act to make sure people leave at the end of their visas. Across the spectrum, from the student route to the family and work routes, we will build a system that truly puts you, your family and the British people first.

Our plan of action:

We will regain control of EU migration by reforming welfare rules

Changes to welfare to cut EU migration will be an absolute requirement in the renegotiation. We have already banned housing benefit for EU jobseekers, and restricted other benefits, including Jobseeker's Allowance. We will insist that EU migrants who want to claim tax credits and child benefit must live here and contribute to our country for a minimum of four years. This will reduce the financial incentive for lower-paid, lower skilled workers to come to Britain. We will introduce a new residency requirement for social housing, so that EU migrants cannot even be considered for a council house unless they have been living in an area for at least four years. If an EU migrant's child is living abroad, then they should receive no child benefit or child tax credit, no matter how long they have worked in the UK and no matter how much tax they have paid. To reduce the numbers of EU migrants coming to Britain, we will end the ability of EU jobseekers to claim any job-seeking benefits at all. And if jobseekers have not found a job within six months, they will be required to leave.

We will tackle criminality and abuse of free movement

We will negotiate with the EU to introduce stronger powers to deport criminals and stop them coming back, and tougher and longer re-entry bans for all those who abuse free movement. We want to toughen requirements for non-EU spouses to join EU citizens, including with an income threshold and English language test. And when new countries are admitted to the EU in future, we will insist that free movement cannot apply to those new members until their economies have converged much more closely with existing Member States.

We will continue to cut immigration from outside the EU

We have already capped the level of skilled economic migration from outside the EU. We will maintain our cap at 20,700 during the next Parliament. This will ensure that we only grant visas to those who have the skills we really need in our economy. We will reform the student visa system with new measures to tackle abuse and reduce the numbers of students overstaying once their visas expire. Our action will include clamping down on the number of so-called 'satellite campuses' opened in London by universities located elsewhere in the UK, and reviewing the highly trusted sponsor system for student visas. And as the introduction of exit checks will allow us to place more responsibility on visa sponsors for migrants who overstay, we will introduce targeted sanctions for those colleges or businesses that fail to ensure that migrants comply with the terms of their visa.

We will strengthen the enforcement of immigration rules

We have introduced a 'deport first, appeal later' rule for foreign national offenders. We will now remove even more illegal immigrants by extending this rule to all immigration appeals and judicial reviews, including where a so-called right to family life is involved, apart from asylum claims. We will also implement a new removals strategy to take away opportunities for spurious legal challenge and opportunities to abscond. We will introduce satellite tracking for every foreign national offender subject to an outstanding deportation order or deportation proceedings. And we will implement the requirement for all landlords to check the immigration status of their tenants.

We will tackle people trafficking and exploitation

We have already re-introduced a proper system of exit checks across the country, passed a Modern Slavery Act that will protect people from exploitation, and quadrupled the fines for unscrupulous employers who undercut the Minimum Wage. Now we will introduce tougher labour market regulation to tackle illegal working and exploitation. To crack down further on illegal working, we will harness data from multiple agencies, including Exit Checks data, to identify illegal immigrants and businesses that employ illegal workers. And to incentivise tougher action on employers who do not pay the minimum wage, we will allow inspection teams to reinvest more of the money raised by fines levied on employers.

We will ease pressure on public services and your local community

We are taking unprecedented action to tackle health tourism and will recover up to £500 million from migrants who use the NHS by the middle of the next Parliament. To help communities experiencing high and unexpected volumes of immigration, we will introduce a new Controlling Migration Fund to ease pressures on services and to pay for additional immigration enforcement. To prevent sectors becoming partially or wholly reliant on foreign workers, we will require those regularly utilising the Shortage Occupation List, under which they can bring skilled foreign workers into the UK, to provide long-term plans for training British workers.

We will protect British values and our way of life

We will promote integration and British values

Being able to speak English is a fundamental part of integrating into our society. We have introduced tough new language tests for migrants and ensured councils reduce spending on translation services. Next, we will legislate to ensure that every public sector worker operating in a customer-facing role must speak fluent English. And to encourage better integration into our society, we will also require those coming to Britain on a family visa with only basic English to become more fluent over time, with new language tests for those seeking a visa extension.

Appendix IV

Examples of medical or other failures by immigrant medics/care workers

- Yaha al-Abed removed a pregnant woman's ovary instead of her appendix.

- Madhafar Alhiwidi, a locum consultant at Leicester Royal Infirmary, in attempting a gall bladder operation, punctured an artery three times; a fitness to practice panel ruled he must be supervised when performing surgery.

- Manjit Bhamra, four of whose patients in Rotherham Hospital have between them had payouts totalling £1,005,000. This was on top of £1,058,784 between thirteen other claimants and with ninety-four other claims at that time still being processed.

- Midwife Inegbagha Bioelemoye ignored Heather Paterson Croft's cries so that her baby Riley died with the umbilical cord around his neck.

- Fadzai Jaravazza, an NHS Direct nurse, was struck off after failing to realise a patient had swine flu (the patient died the day after being seen by Jaravazza).

- Camellia Jurcut failed to diagnose that abdominal pain was an ectopic pregnancy and failed to find that an eighty-six-year-old who complained of neck pain, after a fall, had a broken neck.

- Abdullah Khan, father of six, was suspended for a year by the Nursing and Midwifery Council for limiting his care to a ninety-seven-year-old with a broken neck in a care home in Blackburn to two paracetamol tablets.

- Rajendra Kokharne may have been distracted by sports websites while prescribing drugs: as the result two patients died of morphine poisoning.

- Emmanuel Labram went before the Medical Practitioners Tribunal, facing eleven allegations that he 'lied and lied and lied in order to cover up his initial failure'. He was found guilty of serious misconduct and struck off the medical register – for 'behaviour [that] would be regarded as deplorable by fellow practitioners and the public'.

- Nchokhoa Mtetwa arrived here in 2005 from South Africa on a temporary visa. A few years later, Elsie Skelton, eighty-six and suffering from Parkinson's disease, was found face down with Mtetwa leaning over her. Mtetwa told a fellow care worker, 'We will tell them she went while we were washing her otherwise they will be on our backs for the rest of our days.' Mrs Skelton died from 'compression of the neck'. A jury failed to reach a verdict on murder. The Crown accepted Mtetwa's plea of manslaughter.

- Yvonne Musonda-Malata was found by the Nursing and Midwifery Council to have failed to provide appropriate clinical care, after a colleague went to the stationery cupboard for an envelope and found a four-day-old baby, despite protesting, 'I did not put the baby in the cupboard. At all. I did not.'

- Anthony Muyinda was struck off by the Nursing and Midwifery Council for failing to attempt to resuscitate a patient.

- Nigeria-trained Francesca Ogunbiyi advised Jeffrey Wingrove, after he collapsed with severe vomiting and crippling headaches, that he was suffering from vertigo and refused to visit him. He died forty-eight hours later; she subsequently appealed against the warning, which has to be provided to employers for five years.

- Nikolaos Papanikolaou admitted charges as to perforating a patient's uterus as he tried to remove what he thought was abnormal tissue but was part of the patient's bowel; she died. In other cases, he allegedly left swabs in patients but it was held that 'The overall standard of care fell seriously below standards expected of a specialist registrar'.

- Hungarian-born and Egypt-trained Gyorgy Radoczy was suspended by the General Medical Council for injecting a child with too much carbolic acid.

- Nigeria-trained Daniel Ubani gave seventy-year-old David Gray ten times the recommended dosage of diamorphine. The GMC struck him off the register for such and errors in the treatment of two other patients on one shift: it found he had shown a 'persistent lack of insight into the seriousness of his actions'. He still practises in Germany.

- Jacques Vallet, having failed to anaesthetise his patient properly and inform the surgeon, was found by a fitness to practice panel to be impaired; the panel put him under strict conditions with which he did not comply.

- Sabah al-Zayyat was the last doctor to see Baby Peter alive, then not noticing that he had a broken back; she left the country as the GMC's hearing was about to start.

And failings other than medical

- Omar Sheik Mohamed Addow was struck off the General Dental Council for offering to effect FGM. He was not present for the Council's hearing; it seems that following arrest and interview (by the police), he returned to Somalia.

- Mirela Aionoaei drugged dementia patients so that she could get a good night's rest.

- Farhad Allybokus put his hands around the waist of his stroke patient's daughter; the Nursing and Midwifery Council's disciplinary panel found 'a significant risk of the repetition of this behaviour'.

- Badar Masud Aslam was acquitted of sexual assault but the General Pharmaceutical Council decided that his conduct impaired his fitness to practice and was 'satisfied that it is not necessary to send any further message to Mr Aslam. The finding of impairment is by itself sufficient sanction.'

- Asim Ayyub was struck off for downloading pornography while working but asked to be reinstated as such behaviour, he argued, was not incompatible with being a medic.

- Oliver Balico was convicted of attacking a teenager in a side room in the John Radcliffe Hospital and sexually assaulting a foreign student.

- Mohammad Barakat was struck off by the General Medical Council for forging a medical report as to his wife; their marriage came apart following her discovery of an indecent photograph of him on a website.

- Care assistants – Sonia Limbu and Pargash Kaur Sahota beat and abused dementia patients.

- Victorino Chua from the Philippines was a nurse at Stepping Hill Hospital but murdered two patients and poisoned another twenty.

- Barend Delport admitted sexually assaulting child patients and pleaded guilty to having half a million indecent images of children on his computer.

- Devasenan Devendra was meant to undertake a trial to develop treatment for Muslim diabetics who fast during Ramadan; he claimed to have sixty-nine subjects for the trial but had only six.

- Nafees Hamid, neurosurgeon, trained in Pakistan but moved here in 2000. He is now serving sixteen years for sexually assaulting six women in either Birmingham's Queen Elizabeth Hospital or the city's Priory Hospital.

- Chuma Igbokwe, Niger's consul to this country, was suspended by the General Medical Council, having lost a tribunal hearing for sexual harassment.

- Humayun Iqbal was struck of the medical register for sexually assaulting junior colleagues.

- Gousul Islam pleaded not guilty to accusations of assaulting women and girls over twenty-plus years; he was found guilty on eighteen counts and sentenced to eleven years.

- Noah Kantoh asked a teenage cleaner to fill in the three-month sex gap while his wife was pregnant.

- Hassan Khan was sentenced to three years for sexually assaulting a patient in a cubicle after she had an epileptic fit; the fitness to practice panel held him to be 'a great risk to patients'.

- Hung Kor was given a suspended jail sentence in 2011 for obtaining property by deception and making false representations; the Medical Practitioners Tribunal Service heard that he faked prescriptions to feed his drug habit.

- Anthony Madu was taken on by Cardiff and Vale University Hospital in August 2009. Two months later he was suspended. From the start of 2010, he submitted sick notes but worked at Sandwell General Hospital, Scarborough General Hospital and The Royal Oldham Hospital. He transferred £98,000 to a bank in Nigeria.

- Shabbir Merchant was suspended by the General Dental Council after admitting various charges including poor treatment and suggestive comments to a nurse less than three years after being jailed for submitting false invoices to the NHS.

- Nontuthuzelo Ngetu was dismissed by Avon and Wiltshire Mental Health Partnership NHS Trust after leaving confidential patient records in bags of food.

- Sunil Parmar falsely invoiced Maidstone Hospital for locum services. He received a suspended jail term and by the Medical Practitioners Tribunal Service was banned from practising for nine months.

- Freddy Patel trained at the University of Zambia. He was the pathologist who effected the first post mortem examination of Ian Tomlinson, who died after being knocked to the ground by a policeman at the G20 riots. He has been declared unfit to practise, 'having brought the profession into disrepute' and breached one of the 'fundamental tenets of the profession' through his dishonesty; apart from the Tomlinson post mortem there were other cases in which he acted 'irresponsibly'.

- Raghuvir Patel was reprimanded by the General Dental Council for throwing a broken dental brace at his patient's mother. In response to his lack of recollection, the Council stated, 'It was incredible that you could not remember such a unique experience.' He was cleared of making comments of a sexual nature to a member of staff.

- Naraindrakoomar Sahodree raped a wheelchair-bound patient in the National Hospital for Neurology and Neurosurgery. He had got a job there despite previously having been convicted of indecent assault.

- Savi Sondhi ran an out-of-hours service for Londoners from his home in Norfolk and drew £100,000 he was not entitled to. The police want to interview him but believe he may have left the country.

- Jahangir Taghipour was acquitted of sexual assault – allegedly groping a patient and telling her that 'westernised women open their legs too easily'. The Medical Practitioners Tribunal Service found his behaviour inappropriate and sexually motivated.

Appendix V

Paragraph 549 of the judgment as to Mohammed Rahman securing the mayoralty of Tower Hamlets in 2014 by corrupt and illegal practices: *see* V is for Vote rigging.

Bearing in mind that any grammatical infelicities are the responsibility of the translator and not the authors of the Bengali original, the text of the letter is as follows:

BE UNITED AGAINST INJUSTICE: MAKE LUTFUR RAHMAN VICTORIOUS

Creating opportunities, making provisions and providing services to the citizens on behalf of Her Excellency the Queen. In this case everyone has a freedom of right to choose a candidate who is suitable and able to provide the services. However we are observing that the media propagandas, narrow political interests etc involving the Mayoral election of Tower Hamlets Council have created a kind of a negative impression which in turn have created confusions amongst the public, divided the community and put the community in question. We are further observing that today's Tower Hamlets have made significant and enviable improvements in the areas of housing, education, community cohesion, inter-faith harmony, road safety and youth developments. In order to retain this success and make further progress it is essential that someone is elected as mayor of Tower Hamlets Borough on 22 May who is able to lead these improvements and who will not discriminate on the basis of language, colour and religious identities.

We observe that some people are targeting the languages, colours and religions and attempting to divide the community by ignoring the cohesion and harmony of the citizens. This is, in fact, hitting the national, cultural and religious 'multi' ideas of the country and spreading jealousy and hatred in the community. We consider these acts as abominable and at the same time condemnable.

With utmost concern we observe that by shunning the needs and opportunities of the Tower Hamlets Council and its citizens, Islamophobia, which is the result of the current political stance and which has derived from false imagination, has been made an agenda for voting and voters. The mosques and religious organisations have been targeted. It is being publicised that any relationship [involvement] with the religious scholars and clerics are condemnable and is an offence. Religious beliefs and religious practice are being criticised. One of the local former councillors of the Labour Party has stated in the BBC's Panorama programme that 'Religions divide people'. Even in the same programme the honourable Imam of the Holy Kaba Sharif was presented in negative and defaming ways and thus all the religious people, particularly the Muslims, have been insulted and thrown in to a state of anxiety. We cannot support these ill attempts under any circumstances. We believe that it is not an offence to be a Muslim voter, an imam or Khatib of a mosque and have involvement with all these. Under no circumstances it is acceptable to give a voter less value or to criticise them on the basis of their identity. As voters, like in any other elections we also have a right to vote in the forthcoming Tower Hamlets Mayoral Election and we should have the opportunity to cast our votes without fear. As a cognisant group of the community and responsible voters and for the sake of truth, justice, dignity and development we express our unlimited support for Mayor Lutfur Rahman and strongly call upon you, the residents of Tower Hamlets, to shun all the propagandas and slanders and unite against the falsehood and injustice.

Appendix VI

Multiracial myths? by Raymond Honeyford and published by the *Times Educational Supplement*, November 1982.

(The copy I have has some corners etc. missing. I think I have been able to work out nearly all of what is missing, but, where I haven't, I have shown the gap with an asterisk: if I have departed from the original, there was no mischievous intent.)

> Multiracial education is attracting increasing interest. There is now a National Association for Multiracial Education: the educational journal of the Commission for Racial Equality frequently carries articles by both indigenous and minority group teachers which claim there is a 'theory' of multiracial education to which all those training for and currently working in schools must be exposed: there is a plethora of ethnic voluntary groups with interests in the school curriculum: local authorities are rushing to appoint advisers in the subject: others are anxious to appoint very highly paid 'experts' to oversee and investigate employment policies and there is a sizeable, if somewhat dubious, corpus of research now available.
>
> The tone of the debate is often strident. Claims and counter-claims are being heard from various sectional interests and there is sometimes a note of intolerance. The chairman of one of the sub-committees of a large metropolitan area recently and publicly declared that any headteacher failing to accept the multiracial policy of the L.E.A. – a policy which manifestly did not exist – would be sacked. So it is difficult to resist the feeling that a very considerable bandwagon is now underway.
>
> But some teachers regard the whole notion of multiracial education with scepticism and * resentment. They would argue that the responsibility for the adaptions and adjustments involved in settling in a new country * with those who have come here to settle and raise families of their own free will. A large majority of the Asians come from a country which is not even a member of the British Commonwealth. They have exercised their legal right to British citizenship, conferred as a direct result of living in territory formerly part of the British empire.
>
> They enjoy all the rights and privileges of equal citizenship, including immediate and unlimited access to the welfare state. In return, they are obliged to bear the corresponding duties and responsibilities of the

citizenship of their chosen land including the duty to send their children to school regularly.

Their commitment to a British education was implicit in their decision to become British citizens. Maintenance and transmission of the mother culture has nothing to do with the English secular school. If they want their children to absorb the culture of Pakistan, India or the Caribbean, then that is an entirely private decision to be implemented by the immigrant family and community, out of school.

Communities of immigrants from Poland, Hungary, Yugoslavia, the Ukraine and the innumerable Jewish settlers in this country have survived and flourished because they insisted their children get the best possible English education, while maintaining their cultural identity through private initiatives. The same pattern is also appropriate for children whose parents come from the New Commonwealth.

This is pragmatism, not prejudice, and it is based on equality. There should be a welcome for the strangers in our midst, but no attempt by the education service to confer a privileged position on this sub-culture or that.

But this non-interventionist approach is frowned upon by the multiracialists who argue for radically new approaches to schooling. Much of their argument rests on the belief that this country has a moral need to expiate its imperial guilt by providing a special form of education for the children of Commonwealth immigrants. This stresses the validity and achievements of Asian and Caribbean history and seeks to enhance the status and self-respect of settler children by teaching the culture of their parents' mother land and a critical view of British imperialism.

This confuses education with propaganda; makes questionable assumptions about the self-concept and actual cultural experiences of children born and bred here; stems from an historical perspective which is at least questionable; and could prove divisive in its effect. Moreover, guilt and recrimination about the past hardly seem constructive foundations on which to build a sense of harmony and reconciliation.

Those who argue for positive discrimination want more spent on the education of black and coloured children; lower admission standards for higher education for such children and quotas to ensure more immigrants get into the professions.

It is difficult, to see how positive discrimination could, in the long run, benefit the immigrant communities. It might well, indeed, exacerbate their difficulties. Would not other minority groups resent the favouritism and demand similar provision for their children? And would the public respect a professional class which has had privileged treatment in the process of selection for training? Would there not, indeed, be a danger of the public assuming lower level of professional competence? And would it help the cause of racial harmony?

The effects of a quota system based on the colour of the failed indigenous candidate needs to be spelled out.

Racial prejudice exists but is emphatically not a white versus black phenomenon. There is plenty of animosity between Asian and West Indian communities in this country as the Home Office survey of racial attacks (November 1981) showed.

Neither is prejudice the cause of the comparatively poor academic performance of black children in English schools. Unless those who say otherwise are allegis that there is greater hostility among teachers towards black pupils than brown, then we are left with an uncomfortable truth – the significantly better average results obtained by Asian children compared with those of Caribbean origin.

My view is that the cause of comparative black failure is located at the point where unfortunate influences overlap: lack of support for the school and its values among West Indian parents and the support given by some teachers to the idea of a multicultural education movement.

Within the multicultural education movement there is a strand of thinking which might be termed 'cultural revisionism'. This expresses itself as a demand for all books and materials in schools to be rigorously vetted. All references to black or brown immigrants and their homeland, which could be thought to give offence, must be expunged – which, in reality, means throwing away the noxious material. Linked with this is a demand to bowdlerise the language so that all words which suggest a link between colour and negative references or feelings should be abolished. This attempt to sanitize culture is reminiscent of totalitarian regimes' attempts to rewrite history. It is a fundamentally misguided approach in a free society and risks a backlash.

These strident demands for literary purity may well be self-defeating. Gillian Klein's *Kids Schools and Libraries*[1] is a good example of this literary McCarthyism.

This is not to deny that some offensive material has been produced. All minority groups have suffered from ignorant forms of stereotyping: Jews, Italians, Irish and Germans have all been subjected to the distortions of prejudice, as well as people from the former territories of the British empire.

This deplorable crudity is not difficult to recognize at the extremes; no one would deny the malign intention behind National Front propaganda, or the anti-white motives behind some black consciousness publications. But what about works of acknowledged literary excellence? What about Kipling, *The Merchant of Venice, Othello*. What indeed, about certain verses in the Bible? Are these too to be outlawed in the name of the new orthodoxy?

The problem in attempting to dictate acceptable culture forms is to know where to stop. There is already some evidence that publishers are laying down guidelines for the writers of children's stories which, if they are not resisted, will almost certainly mean that second-rate material which toes the prescribed line will stand a better chance of publication than better stories thrown out because their authors reject the notion of external control of the writer's imagination.

Black children in English schools are said to have a defective picture of themselves, negative feelings about their worth and low expectations of their scholastic potential. The English school is not only blamed for damaging their self-image, it is also expected to put the matter right. One West Indian educationalist, Bernard Coard,[2] even alleged that English schools caused a disproportionate number of black children to become educationally sub-normal. This was an absurd and deeply offensive allegation against the English teaching profession. But, for many years, the charge stuck.

A mixture of liberal guilt and political opportunism – both powerful influences in the education service – combined to project the notion that black children were failing to fulfil their potential because English school teachers were 'racist' and consistently held low expectations of black children. Poor black performance in schools was simply the predictable outcome of a negative self-fulfilling prophecy.

This sort of notion can be shown to be false through the daily experiences of teachers working with black children. I have seen countless such children do extremely well both in sport and academically – when the school has had support from the home. For this is the key factor.

Maureen Stone, a West Indian Sociologist, virtually dismisses the research on which self-concept theorists rely as both invalid and unreliable. In *The Education of Black Children in Britain: The Myth of multiracial education* she concludes:

'The research...is generally inconclusive and contradictory...there is no coherent body of research or theory on the development of self-concept in minority group children in Britain.'

Yet such research has not only helped to determine the way people think and talk about black pupils, it has actually influenced policy decisions and the allocation of public funds. Schools are being obliged to preserve and transmit the culture of immigrants. This is not only questionable in principle, it is almost certainly impracticable for the blindingly obvious reason that English schools are embedded in an English culture and history with staff whose culture is European.

Attempts to teach an immigrant culture by people manifestly not part of that culture is not only doomed to failure; it may well, however well-meaning, give positive offence by shabby imitations and the worst kind of patronizing tokenism.

Moreover, the assumption is often made that the culture of the first generation of immigrant parents – born and bred in the homeland – is identical with that of his settler offspring, born and raised in Britain. This is manifestly not so. The average second generation Caribbean or Asian child, has been raised in a world quite different from and in some important respects opposed to the culture which shaped his parents. The Muslim child attending the mosque for an hour or so each night is likely also to have experienced lengthy exposure to British and American television, to read English comics and to support his local football team.

Similarly with the West Indian child, whose parents use Creole as the medium of communication and whose big brother is a Rastafarian. He will be well aware of his origins but will have distinctive British interests and loyalties, too. These children are essentially bicultural, just as they are often bilingual. This is an inescapable result of their parents' decision to settle in a new country.

The desire of their parents to perceive their own cultural background in the behaviour and interests of their children is a perfectly understandable human response. But the emotional and psychological price to be paid for emigration is the pain of change and adaption. The children know this from first-hand. They know that to flourish in the culture in which they live out their lives outside the home, they must first master it.

The advocates of cultural continuity may, for the best of reasons, be overlooking this. They may well be involved in a process which actually limits the settler child's chances in a pretty ruthless meritocracy – which is what our society is. And they are thereby delaying the emergence of a 'black' professional and managerial class, which could play such a vital part in establishing a truly equal and harmonious society.

None of the key ideas underlying multiracial education bears critical scrutiny. It is very doubtful that the bandwagon now vigorously underway will achieve anything positive; it may well, indeed, help to generate a wholly artificial and harmful colour consciousness in our schools. We need a much simpler approach; one which emphasizes the common needs of *all* children. By emphasizing sectional interests, the multiculturalists may well be exacerbating the very problem they claim to be trying to solve – the tendency we all have, whatever our colour, to adapt a narrow and rejecting view of others.

Notes to Multiracial myths?

1. In *The School Library for Multicultural Awareness of 1985*, Gillian Klein wrote:

Not only is the United Kingdom of today multicultural, multiethnic and containing peoples of widely different faiths and beliefs: in one way or another it has been so for many long centuries. For instance, the actual proportion of black people living in major centres of population such as London has surprisingly not greatly altered since the first Elizabethan age …

If only because of the recent increase, that seems unlikely and today DNA investigations show it to be false. Wikipedia has it as follows:

At the 2011 census London had a population of 8,173, 941. Of this number 44.9% were White British … the total black population stood at 1,088,640. This is a rise of 39% from the 2001 census …

And Jeremy Paxman in *The English* (first published by Michael Joseph in 1998) put it this way

[Sir Arthur Bryant and Enoch Powell] were certainly right about its suddenness. In 1951 the total population of Caribbean and South Asian people in Britain was 80,000.....Twenty years later it had reached one and a half million. Forty years on, the 1991 census put the ethnic population at just over *3 million*. It is quite an explosion.

2. In 1971, Bernard Coard, born in Grenada, wrote *How the West Indian Child is Made Educationally Subnormal in the British School System.*